Connemara

Connemara

A Little Gaelic Kingdom

TIM ROBINSON

PENGUIN
IRELAND

PENGUIN IRELAND

Published by the Penguin Group
Penguin Ireland, 25 St Stephen's Green, Dublin 2, Ireland (a division of Penguin Books Ltd)
Penguin Books Ltd, 80 Strand, London WC2R ORL, England
Penguin Group (USA) Inc., 375 Hudson Street, New York, New York 10014, USA
Penguin Group (Australia), 250 Camberwell Road, Camberwell, Victoria 3124, Australia
(a division of Pearson Australia Group Pty Ltd)
Penguin Group (Canada), 90 Eglinton Avenue East, Suite 700, Toronto, Ontario, Canada M4P 2Y3
(a division of Pearson Penguin Canada Inc.)
Penguin Books India Pvt Ltd, 11 Community Centre, Panchsheel Park, New Delhi – 110 017, India
Penguin Group (NZ), 67 Apollo Drive, Rosedale, Auckland 0632, New Zealand
(a division of Pearson New Zealand Ltd)
Penguin Books (South Africa) (Pty) Ltd, 24 Sturdee Avenue,
Rosebank, Johannesburg 2196, South Africa
Penguin Books Ltd, Registered Offices: 80 Strand, London WC2R ORL, England

www.penguin.com

First published 2011
1

Copyright © Tim Robinson, 2011

The moral right of the author has been asserted

Set in Bembo Book MT Std 12/14.75 pt
Typeset by Palimpsest Book Production Limited, Falkirk, Stirlingshire
Printed in Great Britain by Clays Ltd, St Ives plc

A CIP catalogue record for this book is available from the British Library

ISBN: 978-1-844-88237-3

www.greenpenguin.co.uk

Contents

Author's Note

Although it is the last part to be written, *A Little Gaelic Kingdom* takes second place in the *Connemara* trilogy, between *Listening to the Wind* and *The Last Pool of Darkness*. It is concerned with the Irish-speaking areas, and in writing it I have been reminded again and again not only of the debt I owe to the experts I have consulted in various fields, but of the dozens of people in those hospitable realms who guided me round their own neighbourhoods and kept me going with food, drink and encouragement. In many cases an indication of their contributions will be found in the Sources at the end of the volume. In the following list their names occur roughly in the order they come to mind as I read through my manuscript: Brian Ó Curnáin, Arndt Wigger, Helen Spellman, Paul Mohr, Mary Keane, the late Michael O'Toole, Marie Reddon, the late John Barlow, Donncha Ó hÉallaithe, Virginia Blankenhorn, Lillís Ó Laoire, Ríonach Uí Ógáin, Treasa Uí Chonaire, the late Anthony Betts, the late Dick Scott, Sgt P. Ó Conghaile, Niall O'Carroll, John McDonagh, Richard Fitzgerald, Kieran O'Halloran, Angela Bourke, Dáithí Ó hÓgáin, Phyllis O'Donoghue, Séamas Ó Concheanainn, Seán Ó Guairim, Micheál Ó Conghaile, Michael Gibbons, Eoghan Ó Néill, Josie Gorham, Micheál Ó Cuaig, Seosamh Ó Cuaig, the late Pat Sullivan, Máirtín Ó Catháin, Peter Flaherty, Paul Ryan, the late Mícheál Bairéad, Dónall Mac Giolla Easpaig, Padhraic Faherty, Seán Ó Mainnín, Fr Audley, the late Johnny Chóil Mhaidhc, John Donnelly, Fr M. Lang, Martin J. O'Connor, Laillí Lamb, Éamon de Buitléar, Derek and Liz Hawker, Pádraig Ó Maoilchiaráin, Pádraic de Bhaldraithe, Tom Folan, Tomás Ó Maoláin, Paul Kerrigan.

Brendan Barrington has edited my text with his customary judicious incisiveness, for which I am truly grateful. I thank the following for permission to quote from various works, as detailed in the Sources: Cathal Ó Luain, Micheál Ó Conghaile (Cló Iar-Chonnachta) and Anne

Korff (Tír Eolas). I am also aware of how much I owe to people met on the road who gave me some priceless scraps of local knowledge and whose names, regrettably, I failed to note.

In everything to do with language and song Liam Mac Con Iomaire has been a constant and generous support as well as a steadfast friend, and I dedicate *Connemara: A Little Gaelic Kingdom* to him with gratitude and respect.

TR

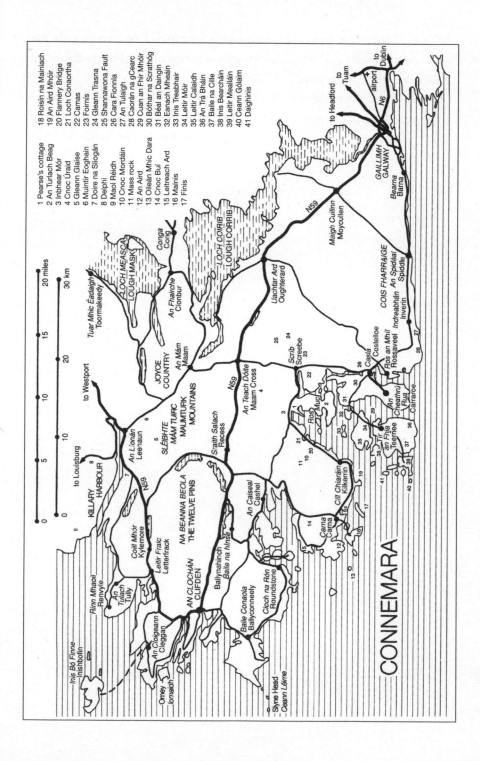

1 Pearse's cottage
2 An Turlach Beag
3 Inbhear Mór
4 Cnoc Úraid
5 Gleann Glaise
6 Muintir Eoghain
7 Doire na Sliogán
8 Delphi
9 Maol Réidh
10 Cnoc Mordáin
11 Mass rock
12 An Aird
13 Oileán Mhic Dara
14 Cnoc Buí
15 Leitreach Ard
16 Mainis
17 Finis
18 Roisín na Mainiach
19 An Aird Mhóir
20 Flannery Bridge
21 Loch Conaortha
22 Camas
23 Foirnis
24 Gleann Trasna
25 Shannawona Fault
26 Cara Fionnla
27 An Tulaigh
28 Caorán na gCearc
29 Cuan an Fhir Mhóir
30 Bóthar na Scrathóg
31 Béal an Daingin
32 Eanach Mheáin
33 Inis Treabhair
34 Leitir Móir
35 Leitir Calaidh
36 An Trá Bháin
37 Baile na Cille
38 Inis Bearcháin
39 Leitir Meallcáin
40 Ceann Gólaim
41 Daighinis

CONNEMARA

PART I

Roads to Freedom

Preface

This Road Before Me

One day a hundred years or more ago Patrick Pearse and a friend were contemplating the waters of Galway Bay glistening through a screen of trees. 'As was usual with him,' wrote the friend later on, 'he seemed inclined to silence, but suddenly he spoke: "We could have here a little Gaelic kingdom of our own."' The scene was in Cois Fharraige, which means 'beside the sea', the arm of the Irish-speaking south of Connemara that stretches along the coast towards the city of Galway. But if there had come to be such a kingdom its capital would have been further west, in Ros Muc, where its ruler was to build, write and plot, and to foresee his death.

In his short stories Pearse often used the topography of Ros Muc symbolically, almost as if he could assume that everyone else was familiar with it, as Dante could rest on certain commonplaces about Jerusalem and Rome; this was overweening in Pearse, but the quality of his stories is not negligible and there are of course extraliterary reasons for examining them. So I will begin by locating Ros Muc, the innermost complication of the topographical knot of south Connemara. A low-lying, south-pointing peninsula (*ros*) some five miles long, pinched into narrows here and stretching out into subsidiary peninsulas there, it has to the north of it a great tract of bogs and hills beyond which the Twelve Pins form the skyline; to its west is a much larger peninsula bearing the villages of Cill Chiaráin and Carna and backboned by the long hill of Cnoc Mordáin; to the east and separated from it by the narrowest and twistiest of sea channels is the hill of Camas and its hinterland of yet more bare hills; while to the south a proliferation of islands spills out into Galway Bay, some deserted, others, joined to each other and the mainland by causeways, having their own dense network of roads, villages and little harbours.

'There's not a foot of Ros Muc that isn't woven into Pearse's writings,' as one of his young disciples from that locality was to put it; the phrase he uses is the expressive *fíte fuaite*, woven-sewn. Pearse's story 'Na Bóithre' ('The Roads') is particularly full of placenames; it mentions almost every townland and village in the neighbourhood except Ros Muc itself, which always appears in his fiction as Ros na gCaorach, the peninsula of the sheep, rather than the peninsula of the pigs. Perhaps he felt that sheep were more poetically suited than pigs to his rather pastoral vision of life in Connemara, or perhaps he was just oversensitive to mindless English or Ascendancy jokes about the Irishman and his pig. In any case it is likely that *muc* refers to the small hogback hills of the locality rather than to pigs.

To understand 'Na Bóithre' and to extract from it some significances Pearse himself may not have been aware of, it is necessary to go into details of its setting and the occasion that prompted it. Nóra, the girl-child heroine of the story, lives in An Turlach Beag, near the school, from which roads diverge to various villages that figure in the text primarily as places people come from or go to; they name directions, like Guermantes in Proust, and they represent the choices or destinies life offers. But Pearse is extremely repressive in the choice he thrusts upon his heroine, and was in fact more concerned with his own destiny while writing this story, as I shall show.

The story begins with a *fleá*, a festivity, in the school, organized by a regular visitor known as the Man from Dublin. Nóra is told to stay at home and mind the baby while her parents and brother go off to enjoy the fun. Rebelling against her lot, she cuts off her hair to look like a boy, and ventures out into the darkness. She hears the voices of people dispersing from the *fleá*, hides herself from them and then takes the road that would lead out into the wide world. But by the time she has passed the haunted graveyard called Cill Eoin and reached a place Pearse calls Eileabhrach she is tired and frightened; she steps aside into a wood there, and faints, and has a vision of Christ's agony in the Garden of Gethsemane. She longs to help carry the Cross – but at that moment her father finds her, and takes her home. She is wandering in her mind for a month, but when she comes to herself she asks for the baby to be put in the bed with her, and vows never to leave her family again. The message is unambiguous: stay at home, girl, and bear children; the excitements and sufferings of the roads of life are Man's portion. But under this bit of patriarchal indoctrination is another level of significance, only legible in the light of the real-life event that prompted the story, and the detailed geography of Ros Muc – both matters few of Pearse's readers could be aware of.

First, the event: Pearse himself had organized such a *fleá* in the school of An Turlach Beag, in opposition to some entertainment of too English a tone mounted by the Viceroy, Lord Dudley, who used to come for fishing holidays to Inver Lodge, on a lake island just north of Ros Muc. Pearse was delighted with the success of his evening, and later based the story of 'Na Bóithre' on it (he finished it only in the summer of 1915, and it was published a few months before the Easter Rising and his own execution). So the 'Man from Dublin' of the story is Pearse himself. Second, the microgeography of Ros Muc, the next layer of the labyrinth, to be imagined as wrapped around the schematic map of the story. Eileabhrach is in fact the wooded area south of Loch Eileabhrach – the name is properly Oiriúlach, perhaps from *foithriúil* and signifying a place of thickets – which lies in the angle between the road leading out of the Ros Muc peninsula and the main road passing by from east to west. The Ros Muc road goes around the east of the lake, and Pearse's cottage was rather isolated, on the west of the lake. So, if Nóra's hallucination of Christ had been prompted by her actually seeing a man in the wood there, that man would most likely have been Pearse himself, taking a shortcut home after his *fleá*. Since Nóra is a fiction, so is her vision, and as for any rationalization of it, it exists only in our reconstruction of Pearse's mind. His self-identification with Christ the Redeemer is well known; here is an unusual demonstration of it, emerging through an interpretation of a projection into a hallucination in a fiction. He must have been full of forebodings of his forthcoming Easter self-sacrifice at the time of writing this story. The wood of Eileabhrach was his Garden of Gethsemane.

1 The Roads

A rush of talk like the whirl of starlings coming to roost, as if time had caught up and amplified those voices Nóra heard in An Turlach Beag that evening of Pearse's entertainment, fills the air as I approach the village on this summer afternoon of 2008; then silence falls as the fifty or more teenagers who have been exercising their limbs and lungs in the playground sit attentively around the foot of the steps of the community hall, and answer one by one in Irish to the calling of the roll. An Chrannóg is the name of the hall, harking back to the lake dwellings of heroic times and hinting at a defensive function, and indeed the Irish-language courses that convene in such halls here and there throughout the Gaeltacht are crucial to the life of the language. They are also an economic staple of their localities – the students being lodged and fed by families living nearby – while for many of the youngsters themselves these courses are a rite of passage, a summer season of discovery of themselves, their peers and their loves.

Opposite An Chrannóg, on the banks of the little lake that centres the village, is a monument that refers us to another heroic epoch, a great slice of granite engraved with a remarkable list of names, members of the Ros Muc branch of Conradh na Gaeilge, the Gaelic League:

Pádraig Mac Piarais	1869–1916
Pádraig Ó Conaire	1882–1928
Colm Ó Gaora	1887–1954
Pádraig Óg Ó Conaire	1893–1971
Criostóir Mac Aonghusa	1905–1991
Máirtín Ó Cadhain	1906–1970
Caitlín Maude	1941–1982

The inscription goes on to tell us (in Irish) that four of these 'Gaelic Leaguers, writers and patriots who stood for the rights of the local

Gaelic community' were from Ros Muc itself and the three others spent parts of their lives here. In exploring this unique cluster of luminaries and the tracery of mutual influences that holds them as a constellation, and to set it in the topographic web of Connemara, where better to start than this little out-of-the-world's-way corner?

First, the starting point. Officially this townland is An Turlach Beag (the *beag*, 'small', merely distinguishes it from a much more extensive townland just to the north of it called An Turlach Mór); but the old people say '*túr-*', not '*tur-*', and in any case there is no geological possibility here in the south Connemara granite country of a *turlach*, a lake that in dry seasons disappears down its own internal springs, as happens in the limestone Burren, for example. A *tuar* is a pasture or a bleaching green for spreading linen on; perhaps the name means 'the small place of greens'. And there are green slopes around the lake (which is hardly bigger than a village pond) where it is not invested with copses, and alongside the three roads leading away from the lakeside and the hall, school, bar and a few houses near it, there are little meadows. This is a relatively soft little nest of a place, in contrast to the generally harsh landscape of south Connemara over which the last Ice Age seems sometimes only yesterday to have desisted from excavating, dragging and dumping boulders at random. I will follow out each of the three roads in turn, starting with the one that runs down to the south-western point of the Ros Muc peninsula.

For any sensible pedestrian the walk through Ros Céide (peninsula of the flat hill), as the south-western townland of the peninsula is called, is a stroll of about three miles each way, past a loose handful of houses and (nowadays) a glimpse of a small clutch of holiday homes off to the right of the road. But if one insists on following the ins and outs of the shoreline north of the road, as I did when first exploring this area in October 1980 during the making of my map of Connemara, clambering over field wall after field wall, floundering across muddy inlets, tramping through banks of washed-up seaweed, to the very fingertip of the land, and returning by the similar obstacle course of the southern shore, it is exhaustingly longer. However, that particular day of my one-foot-in-sea-and-one-on-shore pilgrimage around south Connemara, constant only to the inconstant coast, was blissful:

an October sun, a late hatching of painted-lady butterflies, a succession of tiny geographies to be noticed. Looking now at the tattered and faded photocopy of the six-inch Ordnance Survey map I carried with me that day to note my discoveries on, I find a dozen little landing places marked on a single mile of the shore south of the road; some of these would have been mere clearances made by shifting a few stones out of the way, or quays consisting of stones piled into a low bank, all covered in seaweed and hardly distinguishable from the rest of the shore until one's eye becomes attuned to its minutiae. Here and there great silvery tangles of bog-deal roots are half exposed in little cliffs of black peat, where the sea has eaten into a patch of bog; sometimes these natural hooks and handles serve as bollards for a tiny harbour.

It was on that particular day, when I was grumbling to myself that for all my pains I had found nothing of archaeological or historical interest, I realized that the whole shoreline was an archaeological and historical site of the greatest interest, formed and reformed over centuries by the moving of a stone here and there. All these shore features have names; among those I learned from a farmer-cum-boatman I met on that exhausting ramble were Lochán an Phríosúin, the pool of the prison, a little rock-bound lagoon of the north shore one could float a boat into at high water but not get it out of once the sea had begun to sink away again, and An Crompán Bréan, the stinking creek, on the south shore, into which winter storms pile mountains of seaweed and leave it to rot through the summer. The life-giving significance of the two primary features of the south Connemara coast, its fractal complexity and its vast biomass of seaweed, will become apparent as I work my way around it and through this book. Here I will note in passing a heap of stones on an islet at the end of the outward journey and a few yards off the tip of the peninsula, Oileán an Mhada, the island of the dog (the name probably refers to the *madra uisce*, the otter, rather than the domestic dog). A century or so ago there was a cabin here for a watchman guarding nearby oysterbeds for the then landlords, the Berridges of Ballynahinch; the spat would begin their life in these beds and then be moved into deeper water further up the bay to fatten. Shellfish beds of various sorts, now happily in the hands of local cooperatives, are still important factors of the south Connemara life-equation. And then, at the end of the return journey along the southern coast, is an old stone-built and grassy-topped quay flanking a narrow-necked harbour pool, which the last time I saw it was almost filled by ten *climíní*, circular pads of seaweed each about ten feet across and a few feet deep. This seaweed would have been cut from coastal rocks and offshore islets when the tide was out, roped into these flat bundles, floated off by the rising tide (it is a remarkable sight, men leaping from one of these swampy rafts to another as they pole them out of the shallows) and towed harbourwards behind wooden rowboats – very slowly and effortfully in the days before outboard engines. In the past the seaweed would have been used locally as manure, sold to farmers on the other side of Galway Bay, or burned to kelp (a vanished industry whose meagre traces will be considered later on); nowadays it is taken by lorry to the alginates factory in Cill Chiaráin. And so, this walk provides a first glimpse of the amphibious mode of life of Ros Muc past and present, the work of muscle and blood, background to the intellectual effort of the stars commemorated in An Turlach Beag, to which I now begin to turn.

The quay mentioned above is Céibh na Gairfeanach, from the name of the little townland we are in here, An Ghairfean, the rough ground. A tree-shadowed boreen between walls of impressively massive boulders leads from it up to the road a mile south-west of An Turlach Beag. On my first visit to Ros Muc, when I was told that there was a shop in An Ghairfean I thought I was being sent on a fool's errand: how could a shop thrive at this nether end of a remote peninsula? But look at a map or, better, a sea chart: Céibh na Gairfeanach is at the hub of a tentacular twenty-mile-wide complex of waterways winding north-eastwards to Scríb and Camas, north-west to Inbhear, south to An Cheathrú Rua and Na hOileáin, and south-west to Cill Chiaráin and Carna. The shopkeepers, the Ó Conaire or Conroy family, brought in their goods from Galway in their own sailboat, familiarly known as *Bád Chonroy*, a forty-foot hooker built in 1911 by the most famous of the Connemara boatyards, Gheárd na gCathasach, Caseys' of Maínis. The Conroys' nearest rivals would have been the Mac Dhonncha family, the MacDonaghs, who had a shop on An Chnapach, a little island, now uninhabited, near the south-western extremity of the archipelago of Na hOileáin.

Even after I had been assured that there was a shop in this vicinity it took me a little while to find it, as the spreading sycamores and horse chestnuts and the almost titanic stone walls just inland of the harbour suggested a demesne, an ancestral home jealous of its privacy. But when I followed the driveway I found a single-storey dwelling with battlements that looked too large for it over the porch and around the bay of a living-room window, and a gated courtyard between slate-roofed outhouses swagged with Virginia creeper, in the windows of one of which a few tins of beans and packets of biscuits indicated that this was indeed the shop. The elderly, distinguished and affable gentle-man behind the counter, Micheál Ó Conaire himself, told me that he was about to close as he had to hurry off to the Raidió na Gaeltachta station in Casla to give a talk on local history; nevertheless he couldn't stop talking to me as he took me into the kitchen at the back of the house to make me a coffee. Looking around at the huge, tall old room, the vast clothes-airer overhead, the walls hung with dully gleaming pewter dish-covers and big copper dishes with reproductions of Gains-borough's *Blue Boy* in the centre, I felt I was seeing Pádraic Ó Conaire's own kitchen, or rather his uncle's, the one poor little Pádraic was not entirely welcome in, from a couple of long generations ago.

Ó Conaire was born in Galway in 1882 or 1883, wrote stories, novels and plays that brought the Irish language into the ambit of modern literature and exposed it to the force-fields of Dostoevsky, de Maupas-sant and Robert Louis Stevenson, and died in 1928, possessed only of his pipe and tobacco and an apple. Albert Power's statue of him – a small, round-headed man in heavy boots, evidently noting down some fleeting thought while sitting on a roadside bank – was (until its recent removal) the sole lovable feature in the municipal wasteland of Eyre Square that he would have hated so much, in the city of Galway. Criostóir Mac Aonghusa gives his background neatly; I translate:

Pádraic is the only Irish-language writer to have been born in a big town where a good deal of Irish was spoken. His people were very well-to-do and lived in Ros Muc, one of the poorest places in Europe in Pádraic's youth.

His grandfather had been in a position to spend money on his family. He made one of his sons a lawyer, another a priest, a third a doctor; he bought pubs for two more, gave handsome dowries with his three daughters (one of them an abbess) and left a thriving shop to the son who stayed at home . . . Pádraic's father Tomás was a publican, and unlike the rest of the family he was not a diligent man. He married and had three children, Micheál, Íosóg and Pádraic. But he was given to the drink, and one day he abandoned everything, took ship for Boston, fell sick on the way and died there six months later. His wife died soon afterwards, and Íosóg and Pádraic were sent out to their grandmother's house in Ros Muc . . . Pádraic was sent to school, and he worked for his relatives too. He used to go around with a donkey and cart delivering goods from the shop . . .

. . . and it is with a donkey that he is immemorially associated in minds of all who loved or suffered Irish at school. A generationally worn copy of *M'Asal Beag Dubh* ('My Little Black Donkey'), carefully covered in brown paper, has been many a schoolchild's first literary property, and I have met old men in the Aran Islands who could proudly intone its rhythmic opening sentence, '*Ig Cinn Mhara a bhí mé nuair a chuir mé aithne ar m'asal beag dubh i dtosach*' ('In Kinvara it was that I first got to know my little black donkey'). The book is a transposition of R. L. Stevenson's *Travels with a Donkey in the Cévennes* out of the highlands of European culture with its abbeys and long-historied demesnes into the folkworld of the West of Ireland's lanes, fairs and public houses. Its spell has spread into tourist brochures: today in the Merriman Hotel in Kinvara, under 'the largest thatched roof in Ireland', one can drink in the M'Asal Beag Dubh Bar. When an eighteen-year-old called Orson Welles came looking for a job in the Gate Theatre in Dublin and was boasting of his achievements to the spellbound Micheál Mac Liammóir and Hilton Edwards, he said, 'I've toured the States as a sword-swallowing female impersonator. I've flared through Hollywood like a firecracker. I've wafted my way with a jackass through Connemara . . .' He had surely been led on this last adventure by the legend of Pádraic Ó Conaire.

The Conroys of Garafin House were an English-speaking family ruled by a puritanical mother, the children educated by private tutors;

young Pádraic was a burden to them, and it was in the school of An Turlach Beag, and in his donkey travels, that he learned Irish. When his grandmother died and his uncle married, Pádraic was sent away to school, first to Rockwell College in Tipperary and then to Blackrock College in Dublin, but he took himself off to London without taking his exam. He got a job as a clerk in the Ministry of Education, doing little work for little money, and taught Irish to exiles in evening classes organized by Conradh na Gaeilge; sometimes he was paid and sometimes not. When the London County Council began to run Irish classes Pádraic became their teacher, at the exceptional rate of ten shillings an hour. He was close to the young Michael Collins at this period, and was sworn into the Volunteers. But by nature he was 'unsteady'; he consorted with tinkers, Gypsies, the down-and-outs of the embankment and 'vagabond poets who lived their poetry but rarely wrote it', according to his friend the poet F. R. Higgins. He was a socialist, and, for all his gentleness, liked to scandalize his hearers by looking forward to the day when the last capitalist would be hanged in the guts of the last bishop. He loved to talk, especially to women; everyone loved him and his stories, even his long-suffering wife and children, one of whom later described how if Pádraic passed a flower-girl on his way into a pub, he would send them roses 'on tick'. And he was devoted to the *crúiscín lán*, the well-filled and soon emptied jar of whiskey.

In 1914 Pádraic deserted his family and returned to Ireland; perhaps he was avoiding conscription, like many another London-Irishman. Thenceforth he led a wild and wandering life, teaching Irish and writing. In literature it was Pearse, he said, who gave him courage, but Ó Conaire's demonstration that Irish could be one of the literary languages of modern Europe far exceeds the formal and expressive scope of Pearse's child-centred stories. He was attacked for the frankness of his treatment of sexuality by the well-known Irish-language writer Peadar Ó Laoghaire (Canon Peter O'Leary), whose prim and folkloristic tale of a country cobbler's struggles with the Devil, *Séadna*, had been replaced in the matriculation curriculum by Ó Conaire's *Deoraíocht* ('Exile'), a harshly modern-day novel of a young Irishman disabled by a car accident in Britain, and despite a courageous defence of it by Douglas Hyde, Ó Conaire's book was in its turn replaced, by

Pearse's religiose fable 'Íosagán'. But his definitive work for my web-weaving purpose is his response to the events Pearse helped to precipitate in 1916, a collection of short stories called *Seacht mBua an Éirí Amach* ('Seven Victories of the Rising').

In some of them the Rising erupts quite unexpectedly, diverting the flow of events or even totally demolishing the plot just as it moves towards a resolution. And these plots tend to the bizarre; one could imagine that Poe had a hand in that of 'Ceoltóirí' ('Musicians'). A young man becomes acquainted with the reclusive blind master of the local Big House, on the basis of their shared love of the violin. One night on his way home, where it seems inevitable that he will learn the secret of his birth and that it was his mother, as a pregnant, betrayed and vengeful girl, who flung the acid that blinded his friend, he sees from a hilltop Dublin aflame, and goes off 'drunk with nationalism' to join the rebels, leaving his story unheard. In 'Anam an Easpaig' ('The Bishop's Soul') the bishop is on his way to Dublin on business concerning a curate whom he feels he should reprimand for consorting with enemies of the state. In a series of almost farcical misadventures he becomes separated from his car and driver on a dark road; he too sees from a hilltop the flames of revolution, and the light of patriotism breaks in on him. Later, when the military authorities press him to discipline the nationalistic curate, he replies that he is a bishop, not an official of the state, and amazes the curate by offering him a better parish. Ó Conaire may have agreed with Pearse that 'a living modern literature cannot be built up on the folktale', but there is a round-eyed, wondering, fireside tone to his spinning of these yarns; I can imagine them told in that great Garafin House kitchen or over the counter in the shop.

Pádraic Ó Conaire himself entered the land of legend in his lifetime; he was for many 'the Pan of Gaelic', awakening the magic of youth in them through his tales and his example. But drink and rough living wore him out by the age of forty-six. His latter days were pitiable. On the occasion of the opening of the Taibhdhearc, the Irish-language theatre in Galway, Pádraic turned up with a few drinks in him and insisted on joining the eminences of the Gaelic cultural world on the stage. An overexcited Liam Ó Briain, the director of the theatre, ordered him off and gave him a couple of blows. Pádraic left in tears, and later that night was seen weeping in the street. A few weeks later he was beaten up in Galway, and kicked in the belly. He set off for Dublin where as he expected he would die in hospital. On the way he called in on Liam O'Flaherty in Wicklow; according to O'Flaherty they talked of 'the damned loneliness of the poet, with only an occasional grip of the hand from some other poor lonely poet', and wept and confessed their sins together. Liam offered to drive him into town, a distance of forty miles, but Ó Conaire declined: 'The one thing on earth that always gives me solace,' he said, 'is a solitary walk on a mountain road.' And off he went, pipe in his mouth, to Dublin, where he died within a week.

I dislike returning by the way I went, so let me, powered by memory, take a roundabout way back to my starting point. There is a long straight road eastwards across the peninsula from Gairfean: Bóthar Cheaimil, after one Campbell, who was in charge of its construction, which the Ordnance Survey map of 1899 shows in progress – a year or two too late for it to have been a useful shortcut for Pádraic and his donkey. It crosses a bare terrain of cut-away bog, one section of which is called Straidhp an Tae, the tea stripe, from the inordinate amount of tea drunk there by men cutting turf to ship to the Aran Islands from Céibh na Gairfeanach. Nowadays very few people cut turf here and the exhausted land is beginning to regenerate itself; a friend living nearby tells me he hears the sweet whistle of the snipe and the plaintive piping of the lapwing here at night. On a recent visit I noticed a clump of the yellow composite fleabane by the side of the road – a plant that is apparently becoming rare and that I have seen in only three other spots in Connemara. After a mile and a half this road joins one running down the eastern shore, to another fine old harbour, called An Siléar, the cellar; the name recalls a long-vanished kelp store by the quayside. From here a very narrow and tortuous branch of the sea, Cuan Chamais or Camas Bay, winds northwards between Ros Muc and the broad promontory of Camas – the basis of these names being *cam*, crooked. An island, low, flat and boggy, and long deserted, lies in this waterway: Cladhnach, place of field walls; one can reach it at low water by splashing across a few yards of mud. To the north-east of it a series of rocks that only a giant could use as stepping stones leads across to Camas; the gaps between them are called Na Léimeanna, the leaps, not because one could jump across them but because with a falling tide the waters of the bay come leaping down in waterfalls between them. From the Ros Muc side they are, first, Léim na hEilte, the doe's leap, then Léim an tSagairt, the priest's leap (the priest used to have seaweed rights on the rock beyond it), and finally An Léim Bheag, the small leap. I also hear of Léim Tíre, the land leap, and An Léim Cham, the crooked leap; I don't know exactly where these are, but to the boatmen they are no doubt as familiar and as negotiable or wearisome as are city roundabouts to the commuting car driver.

This south-eastern corner of the peninsula is the townland of Ros Muc proper, from which the name has spread to cover the whole of the peninsula and a clutch of mainland townlands north of it. The *muc* in question is perhaps the rounded hill occupying the centre of the townland, from the top of which the Catholic parish church watches over a complex little world of land and water within a semicircle of hills that delimits the parish to the north and east. Or at least that was its outlook when it was built in 1844 (replacing a little chapel-cum-school the ruins of which can be seen south-west of the road junction in An Turlach Beag), for the land was laid bare by poverty in those days; nowadays a few prosperous-looking houses with mature trees in their gardens have come to occupy the slopes around the church and enjoy their own views. There are more trees to the right of the road as one follows it north and then west and approaches An Turlach Beag again.

Totally hidden among them, round the bend of an avenue of over-arching hawthorns, is the birthplace of another Ros Muc writer of the name of Pádraic Ó Conaire, known as Pádraic Óg, young Patrick, to distinguish him from *the* Pádraic Ó Conaire, Sean-Phádraic, old Patrick, as the Pádraic of An Ghairfean is often called. Pádraic Óg was born in 1893, got his early schooling in a Ros Muc already under the influence of An Piarsach (as Patrick Pearse is fondly called in Irish), became one of the first pupils of his newly founded school, St Enda's in Rathfarnham, Dublin, and played the old man Sean-Mhaitias in the school's presentation of Pearse's 'Íosagán' in the Abbey Theatre. For many years from 1910 onwards he worked for Conradh na Gaeilge as a travelling teacher of Irish; a toughly built man, he was better fitted than most for this strenuous bicycling role. When he was summonsed for not having a lamp on his bicycle, he refused to speak English in court. Sworn into the secret Irish Republican Brotherhood in 1913, he was marginally involved as a messenger in the Easter Rising, and later took part in the War of Independence. In the mid 1920s he ran Irish classes in Ros Muc, along with two other Irish writers to be, Colm Ó Gaora and Criostóir Mac Aonghusa. He organized yearly pilgrimages to Pearse's cottage after it became a museum, and did not neglect the pilgrimage to Cruach Phádraic either; in fact he climbed the sacred mountain for the last time just a week or so before death struck him down while out fishing from a sailing boat in Cuan Chasla in 1971.

Pádraic Óg is not nowadays so highly regarded an author as his namesake – he worked diligently and perhaps hastily to supply matter for a newly literate Irish-language readership – but his books are rich in conversations about every aspect of Connemara life. At the beginning of his prize-winning novel of 1938, *Ceol na nGiolcach* ('The Music of the Reeds'), set in the year 1908, we learn that the girls are being taught a skill that earns them good money in the local lace-making school, one of several set up in the Irish-speaking areas under the patronage of the Viceroy's wife Lady Aberdeen, but that most of them are saving up to buy their passages to America. On her way home from the school the sensible and modest young Máire meets Marcus, son of a prosperous farmer, on his handsome Connemara pony; it is immediately clear that the book will end with the marriage of these two, despite the competition of another farmer's daughter who would bring with her a large dowry in land and stock, and of the smart and sophisticated lace-school mistress, who is a *bean hata*, a hat woman, as opposed to Máire who is definitely a *bean seáil*, a shawl woman. And so indeed it turns out, after a sequence of incidents that hardly adds up to a plot but rambles talkatively through all the characteristic scenes of Connemara life: the race day, the *buaile* or summer milking pasture, the big shop (no charitable institution to the poor), a wake, and so on. The marriage signifies the perpetuation of all that is healthful and proper about Connemara; it is an act of trust in the future. And in that it contrasts painfully with Pádraic Óg's late work, *Déirc an Díomhaointis*, published in 1972.

When I first read this novel I thought that the one or two effective scenes in it were the result of accident, its construction being so haphazard, but now I feel that its fragmentation into short bursts of conversation presented almost without setting or commentary is an invention in itself, a response to a world in which nothing comes to good. It begins with the theft of a few sheep off an islet which one can take to be somewhere south of Ros Muc; their owner moves the ram and the one remaining ewe to an inland pasture to the north for safety, but the tougher sheep of the mountain drive them into a river, where they drown. A lad sells his cow at the fair of Maam Cross, drinks the price of it in the pub, and in fuddled despair sets off for England; much later his body is found in the vast quaking bog north of Ros Muc. A 'Yank', a retired Irish policeman, returns from America and is shocked by his neighbours' dependence on the dole, '*déirc an díomhaointis*' ('the alms of idleness'), as he sarcastically calls it. When he tries to organize a bit of communal land-reclamation only two of them turn up for the work. Later he falls ill, through accidental contact with a rat he was taking out of a trap; in hospital he falls in love with a bright young nurse, but does not reveal his feelings, and dies. The voice of this remarkable novel is that of honest disappointment and waning faith in the future of Pearse's 'little Gaelic kingdom'.

But if the children of the Gaeltacht seem to be turning their backs on Irish, many of their peers in Dublin and elsewhere are still keen to learn the language in its own habitat. Just beyond Pádraic Óg's old house we come into the village of An Turlach Beag again, and can hear the vivacity of the Irish-language summer school located in An Chrannóg. This is one of the oldest, most influential and most traditional of all such residential courses. It is run by Coláiste na bhFiann – another name with an antique heroic ring to it, referring directly to the Fianna, Fionn Mac Cumhaill's warrior train, and evoking the Irish Republican Brotherhood, the nineteenth-century rebels also known as the Fenians. The Coláiste, which also runs summer schools in the Gaeltacht area of Meath as well as in Sligo, Carlow and Kerry, was founded in the heady year of 1968 by Domhnall Ó Lúbhlaí, a charismatic figure to the idealist young, an impassioned disciple of Patrick Pearse, formerly a soldier in the Irish-speaking Galway regiment An Chéad Chath, and an IRA sympathizer. It was very nationalistic and militaristic in its rituals, rising early to salute the flag and sing the national anthem, 'Amhrán na bhFiann' (indeed acceptance on a course still depends among other conditions on the student's knowing its first verse and chorus). The Coláiste was described by the Irish-language magazine *Cuisle* in 1998 as 'a semi-secret society' with an ethos that was 'a potent mixture of the language cause, Catholicism and republicanism'. However that may be, it has parted with Ó Lúbhlaí, who resigned in 1986 and does not figure in the history of the college as summarized on its website.

What the college offers its students, according to this website, is not just a course in the 'living breathing spoken language' but the experience of living in an Irish-speaking world. The whirlwind of chatter I caught as I went by was surely all in Irish, for rules are strict on this and a student caught using one whole sentence of English could soon be on the bus home with no refund of fees. There has been much controversy over this rule; in 1997 there was a law case, which the college won, over a girl who burped (in which language is not recorded) and was expelled for her reflex 'Excuse me!' Regulations are less draconian these days, just as time has moderated the college's youthful extremism. Over 50,000 students have taken its courses and nowadays it can boast that many of its recent clients are the offspring of couples formed in those memorable Gaeltacht summers of yore.

Even when the students have flown with the parting summer, An Chrannóg continues to host a remarkable variety of social events, sports and educational opportunities; one senses that, notwithstanding the evident decline in usage of the language and its symptoms of internal decay, something is alive here, a spirit that few villages outside the Gaeltacht can match. A constancy to a vision begins to make itself felt as one continues to explore the network of relations between the stars listed on the Conradh na Gaeilge monument by the lake, and their continuing influence on the life of Ros Muc.

★

The next of these stars whose memory constellates the roads of Ros Muc offers us this pure distillation of the spirit of the 1960s:

> Tabhair dom casúr
> nó tua
> go mbrisfead is
> go millfead
> an teach seo,
> go ndéanfad tairseach
> den fhardoras
> 'gus urláir de na ballaí,
> go dtiocfaidh scraith
> agus díon agus
> simléir anuas
> le neart mo chuid
> allais . . .
>
> Sín chugam anois
> na cláir is na táirní
> go dtóigfead
> an teach eile seo . . .
>
> Ach, a Dhia, táim tuirseach!

. . . which translates simply as follows:

Give me a hammer / or axe / until I break / and wreck / this house, / until I make a threshold / of the lintel / and floors of the walls, / until thatch / and roof and / chimney come down / with the strength of my / sweat . . .

Now hand me / the boards and the nails / while I build / this other house . . .

But, God, am I weary!

. . . although nothing in English can replace the long-delayed consonance between *tairseach* and *tuirseach* in this poem, written by a young woman from Cill Bhriocáin, the daughter of the schoolteacher of An tOileán Iarthach . . . But I run before my donkey to market! Let me weave these placenames into their places first.

If one takes the road Nóra took in Pearse's story, that is, the main road of the peninsula, running northwards from An Turlach Beag, a few minutes' walk brings one to the little townland of Cill Bhriocáin, which mostly consists of a low hill making a promontory to the west, another limb of this sprawling configuration of land. The chapel or *cill* from which it is named, roofless but with its lichen-dappled walls and gables intact, broods like a speckled hen over one of those comfortable-looking and comforting burial grounds, all humps and hollows, bracken and wildflowers, of south Connemara, which looks down to a little harbour whence one might imagine souls setting forth into an eternity of ever-changing waters and mountains. In pre-Reformation times this was the parish church of what is still known as Paróiste Chill Bhriocáin, which nowadays includes Ros Muc and Camas. In even earlier and more legendary days St Briocán or Breacán is said to have come here and founded a church – perhaps this was after his ignominious failure to cheat St Enda out of his due share of the island of Árainn, an episode I have recounted in my book *Stones of Aran: Labyrinth*. But whatever he built here has been replaced by the existent chapel, which is of late medieval date. The holy well close by, however, is of dateless age and magic power. 'Taoscfaidh mé Tobar Bhriocáin ort' ('I'll empty Breacán's Well on you!') was a terrible curse. There used to be a stone here called Leac Bhriocáin, on which people would take their oaths, but it disappeared into the ground when someone swore to an untruth on it. (It was a woman; she swore she had not stolen her neighbour's hen, and as soon as she had done so the hen flew out from under her skirt.)

Two little islands lie off the western tip of the townland of Cill Bhriocáin. From the end of a side road down to the shore a rough stone causeway leads onwards across the *cora*, the crossing place, which is an expanse of muddy and stony seabed or shallow seawater, according to the state of the tide, to An tOileán Mór. This so-named 'big island' is only about half a mile long and less than that in breadth. A grassy track across it leads to another, shorter and more ruinous causeway, passable only when the tide is out; this lands one on An tOileán Iarthach, the western island, which is a little smaller than the other.

When I passed this way in 1982, on a bleak day that promised showers and was as good as its word, there were still two households on the first island. I called in at one of them to enquire about the tides before committing myself to the second, which is uninhabited, and an old lady, half blind, as she told me, brought me into the kitchen while we waited for her son to get up. When he did so at last he said that the tide was already coming in and that I might have to spend some time on the island if I got there; so the kind lady fortified me for the day with a boiled egg and lots of tea, and then I trotted down the path and picked my way across the broken-down causeway. The opposite side of the bay looked quite close – Cuan Chill Chiaráin is only a mile wide at this point – and there was a dark downpour brooding on it, so I hurried round the island, a huddle of wet little fields with a few roofless ruins scattered among them, rimmed by a blackish seaweedy shore, and came out again, having seen little but emptiness and desolation, and feeling that I had skimped my visit. Back on the bigger island I continued to ramble from field to field, finding nothing more inspiriting than a disused burial ground half eaten away by the sea, for unbaptized children, their graves marked by small set boulders only. I had to shelter from a heavy shower for some time in a tumbledown stone-built barn, looking out at the little black silhouette of a wooden currach with an outboard engine towing four *climíní* of seaweed at an imperceptible rate along the boundary between two shades of grey. Was it for this . . .? But later on I found two lads frying up bacon in the other house of the island; they gave me tea and the placenames I needed (with 'remarkably explosive consonant clusters', says my diary), and so rescued the day from despair.

On An tOileán Iarthach I had noticed the roofless carcase of Scoil na nOileán, the school of the islands, by a little quay on the north shore. An account of it has been left by a schoolmaster who taught there in 1930; it was a little thatched building with one small window to the south and a hearth on the floor at the western gable. School hours depended on the tides. The master lodged in a house on the mainland nearby, and would be woken by the woman of the house:

'Get up quick, master, or you'll lose the *cora*'; and as he hurried out of the door, 'Hurry, you little devil, you have the *cora* yet!' There were no roads on either island then. On his first day, as he leaped like a goat from stone to stone around the shore of the first island, the master saw men at work with a kiln, which he learned later was for drying barley for the making of poitín, a trade practised by most of the islands' inhabitants. The following year the redoubtable Redemptorist missioner An tAthair Ó Conghaile (pride of the Conneely family of the Aran Islands) descended on the Ros Muc islands together with the parish priest, going into every house and, wherever they suspected an involvement with poitín, seizing all the holy objects – crucifixes, paintings, statues – putting them out in the yards and refusing at the tops of their voices to release them until the householders promised to give up the unholy business. The people were terrified: they had never witnessed such ferocity in a holy priest before. Over the following days they were to be seen bent under the weight of the implements of poitín-making, making their way to the chapel, where a huge cairn of kegs, pots, stills and copper 'worms' was assembled and then set alight in a bonfire that could be seen for miles, 'the best of poitín feeding the flames'. However, it seems that when this island Savonarola returned three years later the islanders had reverted to their old ways, for the sale of poitín was one of their few resources in those days before any sort of social welfare existed.

In December 1941 a young teacher, May Ridge from Na Doiriú near Casla, took up the post of schoolmistress in An tOileán Iarthach and came to live with her husband, John Joseph Maude, in the Maude family house in Cill Bhriocáin. Soon afterwards the school was moved to An tOileán Mór, and so their three little children only had to trot across the first *cora* with their mother. The middle child, Caitlín, born in May 1941, went on to study in Coláiste Chroí Mhuire in An Spidéal, and in University College Galway, where she took the first place in the French examination in her first year, and so won a scholarship that funded a month's stay in France. A restless young woman, she taught here and there in Ireland and for a time in London, but her heart was with the performing arts and the Irish language; she acted in the Taibhdhearc in Galway and the Damer in Dublin, and wrote a play,

An Lasair Choille ('The Goldfinch'), in collaboration with Micheál Ó hAirtnéide. She also wrote poetry. 'I think poetry is a function of the imagination and the soul and that some contemporary poetry is too intellectual, although poetry is not a function of the intellect in any way,' she said. And she sang in the traditional style known as *sean-nós*, the old way. It is a ghostly and bodily disturbing experience, to evoke her lovely voice out of the computer or CD player; one is invaded by her passionate rendering of such magnificent songs as the slow air 'Róisín Dubh', an old love song that has been turned into a Jacobitic and apocalyptic vision of the liberation of Ireland, with the River Erne in flood, the hills torn open, the sea in waves of red, blood spilt, every mountain valley and meadow trembling – 'some day before my Dark Rosaleen dies'.

She was, I am told, strikingly beautiful. A much-reproduced photograph of her shows a symmetrical face framed in long dark hair and unruly fringe, looking directly at one with challenging eyes and a hint of resentment in the full lips; it may only be an artefact of the photographic process, but she looks pale, as after a fit of weeping, or of rage. In one of her more lacerating poems, 'Sneachta 1968', we are assailed with this:

> Tá mé i bhfad níos dathúla ná thú
> sa gcéad áit;
> Agus sa dara háit is bean mé;
> Agus sa tríú háit is file mé.

[I'm much more beautiful than you / in the first place; / And in the second place I'm a woman; / And in the third place I'm a poet.]

That the vision of An Piarsach was in eclipse, the Gaeltacht betrayed, feminism in retreat, that the revolution foreshadowed by the year of the imagination, 1968, had not come – these things pained her deeply, as her writings show. It was only natural that La Passionaria of Ros Muc would become a member of Misneach (courage), the organization set up by the Republican and novelist Máirtín Ó Cadhain and others to agitate for Gaelic-language revival and rights. Even her admirers were shocked at the verbal violence she together with Ó Cadhain unleashed on a Fianna Fáil minister of state they regarded as a fake Republican and traitor to the language when he turned up at an Éigse, a literary festival, in Dundalk. But she also understood that English is essential in the modern world. A saying drawn from the life of the West of Ireland shore-people is this: '*Is deacair leis an ngobadán an dá thrá a fhreastal*', 'It's hard for the sandpiper to work the two ebb tides.' But it must be done; Irish must be preserved even while English is learned, for, she wrote, 'when people throw away the language they got from their ancestors down through the generations, they throw away the prime aid to the development of heart and mind.'

Caitlín Maude died in 1982 of cancer at the age of forty-one, leaving a husband and a son. Her work has been published in two rather meagre-looking but precious collections, one of poetry and one of prose; perhaps she was too unsettled and conflicted to write more, or perhaps she always suffered from that tiredness named in the poem 'Treall' (a spell, as of work, or a fit, as of weeping) with which I introduced her, the tiredness that is the threshold of death.

> Tachtadh beag é
> tachtadh an bháis
> ach is tocht rómhór é
> tocht na beatha.

These last lines of her simple little poem 'Dán' (which means simply 'poem') are hard to translate, given the lack of a one-word equivalent in English of *tocht* – a catch or stop in the throat from emotion, a silence. A small strangulation it is, the death strangulation, but a great stop it is, the stop of life. The death rattle is nothing, compared to the silencing of life. Or the silencing of a language – for English and Irish are not just life's alternative ways of dealing with the same world; rather, an individual life is seeded into the join between a language and a world, grows within and is shaped by both, and shapes them in its turn. The little world of Ros Muc is lastingly inflected by Caitlín Maude's brief life, and the Irish language enriched by her scarce and precious words.

2 The Junction with History

The spinal road of the Ros Muc peninsula winds on northwards from Cill Bhriocáin, passing a few houses, a Gaeltacht Authority office block, and the cemetery of Cill Eoin with its melancholy old pine trees, which poor Nóra saw full of ghosts. One gets glimpses here and there of the swan-flecked inner waters of Cuan Chamais down to the right, and then after a mile and a half or so the wood of Oiriúlach, Pearse's visionary Eileabhrach, crowds in from the left, with the lake glimmering through it. Ahead is An Gort Mór, the big field, where the road out of the little side world of Ros Muc meets the main road passing by from east to west, and the land rises into bare hills that mark the beginning of inland, central Connemara. There are various buildings on the far side of the main road: a Garda station on the site of a barracks mysteriously burned down in 1971, a national school, a chapel, a factory, and Gairmscoil na bPiarsach, a vocational school named after Patrick Pearse and his brother Willie; also a fine big Gaelic football pitch and stand at the crossroads, which the community owes largely to the efforts of the former national school headmaster here, the late Tomás Ó Conaire of Glinn Chatha, whom I found to be a rich source of local knowledge. The vocational school has sporting connections too; one of its sons is the boxer Seán Ó Mhainnín or Seán Mannion, who in 1984 got as far as a world title bout in Madison Square Garden and is now the main trainer in the boxing club based in An Chrannóg. In fact there is a strong boxing tradition in Ros Muc, stemming from Micheál Ó Flatharta of Camas, an ex-soldier who taught the local youngsters the art and who is commemorated by a rather odd memorial at the crossroads, in the shape of a bronze bust flanked by two boxing gloves resting on the top of a low stone wall with a seat-like step in it.

The national school is my cue for the evocation of two more of Ros Muc's linguistic battlers, before I turn to Pearse himself, whose cottage is to be seen on the far side of the lake. Criostóir Mac Aonghusa was an Offaly farmer's son, born in 1905, who studied Irish under Professor Tomás Ó Máille in Galway, as well as Spanish in Barcelona, then came to Connemara and spent most of his life as schoolmaster in An Gort Mór until his retirement in 1962. But his first posting was on the little island of Inis Treabhair, a mile or so south-west of An Ghairfean, and he married Mairéad de Lappe from the neighbouring island of Eanach Mheáin. Mairéad had a revolutionary past: active in the War of Independence and then in the Civil War, she had seen the inside of Galway Gaol and Mountjoy, and had been released on condition she leave the country. It was on her return after some years in America that she met Criostóir; they had four children, but parted in the 1940s.

Criostóir was a political activist: founder member of Fianna Fáil in the west, county councillor, founder of Cumann na Gaedhealtachta together with Máirtín Ó Cadhain and Seosamh Mac Mathúna, secretary of the Camas branch of Conradh na Gaeilge, member of Misneach. In the early 1930s he and Mac Mathúna proposed the scheme under which Gaeltacht farmers struggling to survive on inadequate holdings could be given land held by the Land Commission in Meath, which led to the foundation of the new Gaeltacht of Ráth Cairn. He was also a writer, publishing a collection of short stories and another of essays. The title of the latter, *Ó Ros Muc go Rostov*, hints at his wide travels in Europe and Russia, and his literary interests from Pádraic Ó Conaire to Chekhov. In it he writes of his great hero, An Piarsach. I translate:

He was a rebel from head to foot. He was a rebel in politics, in educational affairs, and in matters of writing. He was a poet, and his poetry is to be read in all his writings, whether dramas, short stories, verses or political essays. Who can fail to notice the poetry in his essays on Tone, on Emmet and on O'Donovan Rossa? The freshness and depth of vision and strength in the opinions he expressed are poetic, and the deed he did in Easter Week, going into action against the strongest army to be found, himself and a small band of men, that was poetry too.

Criostóir's son Proinsias grew up to be a more worldly, ambitious, successful and controversial figure than his father, and his career filled and exceeded the bounds of the Irish-language movement he was born into. Máirtín Ó Cadhain was his godfather, and he spoke little English until he was thirteen. After studying (through Irish) at the Jesuit school Coláiste Iognáid in Galway, he became a trainee actor and office boy in the Abbey Theatre. Although, as he said himself, he was never more than a fifth-rate actor, he had some opportunities to act in children's plays and read stories on Radio Éireann, and (according to a slightly hostile-sounding summary biography in *Beathaisnéis*) he became a man of fashion, with a silk smoking jacket, a taste for oysters, supreme self-confidence and a gift for knowing everybody. Through a Trinity College Irish-language society he met and married Catherine Ellis, who later rose to become a judge of the Supreme Court. By the 1950s he was writing 'Irishman's Diary' in the *Irish Times* and contributing to the *New Statesman*. With an attractive Italian countess he founded a company to make and sell radio programmes, and gained some publicity over a programme on Ireland's ill-preparedness for an atomic attack, which was suppressed by the government. For Telefís Éireann he headed the first Irish-language programme, featuring interviews with writers and other notables, and edited the current-affairs programme *Féach*. In his column for the *Sunday Press* he was a strong supporter of Charles Haughey, and he wrote in several Irish-language journals such as *Anois* and *Foinse*. A 'Connolly Republican', he became active in the Labour Party, failed to be elected in 1965, was expelled because of his trenchant criticisms of certain TDs, and lost his deposit as an Independent in 1969. The following year he was invited by Seán MacBride to join the United Nations as an adviser and representative. In this phase of his multifarious career he set up a broadcasting system for the South West Africa People's Organization in Namibia, and took part in diplomatic missions to Egypt, Algeria, Zaire and Tanzania, his concerns being civil and human rights.

In 1976 there was a public competition for the post of Head of Raidió na Gaeltachta; Proinsias seemed the right person, but at the last stage he was passed over, it is said, because of the many enemies he had made on the basis that the enemies of his many friends were his enemies too. He became editor of *Féach* when it was revived in 1980, but had to resign when he fell ill in 1985. On the first occasion I met him he foretold, with apparent good cheer, a very short period of survival for himself, but in the event he went on with his vigorous lifestyle as author, adviser to the Arts Council and board member of Cumann Merriman. He attained to the summit of influence in the language movement as, simultaneously, Chairman of Bord na Gaeilge and President of Conradh na Gaeilge – most controversially, since it seemed to many that the role of the latter, non-governmental, organization is to yap at the tardy heels of the former, an arm of the state. I bumped into him at some official occasion at this period, and asked him how he was; '*Beo!*' he said, and added, '*Tá sé nios fearr ná an bealach eile!*' ('Alive! It's better than the alternative.') But the alternative became actual soon after that, in 2003.

If one walks west from the crossroads, with the lake on one's left, a cottage becomes visible on the far side of it through gaps in the trees, lime-white, thatched, nestled into the shelter of a rise in the land behind it, looking down into the blue waters – a vision of the old Connemara, that of Paul Henry and a thousand lesser masters of the far-off view. This is the navel of Pearse's kingdom. It would be merely conventional to call it his holiday home, since the days he spent here were central to his literary life. His oration at the graveside of O'Donovan Rossa was composed and many times rehearsed here, and in the end the cottage became the secret headquarters of his conspiracy against the British Empire. Nowadays it is in the hands of the Office of Public Works and on the tourist trail, and it receives some ten thousand visitors a year. The interior was destroyed by fire in 1921 (an event I will set in a wide context later on), but has been restored and somewhat unimaginatively furnished with iron bedsteads, patchwork quilts, ewers and water jugs, even a spinning wheel (though I doubt if An Piarsach did much spinning) and other items of suitable style and age. No attempt has been made to persuade you that the man himself has just stepped out for a stroll, leaving a book or a manuscript unfinished on the table or a fire dying in the hearth, but the custodians are friendly and well informed; when I called in recently and happened to mention that I'd been puzzling over the meaning of Eileabhrach, Fióna took it upon herself to phone around the old and the wise of the neighbourhood for their opinions.

The architecture and siting of Pearse's cottage are of deep significance. Having found a spot that welcomed the morning sun, mirrored itself in lake-water and hid from the western gales, he opted for a design rooted in tradition. To choose to live under thatch rather than slates, at a time when so many were fleeing rural poverty and turning their backs on all that was associated with it, was in itself remarkable. The scale of the cottage is rather more ample than the local norm, but its parts are in proportion. J. M. Synge, travelling through south Connemara at this period, noted that the new houses being provided by the Congested Districts Board, with iron roofing instead of thatch, were giving some neighbourhoods 'an uncomfortable look that is, I think, felt by the people'. The rethatching of a house was an occasion of neighbourly cooperation, 'a sort of festival', he writes, and house design had a communal element too:

I remember one evening in another congested district – on the west coast of Kerry – listening to some peasants who discussed for hours the proportions of a new cottage that was to be built by one of them. They had never, of course, heard of proportion; but they had rules and opinions, in which they were deeply interested, as to how high a house should be if it was of a certain length, with so many rafters, in order that it might look well.

The names of those who built Pearse's traditionally proportioned cottage are still remembered locally. They understood that he was not a rich man, and that he was working for the sake of the nation, and they charged little, no doubt having had many consultations among themselves, 'in order that it might look well', which it does. However, it seems that Pearse was not in a hurry to pay for the timber and other materials, as Proinsias Mac Aonghusa tells us:

Probably he was not able to meet the bills; he was a man who always had very little money and faced heavy expenses in many places. He was summonsed for this in Oughterard court. I believe the bill had not yet been cleared when the British government put him to death. But it is the man himself and his ideas and way of life that impressed Ros Muc, not the thinness of his purse.

As in the traditional West of Ireland house the central kitchen and living space, entered though a small porch, is open to the rafters. There is a room off it to either side; one would have expected two small rooms in the place of the left-hand one of these, which, curiously, is entered by two separate doors, but I am told that a curtain used to be drawn between the two beds in it. It would also be more usual for the end rooms to have ceilings and lofts overhead, entered by ladder or stairs from the kitchen, which it seems they did formerly, for Pearse's mother mentioned in a letter that on a visit there she had slept in the loft. There is a fireplace in the left-hand wall of the kitchen, and another in the room to the right, so that the two chimneys are symmetrically disposed and divide the roofline into equal thirds. There are four small sash windows, one on either side of the entrance to the kitchen and one in each room, nicely set in the façade, and one in both of the side rooms, to the rear.

Pearse first visited Ros Muc in 1903, and it was not he who called forth the spirit of nationalism and love of the Irish language there, but the local enthusiasm for both causes that summoned him to witness it. In the previous year a branch of Conradh na Gaeilge had been founded by a group of young people, most of whom were attending evening classes in Irish in the school at An Gort Mór. When they read in *An Claidheamh Soluis* ('The Sword of Light'), the organ of Conradh na Gaeilge, that there was to be an examination for would-be teachers of Irish, a dozen of them contributed a half-crown each to pay for an examiner to come down from Dublin by train to Maam Cross, and the schoolmaster of An Gort Mór undertook to put him up. Came the day, came the train. A stranger alighted – a Mayo man who had come to sit the exam – and to his surprise was met by a welcoming party and whisked off in a sidecar to the schoolmaster's residence. Then the real examiner alighted, to the embarrassment of the remainder of the welcoming party. So there is a glint of comedy in Pearse's entrance into the history of Ros Muc. It was not the last of the mutual misunderstandings between ruler and subjects of the little Gaelic kingdom-to-be, for the former came with an ideal of the latter that no one east of Tír na nÓg could ever have lived up to:

Consider the Irish-speaking child. He is the fairest thing that springs up from the soil of Ireland – more beautiful than any flower, more graceful than any wild creature of the fields or the woods, purer than any monk or nun, wiser than any seer . . . The voice of Éire has spoken to him through generations of soldiers and poets and seanchaidhes whose traditions he has inherited with their speech . . .

One youth at least, Colm Ó Gaora, the secretary of the local branch of the Conradh, was deeply impressed by the examiner and came to idolize him. In his autobiographical work *Mise* ('Myself') he describes Pearse as he saw him that first day. I translate:

He was a handsome, well-built young man of medium height. A pale complexion – the complexion of one who worked indoors. Very diffident – the diffidence of people who lack relationships with other people. He was a peaceable, silent man, more ready to listen than to talk. A notable, noble brow and thick black hair. A slight cast in one eye added to his good looks. He was very well dressed, it seemed to me . . . I can truthfully say that I was under the influence of this examiner from then on. Without my realizing it he put me under a sort of spell that I couldn't shake off from that day to this. Pearse gave his affection to Ros Muc in the same way.

Pearse stayed on in Ros Muc the following day and attended Mass, at which he heard the priest announce from the altar that a scandalous matter had arisen in the congregation, but that since there was a visiting gentleman present he would not speak of it that day. The incident became the nucleus of Pearse's story 'An Dearg Daol', of a woman cast out from village society. Thereafter he visited Ros Muc every summer:

It was the cabins of the poor that he frequented, talking of old times with the village elders by the fireside, or more often listening and noting down their lore. It was the rare afternoon on which he wasn't to be seen at the roadside talking to the little children coming home from school – the children he gave his heart to. Yes, An Piarsach was a strange person, in the eyes of the toadies and anglicized folk of the locality – an educated gentleman like him paying so much attention to the wants and the language of the poor, instead of looking down on them.

But the shoneens, the trotters after the nobility, were strong on the ground in Ros Muc. When Pearse discovered that Lord Dudley, the Viceroy, who came down to nearby Inver Lodge for the fishing and shooting each year, was arranging festivities for the schoolchildren and bringing gentlemen over from London to show them films about heroes who had fought for the empire, he decided to strike back. His revenge was the occasion in the school at An Turlach Beag described in my preface. Colm Ó Gaora was ecstatic over it:

No word of a lie, it was an evening for faithful hearts. To crown the evening there was a film projectionist to show films picturing the nobility and wisdom of the Gaelic race. I never saw Pearse so full of talk as he was that night. Songs were sung, tales were told, poems were recited and orations pronounced. The people saw that this man had respect for the language . . . That was the blow An Piarsach struck on his own behalf, in the year 1906, as stout as any he struck in his life. It's many the one he saved by it. The English gentry gave no more festivities after that – much to the annoyance of their local lackeys.

By 1910 Pearse had his cottage on An Aill Mhór, the big cliff, that is, the hillock now known as Cnocán an Phiarsaigh, and which he made the hub of the web of tales he spun over the surrounding countryside. In the early and rather mawkish story 'Eoghainín na nÉan' ('Little Owen of the Birds') it is on An Aill Mhór that the lad sits and communes with the swallows, while slipping decorously and painlessly out of this world. Sean-Mhaitias, the main character in 'Íosagán', a former Fenian who is reputed to have sold his soul to a mysterious 'big man' he met on Cnoc an Daimh, the hill inland of An Gort Mór, was based on Colm Ó Gaora's father, who lived a few hundred yards west of the hillock. Íosagán (the name is a diminutive of 'Jesus') is a mysterious little boy who appears now and again at play with the schoolchildren when the adults are not watching them, and who announces to the recalcitrant but good-hearted old rebel that he will see him again that coming night; later the priest is summoned to Maitias's deathbedside by the same unknown child. The 'keening woman' of the story 'An Bhean Chaointe' lives just beyond Droichead na Glaise Duibhe, the bridge of the black stream, about two miles to the east. Poll an Phíobaire, the piper's cave in the adventure story of that name, is a little cleft in the steep shoreline below the hill of Camas (a site to which I will return). Many of the protagonists of these stories would have been as identifiable as these and the many other places mentioned in them to the people of Ros Muc; it is through personal names and placenames that the stories keep what grip they have on reality.

From the cottage a grassy path leads down through alder trees and bracken banks to the brink of the lake, where there is a bench, as there surely must have been in Pearse's day. The lake is dotted with islands; one is big enough to carry a small wood, most of them just able to support a single bush. There are frequently swans. It is a peaceful and lovely spot. But when I sit on this bench and imagine Pearse deep in thought there, I feel I am sitting between his two obsessions: boyhood and death. There are passages in the majority of his prose works that cannot be read nowadays without alarm, and which must have raised a snigger in generations of schoolboys. In 'The Master', set in early Christian and Celtic times, the master's older pupils happily concur that, having no women there, they make love to their little Iollann, a boy-child. The poem 'Little Lad of the Tricks' confesses to the child that 'There is a fragrance in your kiss / That I have not found yet / In the kisses of women / Or in the honey of their bodies', and that if the lad could read his secrets he would be white with dread; 'He who has my secrets / Is not fit to touch you: / Is not that a pitiful thing, / Little lad of the tricks?' But one can be assured, according to his biographer Ruth Dudley Edwards (no fond observer), that his love of young boys remained 'wholly innocent of lasciviousness':

He never had an inkling that there was anything sexual behind it, and indeed no man of his reticence and obsessional purity of thought and deed could have written as he did otherwise.

Do we still not dare to read the man's own words? In the moving poem 'Why Do Ye Torture Me?' Pearse describes being hunted by his desires 'as a poor deer would be hunted on a hill / a poor long-wearied deer with the hound-pack after him', and says that no satisfaction can come to his desires while he lives. And, without prying further into his secrets, we can read in his poem 'Renunciation' that his escape from the impermissible longings he recognized in himself was ultimately through the orientation towards death:

> Naked I saw thee,
> O beauty of beauty,
> And I blinded my eyes
> For fear I should fail.
>
> . . .
>
> I blinded my eyes
> And I closed my ears,
> I hardened my heart
> And I smothered my desire.
>
> . . .
>
> I have turned my face
> To this road before me,
> To the deed that I shall see
> And the death I shall die.

Purity is embodied in the child; we cannot approach it because of the impurity of our own embodiment; only the sacrifice of desire and ultimately of embodiment itself can purify us.

Pearse's preparations for the event that would define him and lift him above the impurities of life occupied him as much in Ros Muc as they did in Dublin. In 1913, when Bulmer Hobson and Liam Mellowes were staying with him in the cottage, the three of them set up a branch of Fianna Éireann, the Republican answer to Baden-Powell's Boy Scouts, and shortly afterwards Pearse himself established a battalion of Óglaigh na hÉireann, the Irish Volunteers, in Ros Muc, An Cheathrú Rua and Na hOileáin. Soon the lads were drilling (with sticks, for lack of arms), and camping in tents around his cottage. In late 1914 or early 1915 there were manoeuvres. The headquarters was on Cnocán na Móna, the hillock of turf, a mile or so down the peninsula. The quiet-spoken Pearse became a different man when standing on that hillock and issuing his commands; his shout, rivalling that of any sergeant major, amazed everybody and could be heard as far away as An Turlach Beag.

It was in Ros Muc that Pearse composed his celebrated oration to be delivered at the graveside of O'Donovan Rossa, the old Fenian hero whose funeral would, it was hoped, unify the movement towards Irish independence. Again and again he wrote and rewrote it, and tried it out on his brother Willie and his friend Desmond Ryan, to the point that they began to make fun of him. Some of the Ros Muc Volunteers, led by Colm Ó Gaora, travelled to Dublin for the event, and heard Pearse's monitory words: 'Life springs from death; and from the graves of patriot men and women spring living nations . . .' The cottage, with its many visitors, hidden as it were in plain sight of the constabulary barracks at the crossroads, was an ideal forum for discussions between Pearse and the other IRB conspirators who, in the unknowing heart of the Volunteers, were planning the Easter Rising. Proinsias Mac Aonghusa's local enquiries have suggested that James Connolly was probably the only one of the seven future signatories of the Proclamation of the Republic who did not visit Pearse in Ros Muc, and even he may have done so too.

Among the Volunteers, according to Colm Ó Gaora, the only question was, when will the blow be struck? Each member was to equip himself for battle; most could not afford to do so, but Colm bought himself a rifle and fifty bullets. The week before Easter 1916 he went to Dublin looking for instructions, since the Ros Muc Volunteers were under Pearse's especial command and relations between them and the Galway brigade were obscure. An Piarsach responded to his questions with a melancholy smile and a distant prophetic look. After some thought he said that the best thing Colm could do would be to attend the mobilization arranged for the following Sunday in Galway, and Colm took it that he would receive further instructions after that event. That was his last sight of his beloved hero.

On Easter Sunday Colm left Ros Muc at first daylight, walked the twenty-five miles into Galway with his loaded gun and his fifty bullets, attended Mass and then found to his amazement that the mobilization

had been put off. All waited upon the return of a messenger who had
been sent off to Dublin for instructions. That day passed, and the next.
There were rumours of fighting in Dublin and elsewhere; eventually
it was decided to send Colm off by bicycle to Castlebar, but there he
found the Mayo Volunteers were in the same state of doubt and confusion as the Galway Volunteers. Returning to Galway, he found that
the leadership there had been arrested, and he fell into despair. The
next day, the Tuesday, he heard that the Castlebar men were on the
field of battle; his spirits rose again, and off he went to join them. But
the rumour had been false and he decided to go to Athenry where, he
heard, there was fighting. In the village of Cong, exhausted and
hungry, he called in on a family he knew; but no sooner had the door
closed behind him than it was knocked off its hinges by three sturdy
policemen; he drew his revolver, fired and missed; his second shot
jammed in the barrel, and in no time he was on the flat of his back and
the revolver twisted out of his grip.

So ended Ros Muc's sole contribution to the Rising, and Colm's
tour of state accommodation began, a fourteen-month journey
through squalor and brutality which he describes without self-pity
and with a good deal of humour in *Mise*. It started with a cell in Cong
Barracks, then his transfer by horse-cart to Ballinrobe Barracks, by car
to Castlebar Prison, by train to Dublin and on foot through the still-
burning streets to Richmond Barracks. Next, after appearing
(undefended) before a military court and being sentenced to ten years'
imprisonment, he was taken to Kilmainham, the most squalid of all
his prisons, where a guard showed him the bullet holes in the wall
against which Pearse had been shot. Then he was transferred by prison
van to Mountjoy, by cattle-boat to Holyhead and train to Dartmoor,
where he spent seven months in the company of de Valera and others
of his heroes, and nearly lost his eyesight sewing mail sacks. He was
moved to Maidstone, then to Lewes and then Parkhurst, where he
learned that together with the other political prisoners he was to be
released. Finally via Pentonville he attained to freedom and the Holyhead train. The joyous official reception of the returnees in Dublin
told him of the great change that had come over public opinion, which
initially had been hostile to the Easter Rising but now almost amounted

to the resurrection of its martyred leaders – the change charted by Pádraic Ó Conaire's *Seacht mBua an Éirí Amach*. In fact, who should he meet at the reception but Sean-Phádraic himself, who got 7s 6d out of him (which Colm had to borrow) as a subscription towards the printing of that very book.

Within a few years Ó Gaora, ever faithful to Pearse's vision, was in action again, in the War of Independence. But the history of Connemara's participation in that and the ensuing Civil War plays out over a vast terrain of mountains and glens stretching northwards from Ros Muc to Killary Harbour and beyond – a physical geography fitfully illuminated by history and shrouded in myth, which has now to be brought to mind in as much of its complex grandeur and close-grained reality as I can grasp.

3 The Gentry's Roads

A dozen or so square miles of bog inlaid with thirty or forty lakes
(these numbers are shaky estimates, for to define limits to a bog that
seeps up hillsides into stony heathland, or to discriminate between
lakes and ponds, and between ponds and bog-holes, is to go against
the nature of this riddling terrain) ultimately accumulate their waters
into two major lakes just north of the coast road, and then let it pour
through two bridges under the road to the west of Pearse's cottage.
The furthermost bridge, a mile and a half away, that of Inbhear Mór
or Invermore, the big estuary, marks the eastern limit of the old Barony
of Ballynahinch. Inland from this point the boundary wades up the
Inbhear Mór river, which links a chain of lakes, climbs into the mountains and runs from peak to peak along the Mám Tuirc range to drop
into Killary Harbour. The land west of this, to the Atlantic rim, was
in medieval times the territory of the Conmaicne Mara, the people
who gave their name to Connemara; therefore some say the true
Connemara is what lies beyond this boundary, but that is not a claim
the people of the Joyce Country, of Ros Muc and all that we now call
south Connemara, can allow. Eastwards, Connemara defies definition;
I will not indulge it far out of sight of the Mám Tuirc mountains.

Below the Inbhear Mór bridge the river becomes a little delta of
several channels winding and waterfalling through grassy, furzy,
hummocky land, with rough and ready wooden walkways and plank
bridges for fishery officials, sluices and concrete steps for fish, and,
looking out of place in this tousled patch of scrub, a glistening solar
panel to power an automatic fish-counter. For this is the portal to
one of the famous salmon and sea-trout fisheries of Connemara. The
lakes on the inland side of the coast road were and to some extent
still are the appanage of the *boic mhóra*, the big shots, whose angliciz-
ing influence on Ros Muc so riled An Piarsach, Colm Ó Gaora and,
as I will tell, their successors the young activists of Gluaiseacht

Chearta Sibhialta na Gaeltachta, the Gaelic civil rights movement of
the rebellious 1960s.

The principal lakes of these immensely valuable fisheries are Loch
Inbhear Mór, Loch Inbhear Beag just east of it (these two plus a scattering of lakes further inland constituting the Inver fishery), and a
chain of lakes linked by Abhainn Scríbe, the Screebe river, nearly three
miles to the east of the Ros Muc crossroads. Like most of Connemara
these hinterlands of Ros Muc were part of the Martin estate, and when
the Martins were ruined by the Famine they fell into the hands of the
Law Life Assurance, who eventually sold them to the Berridges. The
fisheries had a separate history, that of their various lessees. In 1834 or
'35 the Martins leased the Inver and Screebe fisheries to a James O'Hara
of Lenaboy, near Tuam, who built a lodge on Weathercock Island in
a lake connecting with Loch Inbhear Beag that is now called Loch an
Oileáin, the lake of the island.

In the years immediately after the Famine, Connemara became for
a while a focus of development, as new money flooded in to wash
away the legacy of inaction of the old landlords, now bankrupt. The
first commercial salmon hatchery was set up in Oughterard in 1852,
while the first artificial river was dug through 600 yards of bog to open
up the thirty scattered lakes of the Doohulla fishery near Ballyconneely
in 1854. O'Hara's son, another James, took over on his father's death,
and introduced the new concept of 'pisciculture' to the region. Young
James's 'tidal fish stairs' in the mouth of the Inbhear Beag river, of
which some traces can be seen below the road, were a famous innovation, and were reported on by the geologist and archaeologist George
Kinahan to a Salmon Fishery Congress in London in 1867. This short
river emptying Loch Inbhear Beag into the sea was so shallow that fish
could come up it only on a high tide; O'Hara's fish stairs consisted of
a series of artificial pools that always retained water, separated by steps
the fish could negotiate, and a two-foot wide channel excavated on
the lower shore to direct the fish to the lowest of the pools. O'Hara
also had a salmon hatchery by a little stream feeding into Loch an
Oileáin; it consisted of a number of boxes filled with gravel that had
been well washed and boiled, on which the fertilized salmon eggs were
laid, with filtered stream water washing over them. After a few years

O'Hara felt that he had sufficiently revivified his fishery by these means, and his hatchery was not in use after 1870. I imagine that it was in his time that the long lines of stepping stones known to the locals as *bóithre na n-uaisle*, the gentry's roads, were laid down from lake to lake of the Inbhear system for the convenience of anglers – another web of ways, largely foundered in bog nowadays.

A new hatchery, for sea trout only, was built on the same site as O'Hara's in 1889, and refurbished ten years later by yet another lessee, the adventurer Moreton Frewen of Munga Lodge near Clifden. Mortal Ruin was his nickname, a memento of his wild days as a Wyoming cattle-baron; his wife was the great heiress Clara Jerome, sister to Winston Churchill's mother Jennie. Frewen inaugurated the Inver Club, a coterie of like-minded sportsmen including Earls Cairn and Warwick, Lords Castletown and Dunraven, Sir John Willoughby and Dr Jameson. These last two were heroes of that high point of jingoistic fervour the 'Jameson Raid', an attempt to win the Transvaal from the Boers and annexe it to Cape Province in 1895; the plan, laid by Cecil Rhodes, was for an armed party to make a three-day dash to Johannesburg and precipitate an uprising of English settlers against the Boer government. However, the raiders were tracked all the way by the Boers and after several bloody skirmishes and the loss of seventeen men had to surrender. Dr Jameson was briefly imprisoned in England for this escapade, and was canonized by Rudyard Kipling: 'If you can keep your head when all about you / Are losing theirs and blaming it on you . . .' Released on health grounds, 'he must have benefited greatly from the rest and recuperation he enjoyed at the Inver Fishery,' as Noel Wilkins, the historian of these fisheries, puts it, 'because he returned to South Africa before 1900, and by 1904 was Prime Minister of Cape Province!' He was later made a baronet for his part in the foundation of the Union of South Africa. His comrade Sir John Willoughby, decorated for gallantry in Matabeleland and in the Great War, died in battle in 1918.

It was in about 1903 that the Viceroy, William Humble, the second Earl of Dudley, started to make the lodge on the island the base for his fishing vacations. Sir Henry Robinson of the Local Government Board describes him:

Lord Dudley was a wonderfully good all-round sportsman. He kept a racing cutter at Kingstown for the one design matches, with which he won many flags during the season, and no one could handle a boat better than he in a thresh to windward in hard weather. He was a crack shot, and took Rockingham, the King Harmon seat in Co. Roscommon, for the shooting. He had a fishing lodge in Connemara, and could throw a salmon fly against any man in Ireland. He rode to hounds well and was a good golfer, though not a very considerate one, as he would think nothing of keeping people waiting behind him for a quarter of an hour while he drove off practice shots from the tee . . . Another thing that somewhat affected his popularity was that although he was rich and open-handed in money matters he was utterly careless and indolent about his payments, and kept people an unconscionable time waiting for their money, without ever realizing how inconvenient it must be to them.

How strange it is that while such pillars of British imperialism as the Viceroy and his friends were hoisting salmon out of the water and blasting birds out of the sky in Inver, the man who posed the most immediate threat to the empire was in his cottage over the road, writing stories about little girls and their dolls! Lord Dudley and Patrick Pearse – can one imagine two more unlike creatures? – formed the two magnetic poles of Ros Muc's social and political life. The United Irish League, a powerful organization of smallholders campaigning for the breaking up of the landed estates and closely allied at that period with the Irish Parliamentary Party, had a Ros Muc branch, and Lord Dudley was soon invited to participate in one of its meetings in the chapel after Sunday Mass. Colm Ó Gaora's father, an unreconstructed Fenian, would have nothing to do with the event, but Colm, like all the other schoolchildren, was there, having been drilled in every detail of raising a shout and clapping hands when the schoolmaster should acquit himself of the honour of reading out an address, which it had taken him weeks to write, before His Excellency:

The day came at last. The parishioners were all agog. The parish priest in charge. The shopkeepers and local worthies competing to be the closest to His Excellency. The address was read, and the priest welcomed the noble

Earl as a prop of Home Rule and the foundation stone of freedom. His Excellency gave a meagre, scanty, terse reply. After a couple of words with one or two of those who were pressing around him, into his coach with him and off he went. That was the sum of the trouble his high mightiness put himself to for the sake of the nation.

All the same, Lord Dudley was well regarded; it is remembered that no one in want who had the nerve to approach him would be sent away empty-handed. The lodge employed servant girls, gardeners, boatmen and gillies, and paid them well. Men poached from the well-stocked rivers and lakes, and/or got posts as water bailiffs to protect them. Stephen Gwynn, the Nationalist MP, visited Ros Muc in 1908 for a fishing holiday in the course of which he enquired into every aspect of Connemara life, and describes coming down the drive on his bicycle to a platform on the water's edge, where he had to wait while a liveried butler was ferried across from the lodge to take his card. He was told that the original proprietor built on the island so as to be spared the importunity of the crowds of famished beggars on the quay, but that it was now customary for the day's superfluous catch to be divided among the people, mainly children, who would assemble there on summer evenings; 'and since four or five rods will be bringing in fifty or sixty handsome sea-trout, it will be seen that the kindly custom means the distribution of a deal of good food to people whose diet is of the sparsest'. Later on, it was more for the fun of the '*sciob sceab*' that broke out among them when the fish were divided that the children gathered on the quay. The wives and mistresses of the anglers, with time on their hands, would call in at cottages to buy lengths of *bréidín* or home-spun tweed; their custom was much appreciated, and they must have looked magnificent, sailing along the boreens in their voluminous skirts and wide hats. Connemara Irish had no term for such beings and had to borrow from English, as in, '*Chonaic mé beirt* ladies *ag gabháil siar inné*' ('I saw two ladies going west yesterday'). Lord Dudley's wife Rachel performed a more lasting service to Connemara and other western regions in setting up the Lady Dudley's Nursing Scheme, providing nurses to areas in which there was little or nothing in the way of medical services. Béal an Daingin, immediately to the south of Ros Muc, was with Carna the first place in Connemara to have such a nurse, in 1903; Ros Muc, it seems, did not get one until 1925. Pretty cottages were built for the nurses, one of which, almost unchanged, can be seen by the road about two miles west of Recess. Lady Dudley was awarded the CBE for her good works. In golden retrospect Ros Muc sometimes wonders if it did not do better out of the lords and ladies of bygone times than it does out of the government of today.

In 1908 Lord Dudley was appointed Governor General of Australia, and he and his wife left Ireland. Later on the Dudleys used to come to Screebe Lodge, a few miles to the east, for their holidays, while Inver Lodge and its fishery passed through various hands. The Guinness family had them for a while, and more recently the Millards of Odlum's flour mills. When I called, in the 1980s, the owners were not in residence, but the tenant of the pretty little gatehouse showed me around, leading me across the swaying forty-yards-long pontoon bridge to see the lodge, which peeped out from trees that had been moulded by a century of wind into a protective cowl around it. Soon after my visit it went on sale; I have the *Irish Times* property correspondent's description:

Inver lodge has a comfortable club-like feel – the kind of atmosphere that takes decades of leisurely living to create. The informal entrance is through the conservatory where fishing rods and nets are lined up in immaculate order and log books stand by to record the day's catch. Wood panelled walls in the hall and adjoining study give way to bright reception rooms . . . An unusual winding staircase leads to the upper floor, where the six bedrooms are all pleasant, airy rooms with views of the lake and beyond to the 12 Pins . . .

I haven't followed the lodge's history further. When once more I strolled down the long drive to the lake, in the summer of 2008 (the hedges afire with montbretia blossoms, one of the lodge's gifts to the neighbourhood, as Stephen Gwynn noted a century earlier), I found the way barred by handsome gates of tall black metal bars, with an electronic lock and no obvious way of communicating with the inhabitants of the privacies beyond. I think no one was at home.

★

The Scríb catchment is separated from the Inbhear systems by a range of low hills north of An Gort Mór. The word *scríb* means a narrow strip of land, a scratch or furrow, a journey, or the mark of a course to be run; which sense was originally at play here I do not know, but the place marks the furthest point in the extraordinary detour one has to make to get from Ros Muc to the lands that lie east and south of it, around the head of the long-drawn-out and winding bay, Cuan Chamais – as I am well aware, having done it on foot or on bicycle in so many weathers. In summer, though, the three or four miles from Inbhear to Scríb are to be walked and remarked upon foot by foot, despite the fact that the road has been widened in recent years and bears too much traffic for comfort. Beyond the school, chapel and Garda station near the Ros Muc crossroads there are tree-shaded stretches with occasional prosperous-looking houses on the left, from whose gardens roses spill out and ramble off with the big white-blossomed bindweed along the roadside banks, where there are drifts of white moon daisies, and St Dabeoc's heath, the rare large-belled heather of Connemara, grows up head-high through the furzy hedges. On the right the bay appears beyond a few little fields; often there are a hundred swans adrift on it. The townland after An Gort Mór is Glinn Chatha, which locally is held to mean battle-glen (whereas my late adviser on knotty toponymics, Professor T. S. Ó Máille, tentatively derives it from *caoth*, bog-hole); they say that rustlers from Gleann Iar-Chonnacht (near Oughterard) carried off cattle from Carna, and the Carna people pursued them and fought with them out on the bogs in the east of the townland.

If foot-weary on this road, one can find ways down onto the shore and rest there. A grassy boreen arched over by trees leads to one such secretive spot, where a pile of rounded boulders as big as haycocks, bound together by ivy, forms a little peninsula called Aill na Staileach, the rock of the stallion. Here there is a flat granite outcrop on which I once lay in evening sunshine for an hour, while a peaceably brimming tide crept in and came licking at my feet like a friendly dog. Looking out across the waters from here one has the narrow opening of Cuan Chamais a mile away to the south, with the low-lying Ros Muc peninsula on its western shore and the neat conical hill of Camas on the eastern.

A small vertical streak of shadow is visible at the foot of this hill; I identify it, from my memory of exploring that shore, as Poll an Phíobaire, the piper's hole. Many caves bear this folkloric name associated with a legend of a lost piper whose music is heard from their depths; I know of one in Cregg near Clifden, a swallow hole in limestone, and another that is supposed, quite impossibly, to link Inis Meáin and Inis Oírr. The Camas cave is equally improbably said to come out in the promontory of Muiceanach Idir Dhá Sháile a couple of miles further south. In fact it is just a cleft a few feet deep where the waves have licked out a relatively soft seam of rock – but nevertheless it has its little station in the conflictual ideologies that beset the Irish-speaking west. Patrick Pearse wrote a boys' adventure tale about it, 'Poll an Phíobaire', of which the famous lexicographer Fr Dinneen, no friend of Pearse's, wrote an insulting review, hinting that the title had a double meaning, and ending with a most unclerical pun: 'It is to be hoped that the Píobaire will continue to draw from the stores of his capacious and well-filled arsenal.' Pearse's friends were led by this obscenity to think that he had been typically naïve in his choice of title, and persuaded him to change it to 'An Uaimh', 'The Cave'. The incident is mentioned in Ruth Dudley Edwards's acclaimed revisionist biography of Pearse, and she seems to agree with Pearse's overanxious protectors. But the title correctly echoes local tradition and usage; it was the cleric, not the patriot, who was inadvertently exposing himself. The misunderstanding is symptomatic of Edwards's incomprehension of what the Gaeltacht and its language meant to Pearse, a fault that explains why her biography, for all its professionalism, is such a sapless work.

A little further to the east in Glinn Chatha is the site of another landmark, now removed, that was extremely ugly but became a favourite of mine for its absurd incongruity: the Screebe Electricity Generating Station – a skyscraping pile of huge battered biscuit tins, with a conveyor belt like a giant centipede crawling up one side of it. Heaps of turf, wood chips and pine-tree bark mingled with broken branches lay around its base. Opened in 1957, it was one of four small five-megawatt turf-burning stations on the western seaboard of Ireland whose principal purpose was to support the local economy rather than to provide electricity at any reasonable rate. And in its heyday it did indeed keep about 180 turf-cutters busy, both near at hand and on the commercial-scale cuttings at Maam Cross, earning around £1,000 a year. But it was always on the verge of closure because its electricity cost nearly three times as much as that from large modern stations, and it finally ceased operation in 1989 and was totally dismantled, to my sneaking regret, although I had often fulminated about its discordance with its lovely surroundings.

In its autumnal days the white plume of smoke with which it proclaimed itself to half of Connemara was often not to be seen. Having got to know one of the operatives, I called in on the station one day when, as it happened, it was in its resting mode. At first I thought the gloomy interior was entirely deserted; I clambered to and fro on iron stairs and railed walkways, shouting, and eventually found my friend sitting on a couch down in a rear corner, watching over a panel of automatic pens and switches. He gave me a vivid impression of ever-present danger. Tapping a pipe, he said, with tremendous emphasis, '*Tá* gal *istigh anseo – atá chomh* te – *ní feidir leat é a* fheiceál!' ('There's *steam* in here – that's so *hot* – you can't *see* it!'), and '*Tá sé cosúil le* bomb!' ('It's like a *bomb!*') The station did not operate over the weekends, he told me, and on Monday the fire would be relit, with some rags or whatever was to hand, but it took most of the day to get it going again. Each day a mix of fuels was determined upon, depending on how damp each sort was. The fuel was hoisted up in a chain of buckets and dumped into the furnace; the pine bark, waste from Connemara's forestry operations, was not proving a success as an alternative to turf as the bits of branches in it tended to get stuck in the furnace's gullet. Water was pumped in from the sea for the steam-driven turbine, and after a series of heat exchangers the still-warm water flowed back into the bay, to the joy of the salmon, which, my guide told me, liked to congregate around the end of the discharge pipe. However, at the present moment, as he pointed out, a red flag on the control panel seemed to indicate that the pump was not working. He pressed a button, and an alarm started to ring, which proved difficult to stop. We went out the back door to check that water was flowing from the discharge pipe as it should, which it was. Since all appeared to be well, we left the homely old contraption to its uneasy dreams.

Eastwards again there are no more houses, the roadside areas expand into tracts of bog, and the road crosses Abhainn na Scríbe, the Screebe river, through which a network of lakes to the north fed by countless streams off boggy hillsides pour themselves into Cuan Chamais. A second bridge carries the road across a wide, peat-bottomed channel, An Ghlais Dhubh, the ominous 'black stream' repeatedly named in Pearse's story 'An Bhean Chaointe' ('The Keening Woman'); the house of this deranged and forlorn woman, ever awaiting the return of her son who has been hanged for the murder of an evicting landlord, is situated just beyond the sorrowful-looking stream, which thus symbolically separates her from the community.

Screebe Lodge, now the Screebe House Hotel, is hidden among trees a little further on, near the fork where one has to choose between turning south towards Camas or north to Maam Cross. It is a pleasant old place, a three-storey Edwardian building with marble fireplaces and tall windows and paintings of salmon, set in gardens that modulate from well-kept lawns and flowerbeds to tangly shrubberies and lead down to a rocky shore and a small private harbour. The view of the head of the swan-frequented bay is rendered rather untypical of Connemara, indeed almost classically composed, by two copses of old pine trees, one on an islet and the other on a little promontory of the Camas side of the bay. It is persistently said by local people that the St Georges, who had the lodge at the time, planted the latter copse to spare themselves the sight of the Catholic church being built a little further off in Camas. I have checked: the lodge, the trees and the church are not in a line; the belief is founded on prejudice, that is, faith. As to the picturesque pines on the islet, what I have heard is disillusioning, and therefore probably true: far from their being an aesthetic intervention, the St Georges planted them so that all the 'vermin' (i.e. crows and suchlike) would nest there and could more conveniently be killed off.

Scríb is part of the townland of Doire Bhanbh or Doire Dhá Bhanbh or Doire Átha Bhanbh, the wood of piglets, or of two piglets, or of the ford of piglets, according to different sources. Whereas all the neighbouring townlands formed part of the Martin estate this little corner belonged to the Lynches of Bearna, and at some time in the 1840s was acquired by a Thomas Fuge, of whom nothing is reported but the local tale that he fell asleep on the hills near here, woke up, looked around him and liked the place. The Admiralty chart of 1847 shows 'Fuge's House' where Screebe House Hotel now stands. The St Georges were the owners from 1896 for some time. Theirs was the first motor-car to penetrate the region; when it got stuck in a slough a mile or so short of the lodge the local lads could not be persuaded to go and pull it out as they thought it was some kind of animal that might pursue them. The St Georges, purported obscurers of the Catholic church, had their own little chapel, which was also attended by Lord Ismay's family from Costelloe Lodge a few miles away to the south. I remember finding it, a corrugated-iron hut hidden in a spooky little wood about a quarter of a mile from the house, on the left of the road to Maam Cross; it used to be *galánta*, I am told, painted black with a stained-glass window, but now one end of it was lapsing into the ground and all was rust. 'Teachín na bPrayers' was the locals' rather disparaging name for it.

After the Berridges sold Ballynahinch in 1925 they moved into Screebe Lodge and remained there until about 1960. Burke's *Landed Gentry of Ireland* tells us that Richard Berridge of Screebe, formerly of Ballynahinch Castle, was succeeded by his son, another Richard Berridge of Screebe, who served in the Second World War, rising to the rank of Lieutenant Colonel and retiring in 1948. The Berridges remained at Screebe until about 1960, and after that still retained a small lodge on a boreen running out into the bogs east of Camas. Since then the old place has seen sundry proprietors come and go, and for a long time now it has been in German ownership and functioning as a hotel.

I imagine that Mr Fuge, who awoke to the vision of a charmed spot between a land of cloud-reflecting lakes and a seaway made mild by sheltering, heather-tinged hills, was a sportsman, tired after a long day's shooting or fishing, for killing animals is the *raison d'être* of Screebe. Today it advertises itself as follows:

Screebe House is a magnificent Victorian sporting estate of 32,000 acres set in Connemara's countryside. In the autumn and winter our wildfowl snipe and woodcock attract sporting guests from all over the world. In addition our red deer are amongst the biggest and finest in the world. The estate is suited to Guns who appreciate the West of Ireland's spectacular scenery and rugged wildness together with the challenge of swirling, curling wildfowl.

The fishing is equally prized by the 'sporting guest'; I read of 500 salmon being caught here in 1869, and of a 21-pound cock salmon landed after a fight of almost three hours in 1894. The Screebe catchment occupies the wide, shallow valley followed by the road northwards to Maam Cross, and consists of around fifty lakes threaded together by Abhainn na Scríbe. At high water the sea floods up the river into Loch an tSáile, the lake of the salt water, and Loch Scríbe; the famous Screebe hatchery is by the rocky fall of the river into this latter lake, just above the tidal limit. It was established in 1863 for the lessee of the fishery, a Major Horsefall, by the famous pisciculturalist Robert Ramsbottom of Clitheroe in Lancashire, who had earlier been at work on the Doohulla fishery near Ballyconneely. Ramsbottom's hatchery at first consisted of a number of canals by the waterfall, in which water fed from a pipe flowed over beds of small stones; the fertilized fish eggs were placed on the stones and then covered with slightly larger stones. This arrangement was not a success – it harboured too many other creatures keen on fish eggs – and in 1866 the first permanent, roofed, hatching house in Ireland was built on the same site. When Mr Howard St George took over the fishery in 1896 he refurbished the interior, replacing the old hatching boxes with more convenient ones that stood at waist height like long tables; but he retained the old stone building itself, which is still to be seen by today's very modern hatchery.

One haunting story remains to be mentioned, that of the death of Lady Dudley at Screebe in 1920. Apparently she came down for a holiday in a humid June, told the domestics that she was going for a swim, and later was found drowned. A lady who used to visit the lodge as a child to play with Sally Berridge and visitors' children tells me that there was an enclosed area of sea known as the Swimming Pool, which the workers on the estate were forbidden to approach when the ladies were bathing; that a man heard her cry for help, but instead of running down to the pool he ran into the house to raise the alarm, and by the time she was reached it was too late. Rumours of suicide arose; her marriage had broken down some years earlier, perhaps because of Lord Dudley's affair with a musical comedienne, Gertie Miller, the famous 'Gaiety Girl' and wife of Lionel Monckton. (Lord Dudley made an honest woman and a Lady of her after his wife's and Monckton's deaths.) However that may be, Rachel's plaintive spirit sometimes returns to her favourite Room 4 in the lodge, and has been seen in the roads and woods nearby too, a fading trace of the belle époque of Ros Muc.

4 Crossing the Bog

The bog stretching beyond the roadside lakes of the Inbhear system is immense in the Connemara scale of things, and intimidating, especially when dark clouds are gnawing the heads of the mountains that rim around three-quarters of its horizon. The main Galway–Clifden road passing four or five miles to the north and the few houses along it are invisible in the distance, so that the bog seems to extend unbroken to the feet of the Mám Tuircs and the Twelve Pins. To the people of Ros Muc, with its built-in familiarity of tiny walled fields, meeting-place hillocks and narrow harbourages, this was Otherland, to be visited with circumspection. Colm Ó Gaora describes crossing it on a bright moonlit night during the War of Independence when he was ordered to join his IRA comrades in Baile an Lotaigh, up in a glen among the Twelve Pins. He asked a water bailiff who was reputed to know every foot of the way 'as well as his rosary' to guide him and another man across the bog to Atraí, a village a couple of miles west of Recess. It was hot and close; they had to sit down now and again to draw their breath and dry off their sweat. After three hours' walking, when they should have been nearing their goal, their guide admitted that he had no idea where they were. Although there are hundreds of lakes and rivers in this bog, that night they met 'not a lake or a pond, a river or a ford, a stream or a streamlet' until the break of day, when their guide, after turning his cap back to front and crouching down to examine the ground as if he were sniffing it, exclaimed, 'We have it!' They were approaching the main road at a point six miles east of where they had intended. But when they learned that the Black and Tans had raided Atraí that night, they blessed the *fóidín mearaí*, the 'stray sod', that had kept them out of the enemy's hands.

Criathrach Choirill is the name of this problematic terrain. A *criathrach* is a 'pitted bog', a bog full of bog-holes; the word is supposed to derive from *criathar*, a sieve. According to an anonymous mid-nineteenth-century visitor, a geologist who explored it in search of evidence for his theory of glaciation, and noted the local lore about it, Coireall was a Celtic hero who from the Mám Tuirc mountains flung a huge stone at one Mordán, who was standing on his own hill, Cnoc Mordáin on the Carna peninsula. But Coireall crushed his own finger with the stone, which fell short; it is called Cloch Choirill, and it stands on the brink of Loch Choirill, about three miles into the bog from Inbhear. The biggest erratic boulder in Connemara, it is a fat column (the geologist measured it to be about twenty-four feet high and sixty-six feet around), with a hollow under it (the mark of Coireall's finger) which has been the site of a kiln for drying barley to make poitín, and a den for a water bailiff guarding the nearby lake. The place, says the geologist, 'has a bad name, so it is rarely visited. It is haunted by "each uisge", the water horse, and other dangerous beings – so few people go there except to fish or brew spirits.' Pádraic Óg Ó Conaire paints a most sinister picture of Criathrach Choirill in *Déirc an Díomhaointis*; it is, he says, 'no refuge or hunting-ground for foxes, badgers or stoats since there were no pickings for them there', and 'even the birds of the air cross it keeping high in the sky as if they preferred to avoid it'. In the few odd places where there was a boulder, there would be a grey crow on it. As it transpires in the novel, the crows do have something to eat out there: the protagonists discover an eyeless corpse near the boulder; they cannot identify it, but the reader knows that it is the body of the young man who drank his money at the fair of Maam Cross and drunkenly set out for England.

Of course I visited this landmark boulder in my map-making days. An old track runs north from the western end of the bridge at Inbhear, for about a mile, to a place called Cúng (narrows), where there is a little bridge over a channel linking two lakes of the Inbhear system. The bridge needed repair, and a few men were standing around it, earning *déirc an díomhaointis*; they pointed me on to a line of stepping stones that stretched north-westwards and vanished into the distance. After something over half a mile I passed a little lake they had told me to look out for, called Loch Pholl an Mhaide Giúise, the lake of the hole of the bog-deal, from some notable anciently bog-pickled timber found there, no doubt. The stepping stones continued; they

were just a fraction too close together for my stride, which was wearying. After another half mile the slightly undulant land revealed the
wide levels of Loch Choirill not far ahead, and the steps soon ended
at a small wooden quay. There was a wooded island in the lake, with
a small fishing lodge sheltering among the trees. I am told that it was
built by some sportsman as a studio for his artistic mother, and all its
materials and furnishings were carried in over the stepping stones, but
that she died before it was ready for her. Cloch Choirill stands a few
hundred yards to the north along the lake shore: a huge half-loaf of
granite, lichen-dappled, massive and yet lightly balanced on end on a
little bulge of bedrock. The nineteenth-century geologist opined that
it had been gently deposited here by an ice-float borne on a hypothetical Baltic current from the Arctic; his colleagues of today would
say it came from perhaps only a few hundred yards away, in the grip
of a glacier creeping out of the Mám Tuirc mountains. I looked around,
waited long enough to feel the 'strange loneliness' Pádraic Óg associates with the place, and turned back. At the bridge the men had started
a few smoulderings in the heather, and were standing around a small
heap of sand, looking at it as if it were the last grains in the bulb of an
hourglass.

I have revisited the *criathrach* since that day. On the most recent
occasion I found that the first half mile or so of the stepping stones
had been replaced by an extension of the track, evidently to service
many turf banks that had recently been opened up; large ricks of turf
awaited collection here and there by the wayside. Also a huge area of
forestry had crept down from the north like a green glacier, to within
a hundred yards of the track. Despite these marks of humanity in
extractive mode, the bog was still intimidatingly solitary. Beyond the
fading-out of the track the line of stepping stones had almost vanished
into the soft ground and there were only the faintest indications of
the way. I persevered, but it seemed Loch Choirill would never make
its appearance. If I turned back and a smear of rain came across, would
I be able to pick out the occasional stepping stone among the muddy
hollows and stiff tussocks of sedge and heather? Or would I miss the
end of the track and have to plough my way across 'pitted bog', and
then make a wearisome detour around a lake to find the bridge? I had

been walking with my back to a filmed-over sun; I turned round and marched towards it, hit the end of the track exactly and in no time at all was back at the bridge. The sun suddenly shone forth unveiled; the nearby forest sparkled; I decided to explore a new track that runs north from the bridge and would, I knew by report, eventually deliver one onto the Galway–Clifden road a couple of miles east of Recess.

The first stretches of this way were charming; it winds to and fro between the forest margin on the left and Abhainn Inbhear, here a stream linking a chain of small lakes, on the right. But after a while the track plunged into the grey-green depths of the forest, and I gave up once again. Somewhere far ahead was, I knew, another once-famous boulder, Cloch Leathbealaigh, the halfway stone. I have read of a man from Glinn Chatha who went out to fetch a bottle of poitín hidden near his house, lost his way in the dark, walked and walked, and, he said afterwards, recognized no place until he found himself at this boulder. He was lying – there are several substantial streams between Glinn Chatha and the stone that would have turned him back – or, more accurately, he was using the stone as an emblem of remoteness. The halfway stone, like the Halfway House, the shebeen in the middle of Roundstone Bog, is as far from one place as it is from the other; it is the embodiment of distance. On a difficult journey one cannot reach the halfway point without some feeling of satisfaction at the part completed, or of disquiet at the distance still to be covered. When I write my treatise on the new science of distemics, the study of topographical sensations, or the phenomenology of far-off things, I shall have Cloch Leathbealaigh as a frontispiece. But now it is hidden in ranks of Sitka spruce. A huge wedge of forestry has split Criathrach Choirill in two, and not just Criathrach Choirill, which is the heart of it, but the entire extent of more-or-less intact bog stretching uninterruptedly for eight miles westwards from the Scríb–Maam Cross road.

What is lost? The forest walk has its interest and in places its charm, but it lacks the profundity, the vastitude, the awesome silences, of the untrammelled bog. When the trees were planted in 1985 the then-Taoiseach Garret FitzGerald came down to unveil a plaque by the main road near the northern end of the forestry track, according to which the forest commemorates Irish emigrants who contributed to the welfare of the USA and of Boston in particular. The planting was partly financed through the Irish American Cultural Foundation by generous individuals, who of course were not responsible for its location. Whether there is even a purely economic justification for it is doubtful; a local forestry official told me at the time that he took no responsibility for it, because of the difficulties he foresaw in extracting the timber in such difficult terrain. The idea that forestry might be the saving of Connemara in terms of employment has been a commonplace of local politicians since Independence, but fortunately Coillte, the Forestry Board, has realized the fallacy in this and no longer plants on lowland blanket bog; private forestry too is much restricted in Connemara nowadays. But here the damage is done, and while the recent erasure of an ugly rectangle of forestry on the south flanks of the Twelve Pins shows that such damage can be undone too, and time given its chance to salvage the land, it will be many a decade before the crossing of Coireall's pitted bog can be made without an apologetic nod to the halfway stone.

There used to be another road, or at least a bridle path, across these boglands, a few miles to the east; before the coast road was built in the 1850s it was in fact the only route into the Ros Muc area, and was continuous with the present road running down the peninsula from the crossroads at An Gort Mór. By the end of the nineteenth century developments at An Gort Mór had eliminated a few hundred yards of it immediately north of the crossroads, but much of the rest of it is traceable. A track starting just west of the crossroads leads up through a small patch of modern forestry and joins the old way on the open hillside above. Soon one passes through a field gate beyond which a few bullocks may be waiting hopefully for fodder, and move aside resignedly when one pushes through them; then all that shows underfoot is a muddy and rocky path that dips to follow the eastern shores of Loch an Oileáin. The old name of this lake is Loch Log na gCléireach, the lake of the hollow of the clergy, and it is said that in the days of the penal laws the Mass used to be celebrated secretly in the hills here.

There is a *tamhnach*, a formerly cultivated area in the bog, on a steep slope above the lake shore, with a few wind-maddened hawthorn bushes and the knee-high ruins of two or three small houses caught in a web of fallen field walls. The place has been deserted for over a century, but it is still evident that life here was a struggle against stony earth; patches have been cleared to create little green pastures, but the heaps of stone removed from them occupy almost as much ground as the clearances do. There are many boulders that have defied the farmer; although none of them rival Cloch Choirill several were once huge, for they have clearly been split by frost and lie in overlapping slabs or lean apart so that one can look into their knotty depths, or even walk through them. Like most of south Connemara this is 400-million-year-old granite country, but it wears its age lightly; the rock exposures underfoot are smooth, bright-toned and glittering with flecks of mica. The boulders scattered over the hillsides are older looking, with their fractured forms and niched fern gardens, but they are really much more recent arrivals, having been dropped like luggage abandoned in a rout by the melt-back of glaciers a mere 10,000 or 12,000 years ago.

The land rising to the left, the east, is the townland of Cnoc an Daimh, the hill of the stag or the ox, according to officialdom, although in Ros Muc Irish a *damh* is a bull. I have good memories of days out on these hills that started threateningly, with a cloud base only halfway up the far-off peaks of the Twelve Pins, but then relented and laid a hand of sunshine on one or other of the many shoulders of Cnoc an Daimh or on those of the next townland to the north, Seanadh Bhéara, another uninhabited tract of low hills. 'Béara' is probably an old personal name, and *seanadh* evidently means a hillside, although the word is no longer current in this sense. Tomás S. Ó Máille told me it may more especially mean a smooth hillside, one suitable for a *seanadh*, an assembly or senate; in any case the root is *sean*, old, and indeed the various hillsides so termed in this area – Seanadh na Feola, the hillside of the meat, Seanadh Mhac Con Raoi, the hillside of the Conroys, and others – are rooted in age. One can find the footprints of *brácaí*, the temporary huts built for those who watched over the cattle out on the *buaile*, the summer milking pastures, and other lonely *tamhnachaí* like the one in Log na gCléireach, with tumbled field walls and grassed-over potato ridges dating from before the Famine. Even the old road is in surprisingly good condition in places, with little revetments where it crosses steep slopes, and stone-filled drains to conduct streamlets under it, but it owes its preservation to disuse rather than to any care taken of it.

Although this range of hills has more recognizable landmarks and is a friendlier terrain than the vast mosaic of bog and lakes stretching westwards from it, there are many tales of people going astray in it, such as a gang of poachers who were creeping down to the salmon lakes of Scríb on a moonlit night when they heard a stream of incomprehensible talk but saw nobody; they panicked, turned for home, quarrelled over which direction to take, and wandered all night. Strange sights have been seen here too. Once some people at the *buaile* on An Cnoc Maol, the bald hill, heard a clap of thunder, and at the same moment saw an incomprehensible being on the road from Maam Cross in the valley below; they abandoned their cattle and their milk and ran home with the news that they had seen the thunder coming down the road. (What they had seen, it turned out, was the first bicycle and rider to penetrate the locality.) Otherworldly encounters were to be expected in these hills. Pearse understood this feature of Ros Muc's psychic geography; it was on Cnoc an Daimh that the old Fenian of his story 'Íosagán' was thought to have sold his soul to some being not to be characterized more explicitly than as a *Fear Mór*, a big man. The water horse, fabulous creature of two worlds, has been seen making its way to Loch an Daimh, which lies like a dark secret in a hollow east of the hill – a lake reduced to the elemental, it always seems to me, with scarcely a bush to blur its boundary with the featureless bogland. Colm Ó Gaora crossed these hills on his first journey out of Ros Muc, on his way to the newly opened Irish teachers' training college at Tuar Mhic Éadaigh in faraway Mayo. Resting on the bare slopes of Seanadh Bhéara to take a last look back to his intricate little homeland, and feeling loneliness come over him like the cloud shadows chasing each other across Seanadh Mhac Con Raoi, he is suddenly accosted by a stranger, a long-limbed sinewy bearded fellow with tufts of hair in his nostrils, who frightens him by beating his stick against the ground while showing off his command of English:

> Hoky poky, penny a lump,
> The more you ate, the more you jump!

And, even more alarmingly:

> I am the air
> I am the clouds
> I am the sun
> I am the moon
> I am . . .

. . . at which Colm flees and doesn't draw breath until he is on the main road to Maam Cross. (Some years later Colm was to follow the old road across the hills in the other direction by night, guiding a 'flying column' of the IRA who were to lay an ambush for the Black and Tans at Scríb, an adventure I will recount when a wider scene for it is fully set.)

One hill rather higher than the rest, solitary and sombre, broods over this landscape; from Criathrach Choirill it rises to the north-east, from Cnoc an Daimh, to the north-west. The top of it is almost a plateau, at a little under 1,200 feet. It is of dark metamorphosed gabbro, like those other isolated hills of south-west Connemara, Errisbeg and Cashel, and very different from the sparkling peaks of the quartzite mountains behind it. Even from my studio window in Roundstone I can see it, a grey-blue whale half submerged by the intervening long horizons of various lowland islands and peninsulas. It intrigues me and I feel I have not located its secret. There is always an imaginary all-seeing eye in the head of an isolated hill, such is the persuasiveness of the topography; one feels the urge to climb it and look out from it in all directions, and if the urge is so strong it must drive others too; therefore there is someone up there at this moment looking down at us in the plain below. This hill of weighty presence is called Cnoc Úraid, and it is said that the last battle for Christianity will be fought around it.

Úraid is a little townland with a widely scattered handful of houses on the north of it (which itself may be named from the several drumlins there, hills of earth, *úr*). It is part of the same parish as Ros Muc, Paróiste Chill Bhriocáin, but is cut off from it by the hill and accessible only from the north, by a turning off the Galway–Clifden road. The townland used to belong to the O'Malleys of Mám, a family we shall meet again, and was bought from them by the Congested Districts Board to be divided between four landless families, the Mannions, Conroys and Nees from Ros Muc, and the Joyces from Log an Tairbh in the Twelve Pins; hence it is a little enclave of the Gaeltacht in a largely English-speaking area, and it is as bursting with tales to be told as is Carna. Mythical time being cyclic, perhaps the battle the local prophets speak of is the one said to have been fought here in some past preceding all dates. The exact site of the battle is a matter of disagreement among the local people, but when the Ordnance Survey was at work on the first detailed map of the area in the 1830s, the name of a long straggle of stony hillocks – which looks to me like a little esker, the deposits left by a river flowing under a melting glacier – in the flat cutaway bog to the north-east of the hill was recorded as Tulach na hEirmisce. This the sappers understood to mean 'the hill of the convention', but it could actually mean 'the hill of the dissention or misfortune' and they noted that it was 'said to be once the scene of slaughter'.

One of the O'Malleys of Úraid, Tomás Buí (yellow) figures in two rather more materialistic tales. He arranged a marriage for his daughter with a man of the Joyces, the dowry to be a handful of sovereigns. Joyce suggested that he himself should dip his hand into the coins, and Tomás, knowing that the Joyces were reputed to have slender hands, agreed. However, this particular Joyce had hands so big he nearly emptied the pot. The other tale tells how Tomás came by his pot of gold. For three nights in succession the poor fellow dreamed that if he went to the bridge in Limerick he would find a pot of gold under the second cornerstone in the arch of the bridge. He told his wife of this, and off he set to walk to Limerick, where he spent three days going to and fro on the bridge. He noticed the stone, but he didn't try to move it. On the third day a man who every day drove cattle across the bridge spoke to him and asked where he had come from. Tomás told him the whole story, and the cattleman said that it was nonsense, that he himself had dreamed there was a pot of gold under a thorn-tree at the gable of one Tomás Buí's house in a place called Úraid, but he had taken no notice of the dream. So Tomás thanked him, hurried home and told his wife, and the two of them went out on a moonlit night and dug with picks and spades until the dawn. The next night they continued to dig, and at last they heard the clink of the spade against the pot. They took it into the house and emptied out the yellow guineas that were in it onto a cloak. They had plenty for the rest of their lives, with sheep and cows on the hill, enjoying good luck and good fortune. They lived a long time, and by the time they died no one else was living in Úraid. Hundreds of years later a poor scholar who was teaching in a hedge school nearby took shelter from a rainstorm in the ruins of their house, and noticed the lid of the pot lying on the hearth, covered in soot and dirt. He took it home and polished it up, and found Latin writing on it that meant: 'One side of the thorn-tree is not more lucky than the other.' So he came back to Úraid with tools, found the hole that Tomás had left by the thorn-tree, and began to dig on the other side of the tree. When he had unearthed the second pot of gold he carefully filled in both holes and went home, and enjoyed plenty for the rest of his life, owing to the fact that he could read Latin.

A similar story is told of a Limerick man who went to Boston on the same adventure and learned there that the pot of gold was in his own garden back at home – and no doubt that is the message of the fable. I have met a man in Úraid who claims to know exactly where the thorn-tree was – on his own land, as it happens, or as it always is in such cases. He said that there were other pots of gold yet to be found there, but he had no intention of telling me where they were or of digging them up for himself, in which he showed great wisdom.

I think it must have been on the same day as that meeting, some twenty years ago, after attending the All Saints' Day Fair in the road at Maam Cross, that I climbed Cnoc Úraid for the first time. The weather was perfect, still and keen; in my eagerness I almost ran up the slopes and arrived on the summit plateau hot and sweaty. A biting wind sweeping up the furthermost slope from Criathrach Choirill assailed me, and by the time I reached home that evening I had a cold and sore throat it took some days to throw off. But I had had time to look around me from that height, at the lovely desolation of lakes and bog to the south and west, uninterrupted by forestry at that date, the well-remembered hills of Cnoc an Daimh to the south-east, and to the north the magnificent phalanx of peaks of the Mám Tuirc mountains and the Twelve Pins, some of them wrapped in layers of silver tissue like the precious objects they are. These ranges, plus those beyond them in Mayo – Mweelrea, Sheefry and Partry – used to be known collectively as An tIomaire Rua, the red ridge, and were to be the site of the last battle, not for Christianity this time, but for Ireland. This prophecy was in the minds of some of those who took to the mountains in the War of Independence, the story of which, so far as it concerns Connemara, I will approach by degrees and indirections. For those men were in love with the places and stories of Connemara, as the writings they have left amply show, and to convey their passion in its particularities and peculiarities I need to unfold the multidimensional written map of this vast arena to the north of Cnoc Úraid, so that the mention of Na Lí, to take a placename almost at random, does not merely direct the reader's mind to a location but brings with it something of the legend that invested it in the minds of those hungry, hunted men of 1922. I begin by establishing a symbolic centre to that map of space and time.

5 A Hiding Hole and a Public House

There is a little cave on a hillside near the head of one of the great glens of the Mám Tuirc mountains. A neatly built drystone wall, with a narrow door and a slit window opening, closes off the mouth of the cave to within a foot or so of its roof. The stones are lichen blotched and grass grown; one could pass within a couple of yards of the place and not notice it, especially as the steep and rugged ground demands attention to one's steps. The door is about six feet high, with a flat lintel like those of Connemara's early churches, which makes one duck one's head instinctively, and so enter reverently. The interior is six to nine feet high at the front, decreasing to a narrow horizontal cleft at the back, and perhaps twelve feet deep. The window, about two and a half feet high and eight inches wide, is flat topped too; on the inside its embrasure widens out in a splay, again as in an early church, and it has two sills, one below the other, or perhaps one should say one sill with a step in it. To the left of the embrasure is a little cubbyhole at waist height. To the right is a knee-high cupboard-like recess at ground level, and a shelf, a flat projecting stone a foot across, which one could rest an elbow on while seated at the window. The outlook from this window is to the east; its perched site gives it a wide range, but betrays a concern with whomsoever might be coming up the valley below.

Out on the broad flats of the valley below, a meandering stream rips through layers of glacial drift, constantly changing its course, cutting old corners, excavating new diversions. The valley is Gleann Glaise; perhaps this name just refers to the stream or *glais*, but I gather that locally *glais* also means a temporary footbridge, such as a plank laid over a ditch in a bog. On leaving the valley, a couple of miles downstream from the hillside with the cave, the stream winds its way eastwards and joins the Joyce river at Béal Átha na mBreac, the mouth of the ford of the trout, in the Mám valley, at the southern end of which their mingled waters enter Lough Corrib. So the glen has in the past provided a route into the heart of Connemara from the south-east. Henry Blake came this way in 1811, with an armed escort to see him safe through 'the gorges of Joyce country', on his first visit to the estates he had inherited at Renvyle, and found he had to 'ride for several miles in the bed of a mountain torrent, which formed the track by which we were gradually led to the pass of Mam Turc'. Thus he must have passed below the cave and, half a mile further upstream, turned left to follow a tributary streamlet coming down out of Mám Tuirc, the pass of the boar. The source of this streamlet is a little spring close to the saddlepoint, beyond which the route, a very faint path, drops westwards into the Inagh Valley. St Feichín passed by this spring, it is said, and blessed it, on his way to found his monastery on Omey Island.

On a shoulder of the slope below the cave is a half-eroded ringfort, perhaps of Iron Age date, some thirty paces in diameter, with an inner bank of stone and an earthen outer bank. On the boggy flats along the furthermost side of the stream is a close-set row of white quartz boulders, about three feet high, aligned north–south, on a low hummock: a Bronze Age monument, of unknown significance. A mile and a half to the east is a pair of quartz boulders, again aligned north–south, on the summit of a small glacial hill in the mouth of the valley; it can just be made out from the cave window, a spark of white. Near it, but not distinguishable in the view from the cave, is a conical heap of glacial till called Sián, fairy mound; out of respect for the powers that do not be I take it as the earliest mark of settlement in the valley. A plantation of conifers dating from the 1980s obscures the south side of the valley; there are a few cottages down that way, and a farm further up to the west, but otherwise the valley is uninhabited.

When the riverside path was widened to serve the forestry the bulldozer broke into three low mounds that turned out to be *fulachta fia*, the prehistoric cooking places country folk used to associate with Fionn Mac Cumhaill and his hunter-warrior band and which probably date from the Bronze Age. These mounds are accumulations of stones that have been heated in a fire and then dropped into a trough or pit of water to bring it to the boil, and which were thrown aside when they began to crack up after repeated use. Fionn and the Fianna would have been happy here, for Gleann Glaise was of old known for its red deer, and it is said the last of Connemara's wolves was hunted down here. From as late as 1700 we have an account of a deer hunt here, written by an intrepid English visitor to the region. John Dunton was staying nearby with an O'Flaherty chieftain, the clansmen, their ladies and their priest in a temporary dwelling, a 'long cabin, the walls of hurdles plaister'd with cow dung', for it was summer and the O'Flahertys had abandoned their castles by the sea to spend the season with their cattle *ar buaile*, on the upland milking pastures.

One thing I saw in this house perhaps the like not to be seen in anywhere else in the world, and that was nine brace of wolfe dogs or the long Irish grey hounds, a paire of which kind has often been a present for a king, as they are said to be a dog that is peculiar to Ireland. They were as quiet among us as lambs without any noys or disturbance. I enquir'd the use of them and was told that besides the ornament that they were, they kill'd as many deer as pay'd well for their keeping, and they promis'd to oblidge me next day by letting me see how they caught their game. I discover'd some apprehensions of dread to lye among such a number of monsters if they were permitted within doores all night, but they had a cabin for their kennel, and were brought in at supper time only to surprize me with the noveltie.

On the following day the hunting party rode out:

. . . to a pleasant vale called Glinglass, or the Green Vale, of an English miles breadth encompasst with lovely green mountains which were tufted with pleasant groves and thickets of natures providing; on the side of these hills I wonder'd to see some hundreds of stately red deer, the stags bigger than a large English yearling calf, with suitable antlers much bigger than any I ever saw before . . . Oflaghertie gave the word and immediately the company with the dogs surrounded a large thicket, while he and I with two hunting poles enter'd it to rouse the game. The first we saw was a stately stag who secure of danger skipped forth of the bushes; he at first seem'd amazed at the cry which was raised looing the dogs, but he bravely endeavour'd charge through them, and was seized by one of the dogs at the haunch, which threw him on his back. The whole kenel was not suffered to come in for feare of spoyling the skin which the people most value, and never did I see a spanniell more subject to command than those mighty dogs are.

Not only the 'stately' stags but the 'pleasant groves and thickets of natures providing' are long gone, grazed to death by generations of sheep; and the dreary cash-crop forestry, which compromises the splendid wildness of the glen rather than complementing it, is no replacement. But still the airy spaces and prehistoric stones visible from the cave's narrow window hold a potent infusion of the past, which would not have been without deep meaning to the hunted outlaw for whom the cave was prepared. Despite its ecclesiastical style and contemplative overview of the centuries this cave was no anchorite's cell; the man who rested his elbow on the stone shelf held a revolver, not a rosary. His eyes were not so much on the mountains opposite, over which the sun would rise for matins, as on the mouth of the valley where the enemy might appear. But while he could not have been aware of all the dimensions of the past I have sketched above, he would as a sheep farmer's son have known the place, its slopes and bogs and crags, almost as an extension of the web of his muscles; and as to its history, that was a matter of his relatives and neighbours, some of them trustworthy, some not. He was Pádraic Ó Máille, on the run after his arrest during the 1916 Rising and his subsequent escape from prison in England. His 'den' had been built by his brother Éamon, an engineer, and I read its careful detailing as a perhaps unconscious rooting of the struggle for independence in a sacred past. The brothers' home was a couple of miles away to the north-east, on the far side of the mountains that separate Gleann Glaise from Gleann an Mháma, the Maam Valley, which I will now begin to spread before the reader's mind.

For the traveller heading out from Galway to Clifden the next landmark after Oughterard is Maam Cross, in Connemara's virtually uninhabited central lowland. Because of its halfway-house location the crossroads even a couple of centuries ago boasted an inn, which became a stage for Bianconi's horse-drawn car service in the 1830s and in 1895 acquired a neighbour, a station of the Galway–Clifden railway line. It seems that the inn, Butler's Lodge, burned down at some period before 1839 (the Ordnance Survey map of that date shows it as 'in ruins'), a calamity from which the place got its Irish name, An Teach Dóite, the burnt house. Later the rebuilt inn became a hotel, known as Peacocke's; there were, I think, three generations of Peacockes there before the old rookery of a building was bought and refurbished by the Keogh family of Oughterard in the late 1970s, preserving the institution's distinctive name. A few years after that I called on Mrs Peacocke, an elderly widow who had retired to live in a cottage (the former constabulary hut) opposite the hotel. She told me that the family had preserved a slate inscribed 'Jo Peacock Sept 9 1852', which perhaps gives us the date of the hotel's construction. The Peacockes were Protestants, she said, and before the days of the motor-car they used to have services in their own house, where there was a harmonium. (A priest I knew who had served in Connemara long ago had a good anecdote about the Peacockes: once when a new Catholic bishop came out from Galway to test the local children's preparedness for confirmation and asked one of them, 'How many religions are there?', he was puzzled by the answer he got: '*Péire: an creideamh s'againne agus creideamh na bpéacóg*'– 'Two: our religion and the peacocks' religion.')

Over the years the crossroads also accumulated around itself a short-lived seaweed-processing factory lodged in the former station of the discontinued railway line, a huge tract of developed bog supplying machine-cut turf mainly to the ESB station at Scríb, a petrol station, a tourist shop, a dancehall (venue of the annual Bogman's Ball), a cattle and sheep mart, a viewing tower, a replica of the thatched cottage used in the filming of that epic of Irishry *The Quiet Man*, and the beginnings of a holiday village ironically advertised as being in the heart of unspoiled countryside. The Keoghs' compilation of enterprises suffered bankruptcy in 2005, but after a period of silence the place is in business again under new management and the old name. Even the traditional Maam Cross horse fair at the beginning of November (Samhain, the immemorial autumn festival of Celtic Ireland) was revived in 2008. Once again surprised tourists driving to or from Clifden find themselves in a long tailback as Connemara ponies are made to prance and circle in the middle of the road, palms are spat upon and slapped together to seal a bargain, weathered countrymen browse the rows of Travellers' stalls for cheap tools and other goods of dubious origin, and Guinness is swilled in Niagaran volumes. And out of this crux of commerce and crack a road climbs northwards, into the unshakeable solemnity of the hills.

The pass this road leads through is Mám Aodha, named from some otherwise forgotten Aodh or Hugh. On the right is the steeply rearing ridge of Leic Aimhréidh, rugged flagstone; on the left, the rounded southern face of Corcóg, beehive, the lower reaches of which are known as Seanadh na Gréine, the slope of the sun – as if to point up the fact that from the summit of the pass we descend into one of Connemara's great raincloud traps. Even in clear weather the view from the saddlepoint is somehow turbulent, as if the ground itself had been blown about and heaped and hollowed. This is Gleann an Mháma, the glen of the mountain pass – but which of the valley's several lofty thresholds is referred to in this name is unknown to me. To the east is the proud sequence of peaks, Sléibhte Mhám Tuirc, the Maamturk Mountains. Few of their names are given on the old OS maps, not even the grandest of them, the 2,307-foot, prosaically named Binn Idir Dhá Log, the peak between two hollows, and I collected them as best I could in the 1980s from dwellers on either side of the range, the problem being that the summits in themselves are not of great interest to the farmers, who are more concerned with and only have names for the slopes on either side of them; also the aged shepherds who know the names of the heights cannot climb them, and trying to distinguish further-off peaks from nearer spurs by pointing at them from the lowlands is an uncertain procedure. The eastern boundary of the old Connemara, the land of the Conmaicne Mara, runs along the watershed here (one of the heights, just to the north of Mám Éan, I hear called Binn Mhairg, which perhaps means boundary peak), and so the Maam Valley properly belongs to the Joyce Country, although nobody nowadays would deny it a part in what we now know as Connemara.

Looking up the valley from Mám Aodha I am reminded of many other heights and slopes whose names express wildness, irregularity and difficulty: Mioscán, heap; Leic na bhFaol, flagstone of the wolves;

Anacair, obstacle (there are at least two of these); Marbhtha, killer cliff; Smuilc, snout; Nead an Iolra, the eagle's nest; Roighne, tough one; and far away to the north, Magairlí an Deamhain, the Devil's testicles. Glaciers have been at work everywhere, quarrying the mountain walls and spreading their spoils on the broad valley bottom. There is a great corrie on the north-east face of Corcóg, to the west of Mám Aodha, and fertile green drumlins here and there in the bogs below, and a trident of rivers that have to wind in all directions through drifts of till before uniting to enter Lough Corrib, which is still hidden by the great blade of Leic Aimhréidh to the east.

From the pass the road drops quite steeply towards the nearest handful of houses, crossing the first of the main rivers, anciently known as the Failmore (which I think must be Faill Mhór, big cliff, deriving from the cliff of Binn Mhairg that broods over the river's first tricklings among the mountains; nowadays it is usually called the Teernakill river for it flows through the townland of Tír na Cille, the land of the church). Just beyond the bridge and hidden away down a lane to the left is a holy well dedicated to St Feichín, and a disused burial ground for unbaptized children, now just a patch of bracken and boulders. A small copse of hardwoods adds to the sense that this is an old and long-settled place. The school is to the left, and opposite it is a house that I am told used to be an inn or perhaps a shebeen, although the landlord did not know this as the licence notice was taken down every time he came around, lest he should raise the rent.

The last half mile of the road runs straight and level across the floor of the valley, bridges another river, Abhainn Bhéal Átha na mBreac, and forms the stem of a T-junction with the main road running up the valley. Cong is some fourteen miles to the right here, and Leenaun nine miles to the left. Keane's bar and shop stands on the far side of this road, facing the bridge, and in its situation and history can be taken to represent the opposite pole from Pádraic Ó Máille's den, being the Maam Valley's official welcome to the outside world, as opposed to its secretive and fearful self-concealment. The road links the fertile limestone lowlands east of Lough Corrib with the rain-soaked sheep-runs of the Joyce Country. In fact a narrow arm of the great lake comes cranking into the valley to within a mile of the junction. Below the bridge is an old slip, off which lie the remains of the last coal boat to come up the lake from Galway, in 1909; it sank when it was left overnight, half unloaded from one end. A little paddle-steamer, the *Eglington*, used to make the trip, and the Bianconi cars used to stop here too.

The two-storey building now housing Keane's originated as Corrib Lodge, built by the mighty Alexander Nimmo in the 1820s when he was employed on laying out the road system that has served Connemara since then. Nimmo was responsible for the typically bold topography here. His lodge was bilaterally symmetrical, its roof rising in a shallow square-based pyramid to a central chimney, and it is in alignment with the bridge and commands the long perspective of the approach road from Maam Cross; thus it occupies the one site from which the symmetry of the T-junction can be overseen, and by its positioning copperfastens the order he imposed on the wild and rebellious scenery. Nimmo used the lodge as a temporary residence during his work in Connemara, and as a pay office, in which, again, symmetry ruled: payments were made on a balcony to which the workers ascended by stairs on one side and descended by stairs on the other, so I am told.

Nimmo's bridges have had an unimpressive history in Connemara; like the one in Leenaun and another at Tullywee near Letterfrack, the Maam bridge was destroyed by floods, and Nimmo's handsome limestone arch was replaced by an iron span. This too eventually failed to bear up under modern traffic, and in 1985 was bypassed by a new bridge that veers off the line of the approach road as if in a tearing hurry to get to Leenaun. Nimmo's piers can still be seen on the south side of the new bridge; there is also a great stone quatrefoil plaque mounted on the façade of the bar, which I think must have formed part of Nimmo's bridge as it is very like one on his Pollaphuca bridge in Wicklow. But the grand regularity Nimmo's imperious eye forced on the terrain has been lost, and with it something of the significance of the place. If I insist on the symbolism I find in such places as Ó Máille's den and Nimmo's bridge it is because the flood of change threatens to bear away all such constructs of meaning, and it is the task of the topographer to shore them up. Without the occasional renewal of memory and regular rehearsal of meaning, place itself founders into shapelessness, and time, the great amnesiac, forgets all.

Nimmo's lodge went on to play a modest part in the anecdotal history of the valley. After his death in 1832 it became the Maam Hotel under his former servant, Mr O'Rourke, a Scot. Maria Edgeworth and her party dined there on 'hare soup, such as the best London tavern might have envied', during their tour of Connemara in 1833. Mr and Mrs Hall also extol the cuisine in their Irish tour-book of 1843, and tell us that O'Rourke had previously been a waiter at the Gresham Hotel in Dublin: 'He is consequently not above his business, which he "condescends" to look after himself . . . Indeed he has introduced the elegancies of "Gresham's" into Connemara without its rates of payment – its "bill of fare" without its accompaniment of prices.'

Mr O'Rourke married an Ann King from further up the valley, and after his death the hotel passed into the hands of the King family. Their landlord was the more than slightly crazy William Clements, third Earl of Leitrim, who owned much of the Maam Valley; a notorious tyrant, in 1878 he was shot and clubbed to death on his way to oversee evictions on his lands in Donegal. Lord Leitrim let the inn on condition that he should have exclusive rights whenever he chose to stay in it. In the mid 1850s a visitor of the name of Arthur Gough had occasion to observe Leitrim's outrageous behaviour. Gough and a friend had had to wait for their room until Leitrim and his ladies had left for his lodge at Fairhill in Mayo. But Leitrim and party returned unexpectedly because a bridge on his route had been swept away, and Mr King was ordered to throw out Gough and his friend. They refused to give up their room, and in the morning from their window saw Lord Leitrim revenge himself on the blameless Mr King by dragging some 200 fleeces out of King's wool store and throwing them in the mud of the yard.

Shortly after that incident the Maam Hotel became notorious through press reports of a visit to the west by the Lord Lieutenant, Lord Carlisle, and John Bright, MP; they had intended to stay overnight at the hotel, but Lord Leitrim ordered his own servants and tenants to occupy all the rooms, so that Carlisle and his party had to press on through the night to Cong. It seems the long-suffering Kings had no lease, and in the 1860s it was rumoured that the landlord intended to convert the hotel into a fishing lodge or summer residence for his own use. But this did not happen; instead, I am told, Peter King decided that his sister should marry a Wallace and manage the inn. The Wallaces' daughters eventually took over and ran it until they were old ladies. The Keanes took it over from them in 1965 and added two wings to it, happily preserving its symmetry.

The hotel register preserves nearly a century and a half of visitors' comments. Among them I note, from 1905, a word of thanks from a J. W. Clarke for the management's kindness when 'death overtook a member of the party'; this refers to the fall of a young English woman from the frightful precipice (known ever since this episode as 'Aill an Lady') on the corrie face of Corcóg. There are also the signatures of two innocent Gaeilgeoirí taking a walking tour together, Máire Ní Aodáin and Pádraic Mac Piarais. They were an unlikely couple (as she points out in her diary, had she married very young, Pearse could have been her son), but there were those who doubted the propriety of what she calls the 'solus cum solâ' nature of their holiday. Their time was mainly spent at Letterfrack, but clearly the Maam Hotel pleased them, for they added a sentence in ancient Greek that I am told means 'Beautiful indeed I consider such a place where men are well disposed towards all strangers.' However, a decade or so later, after 1916, the valley was to become extremely unwelcoming to strangers. Connemara's part in the War of Independence unfolded its wings over all the surrounding mountains, but it hatched in Gleann an Mháma. But before I turn to that story I will complete the traverse of the valley and search out its two dominant families, the O'Malleys and the Joyces.

6 The O'Malleys and the Joyces

Houses are frequent along the first few miles of the road from An Mám to Leenaun, but after the little townland of Na Braonáin they are less so, and the way is lonelier. Odd stories I have picked up here and there enhance the mood of antiquity, of centuries of continuous folklife, that seems to pervade the valley. Na Braonáin gets its name, says a well-informed local man, from a traveller called Ó Braonáin and his daughter, who stopped here for the night, during which the girl died. The people said they would bury her wherever the cows had lain overnight, for that would be a dry place. The graveyard, with its old gravestones of local schist, owes its lovely situation down by the river to this curious decision.

The next townland is Coill Mhíolcon, the wood of Míliuc, an old personal name, according to the scholars; locally it is called Béal Átha na mBreac, the mouth of (i.e. the approach to) the ford of the trout, for here a side road branches off to cross first Abhainn na Seoigheach, the Joyce river, and then Abhainn Bhéal Átha na mBreac itself, the river that orig-inates in Gleann Glaise. This townland has some ecclesiastical history. It was probably given by a Joyce (for we are in the heart of Dúiche Sheoigheach, the Joyce Country, here) to the nunnery of Kilcreevanty near Tuam, and then in 1560 was granted to that Earl of Clanrickard who did so well out of the dissolution of the monasteries under King Henry VIII. There is a small church by the road here; it was built in about 1840, replacing a thatched stable on the same site that belonged to the O'Malleys of this townland and had been used as a church, probably since the ending of the Penal Laws with the Catholic Emancipation Act of 1829. It is worth going in to see the stained-glass window by Evie Hone, dedicated by the O'Malley family of Coill Mhíolcon and depicting St Brendan on the island of Inis Glóire off north-west Mayo, part of O'Malley territory in medieval times. This brings us to the notable presence of the O'Malleys in Gleann an Mháma.

The O'Malleys of Mám claim descent from Grace O'Malley's cousin Tomás Rua, whose son Dubhdara, having participated in the Battle of Kinsale, the historic defeat of Gaeldom in 1602, forfeited his territories in the north-west and was forced to move to Bally-loughmask in the south of Mayo. His great-grandson Éamon Saighdiúir (soldier) lost even that holding in the punitive confiscations that followed on the defeat of King James II in 1690, and removed to Coill Mhíolcon. His son had a very different nickname: he was Éamonn na mBó, Éamonn of the cows; his family home was and is on the east side of the road a few hundred yards south of the church, and the hill behind it is still Cnoc Éamoinn. By the time of Lord Leitrim the O'Malleys were prosperous cattle and sheep farmers, leas-ing 10,000 acres. Peter James O'Malley lived in Coill Mhíolcon and his brother Michael lived in Muintir Eoghain, two miles further up the valley; the sons of the latter were the patriotic O'Malleys whose doings in the War of Independence I will be following shortly, while the descendants of the former were the famous dynasty of medical O'Malleys. The St Brendan window commemorates Peter James O'Malley's eldest son John Francis, a well-known ear, nose and throat surgeon of University College Hospital in London; he invented the O'Malley guillotine, a device for slicing off tonsils. His brothers Michael and Conor became Professors of Surgery and of Ophthal-mology, respectively, in University College Galway. Michael's son Eoin was Professor of Surgery in University College Dublin and President of the Royal College of Surgeons. Several of the younger generation have been equally eminent in Ireland and in the United States; a history of the O'Malleys published in 1988 reckons that forty members of the Coill Mhíolcon family had been medical doctors up to that date.

In the days of the Penal Laws, and before the O'Malleys' stable came into use as a chapel, the Catholics of the locality worshipped within the ruinous circumference of an ancient dún or stone cashel by Abhainn na Seoigheach, to the left of the road a mile and a half nearer to Leen-aun. An anonymous English traveller in the 1820s gives a wildly romantic picture of the ceremony:

By this streamlet's side, raised but a few feet above the surface, there stood the mossy stones of one of the oldest ruins in the west country – the remnant of a banquet-hall and a chapel – the former memorable in tradition as having been the scene of many a Bardic meeting; the latter sacred as the only spot for twenty miles around where the service of the Roman Catholic Church was performed. Many hundreds of the peasantry, clad in their gay purple and scarlet dresses, were grouped along the sides of the mound on which the ruins of the chapel stood. The wind was so still, it moved not the tapers that were lighting on the rude stone altar. The officiating priest, a venerable St. Omers, of the days gone by, had raised above his head the consecrated wafer, which the whole congregation, uncovered and bowed to the earth, received with one long and loud 'Mille Failté Criosd na Slanaightheoir,' 'A thousand welcomes, Christ our Saviour,' that broke from every lip and rang through that peaceful and secluded dell.

The site of this almost ghostly scene is a low knoll between the road and the nearby river; the indistinct, mossy remains of the old cashel's single stone rampart are overlain by a much more recent field wall. It is said that when Grace O'Malley was besieged by the English in Caisleán na Circe on Lough Corrib, she got a messenger through to this stronghold, where a beacon was lit, the first in a chain of beacons that bore her message to Clare Island and brought her kinsmen from there hurrying to relieve her.

Just beyond the dún a stream, Sruthán na Lí, joins the Joyce river from the west; it drains a small side valley known as Na Lí, which perhaps means 'the standing stones', and leads up to Mám na Lí, the pass leading over into Gleann Glaise. A mile or so up the valley is a huddle of buildings, now roofless and converted into sheep pens, associated with a character who aroused the curiosity of various nineteenth-century visitors: Pádraic na mBan, Patrick of the women. I am told locally that his surname was Breathnach, and that he was a generous man who took in destitute women; however, in an account of Connemara published in about 1850 he figures as 'a grazing farmer . . . said to possess considerable wealth and to live in a style more patriarchal than consistent with the laws of modern society'. In fact he is reputed to have had twelve wives, each in a separate dwelling, and twelve cradles rocking.

As the home of Pádraic Ó Máille, the IRA man who hid out in the cave, was in the fork between Sruthán na Lí and Abhainn na Seoigheach, he would have gone up past Pádraic na mBan's former harem village on his way to Mám na Lí and his den in Gleann Glaise. The Ó Máille house lies at the southern limit of the next townland of the Mám valley, Muintir Eoghain, Eoghan's people (I do not know who this patriarchal Eoghan was). With 300 acres of grazing, a two-storey house, stables and barns, employing farmhands, the Ó Máille family was prosperous and had time for mental cultivation, which did not alienate them from their native place but led to a passionate identification with its landscape and language. It was a bilingual family, and Pádraic's father was also a Latin scholar. His mother, a Joyce from Leenaun, had many children, of whom nine survived: Mícheál, Máire, Caitlín, Sinéad, Sorcha, Peadar, Pádraic, Tomás and Éamonn. They were educated by private tutors, together with their cousins of Coill Mhíolcon.

Four of the brothers are involved in the story I am pursuing. Éamonn I know least about. He was an engineer; the curious flat-roofed church at Recess and a similar one at Finny in Mayo are his work. Tomás was the most scholarly, obtaining his BA as a private student from Queen's College Galway in 1902 and going on to the newly founded Scoil an Ard-Léinn Ghaeilge in Dublin, where he pursued Celtic studies under Kuno Meyer and John Strachan. A travelling scholarship took him to Manchester, which awarded him his MA, and then to Liverpool, Berlin and Freiburg, where he studied under Thurneysen and obtained his doctorate. In 1909 he was appointed Professor of Modern Irish in the recently founded University College Galway (an official portrait photograph shows him looking too young for his professorial robes). His love for the spoken language of Connemara shines in his invaluable and engaging book *An Béal Beo* ('The Living Tongue'), a compendium of homely words and phrases, the fruit of years of listening in the homes of Connemara, for like An Piarsach he was more of a listener than a talker.

Mícheál was a teacher and journalist, and together with Tomás published a collection of traditional songs from the Joyce Country,

Amhráin Chlainne Gaedheal. He died young, from blood poisoning after a bicycle accident, and his essays, first published in *An Claidheamh Soluis*, were later collected by Tomás. From that little book (entitled *Diarmuid Donn*, Mícheál's pen name) I have long treasured the proposal that every village should build a spacious library in a sunny spot, where people could spend part of the evening after work without being stifled, so that the lads would not be hanging around street corners nor the girls gossiping about the neighbours.

Pádraic was the politician and fighting man; photographs give him a shrewd but heavy-headed, bull-like look. Gaelic League and Sinn Féin organizer, founder with Pearse of the Volunteers in Connemara, member of the IRB, he went through all the stages that would have culminated in the Easter Rising, had not Galway's participation been frustrated by the confusion it was thrown into by Eoin Mac Neill's countermanding orders. In the aftermath of this debacle Pádraic was interned in Frongach in Wales, whence he escaped, with the aid of a young Welsh girl and dressed as a priest, it is said. Rearrested, he was interned in Wandsworth Prison until the amnesty of 1917. In the following year, as the world war reached its crisis and Ireland was threatened with conscription, the authorities concocted an imaginary 'German Plot' to justify a round-up of Sinn Féin and Volunteer leaders, including Griffith and de Valera. Pádraic, as a member of Sinn Féin's Ardchomhairle or high council, usually took the precaution of sleeping in one or other of the neighbours' houses, but one evening, tired after a long trek, he was persuaded to risk a night in the family home, along with Éamonn. At two or three in the morning he was aroused by the sound of movements outside, and when he asked who was there an English-accented voice said, 'Come down. I have a message for you from the Irish Republic.' 'I'll soon send you a message,' replied Pádraic, and he and Éamonn began to fire from the windows – the first rebel shots since the Rising of 1916. The police took refuge at the gable end of the house and returned fire, but in the echoing dark they thought they were being shot at from behind a nearby tree, and fled to their van. When they had gone Pádraic and Éamonn climbed to the top of Leic na bhFaol, and they spent the following day there before crossing the hills to Gleann Glaise, where they slept in a *scailp*, a little nook in the rocks, and got thoroughly wet, while police combed the glen for them in vain. It was after this first night on the run that the people of the glen prepared a better hiding place for them, evicting a family of badgers from the *scailp* mentioned, or perhaps another one, enlarging it by blasting, and furnishing it with a low iron bedstead and a feather mattress. I am told that it was Éamonn, the engineer, who built up the façade with its carefully constructed doorway and window opening.

In the elections of December 1918 Pádraic stood for Galway as the Sinn Féin candidate, opposing William O'Malley of Ballyconneely, the long-established Irish Party member, and won handsomely, as did Sinn Féin nationally. And then Sinn Féin, instead of sending its victorious members to Westminster, anticipated history a little, as revolutions have to do, by forming Dáil Éireann, the Parliament of Ireland, and issued a Declaration of Independence; thus Pádraic Ó Máille, farmer's son of Muintir Eoghain, became the Galway member of that momentous First Dáil. His further adventures I shall weave into my account of Connemara's little chapter in the War of Independence; for now I turn to the other great family of Gleann an Mháma.

Before the Cromwellian period Muintir Eoghain belonged to a Sir Thomas Blake, and after the confiscations it went in part to Trinity College, which acquired much of the Inagh Valley and various other lands throughout the Joyce Country at that time. But the ancient masters, the Joyces, survived in this neighbourhood as graziers and middlemen. A substantial but long-derelict farmhouse in the north of Muintir Eoghain was called Joyce Grove, and close by it is an ancient burial plot, perhaps an early church site, known as Na hUltaí Beaga, the little tombs, with many uninscribed stones marking children's graves, and a plot devoted to the Joyces in which the tombstones bear mid-nineteenth-century dates. A poet of local renown, Dell Allen, *née* Joyce, was born in Joyce Grove; she died in 1985 and is buried in Leenaun, and her simple and attractive verses are collected in a small volume with the lovely title *Before the Rain Began*.

According to James Hardiman, the historian of Galway, the Joyces were of Welsh and English origins; the first of them to come to Ireland was a Thomas Joyce who sailed with his fleet from Wales to north Munster in the reign of Edward I and there married Onora, daughter of the O'Brien chieftain of that territory. Then he sailed on to Iar-Chonnachta, and acquired considerable tracts of land. A son was born to the couple during the voyage, whom they christened Mac Mara, son of the sea, and from him is descended the sept of the Joyces. Their descendants settled in an area west of Lough Mask later known as the Barony of Ross, where they were tributary to the O'Flahertys and 'did usually yield them risings out to all hostings, roods, and journeys for the princes service'. The words are those of a document of 1607 setting out the boundaries of County Galway, and incidentally transferring Ross from the County of Mayo to that of Galway, because of this close relationship with the O'Flahertys. The town of Galway feared and distrusted the O'Flahertys, but accepted the Joyces because of their British origins, and later, as the 'Merry Joyces', they were numbered among the thirteen Tribes of Galway. Joyce Grove was the principal seat of their country cousins in reduced circumstances, in the second half of the nineteenth century and after.

Not far beyond Joyce Grove the long, fiord-like sea-inlet of Killary Harbour begins to come into sight, with the mountains of Mayo magnificently ranged beyond it. From this approach it looks like a lake at first, for its opening into the Atlantic is eight miles away to the west and hidden by the bulk of the Mám Tuirc mountains, which here press close to the road. After ascending gently to the head of Gleann an Mháma the road winds down into the pretty seaside village of An Líonán or Leenaun, on the south shore and near the head of the Killary. All nineteenth-century travellers have tales to tell of the Big Joyces of Leenaun. From the time of Mac Mara himself the Joyces were renowned for their mighty build. When Henry Blake passed through their territory on his way to his Renvyle estate for the second time, in 1811 or '12, he met a Martin Joyce at Béal Átha na mBreac, who was 'returning from some farms which he held under the late General Miller [the Thomsons' predecessor in the Salrock area], accompanied by a horse load of oysters, and another of scallops'. This man took a liking to Blake and offered the party his guidance and protection, but insisted that instead of crossing the Mám Tuirc pass they go up the

Maam Valley to Leenaun, where they could call on the head of the clan, 'a person emphatically called Big Ned Joyce', before sailing down Killary Harbour to Rosroe. But first the party had to be entertained in Martin's little cottage:

If you imagine the dirtiest pigstye in all England, you will not yet have reached what appeared to us to be the state of this cabin. The smoke rolled in dark volumes, 'above, about, and underneath', pouring out of the door with force enough to turn a smoke jack that would have roasted an ox. In the mean time our friend Joyce began to open his oysters, which he made us eat *au naturel*, without bread or potatoes. Our sumpter horse having gone on some time before us, there was no resource, and we were obliged to wash them down with native *Potsheen*, less adulterated with water than we could have wished. Nor did this suffice; Martin deemed himself a cook, and set about dressing scallops for our entertainment. He opened them, called for butter – and such butter! It was added to the fish, which were fried in the shell, and we were actually obliged to eat of this ragout, until I saw my companion's face utterly discomposed by the extremity of his distress.

Later in this visit Mr Blake made a boat trip up the Killary from Renvyle, and sampled Big Ned's hospitality:

He had at one time been a wealthy middleman, but from extravagance and mismanagement, was nearly reduced to the level of a common peasant. The fire-side however was more comfortable: there were chairs and a table in the room: from the roof hung down stores of smoked geese and mutton, instruments of fishing, and other articles which shewed the remains of former prosperity. The cattle were not allowed the privilege of parlour boarders, and on the whole every thing was in much better style than the outside of the cabin had led us to expect. Dinner was served up in due course, consisting of a goose fresh from the bay, smoked mutton, fish, potatoes, and eggs. It was however Saturday [*recte* Friday?], and neither our host nor Martin would take the meat. The only bed in the house was allotted to my companion and myself; the two Joyces sat up all night, talking incessantly. My friend, who as usual could not sleep, was much amused by their conversation, which was carried on partly in English, partly in Irish, and interrupted by continual inquiries whether it was yet twelve o'clock. That happy hour at length arrived, and the clatter of knives and forks very plainly announced that an attack was commenced on the remains of our evening meal. That they played their parts pretty well was fully ascertained the following morning, for, as I well remember, we fared miserably at breakfast.

There was at that period a highly productive herring fishery in these parts; the Blakes heard that there were sometimes 300 or 400 sail in the Killary, and two sloops of war for their protection; Big Ned it was who would 'row from ship to ship to lay down the law, and settle the price of herrings for the poor fishermen'. But then the capricious shoals deserted these waters for a dozen years, after – and because of, according to local belief – 'the great drowning', a tragedy caused by a sudden savage wind that drove the boats against one another and broke them up as the crews struggled to save their precious nets. During that period, to Big Ned Joyce there succeeded Big Jacky Joyce. In 1833 Maria Edgeworth and her touring companions, leaving Connemara for Westport, were well entertained at his 'cabin or lodge as it is styled' while they waited for the tide to go out so that 'Big Jacky Joyce and his merry men' could manhandle their carriage across the sands, Nimmo's bridge just north of the village having been swept away in winter floods because, Big Jacky told them, Nimmo had built it in the wrong place, against Big Jacky's advice. Another traveller, Caesar Otway, describes Jack as he saw him in his prime:

He made his appearance just as I drove up to his door, bouncing over the wall that divided the potato garden from the front of his house, and I think a finer specimen of a strong man, tall and yet well-proportioned, I could not conceive. The great bullet-head, covered with crisp curls, the short bull neck, the broad, square shoulders, the massive chest all open and hirsute, the comparatively small sinewy loins, and pillar-like limbs all bone and muscle – Milo of Crotona might have shaken hands with him as a brother, and the gifted sculptor of the Farnese Hercules might have selected Jack as his lay figure.

But when Otway journeyed up the Maam Valley on a return visit in the late 1830s he was surprised to find Big Jack running a public

house in 'a coarse, raw, ugly, unfinished edifice', which one can deduce
was Joyce Grove. Calling in on him there, Otway learned that Big Jack
had been put out of his lodge in Leenaun by an attorney supposedly
acting for the Provost of Trinity College, but who was (in Jack's opinion) cheating him 'entirely, entirely' by concealing the existence of
hundreds of acres from which the attorney was extracting rent. To
prove that his famous race was not degenerating, Big Jack whistled up
a son of his from a distant field, 'and certainly a taller and more comely
stripling, of about twenty years of age, I have not seen. He was at least
six feet four inches in height, and I am sure, if fed on animal food as
an English farmer's son would be, he would prove a great specimen of
the human race.' Later, on the road to Leenaun, Otway fell in with
local people who told him that Jack was not a favourite, being 'too
apt to resort to his strength to settle disputes, when the fist he threw
into the balance made the scale descend in his favour'. Indeed Jack
himself had told Otway that in the absence of a Justice of the Peace
he 'used to settle differences amongst the neighbours by taking the
parties at variance by the nap of the neck, and battering their heads
together, until they consented to shake hands and drink a pint of *potteen*
together, which, of course, it was Jack's office to furnish for a consideration'.

Although the herring shoals eventually returned, and in the 1840s
boats from Kinsale and elsewhere were fishing successfully in the
Killary, the Famine loomed, and the inn was closed, as appears from
yet another traveller's account:

A more wretched village than Leenane I have seldom seen; it affords neither
entertainment for man nor beast; it was with some difficulty I procured even
a feed of oats for my horse . . . The Killary absolutely swarms with herrings
and fish of all kinds, and yet the surrounding population are starving.

By 1850 the Leenaun Hotel (as it came to be called) was open again,
and even had something to offer:

It is a bettermost sort of a cabin; I daresay has been better than it is; however,
civility and attention goes a great way, even with tired travellers, to make

up for other deficiencies. There were beds – there were porter and eggs, hopes of bacon; a few dogs of sorts, children ditto, a fox, &c. made company.

This is from an account of the West in the dismal year of 1850 written by an English journalist, S. Godolphin Osborne, a well-intentioned enquirer whose heart-rending report on the state of children in the Clifden workhouse I quote in *The Last Pool of Darkness*. But if there were at least 'hopes of bacon' for visitors, the natives' hopes were less ambitious. On leaving Leenaun for Westport in their horse-drawn car, Osborne and his travelling companion found themselves accompanied by the very embodiment of want:

A girl of about twelve years of age, of course bare-footed; dressed in a man's old coat, closely buttoned; ran beside our car, going at times very fast; for a distance, quite surprising; she did not ask for anything, but with hands crossed, kept up an even pace, only adapting it, to our occasional change of speed; we, as a rule, refused all professional mendicants; we told her again and again, we would give her nothing; she never asked for anything: I saw my friend melting, I from time to time tried to congeal him, by using arguments against encouraging such bad habits, &c. He was firm, astonished at her powers, not so irritated, as I was, by her silent, wearying importunity; on she went; . . . the naked spokes of those naked legs, still seemed to turn in some mysterious harmony, with our wheels; on, on she went ever by our side, using her eyes only to pick her way, never speaking, not even looking at us; she won the day – she got very hot, coughed – but still ran with undiminished speed; my companion gave way – that cough did it, he gave her a fourpenny; I confess I forgave him – it was hard earned, though by a bad sort of industry.

Thus spontaneous humanity won a tiny victory over British economic theory. It would be another lifetime or more before Ireland would be in a position to stop 'trotting after the gentry' and apply its own theories to its own wants. I return to the house in Muintir Eoghain, and the beginning of the end of that lifetime.

7 The Battle of the Red Ridge

'We hardly performed great heroic deeds, but all the same we knocked echoes out of the hills a couple of times' is Tomás Ó Máille's throw-away summation of Connemara's part in the War of Independence. But although it was little and late in comparison with campaigns in Cork, Tipperary, Clare and other regions, there was more to it than echoes. A few combatants and bystanders were killed, a few injured, houses were burned down, the land was fearful and sleepless. Colm Ó Gaora claims that the first shots were fired on 20 April 1920, when a handful of the Ros Muc Volunteers decided to burn down the barracks at Maam Cross, from which the RIC had just withdrawn. They mustered their arms – three shotguns – and were in the act of throwing petrol on the floors and roof of the building when suddenly they found themselves in a fire-fight with eight police, who took shelter in a little wood by the roadside. The Volunteers' ammunition was soon exhausted, and their quartermaster was arrested, but they had the satisfaction of seeing the barracks go up in smoke while the policemen watched helplessly from the wood.

When the Volunteers became the Irish Republican Army in 1919, the Connemara force was organized into two companies each subdivided into two battalions. Colm and most of the officers of what was now the West Connemara Brigade were on the run, and made Gleann Glaise their training camp. At a meeting in the Ó Máille house in Muintir Eoghain (which since the death of Pádraic's parents had become the brigade headquarters), Colm was appointed to head the camp. Tomás Ó Máille came to visit the camp now and again – the social niceties of visiting were not neglected in all the subsequent travails of these warriors – and the first thing Colm noticed about him was his capacity for drinking tea; An Piarsach, he writes, used to drink six cups of tea one after the other, and Tomás came close to that. He goes on to describe Tomás:

An innocent man who was as simple as a child, and very easy-going too, was An Máilleach . . . To look at him or talk to him you would never take him to be the great scholar that he was . . . When he was on the run with us we noticed that he paid a lot of attention to the broken rocks that had fallen from the cliffs and to the water of the little lakes left on the summits or in the hollows of the hills.

There were twenty-two men in the Flying Column, as it came to be called, half a dozen of them from the Roundstone area and most of the rest from Gleann an Mháma; they included a doctor of medicine, a teacher, a travelling salesman, a smith, a butcher, a baker, a member of the Dáil, a shepherd, an engineer, a tour guide, a cobbler and a tailor. Tomás and his brother Éamonn were not members, but had to go on the run with them, as we shall see, and so we have two splendid personal accounts in Irish of their doings: one forms part of Ó Gaora's *Mise*, and the other is Tomás's *An tIomaire Rua*. There is also their commanding officer Peadar Mac Dónaill's memoir in crisp military English. I shall weave all three together, with some details from Kathleen Villiers-Tuthill's objective history of these events, and other sources.

The first engagement of the Flying Column was part of a spiral of killing – a coil with no assignable beginning but hopefully with an end – that included the assassination of British intelligence officers in Dublin by Michael Collins's death squad in November 1920. A young man from Clifden, Thomas Whelan, was arrested, tried, condemned and shot for his alleged participation in this deed, despite good evidence that he was actually attending Mass at the time. Early in the following year the men of the Flying Column assembled in the village of Doire na bhFlann on the southern slopes of the Twelve Pins (many of them having crossed twenty miles of bog and hill to get there and been battered by hailstones). They were still full of rage over the injustice of Whelan's execution, and resolved to avenge it in Clifden, which they saw as in the hands of the enemy. They set up a temporary base in a long-deserted bailiff's hut in Aill na bhFiach, the cliff of the ravens, in the heart of the Pins and five miles as the raven flies from Clifden. From there on the evening of 16 March they stole into the little town.

Three or four of them (their names have never been revealed) walked up to two constables on patrol and shot them at close range. Constable Reynolds was killed instantly, and Constable Sweeney wounded in the left thigh and leg. Finding that the barracks was too stout a building for their explosives to penetrate, the IRA men withdrew, taking the two constables' weapons, and struggled up the swampy slopes to Aill na bhFiach, and after drawing their breath and cooking up what little food they had, set out across the mountains for Gleann Glaise. Meanwhile Constable Sweeney was transferred to a hospital in Galway, where his gangrened leg was amputated and he died of shock and blood loss, at the age of twenty-two.

The day after the raid was St Patrick's Day, which perhaps further provoked the military's thirst for revenge. Thirty Black and Tans came out to Clifden by special train from Galway while other soldiers came by road, and a night of looting and drinking, fire and terror ensued. McDonnell's Hotel went up in flames; Mr McDonnell's son John, just back from war service with the Connaught Rangers, was shot while running up the street in the dawn to the smouldering ruins. A gang of Black and Tans demanded drinks in Clancy's public house, shot young Patrick Clancy and burned the place down. Patrick survived bullet wounds in the throat and jaw; a horse and two cows were burned to death. In all, fourteen houses were destroyed and others damaged. I have heard that the drunken marauders broke into a women's haberdashery, and danced in the streets with corsets over their uniforms. Colm's view of the outrages was that Clifden had always been faithful to the law of the Sassenach, and got the reward of its faithfulness that day.

The next engagement of the Flying Column was an attempt to arm themselves at the expense of the enemy. It was known that two or three times a week half a dozen police and Black and Tans with rifles, revolvers and hand grenades cycled down the lonely road from Maam Cross to Scríb on their way to Camas and the islands further south. The lake-strewn and level bogland along that road offered little cover for an ambush except for the scrubby bit of woodland around Teachín na bPrayers, the Protestants' tin chapel, just north of the Scríb crossroads. So the men moved down Gleann Glaise, crossed the Mám Tuirc range by the pass of Mám Éan, spent the night in safe houses in Úraid, then tramped the hills of Seanadh Bhéara and Cnoc an Daimh to the ford where the salmon hatchery is and was, and so to Gleann Trasna, where they spent another night. The Ros Muc curate Fr Donncha Mac Cárthaigh came out to hear their confessions at five the next morning. Unfortunately the police came a day earlier than expected and passed by before the men were in position, so they had to spend a long cold day lying in wait for them to return. Some of the IRA men were hidden in rough ground west of the Scríb road near the head of an old road to Gleann Trasna, and the rest in the wood opposite and a little to the south.

At last along came four police, two by two, and a Tan. Orders were that no one was to fire before the enemy was between the two groups of IRA men – but of course some impatient or nervous recruit did so, and unfortunately fired at the Tan, who was the furthest from them, and missed. The rear two policemen flung themselves off their bicycles and ran back to hurl themselves over the wall of Screebe Lodge, one of the others threw his belt and weapons away and called out that he would resign from the police force, and while the IRA men were debating whether to shoot him or not he dived for shelter into the wood and escaped. The Tan nearly escaped too, but was shot in the shoulder and fell. The fourth policeman, a sergeant, lay in a ditch and kept up pistol fire bravely – 'Cowardice was never the police's failing,' says Colm – until he was out of ammunition, whereupon he pretended to be dying. His belt and pistol were taken from him, together with two bottles of poitín he had in his pockets, but when he pleaded for his life, saying that he had a wife and family dependent on him, they let him live. Meanwhile the curate, then in Gort Mór, had heard the firing and came on his bicycle back to Scríb, where the two policemen hiding in the lodge grounds told him a comrade of theirs was wounded. He cycled up the road and found the Tan lying by the roadside badly wounded, the bullet having passed right through his lungs. The Tan called on the curate to protect him by sitting beside him, and it seems that he survived; at least the published accounts make no further mention of him.

It was a relatively successful encounter for the IRA, but again the enemy had their revenge: that evening five lorry-loads of police, Black and Tans and regular soldiers came out from Galway and burned the

Ó Gaora family home to the ground, together with Pearse's cottage, which had lain empty since his death, the schoolmaster's house in An Gort Mór (because he had been a friend of An Piarsach), a house in Doire an Bhainbh near the scene of the ambush, and a cooperative store that had opened a couple of years earlier in Camas.

On their return from this ambush the Flying Column set up camp in and around the Ó Máille house in Muintir Eoghain. In the half-light of dawn on 23 April the man on guard outside the house made out something moving on the road from Béal Átha na mBreac, which soon he could identify as a column of twenty or so police on bicycles. The alarm was raised, the men took up their positions for defence, the women and children were herded into a barn. When they were opposite the house the police began to leave the road and cross the Joyce river by the stepping stones, and as they did so one of them fired at the house; this sparked off an exchange of fire that lasted until midday. The police were pinned down in the sands of the riverbed, one of them was mortally wounded, and when four of the IRA men managed to work their way around and shoot at them from their rear, they seemed on the point of giving up. Colm was already anticipating a good haul of rifles when a car came down the road heading for Mám, the driver seemingly deaf to gunfire; a policeman leaped onto its running board, managed to hold on even when hit by a bullet, and ordered the driver to go as fast as he could. That meant that reinforcements would soon be coming. The IRA men decided to withdraw to less-exposed ground further up the hillside, and managed to scramble up several hundred yards through bushes and bog-holes under continuous fire. At one point Colm looked round and saw that Tomás Ó Máille was carrying something in a pocket handkerchief, and taking more care of it than of his own safety; 'A clutch of eggs,' Tomás explained, 'we'll soon need them badly.' Then a beggar came strolling along the road – the life of the countryside proceeding as if war were unheard of – and the police sent him off to tell the priest in Leenaun that a man was dying. The priest soon came, in the hotel car, and as the IRA men did not recognize him he was fired upon and spent the rest of the battle in a roadside ditch, where he heard the confessions of one of the combatants and of a local lad who had been caught up in the fighting.

Soon lorries full of soldiers were arriving from Clifden and Galway, armed with machine guns. The Flying Column gathered itself together up in the hills and watched as the Tans threw a bomb into the house, setting it on fire, and killed the horses and pigs with another bomb. This was the moment Tomás chose to announce that the war was over, since according to an old prophecy he'd heard from one of the farm-hands the battle for Ireland's freedom would finish on An tIomaire Rua, the red ridge, which name, Tomás had worked out, referred to the whole western massif from Cruach Phádraic in Mayo to the heads of the bays of south Connemara. But a rain shower soon put a stop to his prophesying and drove the IRA men to take shelter among the rocks. As Colm writes, with sardonic hindsight, the fighting was to go on for some time after that, and within two years Gael would be fighting Gael in those same mountains.

The subsequent travails of the Flying Column as recounted by Colm and Tomás have less in common with a military campaign than with the flight of mad King Sweeney. As in that tale of a pagan ruler condemned by a cleric's curse to flit from tree to crag to watercress bed throughout Ireland, a deeply poetic feeling for nature pierces through a narrative of exposure and hunger, especially in Tomás's account of their wanderings. That evening the men slipped down into Cuilleach, where they found rest and shelter in friendly houses, then by midnight and shower-veiled moonlight they climbed north-eastwards between the two hills called Roighne. The strangeness and loneliness of the night, the whirring of the snipe that rose before them, Colm says, made them silent; they knew they had lost heart, that grief and despondency had seized upon them.

They spent three days ranging about the hilltops, sleeping in isolated farms and villages of the Joyce Country; then, on learning that the enemy intended to encircle the Connemara hills and comb through them, they came down to Killary Harbour, and the people of Gleann na nGeimhleach, the glen of the fetters, east of Leenaun, ferried them to the Mayo shore. Then they went up across a shoulder of Binn Gorm to the desolate Log an Choraidh, the hollow of the corrie, which is, in Colm's words, 'swallowed down in a deep dark glen with high sharp hills around it'. There is a *dúloch*, a black lake, in the corrie, 'the strangest lake I ever saw', says Tomás, more than half surrounded and shadowed by 300-foot cliffs with screes of fallen rock at their feet. There, trying to hide among the rocks from the bitter wind and failing to make a fire with wet heather, they passed the longest day of their lives. Hunger was making them sullen and short-tempered with each other; but in the evening they came down to a safe house and were fed and slept in shelter. Log an Choraidh became their day home for some time. They got canvas to make a tent from the McEwans, proprietors of the hotel in Leenaun, and made beds of heather and moor-grass. Every day they hid the tent away. One night some of them went down to the Erriff river, which falls into the head of the Killary, and netted a few of Lord Browne's fine salmon, encountering a water bailiff whom they compelled to help them, but who could not be persuaded that God put fish in the river for anyone who needed them, not just for his masters the 'Sassenach' gentry.

As Easter had passed while they were on the run, they arranged with a priest to hear their Easter confessions in a house near Bun Dorcha, and stayed overnight there in order to hear Mass the following morning. Hardly had they begun their breakfast afterwards when they heard that lorries – twenty of them – were coming down the Westport road. Some of the lorries were then seen to be taking the road along the south side of the Killary, and meeting up with others from Clifden; the encirclement of the Connemara hills was beginning. Two by two the men crept up a stream-bed and over the hill to Log an Choraidh, thankful that heavy showers were veiling them from the eyes of the enemy. Then they saw two aeroplanes approaching over the Twelve Pins, dipping into the valleys; one of them came across the Killary, turned west to skim the peak of Maol Réidh and then returned to investigate Log an Choraidh. Fortunately the first men to reach the camp had had time to cover the tent with heather and the aircrew did not spot it. At the same time two warships came up the Killary, seizing every currach and rowboat they could see. There were 2,000 troops combing every nook and cranny of north Connemara that day, according to Ó Gaora, and it was only because every man of the Flying Column was outside the ring, attending Mass, that none of them were captured. But it seemed likely that the next round-up would be in the hills along the north of the Killary, and so that evening the men wearily set off northwards, and before sunrise they were on a peak looking down into Gleann an Iomaire, the glen of the ridge, a couple of miles north of Delphi. There was frost on the hilltop, and 'a bite in the wind that would take the nose off a weasel', says Colm; they had to run and jump to avoid freezing, and take turns in keeping each other awake, and they were foul-mouthed and quarrelsome, until at dawn two of them went down into the valley and fetched up two big cans of tea and lots of bread and butter, which made them all as merry as lambs. It was a Sunday, Cruach Phádraic was in view to the north-west, and they fell to talking about the saint and his struggles with the wicked Crom Dubh, who, according to tradition, lived close to where they now were, and that led them to kneel down and recite the rosary – 'on the top of the coldest mountain in Ireland, a thing that was never heard before in that place'.

In the evening they went down into the glen and lodged themselves in various houses, where the people were anxious and unwelcoming as they half expected a visit from the Black and Tans. In fact at midnight word came of such an attack, and the sleep-deprived IRA men had to move on, this time crossing the Delphi Valley and climbing into the vast recesses of Maol Réidh, the mountain that rides steeply from the Atlantic mouth of the Killary. The morning was cold, with heavy hail showers. When they heard that the alarm had been false they came down again and found a warm welcome in Bun Dorcha on the Killary shore. After a couple of days' rest they crossed the water and reached their base in Gleann Glaise following an exhausting trek over the boggy and rocky mountainsides above Leenaun.

For a while then they lived scattered here and there in the glens, and occasionally paid each other formal visits. Tomás and others made a low-walled dugout for themselves above the now-roofless house in Muintir Eoghain, using timbers and bits of iron from its burned-out stable. He describes how, from there, he was invited to spend an evening with another of the band who had a *scailp* on the hillside behind the house, a mere hollow between two rocks that leaned together, and spent an excruciatingly uncomfortable night there on a bed of hay and a pack of wool. In the long summer evenings Tomás often visited the O'Neills of Gleann Creamh, garlic glen, who had proved themselves the most generous and faithful supporters of the IRA men, and there he could enjoy the luxury of a bed withindoors.

The only action the Flying Column undertook during this period was in south Connemara: Colm and a few others went down to Ros Muc and were ferried across the water from An Siléar, made their way to a friendly house near Ros a' Mhíl, and the next day blew up the bridge at Casla, which kept the enemy's lorries out of a large part of the territory. Not long afterwards the Mayo hills and those north-east of the Mám valley were surrounded and searched by the enemy, in the aftermath of a successful and bloody ambush by the Mayo IRA men at Carrowkennedy on the Westport road, in which six Black and Tans died and seventeen surrendered – but once again, the Connemara men were out of the ring. Tomás, Éamonn and others had climbed the fearsome Marbhtha, killer cliff, east of Béal Átha na mBreac, by night, and in the dawn had a narrow escape from detection by military lorries on the road to Finny and by an aeroplane overhead; nevertheless they were enraptured by the sight of the mist rising off Lough Mask below them:

The mist was golden yellow in the light of the sun, and the islands coming into view one by one as the mist rose and dispersed, and the radiance coming over islands and lake and glen. We forgot the aeroplane that had been overhead a minute ago. We forgot our lives were in danger. We ignored everything but the enchantment God had put before our eyes. What we said was that if there is a place as lovely as Loch Measca and Gleann Tréig in Heaven, then Heaven must be a lovely place.

The church in Finny was under construction at that time, and as Éamonn was the engineer in charge of it they nipped down to see how it was progressing; then they were put up and splendidly fed in a friendly house in the vicinity. They would have stayed another night in more comfort than they had enjoyed for months, but two of their comrades who had a *scailp* nearby invited them over, and they felt they had to accept. It was raining, and their hosts had forgotten to inform the local man who was supplying them with food that they were expecting company. The *scailp* was a low space under a huge boulder that rested on a smaller stone, with room for two but not for four. Tomás was given the place for honoured guests, a loft-like ledge that one could worm one's way into feet first, between the huge rock and the smaller one at the back of the *scailp*. In trying to wrap a corner of blanket around himself, Tomás banged his elbow on the big rock and wept with the pain for half an hour. The other three slept in a heap in the main space. It was raining when they got up at dawn. No breakfast was served until the local man arrived with a can of tea and some bread and butter at a quarter to ten; fortunately the hosts held back and left the lion's share to their visitors.

About a month before the truce was declared, orders came from the IRA High Command for the brigade commanders to meet in Gleann Creamh in connection with the founding of a Republican police force. Colm happened to be in south Connemara, and it was on this occasion that he had to make the crossing of Criathrach Choirill already described, to reach Lotaí, the village perched above Gleann Chóchan in the Twelve Pins, where the Flying Column was stationed at the time. The next day, heading for Gleann Creamh, they climbed to the high pass at the head of Gleann Eidhneach, where they were terrified by a thunderstorm in which multicoloured lightning flashes threatened to split the rocks beneath their feet, and they had to stick the barrels of their guns into the earth lest they attract the strikes. On their way back from this meeting they destroyed the Gleann Eidhneach bridge, denying the enemy's lorries access to central Connemara. Shortly afterwards, when word of the impending truce had already got around and precautions were relaxed, Colm was called to another meeting, this time a few miles beyond Leenaun in Gleann na nGeimhleach. His men were full of joy at the prospect of going home soon, but on approaching Leenaun an inexplicable anxiety made Colm call in to a friendly house, where they learned that if they had gone on they would have walked into the arms of three lorry-loads of Black and Tans lodged in the McEwans' hotel. Instead they had to cross the Killary by boat and go round the head of the fiord to reach Gleann na nGeimhleach. There, at last, they received orders to store their arms safely and disperse.

Despite the 'hare's life' that they had led for so long, says Colm, the

Flying Column was always a hearty and light-spirited gang; they had sports and entertainments outside their huts on the hillsides, they sang spiritual songs, comic songs and exiles' songs, and when they were tired of these they made up patriotic songs of their own. One of their number, whom they called 'the poet', had bagfuls of his own lyrics with him and was always asking their opinion of them, until they told him to go and submit them to the judgement of Eilís Ní Chaisil (i.e. Alice Cashel, coincidentally of Cashel House, a Sinn Féin county councillor and author of a nationalistic children's novel of the Rising that became a well-worn schoolbook for a later generation of Connemara youngsters). This he did; they never heard what she had said to him, but thenceforth the creative heat went out of him, he spent less time off on his own, and he used to say that establishing the Republic was easier than composing poems.

When the Truce came, the men of the Flying Column felt proud that they had beaten 'the most powerful and most scheming empire on the face of the earth', but they were sad to part. They looked forward to long rest and peace, but, Colm writes, 'My ruin and my sorrow, that was not what was in store; it was "out of the bushes and into the brambles".' Colm and a few others crossed Cashel Hill on their way home the next evening:

It was the finest evening I was ever out in. Roundstone Bay below us was a sheet of silver and the channels between the islands like tangled chains looped together. Nothing disturbed the solitude but an occasional screech from a frightened curlew on the edge of the strand, or the strange clattering of the waves against the shore, or the *'giúc giúc'* of a corncrake from a nearby meadow. 'Isn't it good to be alive after all the struggle?' we said to one another, seeing the beauty of the world in the loneliness of that evening.

It is easy to understand why there are no accounts of the Civil War in Connemara to match the writings of Colm Ó Gaora and Tomás Ó Máille on the War of Independence. The memory of the national struggle was gilded by victory; Cogadh na gCarad, the war of the friends, though fought with equal intransigence and courage, ended in moral squalor and hastily buried enmities. Colm fought in the hills once again, and it seems he intended to write up that part of his story, but if he did put it on paper it never saw publication; his *Mise* ends with him walking home through the beauty of the evening as described above, and finding that the Ros Muc people turned aside when they saw him coming, because, he later came to understand, word had gone around that he had been killed and they thought they were seeing his ghost. Tomás played no part in the Civil War; he married in 1923, continued his scholarly career, and died, leaving his widow with seven children, in 1938. Pádraic Ó Máille took the pro-Treaty side, and became Deputy Speaker in the Dáil. In December 1922 he and Seán Hales, the Speaker, were in a cab in the centre of Dublin when they were attacked by gunmen. Hales was killed on the spot and Ó Máille received ten bullet wounds. The cab driver went into shock and Ó Máille, with a bullet lodged close to his spine, took over and drove the cab to a hospital. Two days later the government had four leading Republican prisoners shot as a reprisal, including Pádraic's old comrade Liam Mellowes. Ó Máille was appalled by this action and hastened to make his peace with the Mellowes family, who accepted that he had had no part in it. Pádraic's mighty constitution pulled him through this episode. In 1927, having founded his own little Republican party, Clann Éireann, he lost his seat in the Dáil, but later on became a Fianna Fáil senator until his death in 1946.

Most of the West Connemara Brigade opposed the Treaty and joined the Republican side, and when fighting broke out in June 1922 the hills once again became their stronghold, while Clifden, which leaned towards the pro-Treaty side and had been isolated by the blowing up of bridges and trenching of the roads from Galway and Westport, had to put up with their exactions. But when 150 Free State troops suddenly materialized in Mannin Bay to the south of the town and in Kingstown Bay to the north-west, having been secretly shipped from Galway via the Aran islands in three trawlers, the Republicans had to withdraw into the Twelve Pins, and for a time restricted their activities to small ambushes and snipings and the denial, by burning, of large buildings to the Free Staters; this was when the Railway Hotel at Recess went up in flames. Then at the end of October a Republican force mustered from Kerry, Sligo and Mayo, together with the local men, retook the town and with the aid of an improvised armoured car forced the surrender of the barracks. The Republicans did not continue to hold the town; most of them retired to the hills and crossed the Killary into the fastnesses of Mayo, while most of their prisoners were allowed to go their ways. However, three Free State soldiers, Commandant O'Malley of Cleggan, Captain Dick Joyce and Lieutenant Heanue, who had defended the barracks doggedly until it was almost brought down around their ears by mines, were taken off to a house the Republicans had commandeered on the southern shore of Killary Harbour. Their escape from this remote place, Doire na Sliogán, the wood of the seashells, as recounted by the staunchly Free Statist Mr Barlow of Roundstone in an essay he wrote for me in his old age, 'A Boy's Eye View of the Civil War Years', gives me a chance to describe one more epic journey across the mountains – epic, that is, on the Connemara scale of geography and history – ending with a gallant act to close the scene.

The weather was beautiful, according to the story as Mr Barlow heard it in his youth. The three prisoners and the four Republicans left to guard them sat around playing cards. After a day or two, time began to drag on both guards and prisoners. Dick Joyce, a hardened veteran of the old Flying Column and a native of the Leenaun region, enquired if there would be meat for dinner. When the answer was 'No', he said that when he had been in this same house during the 'Tan War' they had never gone short of fresh mutton, and that obviously the Republicans were not organized at all. The guards agreed that two of them should go off and get one of the big wethers belonging to the O'Neills, the great sheep-raising family of nearby Gleann Creamh, and Joyce offered to go with them to show them the way. They declined this offer, and went off on their own. Soon afterwards Joyce pointed to one of the rifles standing in a corner and said, 'That looks like the rifle I had once – and if I'm not mistaken it has a stiff bolt. Pass it across till I see.' The naïve Republicans did so. Joyce examined it, quoted its serial number, tried the bolt, put a round up into the breech and took the three guards captive. 'You are our prisoners now,' he said. 'Gather up any belongings you can get into a kitbag, and a few slices of bread. We are starting out on a forced march to Oughterard. I've lost my wish for mutton!' Oughterard, the nearest Free State stronghold, lay about thirty miles away, across the heartland of republicanism. 'We've got to hurry before the others come back,' said Joyce; 'Just turn the key in the door: they'll think we've gone for a breath of fresh air.' Knowing every inch of the ground, he led them by shortcuts across the slopes south of Leenaun village and then along the north-eastern flanks of the Mám Tuirc range, by Coill Mhíolcon and Tír na Cille, hurried across the Mám to Maam Cross road just north of Mám Aodha, rounded Leic Aimhréidh and so came into sight of the broad expanses of Lough Corrib on their left (but they had no time to enjoy the beauties of nature, says Mr Barlow). Once in Corrib country Captain Joyce felt it safe to stop to eat their sandwiches, and they all agreed they'd never tasted anything so sweet. But the prisoners were now beginning to worry about their future, since just a few weeks previously the Provisional Government had passed an Emergency Powers Act authorizing military courts to execute persons found bearing arms against the Free State. Captain Joyce assured them that if they were court-martialled he would attest that they had treated their prisoners with kindness and courtesy, and that they would have surrendered long before but for their fear of their own officers. On reaching the Free State Army HQ in Oughterard they were met by a mob of soldiers from Clare, 'wild dangerous fellows who wanted to put a bullet in them on the spot', according to Mr Barlow, and the Republicans would have been beaten and kicked had not Joyce prevented it, saying, 'They are my prisoners and I defy anyone to lay a hand on them. I will defend them with my life.'

In the event the two young men were interned for a year or so, during which period Clifden was retaken by the Free State forces, most of the local Republicans were rounded up and, nationally, the war came to an end after a reign of horrors that Connemara was largely spared. Afterwards one of the men captured by Joyce went to the States for a bit, but returned to raise a large family in Recess, and to tell the then-young John Barlow of this adventure. Dick Joyce left the army to become a successful newsagent in Clifden, where John often saw him chatting with his former prisoner, and, John writes, 'I knew that "the Crack was Sound".'

8 The Long March

In the spring of 1974 a fifteen-strong band of demonstrators came striding briskly along the coast road and paused for speeches at the Ros Muc crossroads. Most of them were young activists of Gluaiseacht Chearta Sibhialta na Gaeltachta, the Gaeltacht civil rights movement, and their principal demand was for a degree of Gaeltacht autonomy, as a prerequisite for the salvation of the Irish language. The government was planning to set up a Gaeltacht Authority, but it was not clear if it would have the powers of a county council, and if its board members would be elected in the Gaeltacht rather than be appointed by Dublin. The marchers were accompanied by respected elder figures: the lexicographer Tomás de Bhaldraithe (his famous *English–Irish Dictionary* had appeared in 1959), and the journalist and social theorist Desmond Fennell. They had just completed the first leg of a 45-mile, three-day march from Carna to Bearna, the two villages conventionally taken as marking the western and eastern limits of the genuinely Irish-speaking part of Connemara. The journalist Breandán Ó hEithir was there to capture the moment for RTÉ's Irish-language current-affairs programme *Féach*, and, according to Seosamh Ó Cuaig, one of the movement's founders, he did not do it justice. I translate:

Breandán came out west and made a programme about us that was damnably hostile. He was given his chance by the big strategic mistake we made. Instead of asking a dozen people who would be willing and able to walk from Carna to Bearna we asked the whole community. And of course the whole community did not turn out, nor would they ever except for some terribly huge cause. And because we'd called them out and there was only a little group of us, he showed the little group and emphasized the little group. We were unhappy about that.

Ó hEithir saw it otherwise:

The march was very small, and in some strange way I don't understand to this day the camera was blamed. And there were ferocious letters in the paper – myself and Eoghan Harris and Seosamh Ó Cuaig and Desmond Fennell arguing with one another. But in the end there was nothing in it but 'the battle of the hornless cows', as we all had the same aim, and at least the matter was alive.

In fact, on viewing the old film, it is the very smallness of the group, the evaporation of their oratory into the uncaring breezy spaces of Connemara, that movingly convinces one of their earnestness and the romantic appeal of their cause. As the historian Gearóid Ó Tuathaigh has written:

In the Gaeltacht, as elsewhere in rural Ireland, after the nadir of despair in the 1950s, the 1960s saw the first serious challenge offered to the defeatism and fatalism of a century. A group of articulate young radicals suddenly found voice and began demanding policies to arrest the dissolution and disappearance of its own community. These Gaeltacht radicals were generally well-educated, and like similar groups in Northern Ireland, were part of the global dynamism of youth politics and civil rights movements of the late 1960s.

The most immediate problem facing the various Gaeltacht areas (of which the Connemara Gaeltacht is the natural leader in terms of the number of regular Irish-speakers) was how to bring in investment and employment without further diluting the shrunken pool of the Irish language with floods of English; surely only an elective body drawing members from a community ready to claim its rights to its own culture and intimately familiar with the pain of emigration could square this circle? The movement (An Ghluaiseacht, as it was familiarly called) was a manifestation of what Desmond Fennell had called 'a sharp loss of faith in the "centre" and a corresponding shift of faith to the periphery'.

Fennell himself had been moved by this redeployment of faith to quit Dublin, with his wife and three children, for the island of Maínis (which he liked to think of as Mao-inis), south of Carna, in 1968. There he had launched an ambitious scheme called 'Israel in Iarchonnacht', inspired by the example of the Jews who returned from the Diaspora to recreate a homeland and resurrect an ancient language; similarly, he proposed, the Gaeilgeóirí, the Irish-speakers, of Dublin should relocate to Iarchonnacht (by which he meant the Connemara Gaeltacht), and dedicate their skills and enterprise to the development of three new towns of 7,000 or 8,000 population. But while the film-maker Bob Quinn moved to An Cheathrú Rua in 1969 to set up his studio and cinema, few others heeded the call. Nevertheless, the idea of the Gaeltacht as the locus of social experiment and the object of dedication was inspirational to the young local teachers, factory managers and journalists who founded the Gluaiseacht in that year.

From the beginning the concerns of the movement were both economic and cultural. As to the language, its death through economic starvation seemed imminent; to survive, it had to claim breathing space in the modern media. The new grouping first attracted attention with a peaceful but vociferous protest meeting outside Teach Furbo, a hotel near An Spidéal where RTÉ was recording a quiz programme; that this was being done in English in what was then a strong Gaeltacht village seemed emblematic of RTÉ's neglect of the Irish language. When discussions with RTÉ on its rather grudging concessions to the official status of Irish as the first national language came to nothing, the movement looked for inspiration to Desmond Fennell's proposal for a Gaeltacht-based Irish-language radio. The new constellation of pirate radio stations in Britain, and Radio Free Derry in the North, showed the way forward. In Easter week of 1970 a young engineering student from Cork, Mícheál Ó hÉalaithe, was brought to Connemara with his equipment. Ó Cuaig was not impressed at first sight by this long-haired hippy, but soon realized that he was no bluffer. Ros Muc, because of its nationalist tradition, seemed the right place for this Easter Rising of the airwaves. Ó Cuaig and the journalist Piaras Ó Gaora, son of Colm Ó Gaora, went on the search for an empty house with an electricity supply; they even considered Pearse's cottage, which had been rebuilt after its burning by the Black and Tans, but its very suitability from a symbolic point of view made it too obvious a hiding place for this illegal enterprise. Eventually they bought an old caravan and parked it behind the Ó Gaora house in An Turlach Mór. Because of the necessity for secrecy, few knew of and fewer actually heard the first broadcast of Saor-Raidió Chonamara, Radio Free Connemara, on Saturday, 28 March, but the beacon had been lit.

By April of that year money had run out, and there were no more broadcasts until November 1970, when a festival of culture, Oireachtas na nGael, was held in the school at An Turlach Beag, as part of a campaign to get the regular Oireachtas na Gaeilge, the Gaelic League's annual festival, to relocate from Dublin to the Gaeltacht. This time the radio station operated more openly, and there were even outside broadcasts of music and interviews. The equipment was concealed in the attic of the nearby pub, Tigh Mhadhcó; the Gardaí must have known this, but did not press their enquiries too hard. (In fact, according to Seosamh Ó Cuaig, the sergeant was in the bar downstairs watching *The Six Wives of Henry VIII* on TV, when owing to some technical error upstairs King Henry suddenly started to sing the Connemara boat-song 'Púcán Mhicil Pháidín'.) As a result of the movement's taking the law into their own hands, the government at last moved on the question, and in April 1972 Raidió na Gaeltachta was opened, with a recording of de Valera's shaky blessings on the project and a performance of Seán Ó Riada's Mass.

One of the movement's early concerns was the fact that Connemara's rich salmon and sea-trout fisheries were still, as they had been for centuries, in the hands of 'tycoons from Ireland and abroad'. The first of its 'fish-ins' took place in 1969; over a hundred members of the movement thrashed the waters of the Casla river. To hand was a Sinn Féin pamphlet, *Stolen Waters*, listing the fisheries of Ireland with notes on 'who to guard against' in each case, information drawn from 'The Poachers' Guide to Ireland's Rivers and Lakes', published in a Republican newspaper, the *United Irishman*. In Connemara it was the agents of certain private individuals and of Ballynahinch Castle Hotel, the Zetland Hotel in Cashel and Ashford Castle Hotel in Cong who were to be guarded against. The campaign was resumed in 1975 with a fish-in on the Casla river, when a large attendance watched as thirty pirate anglers went to work and two fish were caught. Similar scenes were enacted on the Screebe lakes, property of the Screebe estate and of a

Mr H. Hodgson of Oughterard, and on the Erriff river near Leenaun, which belonged to Lord Brabourne, cousin to the Queen of England and, as nationalist newspapers put it, the representative of 'British Imperialist interests'. However, these demonstrations have had little effect. Connemara fisheries are still largely in the possession of the big hotels and a few well-heeled individuals; the exception is the Erriff, which is now state owned, and all who can afford to holiday at Aasleagh Lodge have access to its beats.

In the general election of June 1969 An Ghluaiseacht put forward a candidate, Peadar Mac an Iomaire, who attracted enough attention to give Fianna Fáil a scare; Jack Lynch came down to campaign for his party, there was a great deal of shouting about emigration and water rights, and after a turbulent rally in An Cheathrú Rua the Taoiseach jumped on a chair to cry shame on those who were, he said, refusing others the right of free speech. Later the tyres of Lynch's car were punctured by tacks scattered on the road, a deed the movement repudiated. In the event Mac an Iomaire was not elected, but gained a respectable 1,500 first-preference votes. Then it seems that a 'split', notoriously the first item on the agenda of any Irish political grouping, took place. Peadar Mac an Iomaire decided not to go forward as a candidate in the election of 1973; Seosamh Ó Tuairisg, a member of the movement who had been active in the pirate radio venture and had founded the Irish-language periodical *Tuairisc* ('Report'), stood in his place but did not achieve the same level of success.

So, by the time of the long march from Carna to Bearna, the movement had won a significant battle with the founding of Raidió na Gaeltachta, and had met with mixed fortunes in other campaigns. All the same, Bob Quinn's film about it, which includes the old black-and-white footage of the march, is entitled *Splanc Dheireadh na Gaeltachta* ('The Last Spark of the Gaeltacht'). As Desmond Fennell has written, during that period the movement, like so much else in the Republic, was overshadowed by events in Northern Ireland; 'Moreover, as the years passed, the movement's achievement of many of its secondary goals, together with the rising prosperity in the Gaeltacht, lessened the numbers and enthusiasm of the activists.' Today, the fizz of youth is spent, but the movement's founder members are still in the field: Peadar Mac an Iomaire is Chief Executive of Acadamh na hOllscolaíochta Gaeilge, NUI Galway's Irish-language outposts in Carna, An Cheathrú Rua and elsewhere, and chaired the commission that reported on the state of the Gaeltacht in 2002; Seosamh Ó Cuaig is an independent member of Galway County Council, an elected board member of the Gaeltacht Authority and a staff member of Raidió na Gaeltachta; and so on. The replacement in 1980 of a conventional non-elective Gaeltacht development agency, Gaeltarra Éireann, by Údarás na Gaeltachta, the Gaeltacht Authority, most of whose board members are elected, was the outcome of a decade of activism by members of the movement and others. Raidió na Gaeltachta has brought the various Gaeltacht regions of Ireland within hearing of each other and broken down their provinciality, and is regarded as a beacon of endangered-language broadcasting worldwide. An Irish-language television service has come to be, as a result of a history parallel to that of the radio service. This triumph owed its inspiration to an essay by Desmond Fennell on what Connemara could do for itself, 'Take the Faroes for Example'. Donncha Ó hÉallaithe, a lecturer at the Regional Technical College in Galway, and Ruairí Ó Tuairisg had taken this advice literally and sailed off with Pádraig de Bhaldraithe in his small traditional boat to the Faroe Islands, where they were impressed by the TV service, which broadcast in Faroese to seventeen islands for twenty-five hours a week. In 1987 another Oireachtas na nGael in Ros Muc furnished the occasion for an illicit trial of Irish-language TV; hundreds of homes within fifteen miles of the place were able to receive colour TV images of the festival, thanks to a pirate transmitter hidden in An Chrannóg and another secreted among the heather on Cnoc Mordáin and guarded night and day by young zealots. The transmitters cost £4,000, of which £3,000 was raised locally, and the rest, the operators hoped, 'would come in soon'. Inevitably this demonstration eventually led to that high point in the history of the Gaeltacht, the opening of Teilifís na Gaeltachta in 1996, when among its presenters and reporters was revealed the Irish language's secret weapon, a bevy of the finest young women seen in the land since the days of the demigoddesses from whom they were all named.

But, despite this and the other advances won by the civil rights movement and its successors, the Irish language is still endangered, in its south Connemara retreats as elsewhere. Economic well-being – the boom years of tourism, advance factories, the fish-farming industry – has been as bad for it as were emigration and the 'alms of idleness'. Outside the gates of the primary schools the young, globally encultur-ated, decisively opt for English; it is principally for this reason that a recent, massive and detailed study of the Irish of the Carna peninsula by Brian Ó Curnáin – a magisterial work of long dedication – bluntly terms its subject 'a dying language'. But it is not yet dead. There is an ongoing dogged tussle with *ceist na teangan*, the wearisome old 'language question'. I am unqualified to contribute to the sociolinguistic studies, the pressure groups, the educational inventiveness, 'the long march through the institutions', necessary to reverse the almost terminal decline of Irish. I can only offer an act of faith in its continued life, and hope that my own access to Irish, though limited, will allow me to show that language and landscape are the two wings, however bedraggled they be, on which south Connemara flies.

In the rest of this book I shall be roving through two more provinces of Patrick Pearse's dream-kingdom: first the storytelling villages and turf bogs of Carna and Cill Chiaráin, to the west of Ros Muc, and then the islands and peninsulas to the south and east, where topog-raphy splashes like a child in the sea and revels in a complexity that seems to call for the language of mathematics rather than either English or Irish.

PART II

A World of Words

Preface

A Tale Out of Time

One night a man living in Ard dreamed that Mass would be said the next morning at a place he recognized on the mountain. When he woke he dressed quickly and hurried to the spot, where he found many people gathered and was just in time to hear the Mass. But he noticed that the priest seemed disturbed by his presence. Afterwards the priest came over to him and asked him how he had known that there was to be a Mass there. The man explained about his dream, and the priest said, 'Well, no harm done this time. But in future take no notice of such dreams. And next time you go to Mass make sure first it is the right one – for we are all people long gone from this world, and this Mass was not for the likes of you.'

I first heard this in Irish, from a turf-cutter I met out on the level heath north of Cnoc Mordáin, the long hill that forms the spine of the Carna peninsula; he was delighted to straighten his back and answer my queries about the placenames of the vicinity, and when I mentioned that I had heard of a Mass rock on the hill above us he stuck his *sleán* into the ground and gave me this tale. To hear such a story told impromptu out in the archetypal setting of the turf banks on a summer's day was like a dispensation from the forced march of time. I think it was on the following day that I heard it in English, in almost identical terms, from a man in the village of Glinsce, west of the hill. Unlike the dedicated and systematic collectors of the Folklore Commission who combed through the cottages of Carna in the last century, I carried no recording apparatus, and my Irish is limited, but I believe the above transcription is faithful to the core of a story that has been so well shaped by two languages and polished by repetition.

Storytelling walks us out of the comprehensible dimensions of space and place – the route the man might have taken across the hills from An Aird, anglicized as Ard, a dense cluster of dwellings near the southern tip of the Carna peninsula, to the Mass rock up on Cnoc Mordáin, for instance – into those of history and dream and myth. The solace of escapism is a reductive description of one of the drives to storytelling. Seán Ó Súilleabháin, the commission's chief archivist, wrote that 'the parish of Carna had more unrecorded folktales in 1935 than did all the rest of western Europe'. But consider the harsh world into which the tellers of folktales, these oral artists, were born.

In 1898 the Revd Thomas Aloysius Finlay, Professor of Metaphysics at the Catholic University College and a convert to Horace Plunkett's cooperative movement, came down from Dublin to look into the social conditions underlying the 'distress' of that year. He describes a landscape 'of monotonous barrenness . . . a vast sheet of granite . . . broken occasionally by patches of peat and heather'. A coastal strip of the wilderness a mile or two wide was thickly dotted with roughly thatched houses of mortarless stonework, in which a single room served as 'dwelling, barn, cowhouse and piggery'. Seaweed alone was the basis of all that could be called 'productive economy', and the unremitting drudgery of gathering the weed and tending the kelp kilns had until a few years previously provided something of an income. That industry was virtually extinct, kelp having been replaced as a source of iodine by the South American nitrate beds. But seaweed was still needed as manure for the potato crop.

On the occasion of my visit to Carna . . . a biting north-east wind swept across the moors, driving before it clouds of sleet which neither frieze nor waterproof could resist. At half tide, on the ebb, the boats of the weed-gatherers started for their several stations . . . The crew – men and women – slipped into the water, and here, immersed up to the waist, they began the task of cutting the weed from the stones and flinging it into the boat.

When the boatloads had been brought to shore it was the task of women and children to carry the dripping weed in baskets on their shoulders to the potato plots, often for a mile or more over rough and stony ground. 'Meeting one of these drudges toiling along under her slimy load, her thin garments of flannel saturated with brine, her bare feet and arms benumbed by the icy wind, one is tempted to doubt whether slavery established by law may not have its advantage over the slavery accepted from necessity.' The compassionate enquirer goes on to describe the prevalence of pulmonary diseases, for which the district's dispensary doctor prescribed 'according to the rules of his art' but had his prescriptions revised by the relieving officer, who considered Indian meal 'a universal specific'. The local shopkeeper being the sole market for the product of their labours – the few eggs or the bony cow – and paying only in kind, the peasants subsisted in a lifelong state of debt quite beyond their reckoning. On top of all this, the rent. In some places, Finlay records, holdings of six or seven acres, of which four were naked stone, bore a rent of nearly £5 a year. Since the ground could not produce anything like that profit, the money must come from elsewhere, and in fact its source was beyond the Atlantic: 'All the girls of large families who are not married at eighteen . . . are dispatched to America, they become the rent-earners of the households they have left.'

Out of this extortionate regime came an astounding harvest of words and music. A catalogue based on the manuscript collections of the Folklore Department in University College Dublin lists 633 songs recorded from the Barony of Ballynahinch, the majority of them from Carna and Glinsce (and most of them love songs); this does not include the dozens of songs in the 531 copybooks of folk material in the Schools Manuscript Collection gathered by Carna schoolchildren from their own families under the direction of their teachers under a far-sighted scheme in 1937–8. The mountain of manuscript folktales, historical anecdotes, lists of riddles, charms, prayers, jokes and curses from this overwhelmingly voluble parish is something I have shirked looking into; I quail at the thought of the 2,000 pages recorded from Éamonn a Búrc, tailor of this parish, described in 1966 as 'possibly the most accomplished narrator of folktales who has lived into our own times'. The tiny proportion of all this material that has made its way into published sources is more than I can cope with. Lastly, the sheets of the six-inch Ordnance Survey maps on which I recorded my findings when I was mapping this area in the 1980s are scribbled all over with the placenames I heard from the farmers, fishermen, housewives and schoolteachers, who with one accord lamented the fact that I had not come around when old so-and-so was alive, for he or she was the one who had the memory . . .

Iorras Aithneach is the current name of the Carna peninsula: the furzy headland, if the second word is from *aiteann*, furze or gorse, as seems probable and indeed very suitable, since either the soft cushions of *Ulex gallii*, the western gorse, or the scraggy bushes of *Ulex europeus*, the common gorse, are in golden flower in every month of the year. But Roderick O'Flaherty in 1684 wrote it as Irrosainhagh, and John O'Donovan in his letters to the Ordnance Survey in 1839 says that it is 'now distinctly called in Irish Iorras Aintheach', the adjective being from the Old Irish *ainbthech*, stormy. I prefer this version, if I may take the storm to be one of words, the wind of recollection and denomination that blows about every hummock and hollow of this little world of small places brimful of matter for discussion. For such is the intensity of commentary on the land here, even today, that one can feel how in the bygone years of gross deprivation the verbal arts must have created a compensating atmosphere of immaterial sustenance, turbulent with marvels, beauty, laughter, sorrow and wit.

Where to start, though, in presenting this land and its unquenchable talk of itself, and how to proceed, are problems. There is no overarching story other than the dominance of story itself, no dominating theme but the multiplicity of themes. I have notes of hundreds of placenames, legends of saints and strong men of ancient times, curious incidents unforgotten through the centuries – but how do I link them together? Topographically, as they crop up townland by townland from, say, north to south? Chronologically, as sparkling moments in an otherwise subdued and obscure history? Thematically, as if I were a folklorist myself, which I am not? Or by improvisation and association, drifting from tale to tale on the wind of the word? I think of the man in the story I began with, who walks one morning across familiar hills to witness a visionary re-enactment of an event out of a dateless past. His trajectory from An Aird to the eastern flank of Cnoc Mordáin has the rugged reality of bog and granite, but begins in a dream of a place he recognizes, and ends with a forbidden attendance at an incursion of the otherworld into his everyday. It is like, but more complex than, a knight's move in chess; maybe it is a knight's move on some space-time version of the chessboard with extra, fictional, dimensions. An old puzzle (as old as Babylon, I have read) asks one to make a circuit of the chessboard in knight's moves, alighting on each and every square once only. It can be done, with difficulty. Something like that perhaps might answer my purposes, allowing me freedom to drop in and out of the present-day reality of Iorras Aintheach and rove among its histories and fictions, without having to be pedantic about which is which.

Like the dreamer, I will start from An Aird.

9 The Castle

Iorras Aintheach is a stocky peninsula of Connemara's intricate southern coastline, some eight miles long and four to seven miles broad. Ramifying arms of the sea hold it distinct from Roundstone with its harbour, hills and attendant islands to the west, and the Ros Muc peninsula and the fragmentary territory known simply as Na hOileáin, the islands, to the east. The interior is bare, open and boggy, with many little lakes, and some modern forestry on the flanks of Cnoc Mordáin, a ridge paralleling the eastern shoreline and rising to a little over 1,100 feet. Nearly all settlement is close to the shore; a loop of road strings together a thin but almost continuous scattering of dwellings with the two villages of Carna in the south and Cill Chiaráin in the south-east. The peninsula has its own brood of offshore islands too, but apart from these its southernmost point is a low-lying bulge of the shoreline called An Aird, which means simply 'the headland'. Here, narrow roads wander through a small-scale landscape of crooked drystone field walls and whitewashed cottages, many of them modernized into holiday homes. A stream one can step across, emptying into a muddy creek, divides this out-of-the-way little place into two townlands, An Aird Thoir, and An Aird Thiar, anglicized respectively as Ard East and Ard West. The former is also known as Aird an Chaisleáin, for here 400 years ago and more stood one of the six coastal castles that, together with the lake-island castle of Ballynahinch, watched over the lands of the O'Flahertys.

What remains of the castle are some indecipherable unevennesses of the ground in a field by the stream's mouth, and a blunt, jagged fang of masonry a yard or so thick and about three times my height that stands for its east-facing wall. Most of its big irregular granite blocks sprout one or more tousled beards of grey lichen, and there are periwinkle shells embedded in the rough mortar, which was evidently made with sea sand and, according to oral lore, strengthened with ox blood. There is a window a few inches wide and a foot or so high in it, splayed on the inside, under a heavy lintel, and a small squarish recess in the inner face; otherwise there is nothing that suggests accommodation of harsh stone to human needs. This was the stronghold of Tadhg O'Flaherty, who received a knighthood and was confirmed in his possession of the castles of Ard and of Ballynahinch by the Composition of Connaught, drawn up by Queen Elizabeth's Lord Deputy General of Ireland in 1585, as I have recounted in my first volume. But, standing in this bleak little field in a wind off the sea, it is harder to connect these rugged stones with the well-attested historical figure than with the ogre of local legend, for Tadhg na Buile, Tadhg of the madness or frenzy, seems but recently gone.

Apparently Tadhg first tried to build his castle a little further south, on the western point of the island of Maínis, but every night the fairies threw down what had been put up during the day, and so he moved to this spot, now known as An Fhaiche, the green, in Aird an Chaisleáin. He is said to have poisoned the waters of nearby Loch na Faiche to kill the fish, and to have forbidden the cutting of turf within seven miles of the castle. In the 1930s old residents of the neighbourhood were able to give an amateur folklore collector a good description of the castle, which they said still had its roof in the time of Thomas Martin, for they remembered hearing that he had threatened a man with prison for taking its slates. There was a high-walled bawn or courtyard around it, they had heard, to which the sole access was by boat through an arch from the head of the inlet; inside the bawn was a dock with a lock gate. From there Tadhg would emerge in his big rowboat, to go to the Aran Islands or County Clare. This is the traditional story of how the tyrant met his death:

There was a widow's son living in Inis Leacan [the island just south of Roundstone] who was away at sea for a long time, from before Tadhg came to An Aird. When he returned his mother made him a meal. 'I have no "kitchen",' she said. ['Kitchen' is any tasty food to make bread palatable.] 'I have a crock of butter here for Tadhg na Buile and if I didn't have it he would take the cow from me.'

'What sort of person is Tadhg na Buile?' he said. She told him. 'Serve me the butter,' he said, 'and leave it between me and Tadhg.'

It seems Tadhg took the cow. The sailor came across one evening and got into conversation with Tadhg's servant girl. She used to come out in a little boat to fetch water from the well. He asked her if she would let him in when Tadhg had gone to sleep. She said she would not, that Tadhg would kill her.

'Don't be afraid,' he said, 'he won't kill you.'

When Tadhg had gone to sleep she sent the little boat out for the sailor, and he came in through the arch. She showed him the room where Tadhg was sleeping with his wife. (Her name was Síle Ní Fheilpín and it was said that Tadhg had carried her off.) He went in and stabbed him in his bed. Síle was in the bed.

'Take him away,' she said, 'before he spoils my bed.'

So the sailor threw him out of the window, and he was buried where he fell.

This account has much in common with folktales of the killing of giants (young sons of poor widows excel at this, it seems), of which there are numerous examples in the Schools Collection. At the same time there is nothing supernatural in it; in fact it has a ring of truth. How did Tadhg actually die? The Galway historian James Hardiman merely mentions that an inquisition taken after his death in 1607 found that he had owned the castle and the two Ards, half the lands of Ballynahinch and half of Ballindoon. Tadhg's ghost is suspended between the small print of history and the confusions of myth.

About a mile and a half away on the south side of the road to Carna there is a field called Garraí Thaidhg Mhóir, Big Tadhg's garden. Here, according to a scrap of lore gathered in the 1930s, lived an outlaw from Sligo called Tadhg Mór, together with his wife and family, in a sod hut. He was on the run after the suppressed rebellion of 1798, and had come to Iorras Aintheach from the Aran Islands. But the present owner of the field tells me that his mother used to say that it was Tadhg na Buile who lurked here in An Scailp Mhór, a hollow under a big rock, waiting to rob the passers-by. So the *tánaiste*, second only to the chieftain, of the western O'Flahertys has dwindled into an ogre to frighten children with. He might leap out from behind the broken wall of his castle and scare us away at any moment.

★

In September 1588 a watcher on the parapets of Tadhg's tower house would have seen an amazing sight: out of wild weather to the west, tottering palaces of timber and canvas driven before the gale and lurching helplessly towards the rocky shore. These were ships of the Spanish Armada; this was history in the unmaking, its aftermath of suffering. A battle for dominance over Europe, masked as a struggle to save its soul, had been fought out in the English Channel; Philip II's peacock-proud expeditionary fleet of 128 ships had been torn asunder by Drake's hearts of oak and an anti-Catholic wind, and had fled through the North Sea and rounded Cape Wrath. Most of them stood well out into the Atlantic on their way south again and eventually saw home, but a group of twenty-eight or so that had lost contact with the rest headed for the Irish coast, hoping for a hospitable reception from the rebellious Catholic clansmen of the west. Relying on maps that were ignorant of the great westward thrust of Connacht, harried by a succession of Atlantic gales, exhausted from pumping out shot-riddled holds, reduced to squalor by dysentery, hunger and thirst, they staggered among reefs and cliffbound islands. The treatment of the wretches who managed to struggle ashore through the breakers from some twenty-four wrecks off Sligo, Galway, Clare and Kerry was as cruel as the sea, for Queen Elizabeth's functionaries had a firm grip on the chieftains, most of whom were freshly conscripted into the feudal system. What the Crown expected of them was unambiguously spelled out by the Lord Deputy of Ireland:

Whereas the distressed fleet of the Spaniards by tempest and contrary winds, through the providence of God, have been driven upon this coast, and many of them wrecked in several places in the province of Munster, where is to be thought hath not only been much treasure cast away, subject to the spoil of the country people, but also great store of ordnance, munitions, armours, and other goods of several kinds which ought to be preserved for and to the use of her Majesty, we authorise you to make enquiry by all good means, both by oath and otherwise, to take all the hulls of ships, stores, treasures, etc., into your hands, and to apprehend and execute all Spaniards found there, of what quality soever. Torture may be used in prosecuting this inquiry.

Three ships of the Armada were driven into Galway Bay; one of them, the name of which is unrecorded, was abandoned near Galway itself, and the seventy men who escaped to shore were seized by townsmen loyal to the Crown, while, further west, the two other ships fell into O'Flaherty hands. The *Falco Blanco*, a transport carrying 16 guns and 130 men, went aground near Bearna in the territory of Murchadh na dTua, or Sir Murrough O'Flaherty as he had recently been titled, and the *Concepción*, with 225 men and 18 guns, was smashed on rocks off the south-western headland of Iorras Aintheach. The O'Flahertys rounded up the survivors, and it seems did not immediately hand them over, but soon, as the Clerk of the Connacht Council records:

It was thought good by the Governor and Council to set forth a proclamation upon pain of death that any man who had or kept Spaniards should bring them in and deliver them to Robert Fowley, the Provost Marshal. Any man who held them for more than four hours after the proclamation to be reputed a traitor. Whereupon, Tadhg na Buile O'Flaherty, and many others, brought their prisoners to Galway, and for that many other Spaniards were brought to Galway from other parts of the Province, beside those which the townsmen had taken prisoners before, the Governor despatched Robert Fowley, Captain Nathaniel Smythe and John Byrte with warrant and commission to put them all to the sword, saving the noblemen or such principle gentlemen as were among them, and afterwards to repair to O'Flaherty's country to make earnest search for those who kept any Spaniards in their hands and to execute them in like manner, and to take view of the great ordnance, munitions, and other things which were in the two ships that were lost in that country, and to see how it might be saved for the use of her Majesty. Whereupon they executed 300 men at Galway.

The scene of the wreck of the *Concepción*, which Tadhg is said to have lured to its destruction with false signals, is just over a mile west of his castle. The walk takes one out of the neighbourly villages of An Aird onto a stark coastline challenged by the full fetch of the Atlantic.

From An Aird Thoir a network of quiet side roads brings one round by detour upon detour to a small harbour and a few houses in the townland of An Más. (The word means a thigh or buttock, and in placenames connotes a flattish elevated area; here it refers primarily to the low hill that shelters the village from westerlies.) A stout pier of granite blocks, a work of the Congested Districts Board in the 1890s, almost closes off a lagoon – a few acres of black mud rimmed with little cliffs of peat at low water – from a deep sea-inlet. One can slip down the slanting outer face of the pier onto seaweed and shingle and bits of plastic, and follow the shoreline around Ceann Mása, Mace Head. After a hundred yards or so the coast shakes off the sorry particulars of modernity and turns its attention to the wild offshore islands, each a low dome of granite: first Oileán Máisean, a mile out to the south, its village deserted and roofless except for one or two summer homes; then Oileán Mhic Dara, the saint's lonely hermitage, further out to the south-west; and lastly, withdrawn and mysterious as always, Cruach na Caoile or Deer Island, three miles off to the west and the Atlantic horizon. The last time I walked round this headland, in the early spring, breakers, not huge but somehow vicious-looking, were swarming ashore like pirates with gleaming blades between their teeth. Stones from the storm beach had been washed by winter seas onto the grassland around the skirts of the hill, and a few primroses and violets were nestling among them. So much timber had been cast ashore and blown inland, including what a beachcombing friend from Round-stone calls 'roundsticks' – straight pine trunks like telephone poles – that one could imagine the scene was the aftermath of a shipwreck.

On the top of the hill is a bleak little one-roomed building of concrete that appears like an architectural lantern against the sky: a Local Defence Force lookout post from the Second World War. I sheltered from a shower in it and observed the endless armadas of cloud sailing in from the west. Nearby, across a few rush-infested fields with swampy corners, were the two single-storey buildings and two lofty scaffolding towers of the Mace Head Atmospheric Research Station, an outpost of the Physics Department in the National University Galway. That day nobody was there to answer my knock. But here, day in day out, automated instruments sniff the wind for marine aerosols, particulate matter, carbon dioxide and ozone. The best air Europe breathes brings all the ingredients of universal pollution, indices of global warming and forebodings of the wreck of civilization to these skeletal towers.

At the foot of the hill below these ominous lookouts lies the shingle bank still known as Duirling na Spáinneach, the stony beach of the Spaniards, where the *Concepción* flapped its broken wings and died. Any men who floundered through the breakers half-drowned to land would have been hunted over the hill or along the shore; those who were not killed on the spot would have been marched off to whatever hole Tadhg's castle boasted in the way of a dungeon. An oral tradition recorded in the 1970s has it that there were two ships wrecked here (perhaps the other one was one of the many small tenders accompanying the fleet), and that they were lured in by a treacherous signal:

That night a fire was lit on the land to bring the Spanish ships in, to pretend that there was a safe way in to harbour for them. A family called MacDonagh it was who lit the fire, but whether it was the English or Tadhg na Buile who paid them I couldn't say. The ships saw the light and came in, thinking they would be saved, for the night was bad, but they struck the land down on the shore we call *Duirling Beag* and *Mór*. Not a man in them was saved but a young boy and all the bodies that came ashore that night are buried below on the shore.

The same informant goes on to say that the lad who escaped drowning was sheltered by a family called Ó Laidhigh (anglicized as Lee) and eventually returned to Spain. Later he came back in a Spanish boat and moored off Oileán Mhic Dara; people went out to greet him there, and he captured all the MacDonaghs and took them off to Spain, whence they never returned. An earlier storyteller, Seosamh Mac Donnchadha of An Aird Thiar, who was born in the 1880s, had a fuller version of the Spaniard's revenge:

The men who got ashore were badly treated and only one survived, a youth who managed to hide himself in a wood on the south of Cnoc an Choillín [the hill just west of Carna village]. A man from Dumhaigh Ithir [a townland north of Ceann Mása] who was looking for strayed cattle in the wood found him, took him to his house, tended him until he recovered, and brought him up just like one of his own. His name was Fernandez. When he became a young man he said that it was time for him to go home. He made his way to Galway, and it was easy for him to find a ship out of Galway for Spain as there was much trade between Galway and Spain at that time.

Years later a ship came to anchor in the same place as the ship that was grounded, An Poll Gorm in the lee of Oileán Mhic Dara. A boat went out to her from the land, and every man that went on board of her was put down under the hatches. When this man who had reared the youth went on board it seems he thought he half recognized one of the Spaniards on the ship and he pronounced the word 'Fernandez' a couple of times. The Spaniard walked over to him and asked him what put that name in his mouth. He said that it was the name of a Spanish youth whom he raised.

'Are you the man who raised me?' said the Spaniard.

'I am,' said the Dumhaigh Ithir man.

'If it's you, you are pardoned and so are those with you.'

'And it's likely they needed it,' concludes the storyteller, 'for "treachery rebounds on the traitor".'

10 The Song of Granite

One of the glories of An Aird Thoir a century ago was the voice of
Seán Choilm Mac Dhonnchadha, Seán (son of Colm) MacDonagh.
On coming home in the evening from work in the fields or the bog
or on the waves in his currach, he would rest himself against a great
boulder outside his cottage, open his mouth and sing. The air would
surrender itself (so my second-hand memories of that era persuade
me) to the passionate invocations of 'Eileanór na Rún' and 'Róisín
Dubh', or sigh over the local lament for the drowned of 'Currachaí na
Trá Báine', 'The Currachs of the White Beach'. All over the village
people would listen. In the early nineteenth century travellers in
Ireland used to remark on the habitual singing of the peasantry at
work, and after the Famine the silence that had fallen on the countryside was heard as deeply sinister and mournful. By the 1900s evidently
Connemara was in voice again.

Colm Mac Dhonnchadha's was the chief house for music in An Aird
Thoir, and nearby were two other musical houses, that of Joe Pheaitsín
'ac Dhonncha, one of whose ancestors is remembered for having won
a gallon of whiskey for singing a song in Cinn Mhara long ago, and that
of Seán Jeaic Mac Donncha, a master singer whose sons keep the tradition alive, their familiar names – Josie Sheáin Jeaic, Johnny Sheáin Jeaic
– proud roll-calls of their musical forebears. Among the women singers
of the locality Máire Bean Uí Cheannabháin (Mary wife of O'Canavan),
known from the trade of her grandfather as Máire an Ghabha, Mary of
the blacksmith, was treasured for her store of old prayers and religious
songs, among them the heartbreaking 'Caoineadh na dTrí Muire', 'The
Lament of the Three Marys', to which I will return.

Into this nest of songsters was born, in 1919, a Seosamh Ó hÉanaigh,
better known locally as Joe Éinniú or Joe Heaney, who was to become
the most famous of them all. *Nár fhágha mé bás choíche*, 'May I Never
Die', is the subtitle of Liam Mac Con Iomaire's detailed biography of

Ó hÉanaigh (from which the above sketch of the village and its music is derived); the phrase is from 'Amhrán Rinn Mhaoile', 'The Song of Renvyle', which Joe often sang; Renvyle was the place of origin of his ancestors. So many of his friends' and admirers' accounts of Ó hÉanaigh quoted in that book liken his voice, appearance and presence to the granite of his harsh native place that the simile has become part of him, making him the time-resistant icon of the *sean-nós*, the old way, as the traditional style of singing has come to be called in relatively recent days. There was also, behind this intimidatingly rough-hewn sculptural persona, a melancholic and vulnerable sensibility. He could be touchy, arrogant, loud-mouthed and aggressive in drink, and yet he inspired great love and loyalty.

Joe was the fifth child of Pádraig Ó hÉanaigh and his wife Béib Ní Mhaoilchiaráin, and two more children were to follow him into the family. Their house was one of the slate-roofed single-storey dwellings built by the Congested Districts Board in the early years of the twentieth century. Musical instruments were few in Connemara then; An Aird Thoir had nothing but a melodeon, and, as Joe later reminisced:

People made their own music by singing and lilting and storytelling, and that's how we used to spend the evenings, around the turf fire with our mouths open listening to somebody telling stories or singing. And in our house, my father was always singing.

After attending the national school a few doors away from his home, Joe went off to study at Coláiste Éinde, a preparatory training college for teachers, which at that period was temporarily located in Dublin, but he was soon sent home, perhaps for smoking or some conflict with authority that might explain his lasting anticlericalism. He found on his arrival that his father had died:

Well, my father was a very good singer. In fact, he had more songs than I'll ever hope to have. He died when I was thirteen [seventeen, in fact], so I had no hope of getting the songs because I thought I'd have plenty of time to get them off him. But they went to the grave with him. I heard him sing songs that I never heard since and I haven't got myself.

Deprived of an education, he had to do what Connemara lads did, go to work for a farmer in the fertile plains of east Galway. Then, like so many of his generation, he left the country for a life of labouring and odd-jobbing. In Glasgow he lodged with a family from Carna, married Mary, the daughter of the house, fathered four children, walked out on them – he rarely mentioned this abandoned family thereafter – and moved to Southampton and London, where he got a clerical job with a building firm, and was welcomed in the pubs of Kilburn for his splendid voice. He was by this time becoming known as an outstanding *sean-nós* singer and as a storyteller; he won the first prize at the Oireachtas, the Gaelic League's annual cultural festival, in Dublin in 1942, and was recorded by the great music collector Séamus Ennis, who knew the Carna music scene household by household. After he was awarded a gold medal at the Oireachtas of 1955, records of his singing began to appear from Gael Linn. His admiring friends included Roibeard Mac Góráin, the head of Gael Linn; the American folk-musicologist Alan Lomax; Ronnie Drew of the Dubliners; and Peggy Jordan, hostess and concert-promoter; his relationship with Séamus Ennis was close, and rivalrous. In the early 1960s he often performed at the Singers' Club in Kilburn, run by the demiurges of the 'ballad boom' of those years, Peggy Seeger and Ewan MacColl. But all this attention brought him more acclaim than money; he was often short of cash, and his hectic nocturnal life was fuelled by cigarette smoke and whiskey fumes.

In a long interview conducted by MacColl and Seeger in 1964 these cognoscenti of the world's folk music pressed him hard for the inside story of his style, especially the role of decoration.

EM : You decorate in some songs more than in others, I've noticed . . . What tells you which songs to decorate and which to leave alone?

JH : Well, I think it all depends on the scope left for me in the lines of the song . . . What I'm trying to say, if the words of the line don't allow me to decorate, I've got to sing the line. Because I couldn't break up the sentence too much. But if it's a short line with not many words, that allows me to decorate a lot of the words. That's the way I feel it anyway.

. . .

PS: Now, when you're going to mix – when you're approaching a line, and you know that at certain points you're going to decorate, do you ever see the shape of the decoration in your mind?

JH: I do. I see exactly what I am going to do with it before I reach it. I know exactly what I'm going to do and each time I try to do it better. Hm. I do.

PS: You never make a mistake when you're decorating? I do.

JH: Well, not in my own mind I don't. Maybe other people sees it, but I don't because I think it's something that you can't make a mistake at, because everybody decorates different . . . I could sing a song for you now ten times tonight and each time'd be different. But I'll either do it better, or you're – but I'll know exactly what I'm going to do before I reach it.

EM: Do you ever do the first verse very simply with very few decorations and thereafter on the verses which follow, make . . .?

JH: Yes. I try to introduce the song first as clean as I can . . . especially with somebody who doesn't know the song.

On the mysterious quality known (sometimes derogatorily) as *nyaah*, the almost subliminal nasal drone that lurks in the background of the *sean-nós* singer's delivery, he was less forthcoming; in fact the theorists seem to be pressing him for something more specific than he is happy to provide:

EM: Now, what do you call this? Do you have any word for this?

JH: No, I haven't a clue. That's one thing I can't explain. It's there and that's the way it is. I don't put it in, it's just there.

EM: Have you ever thought about it, why it's there?

JH: I have often thought about it and this is one explanation I got for it from an old man. Before they start singing, they start to go 'hm, hm' in the head first, themselves, you know, humming to themselves more or less through the nose first, and that could be the reason they carry it on. Because even now before I sing a song I sing it in my head first, you know, I do, to see will I get the right pitch or . . .

EM: In short, the drone is so much part of you, so much part of your whole personal style and of your regional style, that every song must be part and parcel of that.

JH: That's right.

EM: Now, do you know how you produce this drone? Have you ever thought about that?

JH: I haven't a clue. If you took the head off me now, I couldn't tell you.

In 1965 Joe was a big hit at festivals of folksong in Newport and Philadelphia, and in the following year he emigrated to the States. For the next fourteen years he worked as doorman to an apartment block in Manhattan. Later his disciples arranged a part-time post for him teaching folklore in Wesleyan University in Connecticut. During this period of his life he used to revisit Ireland annually and give a concert performance organized by Gael Linn.

The most eccentric point in the astonishing orbit of this man from An Aird Thoir was his contribution to *Roaratorio*, a composition by the magus of experimental music, John Cage. Could anything be further in origin and spirit from the world of Connemaran *sean-nós*? *Roaratorio* was commissioned by West German Radio and Pierre Boulez's avant-garde foundation IRCAM (Institut de Recherche et Coordination Acoustique/Musique) in Paris, and is based on James Joyce's word-spinning novel *Finnegans Wake*. Cage was looking for Irish traditional music as an ingredient of his own musical recreation of Joyce's work, and when he was told that Joe Heaney was 'the king of Irish music', he pursued him to Norwich, where Joe was on tour, and swept him off to IRCAM's prestigious base, the Centre Pompidou in Paris.

The first performance of the stupendous outcome of this unlikely collaboration was in Paris in 1980 and the second in Toronto in the following year. The bulk of the work consists of a collage of taped tracks, an aural 62-decker sandwich of the sounds referred to in Joyce's novel – thunderclaps, earthquakes, laughing and crying, shouts, farts, bells, clocks, chimes, gunshots, wails, a cock's crow, a motorbike's roar, falling water, shreds of music, breaking glass, as well as ambient sounds captured in a world-wide selection (made according to elaborate instructions based on chance) from most of the 2,462 places Joyce mentions. Almost drowned by this cacophony, this multidimensional *nyaah*, is Cage's reading – or rather intoning, chanting, hissing, shouting, muttering and whispering – of his own text, *Writing for the Second Time Through Finnegans Wake*, which consists of hundreds of 'mesostics', sentences from the novel, again selected by a complicated method of perfectly logical illogicality and arranged so that certain letters appearing one below the other spell out JAMES JOYCE again and again. On top of all this floats a medley of Irish music – Paddy Glacken on the fiddle playing a reel, Liam O'Flynn piping a lament, the flautist Séamas Tansey whistling away, Peadar Mercier and his son Mel thumping their bodhráns, and Joe Heaney, starring as the Mr Earwicker or Here Comes Everybody of this epic concoction, singing his own choice of songs – a riptide of conflicting currents in which Joe's voice often stands out craggily like one of the rocks he knew so well in Cuan na hAirde. According to Paddy Glacken, 'Joe took it wonderfully seriously. He looked as if he understood what was going on. The thing that most surprised me was that he understood John Cage in a way we didn't.' And what does it all mean? Well, John Cage in an interview accompanying the record of *Roaratorio* says that it is to be experienced rather than understood; nevertheless one strives to salvage sense from it, if only to throw one's interpretations back into the melting pot. To me it is the sound of the past, as I evoked it in the preface to my first volume – but a past in collision with some apocalyptically randomized future, and the whole stabilized momentarily, now and again, by a baby's cry, the sound of the present. Ultimately its meaning is that all meanings, like all songs, are mere straws in the wind of the radical incomprehensibility of the world.

In 1982 Joe attained a high point of recognition in America when he won a National Heritage Award for Excellence in Folk Arts. At the same time he took up a two-year post as visiting artist in the Ethnomusicology Department at the University of Washington in Seattle. Perhaps for the first time he felt that his dedication and talent were being recognized. According to Peggy Seeger, who visited him there:

I think in Ireland they don't like you to rise too far above them, whereas Joe was idolized in Seattle. He was the only person singing those songs and who could talk about them and could translate them, and who could charm you on stage while he was doing it. I think he learned how to stand up straighter;

he dressed better, he walked better, and he did give up the drinking. Because he did drink a *humendous* amount. I know that the couple of times that I saw him in the States before that, he was always with beautiful young women, and I think he made a point of turning up with them. Joe was very happy with his work in Seattle. It was as if he was at last getting the attention he deserved as a singer and as a repository of so much knowledge of his area of Ireland.

Two young women in particular among his students in Seattle were to play a large part in his latter years, Sean Williams and Jill Linzee. Both completed MAs on his singing, and when it was realized that Joe's two-year appointment was coming to an end, leaving him with no income to speak of, no medical coverage and nowhere to go, they joined with a few others in raising funds and arranging transport for him to visit schools and libraries around Seattle. At the same time the university founded the Joe Heaney Collection of recordings, transcriptions and documentation, which soon held some 250 songs and a hundred stories, and continues to grow to this day. But early in 1984 Joe fell ill – and, sadly and mistakenly, Sean Williams blamed herself:

I had the flu and I was drinking tea with him . . . And he reached across the table and took my teacup. And I said, 'Don't take that teacup, you're going to get the flu.' He put it to his lips and he said, 'Then everybody will know that you killed me,' and he took a sip, got the flu, and died! And I nearly died too, knowing what had happened.

In fact he was able to come out of hospital and to teach on several occasions during the following two months; it was the years of heavy smoking, leading to emphysema, that shortened his breath and ultimately his life. Sean and Jill and others of his young disciples nursed him to the end. At his memorial service Sean sang 'Caoineadh na dTrí Muire', the exquisite and sorrowful 'Lament of the Three Marys' she had learned from Joe. There was an odd incident at the wake house afterwards, where Joe's body was waiting to be flown home to Ireland. Cáit Callen, one of those who had nursed him, went out and bought an Irish flag and laid it over his coffin, as befitting a hero of the Irish people. But the wife of the funeral director told her she could not do that, whereupon a gentleman in the background very quietly said, 'She can do whatever she wants.' And as this obscure figure was understood to be from the IRA, the flag was left on the coffin.

When the corpse arrived at Shannon (Aer Lingus having been persuaded to fly it home for free) Cáit arranged the flag on the coffin again. A cortège of Joe's friends and admirers followed the hearse to Galway, where it was met by the Mayor and the Bishop, and there was a short ceremony in the cathedral before the procession went on to Carna. An extraordinary representation of the folk-music world attended the funeral Mass and heard the celebrant, the assistant curate, amply demonstrating religion's propensity to miss the point of life. First he forbade the relatives to have the coffin open in the traditional way, but they went ahead and opened it anyway; a photograph shows the aged Máire an Ghabha in her shawl bending tenderly over Heaney's massively sculptured features, in an image of biblical simplicity and grandeur. Then the curate objected to having the Mass 'hijacked' by the singing of folksongs, but despite him the great lament 'Amhrán Mhaínse' and other songs that Joe had brought out of Connemara into the wide world were sung, together with 'Caoineadh na dTrí Muire', to which Máire an Ghabha murmured the sacred words. Finally in his sermon (the whole ceremony being broadcast live on Raidió na Gaeltachta), after having noted the deceased's fame, the curate said (in Irish):

But if we imagine that it's singing or anything of the sort that makes a person important, I think we are mistaken. Undoubtedly, it was amazing the way he was able to sing, and how much he gave people through his singing and things like that. But all the same a person's importance doesn't come from things like that. In the first place he was an important person because of the amount of love God had for him . . .

Fortunately just then the Almighty was too taken up with listening to His new guest's songs to hear these references to 'singing and things like that'.

If Joe sometimes felt that he was not sufficiently appreciated in his native place, it was made up to him after his death. The removal procession stretched three miles west from Carna to the ancient seaside churchyard of Maoras, where there was great singing, piping and fiddle-playing by his grave, an impromptu session that continued deep into the night in the pubs of the village. Two local singers, Micheál Ó Cuaig and Peadar Ó Ceannabháin, were inspired to found an annual festival in his memory, Féile Chomórtha Joe Éinniú, which still flourishes. In 2009, on the twentieth anniversary of Joe's death, the proceedings included a visit to his grave. A recent recruit to the host of Joe's fans, I persuaded a Roundstone friend to drive me there. The approach to the churchyard with its ruined medieval chapel is magnificent: a straight and narrow boreen runs downhill to a crescent beach between grey stone walls and green pastures; the gables of the roofless chapel with its consort of gravestones scattered across a hillocky acre or so of grassed-over sand dunes appear on the left, and the dragon-backed hill of Errisbeg lies straight ahead across a few miles of sea. It was mid May and midday, with posies of primroses in the grass, the tide far out and the sands wide and smooth, the Twelve Pins a dado of mist-blue along the northern horizon, a clutch of rounded, bare, granitic islands to the south, a vast unsettled argument between cloud and clarity overhead.

We were the only people there at first, but by the time we had identified Joe's grave a minibus and a few cars had followed us down the boreen, and soon about fifty people were assembled in a wide semicircle before the tombstone. The ceremony was all and only what it should have been. Josie Sheáin Jeaic led a muttering of Hail Marys in Irish, while a little child kicked up the white quartz gravel on the grave; a bright-faced young woman from Donegal, Máire Ní Choilm, sang a lively drinking song, 'An Crúiscín Lán', 'The Flowing Bowl'; Tim Dennehy from Kerry sang 'Amhrán na Páise', a beautiful meditation on the Passion, the words of which are graven on Joe's tombstone, and which moved a few to tears. Sean Williams, to whom I'd just been introduced, had to step back out of the crowd to sob a little, and I put my arm around her for a moment. Then, after this entirely apposite balance of the spiritual and the spirituous, we broke formation and ranged among the graves and in and out of the old church ruin, greeting friends and chatting. The splendid ranks of clouds had stood back in a semicircle too and the sun, very high in the south, blazed whitely on us like the atomic furnace it is, while high in the north the sky was as blue as the Virgin Mother's cloak. Most Connemara skies are steeped in a decoction of tones wrung out of rainbows, but this blue had been filtered through infinities of depth to perfect purity; in fact I don't believe I'd ever seen blue of such intensity. Colour is a modality we don't need – old films and photographs show that we can get along with greys – and perhaps don't deserve, I thought. It is a gift, an ornamentation; it is the song of matter, delivered in the 'old way', ever new.

After the funeral – for the informal little graveside ceremony I have described seemed like a coda to his funeral although it took place twenty years after Joe Heaney's death – I marshalled a couple of friends and led them off on a ramble northwards along the shore, paying for their company with stories from the contentious past of the locality. I wanted to reacquaint myself with the sites of these stories before trying to dig down through the many-layered deposits religion has left in the loquacious oral and the slim written histories of this south-western corner of Iorras Aintheach. I remember that twenty-five or so years ago when I was exploring the area for the first time I greeted a woman in her garden as I passed down the boreen; I spoke in Irish, but she picked up my English accent and turned away grumpily, saying, 'We got rid of the Protestants a long time ago.' 'So you're all good Catholics now?' I returned. 'Ah, only God knows that,' she sighed. It was untypical of the reception – nearly always enthusiastic and helpful – that I received throughout Connemara when I came poking around and enquiring about everything that could conceivably figure on a map. But this woman had almost within her view the gaunt gables of a church ruined by anti-Catholicism and traces of another sacked by anti-Protestant reaction. And behind these histories lies, I think, the story of a much more ancient and profound revolution in beliefs.

The Irish name behind the anglicized version 'Moyrus' is compounded of *maigh*, a plain, and *iorras*, a promontory. 'Maíros', the Placename Department's modern version of the Irish name, was promulgated, they tell me, after some heart-searching, for it offends against a basic rule of Irish orthography. When I consulted the lexicographer Tomás de Bhaldraithe about the placename he said it should be Maoras, and that is what I will stick to in Irish-language contexts. It is primarily the name of the low-lying coastal townland just north of the hilly

headland of Ceann Mása; secondarily it has given its name to the pre-
Reformation parish of Moyrus, which comprised what are now the
Catholic parishes of Carna and Roundstone.

We looked around the ruin of the old parish church before we left
the graveyard, and admired the virile rhythms of its irregular lichen-
patched stonework. It is a simple rectangular building about fifteen
yards long inside, aligned roughly east–west, with a slim lancet window
in the east gable and a round-headed arch, largely robbed of its fine
cut limestone blocks, in the south wall, grassy floored and open to the
skies above. I was once lectured by the old *seanchaí* Colie 'Scufal' for
writing somewhere that the church is dedicated to St Mac Dara, whose
holy island lies a couple of miles off to the south and seems to watch
over the shores of Moyrus Parish. Whoever told me that, he said, was
making a fool of me: Mac Dara had nothing to do with it; the church
was built by his own people, the MacDonaghs. Well, I call up Roderick O'Flaherty from four and a quarter centuries ago as my witness:

This saint's proper name was Sinach, and patronymically called Mac Dara,
from his father Dara. The parish church of Moyras, by the seashore just
opposite to the island, in the continent of Irrosainhagh, is dedicated to his
name, where is kept his altar stone, by the name of Leac Sinach. His festival
day is kept as patron of Moyras parish, the 16th of July.

The altar stone no longer exists. Lord Killanin, who published a
summary list of the antiquities of the Barony of Ballynahinch in 1954
describes it as a chamber tomb, but I do not believe he actually set eyes
on it, for the Ordnance Survey map of 1899 marks 'Lackshinnagh Altar
(site of)', on the left at the foot of the boreen down to the beach. On
leaving the graveyard we went down to the site; it is now occupied by
a small car park, and is quite blank.

The name 'Sinach' is a puzzle to which I will return, but as to 'Mac
Dara', there is a scrap of folklore that purports to explain the name.
The saint was born in Kent, it says, and moved to Scotland, coming
up the River Clyde against the current in a boat without a sail or oars.
He built a church there, and as the Vikings were at that time ravaging
the land he made a tunnel from the church to an oak tree, which he

hollowed out as a hiding place. Hence he is *mac dara*, son of oak, because he spent time in the knotty entrails of one.

However, even if the church was dedicated to St Mac Dara it could well have been in the keeping of the MacDonaghs, who were anciently the *ceithearnacha* (which here means middlemen, not outlaws as elsewhere) of the area. One of them was a friar, Raghnall, who lived in Dumhaigh Ithir (which means, roughly, sand-dune arable land), a little coastal townland adjoining Maoras on the south, and according to local legend owned a famous hound as big as a horse's foal and as clever as a human. A passing wizard envied Raghnall this hound and put a spell on it, and people used to say that it still lives and can be seen running races from end to end of the great beach below the graveyard. On the other hand it is also said that grave-diggers once came across a stone-lined grave with a dog's skull in it, which prompted a very old woman to say, 'Ha, ha, you met with Raghnall's yellow hound!' She had a story of how Raghnall had been attacked one night and driven waist-deep into the sea by a huge white-headed hound, and his own hound had come to the rescue, signalling to Raghnall to run home; his hound returned in the morning but died on the hearthstone, and Raghnall had it buried in the dunes after a huge wake, in a place that was later incorporated into the graveyard. So the MacDonagh connections of the church are well attested, to give Colie his due.

If there were friars in Maoras down to the time of Queen Elizabeth I, as local tradition holds, that may explain how the townland came into the possession of the Protestant See of Tuam, for after the dissolution of the monasteries under Henry VIII it would have been liable to confiscation by the Crown authorities, whenever they should catch up with the existence of such a remote and insignificant little foundation as this. No doubt the chapel lost its roof and its congregation during the century or so following Cromwell's suppression of Catholic Ireland, when Mass had to be celebrated secretly in private houses or up at the Mass rock on Cnoc Mordáin. Then in the time of the Famine Maoras suddenly became of religious significance again with the 'Second Reformation', marked locally by the coming of the Irish Church Mission Society with their God-given task of facing down popish pretensions throughout Connemara. The first ICMS scripture reader to penetrate this corner of the world, in about 1848, later described how he had been given shelter for the night in a 'cabin', but was thrown out into the howling storm when he offered some improving observations on salvation through Christ. He went to the police for protection but was advised to leave, for 'all the worst characters in the neighbourhood flock into this wild spot to hide themselves from justice, and the sooner you are out of it the better'. It was only with great difficulty that he persuaded a boatman to take him across the bay to Roundstone, for which he had to pay the extortionate sum of twenty-two shillings. The ICMS decided, however, that Maoras should be one of its centres; soon there was a soup kitchen in operation, and, as elsewhere, 'taking the soup' became a euphemism for conversion, spurious or otherwise, to Protestantism, under the lash of hunger. 'Soup-House Mhuighruis', a song composed by Seán Bacach ('lame') Ó Guairim, was passed down in Joe Heaney's father's family; it contains startling lines on the impact of hunger, which 'no one can withstand for longer than a day':

> Ba throime é ná Binn Éadain,
> Bhain priocadh beag dom féin de,
> Scaip sé mo mheabhair is mo réasún
> Agus chuir sé néal i mo cheann.
> Ach céad glóire leis an Aon-Mhac
> Gur chaitheamar an téarma,
> Má cailltear anois féin muid
> Go bhfaighe muid séala breá na ngrást.

. . . which Liam Mac Con Iomaire has translated for me:

> Like the Hill of Howth it strikes you,
> It touched myself, though slightly,
> It scattered all my reason
> And it clouded all my mind.
> But glory be to the Son of God
> We have survived our term this far,
> And even if we die now
> May we get the fine seal of grace!

The next step in the salvation of Maoras was the building of a church. A pious and charitable lady, Miss Moore of Lisburn in Antrim, the sister of Lady Annesley, undertook to raise funds for it:

At this time she worked for about sixteen hours per day, writing letters and addressing circulars, of which she dispatched about 30,000, and kept a registered list of the names of all those to whom she applied. After almost insurmountable difficulties and disappointments, she obtained 6,000 subscribers; and thus blessed and prospered by her God, she raised sufficient funds, from a generous public throughout the United Kingdom, to build a spacious church, school-house, and comfortable parsonage for the missionary clergyman at Moyrus. General Thomson, lord of the soil, having promised three acres of land for the proposed building, wrote to beg she would go herself and choose the site.

In response Miss Moore and the Revd J. P. Garrett, who wrote the above, travelled from her home in Co. Antrim via Dublin and Galway to Salruck House, the General's residence in north Connemara, and with him went to call on the Revd Hyacinth D'Arcy in Clifden for lunch. Then the party proceeded to Roundstone, where they were joined by the Moyrus missioner the Revd P. Moinah, Mr Carroll, a Dublin builder, and a surveyor, and the next morning crossed to Maoras in a small boat, as the Revd Garrett describes:

There was heavy rain, and a very high wind. We had a fearful passage, General Thomson steering; and on the lee side of that little ship sat Miss Moore, in a waterproof cloak, drenched over and over again by the waves. It was thought we could not reach Moyrus, and at times proposals were made to return, but she insisted on going on. One of the sailors said he had known the bay for nine years, and did not remember to have seen a higher sea rushing in from the Atlantic. After some tacking we neared Moyrus, and at last ran into a quiet and sheltered harbour. We had to walk above half a mile before we reached the place proposed as a site for the church, &c. This was a trying walk for her, wind and rain against us; a scramble over rocks, ditches, and heather. Just as we reached the spot, the clouds opened, and rays of bright sunshine burst over the scene. We felt it was an augury for good, and Miss

Moore remarked that 'God was showing He was present, blessing and approving of their work.' On her return home she had a severe illness from the fatigue and exposure she had endured, and lost her voice, which for some years she only partially recovered.

And so an upstanding little Victorian church with pointed windows and a belfry arose a few hundred yards north of the ancient chapel, with a rectory and a school. The tussle over the souls of the unfortunate people of Maoras led to a full-scale riot in 1853, when the school was stormed and taken over for a time by the Carna parish priest Edward O'Malley, backed by his curate and some monks, and in 1855, on the night before the church was to be consecrated and fifty-one converts confirmed, the church windows were smashed. Nevertheless the mission prospered for some years, doing some material good but causing painful ideological conflicts, before all its enthusiasm seeped away into the sands and the converts crept back into their ancestral fold, or emigrated in despair of ever extricating themselves from the briars of theology at home.

To visit the traces of this dispensation of grace, my friends and I walked along the beach a short way and scrambled over a fence into a lush, grassy seaside meadow. Of the rectory some mortared stone walls remain, their doorways roughly blocked with boulders, enough to shelter us from the onshore breeze as we picnicked. Another stretch of wall once formed part of a high enclosure surrounding the church and graveyard. Not even the footprint of the church was visible; it seems to have been most painstakingly obliterated. Out in the middle of this enclosure, now a field like any other, we looked at a tomb with a limestone lid finely and minimalistically carved in the form of a cross, or rather of a ridged church roof with nave, chancel and transept; here, since 1865, lies Archibald Thomas Hamilton, only son of Captain Andrew Hamilton of Glasgow, of whom nothing seems to be remembered but that he was '*deiliceáilte*', and died by the roadside near Carna. The tombstone actually says he died at Carna Lodge, which I think is to be identified with Gowla Lodge, a little fishing lodge six or seven miles to the north occupied at that period by a consortium of sportsmen including his father. (The house known as 'the Lodge' in Carna was, as we shall see, staunchly Catholic.) That is as much as I can put together of delicate Archibald. There is another grave in the far corner of the field, very overgrown with bushes and surrounded by rusty railings, of which we could make out nothing and from which the arrival of a young bull and attendant herd made us move on.

Finally, a field or two further north, we admired the precision of the cut stone of the mission school walls, the angles of which presented knife-like edges to the soft sky. But again the roof was absent, and the breeze wandered through empty window and door openings. It was here that in 1862 the converts gathered to greet some eminent visitors from England, who had just crossed by boat from Roundstone in the course of a tour of the Connemara mission stations: the Revd Alexander Dallas himself, with the Bishop of Rochester, Mr Eade, the superintendent of the ICMS orphanage of Glenowen in Clifden, and the Revd W. C. Plunket, who describes the scene:

I must take you at once into the Moyrus schoolroom, where a crowd of about a hundred converts, young and old, were soon collected together – the children as usual ranged along in front, and the others grouped variously in the background. Often have I been present on such occasions, but never did I see more genuine 'heart' than was manifested in the countenances of these Moyrus people. The delight of the children at finding Mr Eade again among them; the grateful joy of the parents at meeting once more their dear old friend and benefactor, Mr. Dallas; the pride and pleasure of all at the presence of the kind Bishop, who had come to visit their remote region – all these feelings were plainly discernible in the varied expressions of these poor simple hearty peasants . . . I feel, that in order to present you with a perfect picture of this present gathering, I must just tinge it with that additional glow of enthusiasm, which is felt by a rarely-visited people, when their turn comes at length – and once again they see their much-loved friends amongst them.

That occasion perhaps marked the heyday of the mission; even the boatman who had fleeced the pioneering scripture reader fourteen years earlier was blushingly present. But soon after this date the ICMS began to lose impetus. The Land War brought out the latent violence in a rural society suffering many wrongs in addition to the condescension of Protestant evangelism. In 1879, when most of the Connemara missions were under attack and police huts had to be established to protect them, the Moyrus school was wrecked, its Bibles were thrown into the sea, and Patrick O'Connor, the resident scripture reader, was assaulted together with his wife and son. The mission station's boat, on which they relied for access, was damaged, and when Canon Roberts of Moyrus tried to replace it he received a blunt warning letter: 'Sir, If you don't leave that boat aside, you will come to a MISERABLE END. Sir, Good night.'

Some oral history gathered in the 1930s indicates that the plan to starve out the missioners by sinking their boat and then stopping any carriers from supplying them by road was devised by a blind man from Dumhaigh Ithir, Seán Mhac Con Raoi. Seán had gone to work in England and Scotland rather than take the soup at home, and had been sworn into the secret and conspiratorial Fenian Brotherhood. When he lost his sight as a result of working too close to a furnace, or (according to another account) in a coal-mining accident, he had to return home, but his family was scattered by then, and he lived alone for many years. He was always cheerful, however, and could recognize his visitors by their footfalls. He became respected as adviser to the community on all things and as a *seanchaí*, a bearer of traditional lore; for instance, on one evening, it is recorded, a tailor and a working man from Roundstone came to him, the former for the story of Fionn Mac Cumhaill and the latter for information on the beginnings and origin of the world. He also administered the Fenian oath to men of the locality, and it was his band of Fenians that one night drowned a horse belonging to a local man who had taken up a job with the Protestant minister, as recounted in his song, 'Capall Sheáin', 'Seán's Horse'. Satire was the first weapon of the local Counter-Reformation, and in this oral culture it was as effective as muscle or boycott. It is said that it was a satirical song composed by Seán Mhac Con Raoi that drove out the missioners in the end. I have been unable to trace this song, but a Roundstone friend, the late Mícheál Bairéad, once gave me a savage verse on the 'Jumpers' (i.e. convertites) of Dumhaigh Ithir, which seems to fit the bill:

Dá bhfeicfeá Jumpers Dhumhaigh Ithir
Agus iad cruinnithe ar chrocán amháin,
Pota den 'soup' a' dul timpeall
Agus freangach ag snámh ar a bharr . . .

[If you saw the Jumpers of Dumhaigh Ithir / All gathered on one little hill, / A pot of the soup going round / With a dogfish floating on top . . .]

Despite this sort of poetic violence, periodic physical attacks, and practical jokes such as the tethering of a donkey to the church bell-rope so that the bell tolled all night, the Moyrus mission hung on longer than any other of the Connemara missions, although in ever-reducing circumstances. By 1920 one of the last two ICMS teachers in Connemara was John McClelland of the Moyrus mission, and even he was giving his profession as 'farmer' in official documents; his death in 1937 marked the end of the ICMS presence in Connemara. The church and the parsonage had been gutted by fire in November 1922 (an episode steeped in obscurity, like so many of the Civil War period), and as soon as the missioners were gone the local people took the roofs off the church, parsonage and school. Oral history claims that all this happened because of Seán Mhac Con Raoi and the song he composed. The Protestant presence in Maoras was not quite extinct, though. I have been told that the rector of Roundstone used to sail across the bay, ring his bell on the beach, and if a congregation, however small, materialized, would conduct a service. Later on Mr Tinne of Emlaghmore near Ballyconneely, standing in for the Clifden incumbent, would sail across in his own *gleoiteog*, the *Volunteer*; I hear of a Miss Betts of Knockboy playing the harmonium, sheltered from the rain by his umbrella, the very image of faith in adversity.

There are two puzzles connected with the next religious monument we visited that day, a holy well associated with St Mac Dara. About a quarter of a mile north of the deserted mission school a broad lobe of flattish rocky land, scalped by centuries of turf-cutting, called Portach Mhaorais, Moyrus bog, lies to the west of the minor road serving the sparse habitation of this coastal region. A little stream is conduited under the road and then zigzags across the cutaway bog to the sea; the well is close to the southern bank of this stream, about thirty paces from the road. All around it, on either side of the stream, is a scattering of low cairns, probably penitential stations, and short lengths of drystone wall, some of them angled, which I am told were to shelter people from the weather while they were visiting the well or observing a vigil there. The well, long dry, is a small stone-lined hole with a low circle of walling around it; when I first saw it there were a few little offerings in it: bits of broken china and a Punch-like plastic figure. It is a pity that a fence of wooden stakes and barbed wire now runs along the stream bank, dividing the sacred site in two; some local agreement could surely be reached about this. The feature that first catches the eye here is not the well but the stream, which is remarkably straight over a length of forty yards or more and runs between banks of granite so smoothly shelving they look as if they had been chiselled out of the bedrock. The formation appears to be natural, and the 1839 Ordnance Survey map shows that it pre-dates settlement and enclosure of fields in the immediate locality; perhaps it represents a small eroded-out dyke or fault line. At any rate, it is striking enough to demand an explanation, and just as various reefs of white quartz in south Connemara are regarded as saints' roads, and the remarkably linear passage through the rocks into Cill Éinne harbour in Aran is attributed to an angel wielding a knife on behalf of St Enda, so, I surmise, this geological oddity is what directed attention to the spot to begin with, and (predictive folkloristics, this!) that someday a legend will be recorded, of how St Mac Dara created the waterway for his own good purposes.

The holy wells of Connemara are oases of peace nowadays, but the sectarian strife of the nineteenth century was a petty squabble compared with the earthquake – no, the heavenquake – induced in fifth-century Ireland by the soft footfalls of the early Christian missioners. The old Irish gods had to flee, to go underground or take advantage of their own twilight and hide out among the peasantry in the guise of fairies and *púcaí*. Some of them, more daringly, became saints, and so above all suspicion of being outlaws on the run. I think I can hear a faint echo of this slow cataclysm of the elder faith in the name of this well.

'Tobershinnagh' it is called on the old six-inch Ordnance Survey maps; *tobar* is a well, and 'shinnagh' is clearly the name Roderick O'Flaherty renders as Sinach, which he tells us was St Mac Dara's first name. When John O'Donovan was writing up the ancient monuments of Conne-mara in the course of the first Ordnance Survey, in 1839, he 'corrected' the name to 'Sionnach', meaning 'fox':

This puts me in mind of a most extraordinary superstition still deep rooted in the minds of the fishermen of Galway, Aran, and Connemara; they cannot bear to hear the name of a fox, hare, or rabbit pronounced, and should they chance to see either of these animals living or dead, or hear the name of either expressed before setting out to fish in the morning, they would not venture out that day. This is a most unaccountable superstition; and still the name of their great patron is Sionnach, a fox.

The answer to the problem was pointed out to me long ago by Angela Bourke of University College Dublin. The name is not pronounced *Sionnach*; it sounds more like *Síonach* or *Síothnach*, which would associate the saint with *síon*, wind and stormy weather. And that is an ancient connection; witness Roderick O'Flaherty, again, writing about Oileán Mhic Dara, the saint's island:

The boats that pass between Mason-head and this island, have a custome to bow down their sails three times, in reverence to the saint. A certain captain of the garrison of Galway, Anno 1672, passing this way, and neglecting that custome, was so tossed with sea and storme, that he vowed he would never pass there again, without paying his obeisance to the saint; but he never returned home, till he was cast away by shipwreck soon after. Few years after, one Gill, a fisherman of Galway, who would not strike saile, in contempte of the saint, went not a mile beyond that road, when, sitting on the pup of the boat, the mast, by contrary blast of wind, broke, and struck him on the pate dead, the day being fair weather both before and after.

The saint employed gusts of wind to punish the disrespectful on shore too, as the folklore collector Seán Mac Giollarnáth was told by a Carna *seanchaí*. I translate:

The people of Leitreach Ard [a townland just north of the Maoras well] were collecting seaweed on the strand on Síanach's Feast Day. There wasn't a cock of seaweed on the strand that wasn't sent flying, and any man who had a basket of seaweed on his back was knocked head over heels and the seaweed thrown out of the basket. The people of Leitreach Ard never again went to work on Síanach's holiday.

So who was this person with power over the winds? There are no historical records of a St Mac Dara or of the little religious foundation associated with him on the island. The chapel there is early, but not, by centuries, from as long ago as the age in which the saints are said to have converted the Irish. I suggest that Síonach, the stormy one, is in fact much older than that; he is a regional Celtic god of the winds in Christianized guise, a Connemaran Aeolus. According to Roderick O'Flaherty Mac Dara's island was 'an inviolable sanctuary', and in its chapel 'his statue of wood for many ages stood, till Malachius Queleus, Archbishope of Tuam, caused it to be buryed under ground, for speciall weighty reasons'. This archbishop, Dr Malachy O'Cadhla, a Confederate Catholic leader, died in 1645 fighting the Protestant Cromwellians; if I am right, his action in the island arose, however belatedly, out of a much more profound clash of faiths.

And now it is time to visit the saint's 'inviolable sanctuary'.

12 The Sheltering Island

Provided one pays him due respects St Mac Dara is a protective being.
The word-of-mouth annals of the coastline he presides over make
much of the fact that no one has ever been drowned in all the immemorial history of the boat races and the pilgrimage to his island with
which his feast day is celebrated; furthermore, when in 1907 the events
were transferred to the island of Maínis, conveniently accessible by
causeway from the Carna mainland, a boat sank and eight people were
drowned although the weather was fine, which put a stop to that
thoughtless innovation. Those annals also reiterate that, whatever
direction the wind blows from, there is always a side of the island that
offers shelter to the currach men hauling lobster pots offshore and to
seaweed gatherers on its shelving perimeter. And note the forbearance
manifested in this little foundation-legend with its Homeric echo:

A sailing vessel came into Oileán Mhic Dara. It was driven in by bad weather.
She spent a couple of nights there and the crew killed the bull that was on
the island and the ram that was with the sheep. When she sailed out in the
evening she found herself anchored in the same place the next morning. This
happened three times. The crew said to themselves that the island must
belong to some saint and that it wasn't right for them to kill the beasts and
that they should show some honour to the saint. So they built a church in
his honour and St Mac Dara's church is there ever since.

Contrast this with the vengeance wreaked on Odysseus' crew for
slaughtering oxen on the Sun God's island – storm, thunderbolt, utter
shipwreck, drowning without exception, and Odysseus' years of erotic
captivity on the nymph Circe's island of Ogygia.
    By good fortune I found the ideal boatmen for my first visit to
Oileán Mhic Dara. I was working my way up and down the boreens
of An Aird Thoir in the course of making my map, in the autumn of

1981, when two lads came across their fields to see what I was up to. Joe and Máirtín proved so friendly and interested in my work that it occurred to me to ask if they would like to take me out to the island, and they gladly agreed to do so. I met them the next morning, as appointed. They had already been out setting a tram net at seven that morning, and their wooden currach was on the shore below their house. We were soon afloat, with their little wire-haired terrier, Spot, who had gone fishing with them every day for eight years, pottering around on the shipped oars and the thwarts like a crusty old sea-captain. A bigger dog followed us along the shore as far as it could, and then went home. The island, a mile or so off to the west, appeared as a smooth swell of honey-coloured granite, perfect in its bareness, its profile broken only by the saint's little oratory perched as sedately as a periwinkle on a rock, near its eastern end. Joe had rowed us halfway to the island by the time Máirtín got the Seagull outboard engine running. Unlike its dark brother, Cruach na Caoile or Deer Island (the Ogygia of my first volume), which lies further out and is nearly always defended by breakers, St Mac Dara's Island offers safe landing places in nearly all weathers. We came to land on the eastern shore at Aill na hIomlachta, the rock of the ferry, where boats usually tie up to unload cattle; the little oratory is a few dozen yards up the grassy slope inland of this point.

There is a satellite islet just offshore here that can be reached when the tide is out by a *cara*, a rocky crossing place, from which Oileán Mhic Dara has its alternative and older name, Cruach na Cara. That feature is the only exception to the island's austere simplicity and unity of form, from which it seems all complications have been scrubbed away by centuries of wind and otherworldly contemplations. And yet the island is elementally physical and measurable: a shallow dome just over a hundred feet high at its centre, half a mile across from east to west and a third of a mile from north to south. Its shores are bare grey-black rock sheets lumbered with heaps of boulders pushed above the high-water mark by exceptional seas, while its gentle inland slopes are of glacier-smoothed outcrops glittering in sunshine with flecks of mica, and tussocky grass with fistfuls of the tough little flowers that thrive on salt-filled gales.

We first made a clockwise circuit of the island. The expanses of shelving granite outside the storm beach were delightful to walk on; the seaward space was immense, a dim suggestion of the Aran Islands' long profile hardly interrupting the measureless farness of the horizon. Spot found a half-grown seal pup on the shore and barked at it from a safe distance as it snorted and slithered to the sea, where a watchful adult seal was showing its head above the swells. A rock shelf thrusting out into the waves that the lads named for me as An Leic Dheirg, the red flagstone, was a purple-brown field of *creathnach*, a sort of dulse, the sweet edible seaweed the women of coastal Connemara used to gather to dry in the sun and hawk around the hill-farming areas in exchange for wool. Roderick O'Flaherty says, 'On the shore of this island is the captives' stone, where women, at low water, used to gather duleasg [dulse] for a friend's sake in captivity, whereby they believe he will soon get succour by the intercession of the saint.' I gathered a bagful to bring home with me, just in case, and afterwards heard from several local people that picking it here on a fine day causes the weather to break (but it did not). We could not identify the captive's stone, unless it is the massive slab of rock a little further west that my guides called Mullán na bhFathach, the giants' boulder, and which is said, like many other big boulders in Connemara, to have been thrown by a giant, in this case from the Aran Islands. At the western extremity of the island we looked at the blowhole mentioned in my first volume apropos the legend of St Mac Dara's male animals that were stolen away to Cruach na Caoile and jumped back again, the bull falling short and bursting up through the rock sheets of the shore, forming Spout an Tairbh, the bull's spout, and the ram leaving the traces of its hooves on the rocks a few dozen paces to the south, at Léim an Reithe, the ram's leap. The latter was hidden by the inflowing tide when we were there, but the spout was performing, although in a lackadaisical, fine-weather mode, sending up a moderate fountain of foam every time a roller forced itself into some submerged cave below; in a western storm of course it would be soaking half the island in brine. Then we returned along the northern coast, which looks across to the tawny granite hillsides of Mace Head and green dune-pastures of Maoras. The shoreline here is of low cliffs; one that the lads called An Aill Bhuí, the yellow cliff, was golden with lichen. The cliffs are penetrated by deep narrow creeks in which the sea heaves and gurgles ominously, but which make possible landing places for small boats in calm weather; one is called An Fhuaigh Leanúnach, meaning something like 'the persistent creek', because fishing lines tend to get caught in it. And finally, on completing the circuit, we investigated the saint's little chapel, the jewel in the ring.

Teampall Mhic Dara is a strikingly self-confident-looking building. Relative to its small footprint – about fifteen by eleven feet inside – it stands tall, for it has a steep-pitched and sharp-ridged roof with elaborate finials on the gable tops; thus it shows no deference to the power of gales beyond the slight concession of locating itself in a shallow dip in the eastern flank of the island, where it is spared the worst of westerlies. The roof is of stone flags, and is complete, having been restored by the Office of Public Works in 1976. The walls are of bulky granite blocks roughly hammered into cuboids, some of them four or five feet long and over two feet thick; those composing the slightly inward-inclining jambs of the doorway, in the west gable, and the lintel one has to bow under on entering, are crushingly weighty-looking. There is a narrow little round-headed window in the east gable and a flat-headed one in the south wall, both splayed on the inside.

The most interesting features to historians of architecture are the antae: the side walls are continued for about a foot beyond the gable walls so that their ends stand out like pilasters, and, most unusually, these projections are continued up the slants of the gables to their apices – a structurally unnecessary feature that is thought to have been inherited, through aesthetic inertia and fossilization of function, from earlier wooden churches in which a ridge beam was supported at either end by two crucks or angled uprights; hence the church has been described as 'a petrified wooden construction'. The finely carved finials of limestone are reproductions of the lost originals; each is in the form of a pair of divergent cusps, like continuations beyond their crossing point of the two antae; in the centre is a small bearded head, said to represent the saint, and each cusp bears three round bosses of Celtic knotwork. The Belfast nationalist and antiquarian Francis Bigger, who wrote a useful account of the island's antiquities and first

recommended that the church be restored, described the discovery of
an original finial, lying face down in two pieces among scattered stones
a little to the south of the church, by one Charles Elcock, a Belfast
naturalist, in 1884:

Perhaps one hundred people were there collecting seaweed, and on his picking up the stone and showing it, they raised the cry, in Irish and English,
'He's found the Saint, he's found the Saint himself', whereupon everyone
rushed to see the Saint's head. They thought it a wonderful thing that he
should go to the very spot, and find the Saint himself, at once, never having
been there before; while some of them had been coming and going 'nigh
fifty years', and had never seen 'him' before.

At the time of Bigger's own visit eleven years later, the broken finial
was still lying exactly where Elcock had seen it. Where it is now,
nobody seems to know; some archaeologists speculate that it may yet
be rediscovered under a sack of cement in some OPW store.

How long has Teampall Mhic Dara been applying its little chisel to
the yielding Atlantic skies? Features of the church such as the Roman-
esque round-arched moulding over the outside of the west window
suggest it was built in the twelfth century, and this has been confirmed
by radiocarbon dating of mortar from its walls, although there may
well have been some earlier building on the site. Apparently in certain
lights one can make out squares carved on some of the roof stones as
if in imitation of wooden shingles, which reinforces the idea that the
present church preserves the memory of a previous wooden church.
Whether that might have dated back as far as the great scattering of
hermits and tiny congregations of monks throughout the offshore
islands and inland wildernesses of Ireland in the sixth century, the
time of St Mac Dara if such a person ever existed, is unknowable.

Around the church are traces of a typical early Christian ecclesiastical settlement, thoroughly pillaged by time and the occasional greedy
visitor; a length of collapsed wall curving around the north of the
church probably indicates its boundary. There are remains of three
clocháns or stone huts of which the largest, known as Ballaí an Díthre-
abhaigh, the hermit's walls, is circular and about twenty feet across.

There are also a number of little accumulations of stone that were probably penitential stations or altars, as well as a carved cross-slab and broken bits of other crosses, although most of the elaborately carved fragments Bigger describes as lying around the site have been filched. The holy well, just north of the chapel, is long dry. The saint himself is said to be buried in his *leaba* or 'bed', a small rectangular space marked out by a low slab and a few boulders outside the church at the foot of the east gable, while nearby to the west is a rectangular enclosure in which it is said 'none but saints' lie, together perhaps with the wooden statue the Archbishop caused to be buried 'for speciall weighty reasons'.

The island's later, lay, inhabitants, the MacDonaghs, had their own burial ground by the shore to the north-east, but I am told the tide long ago robbed it of their bones. The last person to be buried there was a Risteárd Mac Dhonnchadha, who died some time in the eighteenth century. As late as 1856, it is recorded, a Patrick and James MacDonagh were leasing sixty acres and a house here from the Law Life Assurance Society, owners of the former Martin estate. (The 1839 Ordnance Survey map shows what could be two houses a few yards west of the church; the 1899 map has just one open rectangle on the same spot, indicating a roofless building.) The story of these last tenants of the island, as local memory preserved it, is sad:

There was a man called Páidín Rua [red-haired Pat] on the island with his family. At that time nobody in Iorras Aintheach had more than two cows, but Páidín had seventeen milk cows on the island. That was because of the excellence of the island for cultivation. The price of kelp was seven pounds a ton in his day, and there wasn't a day on which he could not work the two ebbs in the seaweed season. Whatever the wind there was always some side of the island where a man at work had shelter. There wasn't a year in which Páidín Rua couldn't make three or four score pounds out of kelp. He was able to leave the cattle to fatten and if that didn't suit him sell one or two whenever he chose. They stayed until one of the sons married. Páidín had a half-holding in Oileán Máisean and he gave it to the son who married. The other son stayed on the island by himself. In the end his family decided that the island was no place to be, that it was like being in prison. There was a small farm for sale in Cill Chiaráin and they bought it and left Cruach na Cara behind them, and from the day they left until their deaths, and that wasn't many years, they fell back in every way. They lost their health in the end and died. The mainland didn't suit them once they'd left luck behind them in Cruach na Cara. People used to say that too much prosperity is a bad thing.

After that, Joseph Mongan, the wealthy hotelier of Carna, bought the island and, for twelve years, grazed sixty cattle on it for a month each year. Then he left it empty for a couple of years and sold it to the Congested Districts Board, which divided the grazing and seaweed rights between tenants of An Aird Thiar and Más. As an old woman once told Josie Mongan's mother, its fine seaweed is gold lace on Oileán Mhic Dara.

Having done the rounds of the island's holy and secular relics and paid them the dues of our attention we re-embarked, and chugged back to the mainland through a sunlit autumn afternoon. Joe and Máirtín nosed the boat into the seaweed at a point of the shore where they wanted to show me a holy well attributed to Colm Cille (but: another saint, another chapter); then we walked up to the lads' house, and had tea with their hospitable mother. I collected my bike and cycled back to my lodgings in Carna, perfectly satisfied by a day – the memory of it glints like the island's granite in my mind still – of fascinating details, good companionship and protective calm.

A few years after the visit described above I returned to the island on the saint's day, 16 July, to witness the celebrations. In the oldest of the old days this *patrún* or pattern was organized by the people themselves. The sick used to make the *turas*, the pilgrimage, in hope of a cure, and women in fulfilment of a vow made to the saint conditional on his bringing their menfolk safely home from the seas. The rite started with seven rounds of an altar south of the chapel, with recitations of the Ave Maria and the Creed; seven pebbles would be gathered before-hand and one of them placed on the altar at every round. Then the same was done at the chapel, the graveyard west of the chapel, and the holy well, where the sick would take a spoonful of holy water to rub on wherever the trouble was. Finally the pilgrim would go to the saint's bed at the east gable and pray in it. Afterwards there would be foot races, food and drink and sweets. Many people went just for the gathering; the masts of the boats were like a forest offshore below the chapel.

In 1851 the Moyrus missionary with some scripture readers and teachers went out to the island to observe these popular goings-on:

I found a large mass of people assembled, some going round the holy well which was dry, others praying before stone altars, others amusing themselves and drinking in tents. Priest M's Schoolmaster was there and gave the alarm as our boat neared the quay, and as soon as we landed, we found ourselves surrounded by a mob of both sexes, shouting and throwing stones. I began to reason with them, and showed them the folly and injustice of such proceedings – the wickedness of spending one half of the day in prayer, and the other in embruing their hands in a fellow mortal's blood. A few of them stepped forward and took my part; others soon joined these, and though a few fierce murderous looking men swore that I should not leave the island, dead or alive, yet these stood round me and declared they would lose their lives before a hair of my head should fall. At length I got back to the boat amid showers of stones; though, thanks to the Lord, I was only struck by three, and escaped without serious injury . . . From many things we heard, we have reason to believe this was all encouraged by the Priests; and these feelings were not produced from any regard or reverence for them, but from their being led to believe that we came to mock their ancient rites, and to dishonour their holy well.

A few years later the missionary reported that on 16 July, when the bay was full of boats from every part of Connemara, one 'Romanist' whose boat had been cut to ribbons by returning revellers complained to him that 'it is a very bad system to be bringing people together, first, to do penance, and, secondly, to return home drunk, and greater sinners than they were before'. Also, a priest had gone into the island and told the people that he required each of them to pay, which, the missionary rejoiced, 'gave us a grand opening against the money-making inventions of Rome'.

However, the Catholic Church too came to disapprove of patterns and especially their association with drunkenness, and assumed control of the proceedings. By the 1920s it was customary for the parish priest to celebrate Mass on the island, and not many would be present apart from those taking communion and making the *turas*. But with the revival of the hooker races in the 1970s St Mac Dara's Day has become one of the most important dates of the Connemara year, though it still remains a local festival and tourist onlookers are few. My diary reminds me of many details of my own visit in 1984, on a day I seemingly spent with my ear close to the still-beating heart of the oral tradition.

My friend Mícheál King from Inis Ní and his young son Michael called for me in Roundstone and we drove round the bay to Iorras Aintheach. We had heard that the *Ark*, at forty-two feet in length the biggest of all the surviving Galway hookers, was back in Connemara after years of servitude as a houseboat on the Thames and was moored in An Crompán, the creek, near Carna, so we detoured to see her. Fully decked, smartly painted and polished and equipped with a plethora of fancy gear, she was not to me an object of beauty; nevertheless her curves, however often her timbers had been repaired and replaced, were still eloquent of one of south Connemara's great traditions, having been shaped in about 1878 by the master boatbuilder of Maínis, Seán Ó Cathasaigh. In 1988 this venerable boat was to be abandoned in a storm in the Bay of Biscay; one still hopes that she might yet be rediscovered in some little Portuguese fishing port, distressed perhaps, patched and renamed, but with a hold full of stories still.

Then we followed the narrow roads down to the little harbour of Más, where there were a few tatty sweet stalls and a darts booth, and a crowd that looked as if it had been grown in hard stony soil. It was a grey day with a drift of moisture in the air. We waited in a dense pack on the quay for the boatmen to make their infinitely leisurely preparations – sawing a plastic container in half to make a bailer, and so on – to ferry us out. At that period I was writing an occasional column for the *Connacht Tribune* newspaper detailing my finds townland by townland, and it seemed that everyone was only waiting for an opportunity to contribute to my collection of placelore. 'Tim

Robinson? In person?' cried one eager reader, while old Colie Scufal, whom I had met when he still lived on the now-deserted island of Fínis, took me to task over what I had written about St Mac Dara, as described in my last chapter. That worried me; had I got it wrong? The enthusiastic response to my column only weighted me down with a sense of the responsibility I had lightly assumed, in appointing myself the scribe, the hoarder of stories, of a community to which I had no organic connection.

A tentative sun appeared as we got off at last; my spirits lifted with the first lift of the boat on the swells. We landed at the little beach below the chapel. There were already a hundred or so people there, and the boats brought in at least another hundred after us. I sat on a sloping rock with a few *seanchaithe* I had come to rely on: Pádraic Ó Coscardha, a retired schoolteacher who had been overseeing the embarkment at Más and acting as a human stopcock to the flow of people pressing onto the gangplank; Johnny Jennings, the school-master of An Aird Mhóir near Carna; and the boatbuilder Joe Casey. Three priests, including the Carna PP and his curate, celebrated Mass at a little table with a white cloth over it in the lee of the chapel's east gable, with the little round-headed window looking over their shoulders. I didn't get the impression that anyone paid much attention, but the crowd was still and silent, and afterwards the curate's resonant Irish was praised. Then some of us rambled round the island and splashed along the seaweed-slippery *cara* to the little islet offshore to the east of the chapel; Oileán Muirileach seems to be a reasonable spelling of its name, and several of my advisers on such questions agreed that the *muirileach* was some sea plant, perhaps the sea pink that grows on the islet in abundance. The boat races had started, and four of the smaller type of traditional boat, the *púcán*, were rounding a buoy nearby. I was fortunate enough to meet Dick Scott, the historian of the Galway hooker, who pointed out the curiously hasty and untidy way the *púcán*'s 'dipping lug sail' has to be untied when coming about and the spar poked round from one side of the mast to the other as if the crew were knitting a gigantic stitch with it.

Next I fell into conversation with another fount of lore, Séamas Mac Donncha, of the MacDonaghs who used to be buried in the island.

The date of death of an ancestor of his, Féilim 'ac Risteáird Mac Donncha, is remembered for an odd circumstance, he told me: Féilim was on Caorán na hAirde, a little hill in An Aird Thiar, watching three great ships passing northwards out beyond Slyne Head, when he felt a pain in his belly; he died a few days later on 20 August 1798, and during his funeral word arrived of the French landing at Killala. Séamas also spoke about a little recess in a rockface just east of the southernmost point of An Aird Thiar, where a famous strongman of old, Seán an Chóta, used to sit. (The origin of his name comes later in this book.) I was to meet Séamas again a few days later at Roundstone Regatta; he had a list of placenames from the two Airds for me in his pocket, and a family tree, and was anxious to correct some detail in the story he had told me of the death of Féilim 'ac Risteáird. The diligence of such informants, whom I found throughout Connemara, their care to ensure that I had heard the tale of time and had taken it down correctly, was at the time and still is a needful reassurance that my work is worth doing.

With all this talk, we were almost the last to return to the mainland apart from Pádraic Ó Coscardha, who saw everyone off the island before leaving the saint to himself.

13 The Song of Wonders

There are places where place itself proliferates as if abandoned to a self-replicative urge; in Connemara the parish of Carna is the prime example, and in the parish, the townland of An Coillín, the small wood, in particular, and within that townland (which has long lost whatever wood it is named from and is as treeless as the rest of Iorras Aintheach), An Seangharraí, the old garden or old plot, is the kernel of this phenomenon. Maybe it is the amoeboid clustering of little fields brought about by the ruinous pre-Famine subdivision of holdings, still legible in the skeletal form of tumbledown drystone walls, that suggests the biological metaphor.

There are no buildings or other monuments or striking natural features to point out An Seangharraí, so I have to be pedestrian in indicating where it is. The townland is largely occupied by a hill, Cnoc an Choillin, only 331 feet high but nevertheless dominant in this low-lying coastal area. To the south of the hill is the narrow bay, Cuan na hAirde, and to its east, the village of Carna. The little road from the two Ards bridges a river flowing into the head of the bay, then joins a slightly more major road that winds its way across the northern margins of the hill; An Seangharraí lies on the hillside immediately south of this road, about 300 yards east of the junction. The 1839 Ordnance Survey map shows it as a knot of field walls in otherwise undivided land; it is said to have been the first part of the townland to be reclaimed (by dint of clearing stones, spading over the heather-tough sods of the hillside and carrying in backloads of seaweed, no doubt). The 1899 map shows the old field pattern overlain by straight walls running in parallel up the hillside from the road – the signature of the Congested District Board, which had bought out the Berridge estate and was rationalizing holdings for allocation to the former tenants. The network of old walls, thus condemned as irrational and now torn and half obliterated, still holds stories, or their remains, like the husks of flies in a cobweb. One plot is called Garraí Thaidhg Mhóir; here Tadhg the robber, who was either Tadhg na Buile, the monster of Caisleán na hAirde, or has been amalgamated with him by time, lurked in An Scailp Mhór, the big cleft, under a prominent slab of rock, and leaped out to terrorize passers-by. In an adjacent field called Garraí Pholl an Chiste, the treasure-hole garden, a man unearthed a pot of gold; there was an ugly serpent coiled round it, and he was afraid and covered it up again. One knows from the look of the place that all the other fields, or at least all those of the old, pre-CDB dispensation, had their names and legends, if only in the annals of a single family. It is a narrative hot spot; my infra-verbal sensibilities hum and my antennae twitch as I walk along the road below it.

On the other side of the road is level bogland with a small lake named from the old garden, Loch an Gharraí, and a larger hollow full of reeds called An Corcal, the quaking bog, which was a lake until it was drained (sometime in the second half of the nineteenth century, old maps indicate) by Maolra Bairéad and his son Maitias, who had land by this lake that was frequently flooded. With their spades they dug a channel from the lake to the little river that forms the northern and western boundary of An Coillín; when they came up against a huge boulder they could not break up, Maolra went home in a sulk, but Maitias dug a deep hole to one side of the boulder and levered it into the hole, so that when Maolra came back he could not imagine where it had gone. And finally when they opened the channel they netted all the fish of the lake, salted three or four barrelfuls of them and passed the winter happily eating potatoes and lake-fish.

Maolra was 'a fine strong stump of a man' and a great walker and runner. He was known as Maolra na mBeach, Myles of the bees, for in his youth he made a living by collecting honey from wild bees' nests. His method was this. He knew what sort of flowers the bees liked, and he would tie a bunch of them to the end of a five- or six-foot rod, and pour a drop of honey onto them. When he saw a bee he would hold out the bait to it, and the bee would drink so much honey it could scarcely fly, so that Maolra was able to keep up with it for as much as five or six miles. Sometimes he was able to collect five or six gallons of honey from bees' nests all over the mountains of Connemara. When he ran through a rushy swamp his feet would throw the water up in a mist. He would go to Gleann Chóchain, up in the Twelve Pins, 'looking for a kiss from a young woman', and come back the same day – and then he would be the first man to have his kelp kiln lit the next morning. All this without a word of a lie, according to Pádraic Mac Con Iomaire, a storyteller and *seanchaí* of An Coillín, recorded by Seán Mac Giollarnáth in the 1940s or so.

The sober record of Griffith's *Valuation* (1855) lists Myles Barrett as having a house of ten shillings' rateable value in An Coillín; that's Maolra, the almost magical skimmer over bogs, the hunter of bees and kisses, as seen by the authorities. The Barretts owned a mill a quarter of a mile north of Loch an Gharraí on the river mentioned above, which Seán Mac Giollarnáth calls Sruthán na mBreac, the stream of the trout. The OS calls it Owenhid, but I can't make anything of that anglicization; the field-books of the OS sappers in 1839 note it as 'Abhainn Idid', which they understood to mean 'cold river'; but *idid* is no recognizable Irish word. I have heard one odd little story about this river, told me in the 1980s by an elderly man I met in Glinsce, a village a couple of miles to the north: a man from that village crossing the bogs on his way to church in Carna stopped to see if he could tickle a trout in the river, but after a while he felt another hand grip his under the water, which reminded him of his duty; the hand was that of 'a saint or some such person'. Perhaps the idea of 'cold' could be fished out of this story. Also, at second hand, I have heard an old man call the river Abhainn Ainthín, and Ainthín is the saint from whom the parish of Killannin in east Connemara is named. I have spent too much time trying to make these fragments cohere into significance.

All around the skirts of Cnoc an Choillín is a lacework of little fields; one could spend months in chasing after their names and the honey of their stories. One down by the shore of the bay is called Tóin Naigín, noggin bottom; two fields away to the north-west of it is a cluster of ruins on An Choráin, the small headland. Near the southern end of that shoreline of An Coillín is the tiny harbour of Caladh Mhacaí, where the *seanchaí* Pádraicín Mhacaí Mac Con Iomaire used to moor the *Carna Lass*, a hooker trading to Galway. Just east of it is a small cave, yet another Poll an Phíobaire, the piper's hole, which (of course) leads all the way to Carna. At the head of the bay, where the river mentioned above finds the sea after having passed through a small lake, there was another mill, of which Pádraic Mac Con Iomaire gave an enquirer a description in the mid twentieth century. It was of the antique type I describe in *The Last Pool of Darkness* in connection with the medieval monastic foundation on High Island, with a horizontally mounted wheel onto the paddles of which water was directed by a sluice. A vertical shaft from the mill wheel passed through a hole in the centre of the lower millstone and turned the upper one mounted above it. It was typical of the small mills of Connemara and no doubt Maolra's mill was of the same sort. The mill by Cuan na hAirde was in operation until 1900 or a little later.

On the south face of the hill, just above the wall that separates the highest fields from the bare commonage around the summit, is a small transverse valley, Gleann an Tobair, with a holy well: Tobar Mhic Dara according to Mac Giollarnáth; Tobar Mhuire say local people today. Here an outlaw priest used to celebrate the Mass in secret, as he did in An Seangharraí too, and here he was captured. (Whether this priest, named as Sagart Muiltheach, is to be identified with the Fr O'Donnell who marooned the soldiery on Deer Island after being arrested in An Coillín is not clear.) And on the summit itself are slight traces of one of the signal towers built all around the coast of Ireland in 1804 or so at a time when a French invasion seemed likely. It must have looked rather like Tadhg's castle a few miles to the west, being a stone-built square-based structure of two storeys. It would have been in communication by signal fires and by tall flag masts with similar towers on Ceann Gólaim eight miles away to the south-west, Inis Oírr and Árainn in the Aran Islands to the south, and Cnoc an Dúin twelve miles to the west; the last-named tower has totally disappeared, but the other three still stand, and when I come to Ceann Gólaim I will describe their functioning and historical context in more detail. The only story I have heard about the tower of An Coillín is this trivial incident: when the first packet of tea came into the district the woman who lived in the tower (perhaps she was a housekeeper) was asked to prepare it; she boiled the lot, poured away the liquid and served up the tea leaves.

Although the tower no longer exists, it will serve as a pivot on which to reorient my theme of place and story, freeing it from the constraints of historical and geographical fact. Here's a verse from 'Amhrán na nIontas', 'The Song of Wonders', also known as 'An tAmhrán Bréagach', 'The Lying Song':

A's chonaic mé roc i gCill Coca 's é bleán na mbó,
A's eascann ag gor i nead iolra lá gála mhóir,
Chonaic mé seangán a's é fuipeáil míl mhóir i dtír;
A's tá túr Chnoc an Choillín mar *eggstand* ag Maolra a' roinnt . . .

And I saw a ray milking the cows in Kilcock,
And an eel hatching eggs in an eagle's nest on a windy day,
I saw an ant whipping a whale ashore;
And Coillín tower used by Maolra as an eggcup for serving drinks . . .

The composer, this visionary of the absurd, was (according to schoolmaster Dónal O'Fotharta, who published a long version of this song in 1892) a blind harper, Micilín Mhichil Bacaigh, who used to perform in competitions in Connemara, and the Maolra it refers to was indeed Myles Barrett of An Coillín. There are many discrepancies between the various recorded versions of the song, probably because there is not a great deal of sense in it to check the wandering of its words. The occasion of the song, says O'Fotharta, was this: the piper's brother Colm bought the makings of a pair of trousers once, and went to a tailor to have them made up, but for some unstated reason the tailor refused the job. Now, what could be more ridiculous than a tailor who will not make a pair of trousers? The song strives to answer that question, and in the process every impossibility is canvassed. A cricket with a pistol behind the hob, a duck playing the harp, a frog in the ditch with a watch in its pocket, nine rabbits drunk on brandy, the bee and the midge at anchor off Inis Leacan – all the farmyard and country familiars are seen breaking the bounds between the animal and the human worlds. Topography too is disrupted; for instance a piece of Inis Meáin breaks off and passes a south Connemara village:

O, bhí mé lá i gCasla 's bhí farraige ann a's gála mór,
A's cé chífinn ag dul tharam ach Ceann Gainimh
  is é ag iompar seoil . . .

O, I was once in Casla with high seas and a gale,
And what did I see go by but Sandy Head under sail . . .

Galway challenging County Clare with the Sceird Rocks and Dún Gudail as seconds; Cnoc na Sciortán, the hill of the ticks, in Camas, being used as a spinning wheel; Liabhrás, a shoal off Ceann Mása, fishing for trout with a rod; the people of Sraith Salach collecting seaweed on rocks at Mám Éan; a woman netting a stream west of the sun – with the exception of this last myth-tinged effort the seer's reorderings are exercised on familiar places and induce a paroxysm in local geography. The song turns up in Inis Meáin, east Galway, Munster and Ulster, naturalized in each locality by references to specific places and people, for of all songs this is the easiest to adapt by adding or omitting lines, its commitment being not to truth or even verisimilitude but to the foam of fantasy. But judging by the number of recorded or printed versions Connemara is its land of choice; the mention of Maolra seems to bring the one quoted above home to Iorras Aintheach in particular. The excuse for the song, the tailor's unnatural behaviour (hinted at rather obscurely in the song itself and amplified by O'Fotharta's editorial note) is peculiar to this version, and another one recorded in Carna in 1952 is ascribed to a well-known singer, Micheál Mharcais Ó Cualáin of Iorras Mór, who was arrested as a Fenian and promised his freedom if he would compose a song of lies. But this story itself is a lie, for behind it is a Europe-wide and ancient hinterland of folktales in which the hero has to improvise a song of which not a word is true; sometimes he succeeds and sometimes he fails because some element of his invention turns out through linguistic quibble or unforeseeable coincidence to be truthful.

So, I conclude, the history of lies is a history of lies; the finest lie, the one free from any trace of truth, is the most highly prized. In particular the juggling of geography, the skew refolding of the map (too hasty, its ink scarcely dry, so that one place is printed off on top of another) crumples up my hard-won exactitudes, my monotonous refrain of 'A is 250 paces NNE of B', and it does so to a cheery, chatty, trivial, uncaring air. Lies and wonders are what the world wants to hear. I should adopt a sense of place that glides as playfully over the terrain as Connemara's inconstant cloud shadows, as lightly as Maolra of the bees looking for a kiss from a young woman.

14 Bee Flight

Maolra's bee-like flight to Gleann Chóchan would have taken him north-eastwards across uninhabited bogs and between lakes to the village of Glinsce, and thence along the shore to Gabhla and so out of the peninsula of Iorras Aintheach. I will follow him for the first part of the way, with excursions to his left and right, his past and future. The first lake he would have passed is Loch Buaile, booley lake; the townland on its east is An Cnoc Buí (anglicized as Knockboy), the yellow hill, and it was in his time a commonage to which the people of An Más took their cattle for the summer milking season. The lake is about half a mile long from north to south, and nearly as broad; on the map its shoreline is a hedgehog of tiny points and coves, and there are dozens of islets in it. One of these might have caught Maolra's eye, and it immediately takes one back into prehistory; it is round, some twenty yards across, and evidently at least partly artificial. It is edged with a wall that nowadays stands to a height of two to four feet only, but was perhaps higher in his day. This is a lake dwelling or *crannóg*, of the stone-built sort best described as island cashels. It has the remains of a quay on its east side, and there is a corresponding quay or perhaps the beginnings of a causeway off the tip of a little peninsula a hundred yards or so to its north-east. It dates perhaps from the Bronze Age or early Christian Iron Age, and it was first described by the polymath G. H. Kinahan of the Geological Survey in 1872–3. It was customary then for illustrators to show what a romantic sensibility would have preferred to see rather than what the truthful researcher might have described. The engraver who illustrated Kinahan's article took great liberties in the interests of expressiveness and so betrayed this meticulously factual author. He gives us a lofty four-sided tower, but, as a later enquirer complained, it is 'an entirely fancy sketch . . . and as regards the truthfulness of the picture, it may equally well represent Windsor Castle and Park'. I shall write more factually about island cashels in a later chapter when we come to Connemara's prime example of the type, but here I pass on, admitting that the imaginary tower of Loch Buaile stands in my mind as a most striking virtual monument.

There is coniferous forestry on the eastern side of the lake, but not nearly so much as the Ordnance Survey map of 1898 indicates. Instead most of the northern half of An Cnoc Buí is a bare, heathery hillside with occasional bonsai-like specimens of larches two or three feet high – the relics of a failed experiment that provoked much merriment at the expense of the Congested Districts Board. Mr W. L. Micks, former secretary of the Board, ruefully recounted the little history:

Some months before the creation of the Board [i.e. in 1891] a mountain side at Knockboy was offered by Fr. Tom Flannery P.P. to the Irish Government if it would attempt as a Relief work the planting of some hundreds of acres. This tract was exposed to the full strength of the south-west wind, and the Atlantic Ocean only a few miles distant. The Government accepted the offer, as it was felt that, if planting succeeded there it might be tried anywhere. It did not succeed, and for many years the Board was twitted about the Knockboy 'forest' . . . An unforeseen result was that excellent cover was provided by the stunted trees for woodcock and hares.

I am informed by a forestry expert that Micks was wrong to blame the exposure. The main culprit was a deficiency of phosphorus in the soil; only since the 1950s has it been the practice to apply basic slag or rock phosphate when planting in infertile soils. There may have been other causes of the failure too. A manuscript history of Knockboy by Esther Bishop (of whom more below) says that the young trees were imported by sea from the Netherlands but on arrival were left on a quay with the sea washing over them, so that a considerable number of them died; also, the planters were paid by the number they planted each day, and had 'no incentive to make sure that each young tree actually had soil and not just rock under its roots'.

If the first forest here caused some amusement in its dying, the later forestry, planted in the 1960s, hides a hint of melancholy in its flourishing. When I first explored its shady avenues I found in the heart of the forest some shabby sheds made out of the remains of a house the

1898 OS map calls Forest Lodge (an optimistic name, since at that time the forest was knee-high at best), and a little further in, the former stables, converted into a summer home, but deserted and gaping open. The latter building bore these words on a plaque:

Remember as you pass / Cecil Coulter Betts / and / Louisa Alice his wife / who in this place 1918–1946 / met sorrow and adversity with fortitude / and all who came their way with loving kindness / and who in their day / by their vision and their labours / made this wilderness a place of beauty.

Every dwelling carries the invisible inscription 'Here lives a story', but this explicit, if cryptic, invitation to speculate was particularly attractive. I thought I had discovered the cause of their sorrow when I noticed a funerary plaque in the Protestant church in Roundstone, in memory of Cecil Coulter Betts, died 1946, and his wife Louisa Alice, died 1956, and of their younger son, Conrad Coryton, 'observer, Sub-Lieutenant R.N. who was killed while flying over Lemnos in the Aegean Sea on April 17th 1918 aged 19'. I mentioned this in a little book I made out of my *Connacht Tribune* columns, *Mapping South Connemara*, and soon afterwards heard from a Mrs Chloe Stewart in Australia, who kindly sent me a copy of the history of Knockboy mentioned above, written by her mother Esther Bishop, a daughter of Cecil and Louisa. Independently her brother Anthony Bishop called on me in Roundstone and gave me a good haul of placelore. From these first-hand sources and a few official records I extract a prosaic but touching story – typical of Connemara's tenacious little Protestant presence – of dreams and disappointments, adversity and fortitude.

Perhaps the CDB spent too much money on the fine cut-granite stable block, for when it came to build the lodge in 1893, it retrieved two engineers' huts left over from the construction of the newly completed Galway–Clifden railway, brought them to Knockboy and stuck them together; however, the result, a wooden house sheathed in felt and corrugated iron, the cavity between being stuffed with sawdust, was of excellent workmanship, warm and comfortable. In the period between the abandonment of the first forestry venture and the outbreak of war in 1918 the lodge was leased by a young Englishman, Douglas

Thompson (C. of E., farmer, magistrate for Co. Galway, Cambridge BA, born in India, according to the 1911 census). Together with another Cambridge BA of the same generation called Percy Bain, he ran a demonstration farm here, until they abandoned it for military service. In about 1912 someone of the name of Lehmann had the place, and grew sugar beet on the flats north of Loch Buaile for a London manufacturer of condensed milk; Esther Bishop tells us that local women employed in singling the beet were paid 4d a day. That experiment came to an end when the London firm found it was cheaper to pay the freight on beet from the Ukraine than from Connemara.

During the war years the place was mostly empty, but in 1918 Thompson's cousin Cecil Betts, a retired jute broker who had spent most of his life in what is now Bangladesh, took over the lease, and later bought it out. The CDB retained half of the 900 acres of land as turbary for local people, and Mr Betts fought and lost a battle with the Board over shooting rights on it; this became a subject that could not be mentioned in his presence, although it seems he continued to shoot there, no doubt appreciating the 'excellent cover' of the CDB's dwarf forest. He gathered a workforce of forty men to clear a slope below the house of stones and plant it with pine, Sitka spruce and cedar, as a shelterbelt for an orchard of 900 apple trees, 'but he never envisaged the task of selling the fruit nor of keeping the jungle or disease at bay, still less the "troubles" of 1922 when the fencing round the whole estate disappeared'. Although IRA men were thought to lurk in the woods, it does not appear that the family was much troubled by the Troubles. Louisa used to drive into Carna once a week on a flat car drawn by her Spanish donkey and surrounded by all her other donkeys, with a cheque to be changed at Mongan's, and come back with the £100 for the wages in a biscuit tin. 'In those days,' writes Esther, 'in spite of father's flock of pedigree goats, of an unbelievable malevolence, the desert did indeed bloom as the rose, which is almost impossible to believe today.'

The shelterbelt grew into a wood the family called the Everglades, and gradually engulfed the orchard. When Cecil Betts lost all his money playing the stock exchange and had hastily to sign over the house to his wife just before a bank foreclosed, they kept the place going by selling daffodils, apples and vast quantities of Louisa's jam. Cecil also kept bees and produced a honey of unique flavour, which he attributed to fuchsia, others to ling, and the family to the appalling tobacco he smoked in a pipe stuck through a hole in his bee veil. As times grew harder they also took in paying guests attracted by the fishing on the neighbouring lakes. But in 1947 Cecil Betts had to sell Knockboy, and he died a week later.

His daughter Esther had married a Mr Bishop, who was connected with Jameson's distillery; I hear one good story about him, from his son Anthony. When he first came down to Knockboy he was curious to learn something about Jameson's native competitors, the poitín makers of Connemara. After some negotiations a neighbour agreed to introduce him to one of the trade. He was instructed to be on the bridge at Gabhla, with his fishing rod, early one morning. There the neighbour greeted him with some specious enquiry about the fishing, and the pair of them headed into the hills. In a remote spot they found an old man tending a still, who readily answered Mr Bishop's questions about the process, from the buying of the barley corn to the final distillation of the poitín through the spiral copper pipe known as the 'worm'. Thinking of Jameson's old slogan, 'Not a drop is sold until it's twelve years old', Mr Bishop asked how long the poitín would be left to mature. The old man replied, 'Some like to let it cool, but I like it hot from the worm.'

After Cecil's death Knockboy passed through two pairs of hands; the first profited by cutting the fine stands of timber, the second was beset by misfortunes, let it 'get on top of him', and left the place abandoned for a couple of years, after which the Bishops bought it back sight unseen. Arriving in March 1960, they found bullocks looking out of the windows of the wrecked house, the kitchen clogged with broken glass, fallen timbers and manure, and the yard blocked by skeletons of abandoned cars. But, as Esther writes, 'Connemara is ever a place of mysteries':

It was 15 years exactly since my Father's death and we expected that, a new generation having grown up, we should neither know or be known. We had told no one that we were coming and yet, in the middle of all the devastation and dirt, someone had arranged a jampot full of daffodils to soften the edges of our homecoming.

In the following year Hurricane Debbie felled many lovely trees, adding to the utter confusion and exposing the bleakness of the surroundings. But acres of daffodils and rhododendron, and the 'immemorial peace' of Knockboy, recompensed them, and by 1962 they were ready to welcome visitors to share the house's 'odd mixture of monasticism and gaiety'; Esther's typescript history was evidently written for such guests. The house now belongs to her son by a second marriage. There is a touch of England about the place; perhaps it is the fine horse-chestnut trees, a rarity in Connemara. Exploring here with friends from Carna one autumn when the horse chestnuts were lying here and there among fallen leaves, I found that their young son was ignorant of the game of conkers, and had to introduce him to this ancient art of surviving hard knocks.

Heading on from Loch Buaile, Maolra of the bees would have had his eyes on Cnoc Glinsce a mile or so to the north. I too set out in that direction once, and found myself forced further and further to the west in trying to cross a marsh and a deep drainage channel. Eventually I was driven to take off my wellington boots and wade through sinking sphagnum and scratchy dwarf willow – a foolish thing to do, no doubt, lacking Maolra's ability to skim over quaking bogs, but the view from the hill was worth it. The placename Glinsce, anglicized as Glinsk, which also occurs in north-east Galway and Roscommon, derives from an Old Irish word, *glinn*, meaning 'secure', I was told by T. S. Ó Máille, the implication being that these places have natural lookout points. A linguist of a younger generation would prefer a less strenuous derivation, from *gleann* and perhaps *sceach*, thorn-bush. But certainly this hill is well situated to watch over a huge arena of lakes and bogs as well as the many little settlements and harbours along the shoreline of Cuan na Beirtrí Buí, the bay of the yellow oysterbeds, which separates Iorras Aintheach from Roundstone and Inis Ní. From this height Maolra would have run down to the long sea-inlet called Barr an Linnín, the head of the small pool, where nowadays there is a little knot of settlement – a holiday village, a community centre, a restaurant – but in his time only a few scattered cabins, and from there he would have followed the coast northwards out of the ambit of this volume. I part from him here, and follow a train of memories of odd encounters, south-westward along the coast road to Maoras and so to my starting point.

One remarkable denizen of Glinsce was the late James Jocelyn, who lived in an isolated cottage white with the dust of the marble from which he carved little knick-knacks such as paperweights and boat-race trophies. I knew nothing of him when first I knocked on his door, except that he was said to be reclusive. He welcomed me in, and put on the kettle for the tea I needed after a long day's walking. He was a nervous, excitable person with a country-house vocabulary: of a soft place in his little garden, 'you'd sink up to your hocks in it!'; of a lady we both knew, 'as thick as the hills!' He searched around for sugar, and found a little rock-hard deposit of it in the bottom of a squashed antique silver sugar bowl. I glanced around the walls at various framed engravings of country seats, and made some remark on one of them; 'Oh, my grandfather popped that one!' he said. Later I learned that the Jocelyns go back as far as nobility itself; there are baronetcies and chateaux and crests and mottos in their history. James was a younger son of the ninth Earl of Roden of Tollymore Park in County Down; how he came to be living in Glinsce on the scrapings of marble I do not know. 'Last week for the first time in my life I slept in a house that was less than a hundred years old,' he told me, 'and by God you'd know it!'

As I was leaving he invited me to bring my partner M to take tea with him on the occasion of Glinsce regatta, which we could watch from his garden. On that day M and I cycled around the bay from Roundstone. The weather was perfect for tea on the lawn, breezy and sunny. The garden was a tiny stone-walled plot shaped like the bowl of a spoon, but something in the disposition of a few shrubs and clumps of flowers around it gave it the dignity of an ancient demesne. We lay on the rug-sized lawn; at the end of an imaginary perspective of classical fountains and gesticulating statuary we saw the hookers manoeuvring in the bay, far off, no bigger than midges.

There is another demesne, or the leavings of one, about two miles to the south-west in the next coastal townland, Leitreach Ard. (The townland is named in seventeenth-century sources as Litterdeharta and Literdahart, which suggests that the current name is a corruption of Leitir Dhá Ard, rough slope of two heights – and in fact the far end of the townland, forming the north-western corner of the Iorras Aintheach peninsula, is composed of two stubby peninsulas.) 'An Diméin', as it is called in Irish, belonged to a Mac Donnchadha family who lived by a lovely little inlet, Cuan Caorthainn, rowan-tree bay, where there is an old stone pier and the ragged remains of a few walls of 'Demesne Lodge'. According to local history recorded by Seán Mac Giollarnáth they were the descendants of a Maoilre Dhonnchadha an Tuistiúin. They were middlemen, leasing the townland from the Martins of Ballynahinch and subletting to smallholders, and I have been told that the *tuistiún*, testoon or fourpenny bit, was the sum levied by them from their tenants as a sort of social insurance payment. However, when I mentioned this in my newspaper column I received a letter of correction from one of the Clann Donncha of An Diméin, now living in Mountbellew; he tells me that the family was actually descended from a Mac Dhonnchadha na Céise, a *céis* being a young female pig. The foundation-legend is that the ancestral Clann Donncha lived in Sligo, until a raiding party burned their farm and killed them all except for two young boys who hid in a cave and then lit out for the south, one carrying a fourpenny bit and the other a young female pig. Two prosperous families sprang from these meagre fortunes, it seems. I hear of the fourpenny branch in An Aird and in Ros Muc, while the Clann Donncha of An Diméin used to have three hookers coming and going from their pier, which is still known in English as McDonagh's Quay.

This last name, like many others along this coastline, was given to me by the late Paddy Barrett, who lived by another quay further west named Céibh Bhairéad after his grandfather, the foreman on the building of it. When I first came round this way in 1980 and got into conversation with him, he was grumbling about the damp turf that had just been delivered to his door. As soon as he understood that I was making a map he brought me into his cottage and got out an old and almost illegible Admiralty chart in the hope that I could solve a cartographical problem concerning the Sunken Bellows Rock, out in the bay. (Several rocks have acquired similar strange English names, through over-literal translation of the prosaic Irish; *bolg* can mean a swelling such as a shoal, as well as a bellows, and *báite*, merely submerged as well as sunken or drowned.) When Paddy was a fisherman he used to locate this rock (in order to avoid it) by lining up the opening of a certain little inlet with the Protestant church in Maoras, but of course the latter no longer existed. While drinking the whiskey he hospitably poured out for me I tried laying a rusty hacksaw blade, the only straight edge he could find in the house, across the chart from the rock to various landmarks, but none of them lined up satisfactorily. I comforted myself with the thought that since the church had been demolished some fifty years earlier this was hardly an urgent matter.

The next time I passed by he mentioned a holy well dedicated to St Colm Cille on the north-eastern foreshore of Inis Troigh, a little island a few hundred yards out, opposite his house. *Troigh* means foot, 'a word that is transferred to what is stepped on', according to T. S. Ó Máille; here it indicates that one could walk to the island at low water. Since the tide was out and a continuous spread of seaweed and stone lay exposed between the quay and the island I decided to go and look for the well, which by his description was a cylindrical pothole like the ones I have described from Inis Ní in *Listening to the Wind*. Since Paddy was too old and stout to accompany me we arranged a system of signals – one whistle for 'north', two for 'south', etc. – and he pointed out a pair of seagulls sitting on a rock that he said was close to the well. As I splashed and scrambled out over the seabed I passed a couple of men gathering winkles; they told me that the tide was coming in and that I would not be able to return by this same route, but that there was another crossing place from the south of the island that would not be covered so long as two little rocks they pointed out in the bay were still visible. I slithered and staggered onwards until I was near the seagulls. Directed by Paddy's whistles I peered under mats of seaweed and groped in rock pools, without success. Then, as the two little rocks were visibly dwindling in the flowing tide, I got ashore onto the island, hastily crossed it and made my way to the mainland via the gapped and tumbled remains of a ruined causeway. Back at the cottage, Paddy said I had been standing right on top of the well.

My diary reminds me of two more odd encounters, from the days of mapping this shoreline. Once I was sitting on a hillock looking down at an inlet and wishing that there were somebody around to tell me its name, when I saw a car turn up a driveway to a house in the distance, and after a few minutes reappear on the road, coming in my direction. It stopped just below me, for no apparent reason. I jumped up and ran down the hill, and in my eagerness almost stuck my head in at the open window. The driver was a young man with a wild crooked face and curly blonde hair, and his lap was covered in pound and five-pound notes, which he was counting. He didn't know the name of the place, he said, as he was from Leitir Mealláin and was just delivering poitín here. I said I'd be round that way shortly, and would maybe buy a bottle. The price, he told me, would be three pounds.

Later on that same day I saw a woman out on the foreshore, bending among the piles of seaweed. I sat on a rock to speak to her. When I spoke in Irish she thought at first I was someone from the village making fun of her, for the sun was behind me. Then she said, '*Meas tú an bhfuil mé cracáilte, ag piocadh faochain i mo chuid ragannaí?*' – 'Do you think I'm cracked, picking winkles in my rags?' I assured her I did not; in fact I hope I left her convinced that picking winkles was at least as sane an occupation and, at what she told me was the going rate of £12 a hundredweight, a more profitable one than my walking of the tide-line between place and story.

15 The Town of Tall Tales

So much of the folklore I have presented in the last few chapters was first recorded by Seán Mac Giollarnáth that it is high time I brought him forward as a personality in my story. And since his habitat, lair and hide as folklore collector was the bar of Mongan's Hotel I shall approach him through a history of that institution, which in its turn has to be set into an account of the village of Carna as it was and as it is today.

When I came round this way in the course of my first reconnoitre my impressions of the place were so dismal that they almost spelled the abandonment of my then-nascent project, a map of south Connemara. But that was because it was on a May Day beset by all the storms winter had forgotten to unleash upon the 'stormy peninsula'. That morning I had climbed Errisbeg Hill behind Roundstone with the intention of grasping in one perspective the whole coastline from there to Ros a' Mhíl, just as the map I envisaged would, I hoped, capture it on one graspable and foldable sheet of paper. There was a dusting of snow on the Twelve Pins, and I had to shelter under a cliff from a brief snowfall and (in the words of my diary) 'watch the showers scampering away, a brisk west wind yapping at their heels'. Then I came down to my lodgings in the village, loaded up my bike (an old black Raleigh, gearless and puncture-prone) and wobbled off round the bay:

A hard struggle most of the way against the wind and I kept having to put my waterproofs on and take them off again. By the time I got to Carna I was exhausted, the tyre went again just as a final overwhelming storm, great wings of hail flapping, came rushing on from the north. I ran from house to house and finally got b&b in a room with a 5-watt bulb at least. After a brief rest set out to find a tyre; it was difficult to identify a single building along the road east of the PO, none being named, but it was clear that 'Mac's', which had had tyres, no longer did so, so again I got a bucket of water and stuck on another patch. The bar near there offered nothing to eat. Thoroughly fed up.

That was in 1979; I persevered, and the village too since then has emerged from dim times; a young man there told me recently that '*an tíogar Ceilteach*' didn't come to Carna, but in fact the redeveloped east end of the village boasts plenty of those omnipresent gables any architect possessed of a set square can slap on a façade and which will come to be recognizable as the stylistic tic of the boom years. A row of 'town houses'; a neat council-built estate of smaller homes known as Bruach na Mara (the bank of the sea), opened in 2005; the privately owned Carna Nursing Home and the much-expanded hotel, Óstán Charna, both of a relaxed Californian spread but with capacious roofs for the Connemara rain – this new Carna welcomes me readily enough on my rare revisitings, praises my devotion to the old ways and words, but regards me as an oddity.

Moving on eastwards one comes to a clutch of older buildings: a small supermarket and the post office (its trim white frontage with tall sash windows attractively half masked in Virginia creeper) on the left, the church and a pub on the right. The post office was built by the Berry family, descendants of the James Berry mentioned in my first volume in connection with 'The Horrors of the Halfway House'. James was born near Louisburgh in 1842 and in his youth used to visit his uncle Fr Ned O'Malley, the parish priest in Carna at the time; thus he came to meet and married a Sarah Greene of this parish, and settled here. In the words of the editor of his works, 'he raised his family, toiled as a farmer to support them, and persevered in his lifelong devotion to the art of storytelling'. His writings were published in the *Mayo News* in the years 1910–13 and resurrected under the title *Tales of the West of Ireland* in 1966. These tales of the extraordinary, cooked up out of the fireside traditions of Connemara and the Mayo of his youth and his own Gothic imaginings, are frustratingly indissoluble amalgams of oral history, folklore and literary invention; one ignores them at peril of missing some clue to a genuine past, or at least to some lie old enough to have matured into an interesting story, but they leave one with the same queasiness as those 'restored' ancient monuments in which the joins between archaeologically advised conservation and speculative reconstruction are left unmarked. His daughter Miss Helena Berry, in the 1960s, recalled that her father spent many night hours in recording traditional tales in notebooks, and that when he was dying he made his wife burn a heap of ledgers containing the stories he was still preparing for publication – and so the manuscript evidence of the location of those textual joints is dispersed to the winds. Nevertheless I will call on his witness, with due caution, here and there.

The sea is hidden by trees from this end of the village but is near at hand. Between the church and the pub a lane leads down to an inlet made dismal by the roofless walls of a disused boys' national school, and by exposures of mud when the tide is out; a digger was groping in black seaweed and heaping it onto a lorry the last time I was down there. St Mary's church, Teach Pobail Naomh Muire, dates from 1845 and after recent restoration shows no sign of its beginnings in such a year of want; it is a pleasantly pale cream-washed building with a long slate roof and a little belfry, set in neat grass-and-asphalt grounds, insulated by mature trees from traffic on the road. The story of its building was recorded from an old *seanchaí* by Seán Mac Giollarnáth. When the walls had been completed the craftsmen asked the priest if he had the wood to roof it. The priest said, 'God will send us the wood.' And the next morning every creek was full of timbers from a ship wrecked on Na Sceirdí. Such are the inscrutable ways of Providence.

The road – surprisingly busy at some times of day, with commuters to Galway, and modern-looking school buses darting to and fro – runs straight on eastwards, with a fine sports pitch on the right and a few big dormer-windowed houses in suburban gardens on the left, some of them, I'm told, let out to Filipina nurses working in the Carna Nursing Home. A side road to the right leads down to Carna's main quay, Céibh an Chrompáin (a *crompán* being an inlet), and the clustered buildings of the Martin Ryan Institute's marine research laboratory: an old fisheries store of the CDB era, the plain single-storey premises of the original laboratory opened in 1975, the recent and relatively glamorous Marine Innovation Building with its eye-catching curved steel roof, and, behind all these, jungles of pipes and pumps and sumps and tanks. This outpost of NUI Galway not only provides employment itself but also serves the fish-farming industry that many south Connemara communities depend on.

When I first knocked on its door, unannounced, in the course of my marathon walking of the south Connemara coast in the 1980s I was hospitably received and shown around, though the then-director, John Mercer, has since told me of his surprise at my approach, not by the road but struggling over the rocks and seaweed of the foreshore from the east, and then my departure westwards in the same mode. At that time the focus of the laboratory was on salmon farming and the shellfish and lobster fisheries – I remember mechanically jiggled trays of glass beakers each holding a lugubrious lobsterling – and I am told by Richard Fitzgerald, today's research manager, that John Mercer, now retired, and the late Professor Ó Céide did much good work for the nascent industry that has not been adequately recognized. Currently the Institute is developing the technology of codfish farming, which may prove less controversial than salmon farming with its sea-louse-infested cages. There is also a project concerning the breeding of ballan wrasse, which like to nibble the sea lice off salmon; it is reckoned that one wrasse can groom a hundred salmon in this way, and their intro-duction into the cages may solve the problem of infection of wild salmon and sea trout that has led to such animosity between sports fishery interests and the fish farmers. These researches call for a blend-ing of advanced technology and hands-on bricolage; in the vats containing young wrasse wads of black plastic bags play the role of the broad-fronded *Laminaria* seaweeds they shelter under in the wild, while a €50,000 DNA analyser keeps track of their family trees. Rich-ard tells me that wrasse are a pleasure to work with, being lively and intelligent fish compared to the rather dull cod, but if one bends too closely over their vat they do tend to leap out of the water and try to snap off one's nose.

Another experiment that caught my attention as I was being shown around the Marine Innovation Building's watery labs was concerned with what might become an important local industry, seaweed farm-ing. One vat held hanks of thread wound on square frames, immersed in soupy-looking water full of the microscopic spores of seaweed. When the spores have settled on the thread and begun to grow, the thread will be wound spirally onto lengths of rope, and then when the plants have developed further the ropes will be pegged out on the foreshore. Harvesting is easy: the rope is simply pulled through a ring that slices off the seaweed. This made me think of the generations of Connemara men who have racked their bodies wrenching seaweed off submerged rocks with long poles and rowing boatloads of it to shore.

From Céibh an Chrompáin the side road continues over causeways to the large and densely inhabited island of Maínis – but for now I return to the main road. Immediately east of the junction mentioned above is a cluster of buildings, the first, largest and most significant being Tigh Mheaic, Meaic's house, named from Meaic Moylette who opened it as a pub and a hostel in 1978. Attached to a corner of this building is a short remnant of a high stone wall with battlements and a Gothic arch in moulded plasterwork, which once closed off its grounds from the road and most of which has been ripped away to reveal a deeply uninteresting parking lot. This stub of Old Decency dates from the time of the Moylettes' predecessors the Mongans, under whom the building was just 'plain and honest Mongan's Hotel', in the words of a member of its clientele, Seán O'Faoláin, and to the villagers the prestigious site of political power and patronage.

Deeper in the historical background of this building is Loideán Mór, Martin Lydon, who had his house here, owned several islands and other properties, and was Carna's primary accumulator of capital. The Lydons' wealth was founded on their extensive smuggling business with Guernsey, whence they brought in rum, indigo dyestuff, tobacco, brandy and silks. Folklore tells of the tricks they used to evade the King's revenue cutters; once one of them had to dodge in among the islands on the east of Cuan Chill Chiaráin and shelter under a cliff of Leitir Calaidh, where he shifted all his cargo to one side of his boat, attached tackle to his mast and winched it down until it touched the rocks and was out of sight of his pursuers; the place is known from this adventure as Brandy Harbour. Another Lydon in a two-masted schooner effected a similar disappearance in one of the rocky passages between the islets off Slyne Head, by sawing down his masts, a sacrifice his cargo made very profitable. Related by marriage to the McDonaghs, shopkeepers of An Chnapach who rose to become Galway's principal merchant family, and to the Conroys, shopkeepers of Garafin in Ros Muc, the Lydons were powers in the economy of south Connemara and were regarded by their social inferiors as *lucht an ghaimbín*, profiteers, gombeen men. Such men represented the only access to markets for the small farmers, and their mode of operation was described in T. A. Finlay's report on the economics of Carna in 1898:

He will buy cattle, which he turns loose upon the mountain areas which he rents and reserves; he will buy pigs, which, when he has a sufficient number collected, he can send by train or sea to Galway; and, in the same way, he is open to purchase of poultry or eggs. For the seller there is, however, one grave defect in this system – the element of competition is wholly eliminated . . . Moreover payment is not made in cash, but in kind – in tea and sugar and Indian meal. And the seller has to take these necessaries, in the quantity, and of the quality, which the purchaser determines to be the equivalent of the animal sold. He is already deeply in debt to the shopkeeper; he owes £5 or £6 – the usual limit to which his credit extends. These transactions are all duly recorded in the book of the shopkeeper; but no record of them passes into the hands of the debtor.

'The Lydons are strong in herds and boats,' says a song by Seán Bacach Ó Guairim called 'Bád Dóite Loideáin', 'Lydon's Burnt Boat', which seems to commemorate the revenge of Martin Lydon's poor neighbours on him in 1880 during the Land War (nothing had properly happened in Carna in those days until a song had been made of it). 'Whoever burned the boat, Cromwell had a hand in it,' says the song, but reveals nothing more of the inside story of this event. In the same year Martin Lydon, described as 'blacksmith', claimed compensation for the burning of a 'house and lodge' because he had paid rent to Carna's landlord, Mr D. Leonard of Tuam.

It was a daughter of the Lydons, Honoria, and her husband Máirtín Ó Mongáin who opened Mongan's Hotel in 1895. Initially it was, says Finlay, 'a small, squat building' attached to a grocery shop, and in grandeur was eclipsed by the nearby constabulary barracks, built in 1867:

The barrack of Carna is one of the most striking examples of police architecture of which this much-governed country can boast. It belongs to what we may describe as the severe pepper-box style. It is a gaunt quadrangular pile, devoid of windows below, as befits a military stronghold, broken by windows of various outlines in its upper storey, and terminating aloft in an arrangement of turrets, gables, and chimneys which amply compensates for the lack of structural adornment at the base.

This exotic pile attracted a theory that the plans for the Carna and the similarly ornate Caherciveen barracks were muddled up with those for two forts designed for the North-West Frontier in India, where plain Irish barracks were built in their stead; I have heard the same silly but incorrigible tale told of the old Ballyconneely barracks. In fact quite a few rather fanciful and defensible barracks were built during a period when fears of a Fenian revolution and a taste for the medieval were both rampant. The Carna barracks was also said to be haunted by a policeman who was drowned while fishing in a nearby lake; whether his ghost transferred itself to the uninteresting new Garda station when the barracks was pulled down in 1955 I do not know. (This present station has been boarded up for some time following an arson attack, an unsolved crime that blotches the reputation of the village.)

Mongan's Hotel knew its best days after Independence, under Honoria's son, the well-known nationalist TD Josie Mongan. It was the centre of the village, having the court, the barracks and the dispensary all huddled around it like a little cabal. *Dlí Charna*, Carna law, was a byword for the ordering of all local affairs through a few words, explicit or allusive, exchanged in the discreet comfort of the hotel dining room or the privacy of its trout-lake beats. Politically the hotel was especially favoured by supporters of the Treaty, members of Cumann na nGaedheal and later of Fine Gael; W. T. Cosgrave stayed, and Earnán de Blaghd, while James Dillon met his future wife here. Josie's artistic guests included Micheál Mac Liammoir, Hilton Edwards, Margaret Burke Sheridan and John McCormack. Their genial host was devoted to the Irish language – he refused to speak a word of English in the Dáil – but no singing was allowed to disturb his respectable clientele, whereas his brother James's pub, over the road from the hotel, was hospitable to the old songs; it was in Tigh James that men would gather for a drinking session after a hard day's work ferrying

Josie's cattle to or from his islands. However, the decorous business of collecting folklore could be carried out in the hotel, and here it was that Justice Sean Forde, having heard many a tall tale in the courthouse, would become Seán Mac Giollarnáth and lend a generously attentive ear to storytellers of Carna, selected for him by Josie.

Sean Forde was born in 1880 into an east Galway family with a shop and a small farm; they did not speak Irish but there was in the house a servant girl, a Conroy from Ros Muc, from whom Seán would have heard the language and perhaps some of the songs and stories she must have brought with her. In London as a young man he met Pádraic Ó Conaire through Conradh na Gaeilge, of which he became a member, as well as such enthusiasts for the culture of the west as Stephen Gwynn, Robert Lynd and Mícheál Breathnach from Cois Fharraige. He also became a member of the secret Irish Republican Brotherhood and then of the Volunteers. On his return to Ireland he became editor of *An Connachtach*, 'The Connachtman', a short-lived monthly journal. In 1909 he succeeded Patrick Pearse as editor of *An Claidheamh Soluis*, the organ of Conradh na Gaeilge. He once conducted Edward Martyn around Connemara, and sometimes stayed in Pearse's cottage in Ros Muc – in fact it was he who was witness to Pearse's dream of a 'little Gaelic kingdom', mentioned in the opening lines of this volume. He was at home during the Rising and took no part in it, though he was arrested twice for carrying messages for the IRA, of which he was a member. Taking up law when *An Claidheamh Soluis* closed, he qualified as an attorney in 1920, and was the first judge to be sent to the Connemara Gaeltacht on the foundation of the Republic. He retired in 1950 and died in 1970, leaving his wife Rebecca and three sons. As Criostóir Mac Aonghusa wrote in an obituary of him:

He was good at his work. No one was in fear and dread before him. Often in court you'd think you were listening to a group of friends spinning stories. One would say to him, 'Now, Seán Mac Giollarnáth, this is how it happened . . .' When he retired on his pension he told me, 'The Doire an Fhéidh court was the best. That's where the Gaelic speakers of Na hOileáin came, and they were the ones who could spout talk.' But he was no soft touch. It wasn't easy to fool him. There was a man in one day when I was in court. He was giving out furiously. Seán let him go on. Then he said to him quietly, 'I see you here often.' 'You do,' said the man. 'And you see me winning often.' 'I understand,' said Seán. 'You won't be able to say that in future.' And the case went against him.

He was good friends with all the storytellers out west. One of them was charged with having poitín in his house. Seán found against him. But if he did, he paid the fine himself. He often did that for people who were too poor to pay themselves.

Not always, though. Tom Nan Choilm Ó Lochlainn of An Trá Bháin in Na hOileáin was at work at his poitín still one day, confident that there were no Gardaí nearer than An Tulaigh, when a crowd of them fell on him at dawn. Condemned to two months of prison and the miserable task of picking oakum (teasing old ropes apart for the fibres used in caulking boats), he amused himself by composing the song 'Ócum an Phríosúin', of which this is the first verse:

Ó molaim sú na heorna go deo deo 'gus choíchin
Nach é an truaigh nach bhfuil tóir ag Rí Seoirse ar a dhéanamh
Seán Forde a bheith ina ghiúistís 's go gcomhairleodh sé na daoine
Mar 'sé a chuir mise ag foghlaim ar an ócam a spíonadh.

Oh I praise the juice of the barley for ever and for ever
But isn't it a pity that King George has no taste for making it
And Seán Forde is a justice and adviser to the people
For it's he who put me learning how to pick the oakum.

Mac Giollarnáth's publications include works on bird life, children's tales, articles for *Béaloideas* (the journal of the Folklore of Ireland Society), *Peadar Chois Fharraige* (a collection of tales and reminiscences taken down from an old Galway working man) and *Mo Dhúthaigh Fhiáin* (a lyrical evocation of his 'wild native land' of Connemara's lakes and islands as seen through the eyes of an angler and fowler). Then there is *Loinnir Mac Leabhair agus Scéalta Eile* (1934), a collection of hero-tales taken down from four Carna *seanchaithe*, which includes episodes from the Fionn cycle and other wondrous stories narrated in the most down-to-earth style. Here's the beginning of the title story, 'Loinnir Mac Leabhair' (a strange name – it seems to mean 'Brilliance Son of Book'). I translate:

There was a king who was High King of the whole world. The King of the Eastern World and the King of the Western World said he couldn't be in authority over the whole world. They agreed between themselves to get round him one day and take his authority and his club of life [*comán beatha*, penis?] from him. They came, and they sat around him, and they cut off his head and his club of life and those of all his army. He had just one son and his name was Loinnir Mac Leabhair, son of the High King of the whole world. He was such a handsome man that they consulted their consciences about cutting off his head and they let him go free.

   And here's another beginning, of the story 'Cú Mac an Ghabha' ('Hound Son of the Smith'):

There was a king here once in Ireland and one day he was out walking in the hills when he met a child on a mountain arable patch who had a fillet of gold on his brow and a fillet of silver on the back of his head, and he had never seen a more beautiful child than him. He carried him off home with him. He thought it would be a great shame to leave him there. He told his wife he had found such a one, and he had no idea what was best to do with him. They said that it would be best to give him to the blacksmith's wife, who had no child of her own . . .

I find these rambles rather tedious, however ancient their lineage and however rich they may be in the motifs folklorists have arduously catalogued and numbered. I value the book more for its introductory essays on the four old storytellers – including the old Fenian Seán Mhac Con Raoi – and its dim photographs of these almost fabulous beings in their great beards and thick waistcoats and heavy boots.

   Finally there is the book I have mined for the present work and for which I owe Mac Giollarnáth an immense debt, which I hope to repay someday with the help of Liam Mac Con Iomaire through translation and republication, as it is long out of print: *Annála Beaga*

ó Iorras Aithneach, 'Brief Annals from Iorras Aithneach', published in
1941. This book presents a treasury of material taken down from eighteen custodians of the oral traditions of the Carna region. Just as this
recalcitrant terrain has been rendered habitable by spreading seaweed
on it year after year for centuries, so this stuff of words dredged up
from communal memory and the collective subconscious has fertilized
an otherwise unbearably impoverished life. ('Carna' means cairns or
heaps of some sort; for myself I associate the name with the place's
extravagant heaping up of stories.) Anecdotes of Connemara's saints
and their offshore islands; historical or pseudo-historical episodes of
the break-up of the old Gaelic order such as the tyrannical deeds of
the O'Flahertys and the coming of the Martins; the Year of the French
and the men on the run in its aftermath; the Torys, the rural terrorists
who enforced resistance to extortionate landlords and bailiffs; strong
men and their amazing feats; robbers and their buried hoards; smugglers and their brushes with the revenue cutters; poor wandering
scholars; revered priests; events linking people and places, such as the
marooning of women on Na Sceirdí, as told in my first volume; boatmen and their perennial concern, timber; food production – mills,
fishing, booleying, etc.; a plentiful heap of '*sifíní*', 'straws', little tales
such as this of St Paul in Rome: when his head was cut off it bounced
three times and three springs of fresh water appeared where it touched
the ground; and finally tales of the traditional memorialists and storytellers themselves. One missing category is that of material concerning
the collector himself, of whom tales are plentiful. Also, more seriously,
where are beauty, love, sex, desire? Mac Giollarnáth was acutely alive
to the loveliness of the Connemara landscape and had a judicious regard
for the Connemara girls too; censorship is not in question, I think.
These omissions from the prose register are amply made up for by the
song tradition, which is full of passionate joys and longings. But the
world conjured up by *Annála Beaga* is no pheromonal Ovidian playground of nymph-haunted pools and lecherous gods. It is rough and
ready, practical and to the point even in its myth-making; it is as raw
as the wind, as poitín, as granite.

16 A Necklace of Islands

Maínis, Fínis and a handful of little ones – to tell them like beads, these islands dependent on, or from, the shores south of Carna, would be to scant their individualities; instead I shall polish up a few facets of each. Two of them are inhabited and linked to the mainland by causeways, and another is close enough to one of these for a shout to summon a boatman to come and fetch you out to it, or so it was until the last family left, a couple of generations ago. A fourth can be walked to when the tide is low. The rest are free-standing but rooted in the same granite as the mainland. None are free-floating, as Inis Bó Finne once was, except perhaps one that was created by a god in an emergency. One was the subject of legal argument as to whether it is an island or a rock.

Maínis, the chief of these islands, is reached by the side road from Carna, which having passed the quay and the shellfish laboratory at Crompán turns into a causeway to cross a terrain as perplexing as a spilt jigsaw puzzle: a salt marsh fragmented by winding tidal channels with black banks of peat. This brings one to the first island, Roisín an Chalaidh, the little peninsula of the harbour, which is a straggle of boggy fields carrying a few houses and deeply penetrated by muddy inlets. An almost enclosed lagoon on the south-eastern shore of the island is called Loch na Lannach, the lake of the mullet, a recurrent placename in the tangles of south Connemara's coastal fringes; shoals of these big fish come into such waters in the summer, creating strange disturbances in the shallows, and people used to build walls across the mouths of lagoons like this, with a narrow gap in the middle where the fish could be netted. The westernmost house in Roisín an Chalaidh was formerly the police barracks, and the shore beyond it was known as Step na bPeelers from the stepping stones by which the 'peelers' would cross the next 500 yards or so of tidal rocks on their way to drop in upon the poitín-makers of Maínis. In about 1893 this ancient footpath was built up into a causeway incorporating a couple of islets, so that nowadays a good road brings one to shore on the north-eastern tip of the island. From there it is about a mile and a half down to the end of the island's broad southern promontory, and a bit less to its narrow western point.

The inconstant topography this causeway crosses, mapped out with dazzling clarity by flood tides and abandoned as a shapeless waste of mud and rock by ebbs, is a natural forcing house for the seaweed growth the islanders depended on formerly, providing vast tonnages of 'yellow-weed' (knotted wrack or *Ascophyllum*) for fertilizer and for burning to kelp. Around the time of the building of the causeway there was much disputation over this resource between the landlord, Colonel Nolan of Tuam, and his tenants in Maínis and Roisín an Chalaidh. Nolan, a veteran of the British campaign in Abyssinia, war correspondent for the *Daily News* and a Parnellite MP for Galway, took a case against some fifty tenants who were objecting to paying rent on seaweed gathered on the shore, which led to a widespread dispute throughout west Galway. The Carna parish priest, Fr McHugh, accused him of also charging rent on seaweed gathered far out at sea, but this was denied. A native of Maínis, the Irish-language writer Séamas Mac Con Iomaire (of whom more shortly) tells us that one of the islanders had to demonstrate to the court how weed was wrenched off the ocean bottom with the *croisín*, a long pole with a little crosspiece near one end:

Mícheál Shéamais took off his clothes down to the trousers and his shirt. 'Keep out of the way,' said he to the crowd around him, although all he had below him was the bare dry floor. He was twisting and pulling, now and again wiping his forehead with his sleeve. Someone threw his *báinín* under the knife of the *croisín*. It didn't take him long to get a twist in it, to lift it high, the judge looking on all the time; but the end of the story was a judgement of a couple of pounds each boat, about a quarter of what was demanded.

The United Irish League (a powerful smallholders' organization campaigning for redistribution of the estates, soon to be absorbed into the Irish Parliamentary Party) considered the matter at their Galway

AGM in 1901 and called on Nolan to resign from Parliament; he had, it was said, been elected under the banner of the League but had betrayed it. He was defeated in the next election, in 1906, and withdrew to his ancestral home near Tuam, where he died in 1912. The Maínis view of landlords (seaweed-lords in this case) like him is roundly expressed by Mac Con Iomaire:

The kelp makers were working for the landlord. The rent money – about four hundred pounds a year – wouldn't last him long. He was getting between sixty and eighty pounds from the kelp makers. Those in the know who had dealings with them said that four hundred pounds wouldn't last a year for some of them going about their business in England, between horses and drink, revelling, sport and fun. They thought little of the amount of sweat lost by the poor creatures who earned it for them. They were feeding and fattening themselves and having a good life on the backs of the poor, like insects sucking the blood and the marrow out of an old sheep, bringing themselves to a state of bursting with fatness.

Despite the hardships of life there, Maínis has inspired passionate nostalgias. In prose as vigorous as the exertions of the seaweed-gatherer in court, the writings-in-exile of Séamas Mac Con Iomaire channel the joyous physicality of island life. He was born in 1891 into a family that owned a small shop in the south of the island and imported their goods from Galway in their own hooker, *An Áirc* – the famous old *Ark* whose return from exile and subsequent disappearance I have mentioned. At school, having little English, he suffered under a teacher with no Irish, a cog in the educational system Pearse called 'The Murder Machine': the strap-driven suppression of national and personal identity, and the imposition of an imperialist ideology in place of the immediacy of the child's home life and language. A ludicrous instance of this last is recounted in Mac Con Iomaire's English-language collection of reminiscences, *Conamara Man*. A school inspector from England, who roared at the children because they could not understand him, ordered them to write a short story on His Majesty. Young Séamas knew His Majesty as a feature of his life-world: it was a rock about five miles out to sea to the south. What he did not yet know was that its real name was (and is) Carraig na mBod, the rock of the little fish known locally as the *bod gorm*, literally 'blue penis', 'His Majesty' being a euphemism used in the presence of women. Séamas's lively little essay in which the black cormorant stands on His Majesty's head and 'dirties' on it was of course incomprehensible blasphemy to the inspector, who tore it up and flung it in his face.

Perhaps it was school's systematic insult to home that woke Séamas into an awareness of the revolutionary values emanating at that period in Connemara from Pearse's disciples in Ros Muc and such Fenians as Seán Mhac Con Raoi of Dumhaigh Ithir. From an early age Séamas was devoted to the songs and stories in which his everyday life was wrapped, and wrote them down from the lips of his old neighbours. As a young man he joined Sinn Féin and the Volunteers, and in 1919 the family home was raided by soldiers and peelers, who confiscated his collection of folklore, perhaps suspecting that the Gaelic script concealed insurrectionary secrets; after that he took to burying his notes and writings in boxes in the sand dunes. Then, following Colm Ó Gaora's example and advice, he went to the Irish college in Tuar Mhic Éadaigh to train as a travelling teacher for the Gaelic League. He taught in Roscommon and Wicklow, obtained a Gaelic Diploma from Rinn College in Waterford, was arrested once or twice and had some narrow escapes from the Black and Tans. When he was denied a permanent post because he refused to take the oath of allegiance the British Empire required of its servants, he decided to emigrate. In the States he found employment with a railway company, working underground and hardly seeing the light of day for months. He contracted TB, and it was while flat on his back in a New York hospital that memories of his island home came back to him with the intensity that shines through the resultant writing.

This work took a most unusual form. *Cladaí Chonamara* (recently translated as *The Shores of Connemara*) is arranged as a field guide to the plants and animals of the seashore, but is transfused with a boyish delight in the colourful oddities to be fished out of rock pools. It appeals simultaneously to the classifying and identifying urge, and to the tactility of the encounter between a self and a fellow creature recognized as a self in itself. Here he is, for example, on the shrimp or *ribe róibéis*:

'*Ribe ribe róibéis, tabhair dom greim ar bharr do shlaite bige agus tabharfaidh mé duit arís amárach é*' ['Shrimpy-shrimp-shrimp, give me a grip of the top of your little rod, and I'll give it back to you tomorrow']. That's what we'd say long ago when trying to deceive this little creature which would swim to and fro in the pools on the bottom of the shore. It wasn't easy to see them as they are the same colour as the sand on the bottom, but if you put your hand in and leave a small gap between your thumb and index finger saying at the same time '*ribe ribe róibéis . . .*' it would not be long before a group of them gathers around your hand looking as if they are amazed at the piece of flesh, and before long, one of them who is bolder than the rest will put its antenna in the wrong place. I suppose it thinks the fingers are to be eaten, but if you close them quickly it will have a different opinion, as it will be caught between your thumb and index finger. I can tell you that in spite of its small size it will make a great effort to escape from captivity . . .

Mac Con Iomaire's system of classification is commonsensical rather than scientific; if he had included whales, he would have agreed with Herman Melville that they are fish. His three main groupings are: Seaweed (no fewer than thirty-six sorts, but including such animals as sea mats and sponges), Small Shore Fish (lugworms, winkles, crabs and the like, but not including finfish), and Sea Fish (among which he counts the cuttlefish). To equate his categories with recognized species is not always possible – for example some of his types of seaweed are different parts or forms of others – but, if not scientific precision, he gives us the seashore's breath and pulse of life. The ideal translator of this deeply felt work would be someone with certain qualities not to be expected to occur in conjunction: an academic background in Irish, a daily familiarity with the speech of south Connemara, expertise in marine biology, hands-on understanding of traditional boatcraft and a detailed knowledge of local seaways. Fortunately such a person exists: Pádraic de Bhaldraithe, son of the renowned lexicographer of the Irish language, long-time resident of the south Connemara island of Foirnis, with postgraduate qualifications in marine zoology and oceanography, owner of the *Widgeon* (a *púcán* now rigged as a *gleoiteog*), and salt-soused participant in every regatta from Kinvara to Round-stone. So we now have a respectful translation of Mac Con Iomaire's love letter to his home, with annotations that discreetly correct his happy-go-lucky taxonomy, and with a bonus of delicate etchings of sea-creatures by Sabine Springer.

Séamas Mac Con Iomaire also wrote a book of reminiscences of his early life in English, under the anglicized form of his name, Seamus Ridge (*iomaire*, a ridge). *Conamara Man* was published in the States two years after his death in 1967. It recycles and clarifies some passages from his Irish book, so I will quote from it to give an idea of the island and its vivid after-image in the mind of the exile.

The name Muighinis means island plain in the English, and it suits well enough too, for a part of the island is a plain or sandy beach. Yet, other parts are craggy, with heights and hollows, steep cliffs and piles of granite boulders. Wild and exposed the south and west shores are. Where the land was soft, the restless sea in her hours of madness devoured it gradually night and day down through the ages so that she might thrust her arms further into the land. To spite that, however, the land pushed out its hard bare teeth of gran-ite, defying the angry breakers . . . In the summer when the sea around is calm and smooth, my Island is a lovely place. The fine white sand dazzling under the rays of the sun. Patches of rye and potatoes mantled with thick foliage. To the east of our cottage a fine stretch of level green reaches down to the sea. On this grassy bawn, one notices hundreds of tiny buttercups, primroses, daisies and bluebells, each not much bigger than a pin's point . . . Birds in a merry mood from the pleasant warmth flit and coo in the black-berry bushes. Wrens build their nests in the green ivy that clings to the face of the tall cliff. Snowy gulls and terns wheel overhead, black cormorants doze on the rocks and sandpipers rush here and there looking for a mouth-ful. Peace and quiet are all around, as some folks stretch on the sand and others swim in the placid water . . . When the dreary winter sets in, the picture is much different. Blustering westerlies and southerlies rush from the bosom of the big sea in frightful gales, giving the Conamara islands a weird and gloomy look. Sea waves, mountain high, driven by the storm, hurl themselves with foaming manes, hiss and keen against the granite shore.

The surf beat on Long Strand is loud and continuous. Big blobs of white foam are blown around to find shelter in the lee of the dark cliffs. The Atlantic away to the west is like frothing milk, and the cheeks of the Beola Hills are mantled with the fresh snow . . .

In Mac Con Iomaire's day, he tells us, eighty households shared the sea-fraught square mile of Maínis. Rock and sand were its ground, with plenty of seaweed and hand-labour to turn it into a maze of tiny pastures and potato plots. Subsistence farming – or what would have provided a subsistence had the landlord not been drawing on it – had to be supplemented by kelp-burning and emigrants' remittances. But the island had another source of strength and indeed of pride: its boatbuilding tradition. There were in the 1830s over 400 sailboats working out of the various harbours from the Claddagh at Galway to Bun Abhann near Slyne Head. The tannin-red sails and shiny tar-black hulls that now delight us on regatta days were a workday sight, supplying the little seaport shops like Clohertys' of Roundstone with goods from Galway, heading out to the Aran Islands with turf and to Kinvara with seaweed, or setting nets for mackerel beyond Na Sceirdí. These superbly adapted boats were built by local craftsmen, working without plans, either in small boatyards or on any handy flat place by the shore. The Mac Con Iomaire hooker, *An Áirc*, built in the 1890s, was the work of Seán Ó Cathasaigh (Casey), who had learned his trade in Maínis from Seán Ó Laidhe of Leitir Mealláin. It is perhaps relevant that these two centres of boatbuilding lie in similar positions relative to the stream of sea-traffic along the south Connemara coast, which had to skirt Leitir Mealláin, the outermost of a score of tightly clustered islands southeast of Cuan Chill Chiaráin, and would have preferred the narrow shortcut through Bealach na Srathrach or Straddle Pass around the western tip of Maínis to the more exposed route outside of Oileán Mhic Dara. Seán's sons inherited his skills; the remains of their yard can be seen on the eastern shores of Máinis, above the low cliff, Aill na gCathasach, from which the boats were lowered into the sea. In the western arm of the island the Ó Clochartaigh boatyard was in business until the mid 1980s, while another well-known boatwright,

Colm Ó Maoilchiaráin, was at work until a few months before his death in December 2009.

The origins of the Galway *húicéir* are lost in time's wake. Perhaps, like the Dutch *hoeker*, the name of the boat-type associates it with fishing hooks. On little or no evidence the convinced diffusionists have variously derived the characteristics of the hooker from those of Dutch and Norwegian fishing boats, the pleasure boats of the venerable Cork Water Club, and seventeenth-century smuggling luggers; but I see no reason to suppose that the hooker's graceful lines founded on its massive timber frame did not come into being in Connemara, moulded by the demands of the outrageously rocky and complex lea shores of this splintered Atlantic promontory. And not so long ago, for Hardiman's *History of Galway* and the 1836 Fisheries Inquiry seem to suggest that the hooker evolved from smaller inshore craft in the years between 1790 and 1830.

There are two sizes of hooker: the *bád mór*, literally 'big boat', thirty-five to forty-four feet long and capable of carrying twelve to fifteen tons, and the *leathbhád*, 'medium-sized boat', about thirty-two feet long. Both may be fully or half decked, and both have a high-peaked mainsail, a jib and a staysail. And then there are two junior sisters of the family, both from twenty-four to twenty-eight feet long. The *gleoiteog* (perhaps from *geolta*, a yawl, or from *gleoite* and meaning 'pretty little thing') is rigged like a hooker, and is open or has a short foredeck. The *púcán* is an open boat with a small jib and a 'dipping lug' which has to be quickly manoeuvred from one side of the mast to the other when coming about; the late Johnny Jennings has suggested that this action gives the boat type its name, a *púcán* being a wrap or poke, such as a fingerstall.

Even if I don't understand all its terminology I love the craft-language, lean and muscular, with which these boats' lines are described. Dick Scott in his indispensable study *The Galway Hooker* conveys their wavelike swell and swoop thus:

The hull's sharp, clean entrance, deceptive under the apple-cheeked, buoyant, forequarters, considerable tumblehome or belly of up to twelve inches each side, a beautiful run starting almost amidships, and sweeping up to the raked transom, all were distinguishing features of the hooker. The degree and faring off of the tumblehome into the hooker shape was an art, with subtle differences between builders . . . From the chainplates the sheer eased from a steady rise to a more urgent, upward curve to meet the stern head. It was the accentuated sheer and tumblehome that were the first characteristics of a Galway hooker hull. Indeed this very trademark is the magnet that attracts one to linger and study the odd survivor from a quay today.

And Scott himself writes as one who spent most of his life on quaysides, bent forward, hands on knees, talking to the skipper of some boat moored below or scrutinizing the profiles of a choice specimen of the boatwright's craft, as we used to see him every year at the Roundstone regatta, until emphysema denied him this, the breath of his life. He loved to sail too, in earlier days, especially in the hooker *Capall*, 'Horse', with Johnny Bailey, a barrel-shaped, flat-capped, pipe-smoking old boatman who always lay back at his tiller looking as rooted and imperturbable as one of the Twelve Pins. Dick told me how once he had been at the prow of the *Capall* as it was clipping along the coast south of Roundstone harbour and seemed to him to be approaching a rock with alarming speed; eventually he summoned up the nerve to cry out, 'Johnny, there's a rock ahead!' and Johnny removed his pipe long enough to say, 'I noticed that one forty years ago.'

Nowadays the Galway fleet comprises about twenty-five hookers and thirty of the smaller sorts; a good proportion of these turn out to race in the dozen or so yearly regattas centred on various little harbours around Galway Bay – summer visitors, as graceful as shearwaters in the distance, as antiquated and thick-timbered as an ancient church roof when at rest in harbour. A mere forty years ago it seemed that the last of the traditional boats, doomed to unemployment in the age of lorries and small trawlers, would join their forebears whose foundering skeletons were to be seen in a hundred muddy creeks. Then in 1966 a young Dubliner, Denis Aylmer, found the *Morning Star*, an old Kinvara-built hooker, long laid up in Na hOileáin, bought her, made some repairs, and sailed her via the Shannon and the Grand Canal to Dublin. She was later acquired by John Healion of Dublin, restored and brought back by road to Connemara for the St Mac Dara festival of 1976, in which she won the championship. In the same year the first new boat for some forty years was built by Cloherty of Maínis. In the following year the *St John*, bought as a mere hull in Strangford Lough, was also restored and returned to Connemara. The Galway Hooker Association was founded in 1978, and the revival was well under way. Boats long moribund or sold into service elsewhere as yachts re-appeared in authentic form, including the famous *American Mór* and *An Mhaighdean Mhara*, 'The Mermaid'. In 1979 another Ó Cathasaigh-built boat, the *St Patrick*, formerly *Bád Chonroy*, the trading vessel of the Conroys of Garafin House, which had been acquired by Paddy Barry, sailed northabouts from Dublin, summered in Roundstone and completed a circuit of Ireland that autumn. The *Connacht*, thought to be over 130 years old, returned from Belfast; *An Áirc*, the largest of the surviving hookers, revisited from London. And so on; one by one names that have since become summer familiars were added to the regatta programmes: *Mac Dara*, *Truelight*, *Naomh Máirtín*, *An Tónaí*, *Star of the West*, *Morning Star*, *Ave Maria*, *Hunter*, *Volunteer* . . .

There were also tragic losses. At Kinvara's festival, Cruinniú na mBád (the gathering of the boats), in 1988 the new-built *Meaircín Joe* was overset by a squall and her skipper lost; the boat was later raised and returned to her maker, Marcas Ó Clochartaigh of Maínis, for repairs. In the same year, as I have mentioned, *An Áirc* was abandoned in bad weather on her way to the Mediterranean. In 1989 the ancient *Connacht* was lost for unknown reasons, with her skipper and the woman crew-member, on her way round the north of Ireland from Portaferry to Roundstone. In 2002 the *St Patrick* was smashed on rocks near Glandore in Cork when its mooring chain snapped in a storm. And as I write this, in September 2009, news comes of the capsizing of the *gleoiteog McHugh*, en route to Ros a' Mhíl from Kinvara, with the drowning of its skipper Johnny Mac Donncha and near escape of his brother the singer Josie Sheáin Jeaic.

Some spectacular voyages by hooker, far beyond the horizons of the old workboats, have caught the imagination of the nation. Paddy Barry and his crew took the *St Patrick* to New York, to Spitzbergen, and to the west coast of Greenland; photographs and film showed that a world of ice-blue and snow-white had been waiting since Creation for the entrance of those rust-brown sails. In fact film has proved the natural partner of the arts of boatbuilding and boat-sailing. Bob Quinn has coupled Connemara's traditional music with its traditional boats in an early series of documentaries; more recently TV programmes using telescopic lenses and masthead cameras have drawn us shorefolk into the vortex when the big hookers are jostling for position in turning a buoy far out at sea. The film *Húicéirí* by Éamon de Buitléar and his son Cian shows us every stage of John Healion's building of the *Star of the West* for Cian, and culminates in a triumphant and lyrical passage of sailing before the wind, thrilling us with the imperious swell of straining canvas and perilous slant of masts. Just as Connemara's yearling ponies running wild on the hills proclaim the not-quite-yet annulled freedom of its empty quarters, so the former boats-of-all-work in their afterlife of pure play assert the ageless, dangerous, splendour of its seas. May they long do so, until on Judgement Day they all follow *An Hunter*, which the contemporary poet-boatman Seán Cheoinín tells us 'will sail into heaven as she sailed on the day of the great gale' with himself at the helm.

One more voyage, one more song, will bring me back to Maínis. When Máire Ní Chlochartaigh lay dying in Leitir Calaidh, half a dozen miles to the east across Cuan Chill Chiaráin, she composed the finest of south Connemara laments, known as 'Amhrán Mhaínse', 'The Song of Maínis'. In it she bewails the imminent loss of her husband's companionship, worries over the fate of her household as winter draws on, and then arranges her funeral. 'Let my little cap with my ribbon in it be neatly on my head,' she stipulates, and 'there will be three young women from the mountain to keen me when I am laid out':

> Bíodh mo chaipín is mo ribín inti istigh,
> Is iad go ródheas faoi mo cheann.
> Beidh triúr ban óg ó shliabh agam,
> Le mé a chaoineadh os cionn cláir.

She is to be keened for three days and nights, with long clay pipes and kegs full of drink for the mourners. She is not to be buried in Leitir Calaidh for her folk are not from there, but Páidín Mór is to take her back to Maínis ('if the weather is not too rough', adds this practical Connemara woman) for burial in the old graveyard, which looks out to sea over the island's great western beach. The song ends with the magical words '*Beidh soilse ar na dumhchannaí / Is ní bheidh aon uaigneas orm ann*' – 'There will be lights on the dunes, and I'll not be lonely there.'

The low-lying western quarter of Maínis, I was told locally, is called Feithearnach, which perhaps means 'place of watercourses', for Fethernagh in Armagh means 'abounding in little brooks' according to P. W. Joyce's *Irish Names of Places*. I am unreasonably persuaded of the correctness of the interpretation by a clear memory of walking this bit of land on a still day when a high spring tide brimming all around the island incited the obscure, rush-choked drainage channels between the little fields to a murmuring, the source of which I could not at first identify. The final headland of the western promontory is Tóin an Roisín, the back-end of the little point; this is where Tadhg na Buile first tried to build his castle, only to have it unbuilt every night by the fairies. Off the tip of the headland is Carraig na Blaoithe, the rock of the calling, on which people stood to call for a boat to come out from Oileán Máisean, Mason Island, a quarter of a mile away to the west. No use calling these days, for apart from the occasional holiday-home owner in summer, or a man from Más seeing to his cattle, there is nobody there. The name of the island must be related to that of Más, which is only a little over a mile to the north, and in fact Roderick O'Flaherty refers to Ceann Mása as Masonhead.

On one of my visits, in 1983, I got a young man from the last house in Tóin an Roisín to ferry me out to the island. It was midsummer, and as we walked down to the shore children were collecting dried-up furze bushes that had been chopped out of field corners, for the St John's Eve bonfire. The straits between Maínis and Máisean, Bealach na Srathrach or Straddle Pass, once a busy seaway, was glassily calm. We beached the boat on Trá an Éadain, the wide strand that forms the face (*éadan*) the island shows to Máisean, and walked south to Guaire na gCnámha, the sandhill of the bones, where the sea long ago had mined an old burial ground. On the far side of the island we looked at the fine little harbour built by the Congested Districts Board about a hundred years earlier in an unavailing attempt to conserve an already dwindling population. The hundred acres of Oileán Máisean used to be part of a 1,200-acre estate belonging to a Dominick Leonard, which was reckoned to be one of the poorest in the west when the CDB bought it out in the mid 1890s; there were twenty-two families living on the island at that time. The Board rationalized the holdings and divided them among the tenants; one can see on the OS map of 1898 how the new straight and parallel field walls cut across the spiderweb pattern of older walls as if to score out an obsolete way of life. I imagine it was also the Board that built the two grassy roads running across the island and forming a crossroads at its centre and highest point, like the cuts in the crust of a hot-cross bun. Nested into a slight hollow near this point there was once a holy community. My boatman and I examined the waist-high, bramble-protected remains of a chapel seven or eight paces long, with a wall that seems to have enclosed a graveyard. I noted a small pillar-stone of early Christian date inscribed with the outlines of a simple cross, and a small granite boulder with an oval hollow in its upper side and a stone lid shaped like a soda-bread loaf. (Such 'bullán' stones with ground-out hollows were used as mortars, and have come to be regarded as fonts or holy wells as they are often found near ancient ecclesiastical settlements.) There were also a few fine blooms of elecampane, a tall, yellow-flowered composite once highly regarded for its magical-medicinal powers, which I have seen in only two other places in Connemara, both of them, like this, once inhabited and now deserted.

Then we walked on down one of the roads past a few cottages, some of which were abandoned and derelict, some occasionally used by former island families now settled in Más, and one or two spruced up as summer holiday homes. From outside one of the latter a friendly couple greeted us and invited us in for a sup of poitín. They showed us their various island finds: a rusty three-pronged eel-spear, a locally built kitchen dresser, a couple of granite quern stones. Their midsummer bonfire was all prepared on the hilltop, and they evidently felt the lack of a party to go to, being the only inhabitants of the island that day, but we had to catch the falling tide and could not stay. Back on the beach we found the currach high and dry, and had a struggle to drag it down to the water's edge. As we rowed across the straits to Maínis, I remember, sky and sea perfected themselves in stillness, and on the land little points of light appeared here and there as each village lit its bonfire.

After Maínis the largest of the Carna islands is Fínis, a mile-long north–south tongue of land. It lies nearly half a mile offshore when the tide is full, but can usually be reached at low tide on foot over level sands from a beach just east of Carna, as I did on my first visit. In fact it was the experience of 'walking out to islands', specifically Fínis and Inis Bearcháin, in Na hOileáin, that first shocked me into, if not poetry, then poetic prose on the subject of Connemara, in 1981; the resultant pamphlet, *Setting Foot on the Shores of Connemara*, was Lilliput Press's first publication. (In that essay I did not identify the two islands for fear of disturbing the melancholy tranquillity of two islanders, each of them virtually the sole remnant of a vanished community, and particularly of the aged Cóilín Scufal in Fínis, of whom I wrote a close-up portrait. However, time has long relieved me of that anxiety, in its stealthy and inexorable way.) Coming to write about Fínis once again, I realize that writing about an experience is a way of forgetting it, or perhaps of sacrificing it for the sake of writing, for the memory of what one has written overwrites one's memory of the event that inspired the writing. In any case, since I cannot recapture my anything-but-careless if rapturous prose style of earlier years, I will now have to find my way into the island in a more objective mode.

Shifting sands and the timetable of tides necessarily dominate all thought of Fínis. Traces of the early settlers have been bared by wind erosion in several places in the island: blackish layers full of oyster, mussel and periwinkle shells with bits of fire-shattered stone are visible in the sandy cliffs of blown-out dunes; there is a spread of limestone flakes on a recently exposed ground surface, suggesting that stone from the Aran Islands (which are visible on the sea-horizon to the south) has been worked here; rows of small granite boulders set on edge show through the sand here and there, the foundations of round and rectangular houses. The more recent history of the island too is written in sand. Potatoes and corn grown on the sandy soil used to be its prized products, along with scallops dredged from its offshore sand-banks and rabbits from its dunes. When the Congested Districts Board bought out the island from the Leonard estate in the 1890s there were twenty-five households on it. The Board supplied it with a good pier and a fishery store, and resettled the former tenants in stout stone-built, slate-roofed houses. Nevertheless the little community continued to evaporate as family after family moved out to the neighbouring town-lands. I suppose that the reason the island was never linked to the mainland by a causeway, which might have saved it, was the difficulty of building on tide-stirred sands. Nowadays the rabbits pullulate unchecked; they have undermined the walls of the old schoolhouse so that its gable has collapsed, and the dunes are so hollowed out by rabbit burrows that they can founder under one's footstep. The fields are unworked and flooded with sand; in the north of the island they have been denuded down to granite bedrock and the blown sand piled in long parallel dunes along the straight field walls with which the CDB striped the land, creating a gaunt and eerie empty quarter.

On my first visit just one family remained, who were soon to leave, and solitary Cóilín, who seemed to have been waiting for years to show me round the island. When he had done so and we returned to his bare, womanless house he ran in before me and rapped on the door of the bedroom as if to wake those within, and then flung it open with a laugh at his own bitter joke to show me that it was empty. A few years later I found him living by a bog road outside Carna in one of the disgraceful cardboard-box-like chalets that were all the council could provide at the time. For a long time then the island was empty; an entrepreneur bought it with, so we heard, the intention of building a holiday village, but that never materialized. Seen from the mainland against the sky the row of roofless CDB houses stood like dark verte-brae – but the last time I passed by there was an addition to the outline: a new house, built, I am told, by a granddaughter of one of the island-ers, who goes in and out of the island in a four-wheel-drive vehicle, the brusque modern solution to the immemorial problem of access to the island.

The first settler in the island, according to Cóilín, was a Mac Donncha woman. (He himself was a Mac Donncha; his byname

'Scufal' was inherited from his father, who used to sell fish to a dealer called Schofield.) This ancestral personage, who is buried in the little graveyard near the western shore of the island, he told me, was drowned when crossing into the island on horseback; the horse got safely to land but she did not. However, it might be that this lady is mythical, for one of the dangers of wading across the strand when it is partly flooded is that one can stray into a pool of deep water called Poll na Seantuinne, at what looks like the most direct crossing point, and that last word is an archaic term for an old woman. There are a number of places in Ireland with this strange name, some of them blowholes on sea coasts and others watery inland abysses; they are similar to places that used to be named Poll Tí Liabáin, the hole of the house of Liabán, and regarded as entrances to the underworld. The dictionaries give *lia*, a flood or torrent, and *liabán*, a sort of porpoise or a basking shark; and then there is Lí Ban (beauty of woman), a mermaid who escaped drowning when Lough Neagh burst forth in Ulster by becoming a salmon, according to another complex of legends that might be in play here, given the time-blurred nature of the coherencies of myth. The most one can be sure of is that the foundation-story of Fínis concerns the perils arising out of its ambivalent nature, its inconstancy to land and sea.

Perhaps, having so closely attended to the warnings of myth and history, it was inevitable that sooner or later I would myself be caught by the tides here. One autumn day a few years ago I went out in the company of the photographer Amelia Stein, who was in search of picturesque desolation. The sands we crossed on the way into Fínis seemed to spread to the limits of vision and were so firm under foot that one did not think of them as forming part of the sea's bed. Then, as view after view presented itself to the camera, we rambled all along the island's length. I began to think it was time for us to turn back. Angles of gables and empty window frames suggested more shots; the tops of long walls showing along the crests of dunes offered interesting perspectives; the vast span of distant mountains around half the horizon and the dark silhouettes of the outer islands around the other half combined to tempt the lens. When at last we arrived at the north shore, seawater was swilling in from either side – but it was shallow;

we could surely wade across. I trod into it, and the cold grip of the
current immediately told me we could not. Evening was coming on;
the prospect of waiting for the next ebb in eight or ten hours' time in
a roofless building was chilling. We climbed a hillock and jumped up
and down and waved our coats, and it wasn't long before tiny figures
emerged from one of the cottages up near the coast road a half mile
or so away, made their way down a boreen to a quay and got into a
rowboat. Their progress towards us seemed inordinately slow, for all
the effort the two young men were putting into rowing. The reason
for that became clear as we hopped gratefully into the boat: the blade
of one of their oars was broken short, reducing it to a stump. We crept
crabwise across the dark waters of Poll na Seantuihne in a rising wind
that seemed to me to be edging us out into the wide seaways. But all
this was normal to the lads, who in their time had ferried many a fool
out from Fínis.

One fine June day in 1983 I visited the half-dozen lesser islands, rough
but highly individual nuggets, that form an outer fringe to the Carna
archipelago, in one glorious circuit, in the company of the respected
local historian and irascible schoolmaster Seán Ó Ceóinín (alias Johnny
Jennings) and his young son Simon. Seán had arranged with his cousin
Pádraic de Búrca to take us out in his wooden currach. We were late
in starting as Seán was '*roinnt batteráilte*' from the previous night's
midsummer excesses, and his wife Catherine had gone off to the village
in their car. 'Women just don't understand tides!' grumbled Seán, but
he recovered his spirits when Catherine returned in time to drive us
down to one of the little quays east of Carna, where the philosophical-
looking Pádraic was resting on his oars and keeping the boat from
knocking against the bouldery shore. Pádraic started the outboard
engine and wove his way around numerous rocks and shoals, the names
of which he called out for me, between the green sea-meadows of
Maínis to the west and the long sandy finger of Fínis to the east. We
landed first on Oileán Lachan, Duck Island, a low outcrop of rock off
the southern tip of Maínis, and found ourselves treading among dozens
of terns' nests; I regretted that we had come at this time of year, but
Simon was entranced by the sight of a chick pecking its way out of an

eggshell, and I managed to shepherd the rest of them out of the ternery before our clumsy feet did any damage. Pádraic and Simon wandered off picking *creathnach*, for which the island is well known, and I found some sea beet, a big, juicy-leaved wild spinach which M and I used to relish when we lived on the Aran Islands but was new to Seán, being rare on Connemara's shores.

From there to a rather larger island, Inis Múscraí, is just over a mile, south-eastwards. Halfway between the two islands we passed Carraig an Ghloinigh, the rock of the . . . – but no one can affix a meaning to that last word (a linguist suggests the name may originally have been Carraig Loinidh, churn-dash rock). This is the rock that figured in a court case some time around 1860, as Séamas Mac Con Iomaire tells us. It was in the possession of the landlord's agent, but as 'want respects no law' some of the tenants went out to pick dulse on it, and were caught by the bailiff. It seems that the law was such that the landlord's claim would prevail if there were grass growing on the rock, i.e. if it could be classified as land; so the bailiff went out by night and hammered a grassy scraw onto it with a couple of blows of his shoe. Admiring his work by moonlight, he promised himself revenge on the dulse-pickers. In court the next day he was able to swear there was grass on the rock, and the tenants were heavily fined. Early the following morning some fishermen saw a flock of gulls pulling the scraw off the rock and dropping it into the sea as if they resented interference in their kingdom. Not a blade of grass has grown there since; it is a rock, not an island.

The sense of the name Inis Múscraí is obscure too; *múscraí*, according to T. S. Ó Máille, means 'sunset' in Ros Muc Irish, while Ó Dónaill's Irish dictionary gives it as an adjective meaning 'dank, moist, muggy or dull'; it is also the tribal name behind Muskerry in County Cork. We landed there in bright midday sunshine; in fact we all got a little sunburned that day. The island is low and exposed, but grassy, and there were a few cattle grazing on it. Pádraic showed us the remains of the rear wall and the base of a half-underground hovel or den in a sandbank by the island's northern beach, and gave us the name of the western point, Tóin na mBrácaí, the back place of the hovels. This name and the broken-down *bráca* by the beach were relics of periodic temporary habitation from the island's heyday when it was a place of concerted and regular labour, an open-air factory, an outpost of the Industrial Revolution. Its product was kelp, the fused ashes of seaweed, which was the material from which the alkalis required by northern Europe's glass, soap, explosives and linen manufacturers were extracted; later on, when alternative sources of alkalis undercut it, the market for kelp was revived by the discovery of iodine. For over two centuries from the early 1700s the shores of western Ireland, like much of the Atlantic coastline from Norway to Spain, were periodically wreathed in smoke from the kelp kilns. The breeze of nostalgia even brought its tang across the ocean to Séamas Mac Con Iomaire, lying in his New York hospital bed:

At the end of summer and the beginning of autumn the coast of Connemara is alight. There are hundreds of kilns to be seen . . . their smoke rising slowly skywards in the quiet of the evening, submitting to every breath of wind, however slight, to signal to everyone from what quarter of the sky the wind is blowing. The smell from the same smoke is a healthy fragrance.

Inis Múscraí seems to have been particularly dedicated to this toilsome craft, judging by an account given to Seán Mac Giollarnáth by an old Carna man, Micheál Mhac Dhonnchadha, in the 1930s:

When I was growing up life was hard, and it was harder still before that. I spent fourteen years making kelp on Inis Múscraí, summer and autumn. It was as if I lived there for those fourteen half-years, except that we came in [to land] on Saturdays. The island used to be hidden in red weed spread out to dry. We used to cut the seaweed when a big ebb left it dry, and at other times we gathered it from boats with the *croisín*. Two good men with a good boat would gather three tons of oarweed a day. There wasn't a stitch of dry clothing on me from Monday to Saturday.

We were burning kelp on the island day and night. When we had one kiln burned there was another to be built. One year I spent six days and nights burning kelp without a wink of sleep. There was no slavery like it, keeping it burning all the time and stirring it with kelp rakes. Another man and I made nine tons and sixteen hundredweight of kelp one year. We got five pounds ten shillings a ton for that kelp.

There was a house on the island for the foreman and the kelp makers. The foreman and I stayed on the island one Saturday night. The house had a half door. There was a big coffer in the house and we put it against the half door, for the wind would blow it in. We were no sooner in bed than the coffer was thrown against the other wall of the house. We put it back against the half door. We fell asleep heavily. We didn't wake till twelve on Monday morning. It was the six other men coming in on Monday who woke us. They thought we had died when they saw the boat and we were not to be found. I think we would have slept until Monday night if they hadn't woken us.

The kelp fire would be started with turf or brambles or whatever was to hand, stoked with armloads of seaweed, kept burning for eighteen hours or so (later on it was realized that a shorter burning gave better results), and raked now and again; then the molten, glowing mass would be allowed to cool and fuse into a block. This would be broken into several pieces, taken off to be sold to one of the local kelp agents in Cashel or Cill Chiaráin, and shipped in bulk to factories in Glasgow. So the seaweed of Inis Múscraí entered the web of European industry, and conversely the influence on kelp prices of far-off events – the French Revolution, Waterloo, the Battle of the Somme and the consequent call for iodine, the discovery of penicillin – fed back through the channels of trade and was keenly felt on the little island. It was probably sometime in the 1940s that the last of the kelp smoke drifted away from the shores of Connemara. Little if anything remains of the kilns, for they were hardly more than rows of stones laid out to enclose a flat bit of ground a yard or so wide and four or five yards long, which the high tides of winter have long tidied away into the storm beaches they came from. An eye alerted to such traces of the past might notice places by the shore where the surface of the bedrock has been splintered and scarified by fire after fire.

Bior Mór or Oileán Bheara is about two miles to the east of Múscraí. It is similarly low and grassy, a little larger at thirty-two acres, and has a small satellite, Bior Beag, on its north. Bior means a spit or spike or point, which is puzzling, as it is Inis Múscraí that is known in English as Spike Island; some cartographer's mistake, no doubt. In the nineteenth century Bior Mór was leased from the Martin estate by the Cookes of Cill Chiaráin, who sublet to their bailiff Beartla Ó Clochartaigh, and a Pádraig McDonagh. The last of the two households moved out in about 1930, when the Mylottes of Carna bought the island for its grazing.

An episode in Seán Mac Giollarnáth's book *Mo Dúthaigh Fhiáin* ('My Wild Native Land') tells us something of life on the island and how it came to be deserted. He describes walking one day on the beach of Caladh Fhínse, on the mainland just east of Fínis, and meeting a man who had just rowed in from Bior Mór (he doesn't name it but one can deduce which island is in question). They sit down together and chat, for, as Seán remarks, God had given them a fine day and the powers of speech, and was not storytelling a fine craft long before 'the Adversary' brought printing into the world to spoil good company? The Bior man tells him that he has come ashore to send a telegram to the British government asking for the return of his gun, which had been confiscated. His family were tired of eating fish day in day out, and the wild geese and duck he used to shoot had become so tame they were mingling with the chickens around the house. Seán warns him that a telegram would cost a penny a word, and undertakes to write a letter for him instead. In return the islander offers to tell him the story of the King of the Cats (a bloody and merciless story composed, says Seán, to teach kings not to lose their nobility by adopting the low ways of cats). We do not learn what success Seán's intervention with the government has, but many years later when he is climbing the hill behind Caladh Fhínse he is hailed by a sad-looking old man whom he recognizes as the islander. Once again they sit down together to talk. The man now has a farm nearby, as he explains:

My son's family were growing up and their mother didn't like them to be without an opportunity of schooling. Her husband agreed and I gave into the pair of them because I thought I wouldn't live much longer. I sold my half of the island and bought a holding here on the hilltop. The children are near the school and I am far from the island. I have no inclination to the place and my heart won't incline to it until I'm laid in the sands of Maínis . . .

He was not born on the island but moved out there as a married man, and has only fond memories of it:

There were two houses on the island at that time, but my neighbour soon sold out to a mainlander and took himself off. After that there was no one but ourselves on the island. We didn't feel a bit of loneliness or distress, for we had the produce of earth and strand every day of the year. I had my boat to go to Mass on Sundays, for cutting seaweed and fishing and setting lobster pots. It was the boat that brought the turf in for me and took out the bags of winkles and scallops in the winter. I was the happy man out there, not like here with neither road nor boat coming to my door. The cows here are humpbacked from lack of grass and water. There was soft sweet grass on the island, and a well of fresh water . . .

Some sixty years after this man's expulsion from his Eden we found the island settlement mapped out in fallen stone: the roofs of the houses long collapsed and the field walls almost lost in long grass. All the same Pádraic was able to trace out the boundary between the two holdings the islander had named. By one house I found a dozen plants of one of Connemara's rarities, the wild leek *Allium babingtonii*, with its crooked four-foot-high stems and weird medusa flower-heads, which had obviously been cultivated for kitchen use. Cattle, which had been brought out to Bior Mór by raft, had waded across to the lesser island of Bior Beag. We followed them by boat, and when we sat down for our tea and sandwiches I was delighted to find lots of tiny adder's-tongue ferns at my elbow, and fat fluffy seagull chicks tucked in by stones here and there in the tufted grass.

As we left for the mainland Pádraic pointed out a rock far off to the east, called, according to him, Carraig Shiobháin Uí Bhéara, Shevaun Barry's rock, but which other reputable informants insist is actually Carraig Siánaí Bheara, the rock of Bior's mounds or (jocularly) testicles. In similar vein, a pair of rounded rocks, white with seafowl droppings, at the end of a reef running out north-eastwards from Bior Beag, is called Na Briolla, a term that according to the dictionaries refers to various unmentionable lumps of the male or female anatomy; Seán was sure that in this case it was their breast-like appearance that had given rise to the name. There is an old phrase, *taobh thiar dho na Briolla*, 'out beyond the Briolla', used of anything that is very far away. Nevertheless it was only a run of a couple of miles north to Caladh Fhínse, completing the circuit of the outer islands, except for the one we forgot, Oileán Mana, a dot of land two miles off to the east of Bior. Perhaps this is the essential island, there when you think of it, and not when you don't. Here is its legend, so brief it must be matter of fact, as recorded (in Irish) from a Seán Ó Donnchadha of An Aird Mhóir, the headland on the east of Caladh Fhínse, in 1933:

There is a little island called Oileán Mana in Cuan Chill Chiaráin. The old folk say that one day the daughter of Manannán Mac Lir was boating and a great storm came up, she was nearly drowned but when Manannán saw that she was in danger he made the island by his magic so that she got to land safe and sound. The island is there since and will be for ever.

What is it that comes into existence as you step into it and ceases to exist when you step out? The exact answer is your life, of course; but an island is an approximate answer, only slightly blurred by the aura of expectation extending before one's visit and of memory prolonging it. A little jaded from dipping into so many life-sites, we lay on the quay in the sunshine, and Seán sent Simon off to ask Catherine to come and collect us. I was unsure as to whether I should offer Pádraic money or not, and asked Seán to sound him out. Pádraic politely declined payment, saying, '*Ní dhéanfadh sé saibhir nó daibhir mé*' – 'It wouldn't make me rich or poor.' I was charmed by the grace of this refusal, and by its recourse to the ancient magic of the *so/do* (good/bad) prefixes in the Irish language. *Solas/dolas*, bright/dark; *soiléir/doiléir*, distinct/obscure; *soineann/doineann*, fair weather/stormy weather; *sólás/dólás*; solace/dolour . . . I could map all my island findings and feelings in such twinned opposites.

17 Sorrowful Mysteries

Carna's best and worst buildings lie to the east of the pub, Tigh Mheaic, along the road to Cill Chiaráin, in the townland of Roisín na Mainiach, the little point of the shrubbery. To the north of the road, the uninspiring tarmac deserts and one-storey boxes of an Údarás na Gaeltachta industrial estate. To the south, comfortably settled back behind screens of trees and with glimpses of the sea beyond it, the former convent, like a small country house – two storeys, hipped roof, central porch, round-headed fanlight over the door, two tall windows on either side and five above – but with a little square-towered chapel stuck onto one end. Its stones are of a time-worn grey, patched with lichen and moss. On one side of it is the primary school the nuns used to run, and on the other, Scoil Phobail Mhic Dara, the community school, successor to the nuns' secondary school; the old convent sits between them as sedately as a speckled hen among her ebullient brood of chicks. Visually at least, then, the north side of the road is the more attractive, but it hides its own doleful histories.

The convent was the local home of the Sisters of Mercy, an order founded in 1831 by Catherine McAuley of Dublin, which in contrast to the enclosed orders was engaged in social problems; it aimed to help educate the poor, run hospitals and orphanages and provide employment. In 1855 Dean MacManus of Clifden asked the order to open a convent there, to counteract the Protestant missionaries then rampant in Connemara, which they did, and the Carna foundation was initiated by three Sisters as an outlier of Clifden in 1874. In the following year John Yates, an eminent Catholic convert and solicitor from Liverpool, came to Connemara to find out what truth there was in the claims made by the Irish Church Mission Society that numerous Catholics had forsaken their faith, and what he found was reassuring. In Clifden the Sisters were running an infant school, a school for poor children, another for 'young ladies of good position in life' (the daughters of local tradesmen and merchants) and an orphanage, which had recently been registered as an industrial school. About 300 children were attending these institutions, which were all of 'apple-pie neatness' and full of happy youngsters whose physique and piety 'left nothing to be desired'. Of the Carna convent Yates writes:

It is the gift of the generous charity of Major Forbes, who gave not only a furnished house but also a car and horse, cattle, and twenty acres of land. The schools there are now being built chiefly through the exertions of Mrs Forbes, who is an active agent in collecting subscriptions amongst the leading Catholics in London.

But Carna was in much worse state than Clifden in those dreadful years that were soon to usher in the Land War. As the parish priest wrote in a letter to a newspaper at Christmas in 1879, this isolated community was many miles from a workhouse or even a relieving officer; it had 'no board of guardians, no town commissioners, no corporate board, no public body of any sort, to give employment, or raise a sympathetic voice in behalf of a naked and starving population'. Wet weather had ruined the turf trade, the potato crop was a disaster, the demand for kelp was so low that hundreds of tons of laboriously gathered seaweed were rotting by ditches and walls, and many people were not attending the chapel for lack of clothes.

The good Sisters of Mercy residing in the little temporary convent of Carna have within the last six weeks clothed 100 naked children attending their school. But I suppose twice or thrice that number applied in vain for garments to cover their naked and emaciated bodies; and surely, much as these poor children suffered bodily by not getting, the virtuous nuns suffered at least as much mentally by having to refuse, not having any more to give.

The priest went on to warn that if employment were not provided the people would, 'with the instincts and impulses of every living being, arise into anarchy and rebellion'. Part of Westminster's response to such pleas and to the violence that followed was the establishment of the Congested Districts Board, and one of the CDB's minor works was the establishment in conjunction with the convent of a lace-making school, which became a knitting factory when the lace trade fell away. Sadly, like other such schools in Connemara it mainly served to fund young women's emigration, the region being so dependent on remittances from the United States that sheer want persuaded families to export their female young.

By the time the convent closed in 2000 the very name of the Sisters of Mercy had acquired bitterly ironic resonances. Louis Lentin's TV documentary *Dear Daughter* had exposed the merciless regime of Goldenbridge Industrial School in 1996, and the Ryan Commission received many allegations of neglect and physical abuse from former inmates of the order's institutions. Thirty-three complaints concerned the industrial school and orphanage run by the Sisters in Clifden; the details of filthy conditions and scanty food given in the commission's subsequent report are sickening. This report lists no complaints about the Carna convent schools, and I have heard nothing of the sort from the ex-pupils I have spoken with, but their embittered memories suggest that in the early 1960s the educational regime was very antiquated – fear-driven rote-learning, punishment by ridicule and shaming, recreations restricted to long walks two by two in file, tedious retreats with endless Masses and confessions, favouritism shown towards the daughters of teachers or guards over those whose dads were off labouring for McAlpine in Britain, intrusive surveillance and lack of privacy. All this did not quite suppress high spirits: one girl, showing off a new nightdress to her friends in the dormitory, stuffed a pillow under it and waddled up and down as if pregnant; enter Sister Jarlath at that moment, and the following morning the miscreant had to go and knock on the big oak door of the convent itself and apologize to Reverend Mother.

Much of the housework of the old convent school was done by girls brought in from the now-notorious orphanage in Clifden, and I am told that these unfortunates were even more isolated than the school boarders. One of them ran away, and when she was caught her only plea to the Gardaí was that she should be returned to the orphanage, where her friends were, rather than to Carna. This was in about 1960; in later years conditions and practices improved. One person tells me she and her classmates attended the Irish-language summer school the nuns ran 'happily enough'; others are grateful to the order for opening the secondary school in the early 1960s and putting them forward for scholarships to such preparatory colleges as Coláiste Éinde in Galway. 'In homage to the good work done by the Sisters of Mercy in this district from 1874–2000, and especially the last three who were here: Sisters Pius McCanna, Angela Dempsey and Maria Collins,' reads (in Irish) the plaque attached to the convent gatepost. No doubt much good work was indeed done in the grandmotherly old building and its dependencies, but at present the memory of it is obscured by the fog of infamy issuing from the order's very name.

After the departure of the nuns the convent buildings and '*an Teic*', a former technical school a little further east, were taken over by Acadamh na hOllscolaíochta Gaeilge, a department of NUI Galway that provides third-level education through the Irish language, with a focus on community development and Gaelic culture. Since 1998 the old school has housed one of the academy's three outreach centres in Gaeltacht areas (the others are in An Cheathrú Rua and in Gaoth Dobhair in Donegal). Today in these rather ramshackle premises one finds busy classrooms with rows of computers, walls decorated with big bright paintings of Connemara landscapes, cupboards full of invaluable research material on the folklore and song tradition (including duplicates of all the items in the massive Joe Heaney archive that Sean Williams, Laurel Sercombe and others assembled in Seattle), another archive devoted to Seán Mac Giollarnáth and a third to a fine singer from this townland, Sorcha Ní Ghuairim, whose life's passion was the Irish language and the culture it bears and after whom the building is now named Áras Shorcha Ní Ghuarim. I shall have much to say about this rare person, who has become something of a feminist exemplar, and her pitiful death, hereafter; for now, I mention her name only as another hint of a theme, that of suffering womanhood, which I find emergent along the seaward side of this road. The convent itself is empty except for the smell of damp, behind which one can imagine the scent of beeswax and turpentine floor polish and a little glass of sherry for the bishop in the low-ceilinged reception rooms on either side of the hallway, and a must of thwarted femaleness and prayerful tedium in the little bedrooms upstairs. All this will change, it is hoped, when the building becomes a communal archival resource or perhaps a heritage centre, in a future that has suddenly been indefinitely postponed by the collapse of the economy.

Close by to the west of the former convent is the lodge, still known as *Teach an Mhajoir* from Major Forbes, the Catholic landowner who left his estate to the nuns, and remembered by the convent school pupils who had their dormitories in it simply as the Grey House. In January 1868 a curious incident took place in this grim-looking old building. According to press reports the Major's brother, Colonel Forbes, an elderly and ailing gentleman who was the local Justice of the Peace, narrowly escaped being murdered in his bed. A man with blackened face, wearing a long coat and old overalls to conceal the colour of his pantaloons, entered the house, sat with the servant maid for a time – she did not recognize him – and then ran upstairs and started to batter the Colonel with a stone in either hand. When the servant maid ran to her master's aid the intruder leaped through the window, sweeping the glass and sash before him; the maid caught his trouser leg, which tore away, and the man fell the height of two storeys to the ground and escaped. Since the newspaper reports mention that the Colonel had served ejectment notices on some of his tenants, it is clear that this attack was a forerunner of the violence of the Land War.

Local memory supplies a precise motive to the crime, and some folkloresque details, as shown by the version of the tale Seán Mac Giollarnáth published in 1932. The Colonel, it seems, did not get on with one Séamus Ghiolla who lived with his sister Bob in a little house nearby (just east of the present convent building), and decided to evict him. One night Bob dressed Séamus up in a fantastic garb made out of a black sail decorated with ribbons, and set ram's horns on his head. In this battledress he entered the lodge, attacked the Colonel, jumped out of the window, hid his weird get-up under a flat stone on the shore and went home. The Colonel survived, and must have penetrated Séamus's disguise, for he was arrested the next day and was put on trial. Although the Colonel asked the judge not to give his assailant a long sentence, he spent seven years in prison. During this time the Colonel's stables were burned down; Bob was tried for it and given a sentence of five years. Most of the rest of her life was spent working in Ballinasloe, where she was regarded as an excellent clothes-mender. Séamus, it seems, never returned to Roisín na Mainiach.

The lodge is empty nowadays, except for a few rooms used by FÁS, the national training agency, for some craft courses; in one room I saw an upturned, newly built rowboat that looked too big ever to be got out of it. It is a dismal, flat-fronted, three-storey building overlooking a blackish, peat-bottomed inlet called An Murlach, the lagoon. Most of its ground- and first-floor windows are blinded with concrete blocks, and its seven little irregularly spaced dormer windows have the gutter along the eaves passing in front of them. Like the convent, the lodge waits on its resurrection.

Walking on eastwards from the convent and its satellite buildings one finds the view of the many-islanded bay, Cuan Chill Chiaráin, opening wider and wider to the right. Narrow side roads or boreens run down to the shore through a mile-wide coastal zone of small stone-walled fields and a few scattered farmhouses; the third of these boreens, just over a mile beyond the Áras, is straight except for a slight kink to the right, halfway down, which would have alerted one's attention to the spot on the left it skirts around, even before the installation of a little white-painted iron gate in the wall there. Inside the gate are a tiny lawn and a sanded path, always neatly maintained, in an oval enclosure with the road wall on one side and a high privet hedge and some great boulders with montbretia flowering in their fissures on the other. Here is the best-known holy well of the Carna area, Tobar Muire. An almost life-size statue of the Virgin Mary in her sky-goddess blue and white presides over it, in a stone-built canopy at one end of the enclosure. There used to be a plaque – 'Erected to the honour of the Holy Mother of God 15 August 1949 by Morgan Mulkerrin Morgan and Reverend Gerald L. Burke' – but I could not find this on my most recent visit, in 2009.

The tale of the discovery of the well was told to me by an elderly man, Micheál Mac Donncha, whom I met there when exploring the neighbourhood in 1989. Thirteen lads were playing with a ball stuffed with horsehair there, and the ball knocked over a blind boy. He pulled on a tussock of grass to help himself up, the tussock came out of the ground, water flowed from the spot and he recovered his sight. There was a woman whose children were sick living in a house close by. (Micheál pointed out some stones of the foundations of this long-vanished house in the foot of the field wall opposite the enclosure; the family name, he said, was Ó Maoil Chiaráin.) She walked all the way to Bántrach Ard, near Cill Chiaráin, to her sister's house to ask her for milk for the children, but the sister closed the door against her for fear of the fever. Coming back she saw the Virgin Mary at the well, which was flowing with milk. After three days of drinking tea with this milk put through it the children were cured. Micheál went on to say that when the well was being consecrated (in August 1949, on the Feast of the Assumption), a snow shower carpeted a small area around it while the people were kneeling. And when Hurricane Debbie in 1961 knocked down the walls on either side of it and blew the water out of the nearby sea-inlet, the well was spared.

So the well is still a presence in the landscape, an emblem of the Earth's maternal charity. There was a young man kneeling at it the last time I passed. For me it harbours a secular mystery too, for this is a blind well; there is no spring here, just an accumulation of rainwater or dew in a hole in the granite bedrock – but the hole itself is remarkable. It is a cylindrical pothole like the ones I have described in Inis Ní, nearly a foot in diameter and two feet deep, and as smooth and regular as if it had been bored into the rock by a powerful machine. But the Inis Ní examples, like another thirty or more such holy wells I have been shown in south Connemara, are on the foreshore or only just above high-water mark, and the usual geological explanation of them – that they have been produced by a stone caught in a fissure and driven round and round by pounding waves over centuries – is at least credible. But this one is several metres above high-water level, I should think, and I know of another one, in Cladhnach near An Cheathrú Rua, that is a good deal higher. In general the sea has encroached on the land in Connemara since the last Ice Age, and so if these potholes were produced by wave action they pre-date that period; or if they were formed in riverbeds, perhaps those rivers were flowing under glaciers. That the world is explicable is miraculous, and so explanations need not be the undoing of miracles; but in this case I find the geologists' theories as unconvincing as the folklore.

The cult of Christ's sorrowing mother has always been strong in Connemara – there was much in everyday life that answered to it – and its supreme expression was, and is, the lament 'Caoineadh na Páise', 'The Keening of the Passion', now generally known as 'Caoineadh na dTrí Muire', 'The Keening of the Three Marys'. Sorcha Ní Ghuairim's singing of it could conjure tears out of granite. Each line of the poetic text is a slow swooning fall, each repetition of the refrain a low murmur of grief. It begins with Mary going out to look for her son:

> Is mithid dom dul chun an tsléibhe,
> *Ochón agus ochón ó!*
> Is mithid domsa m'aonmhac d'éagnach,
> *Ochón agus ochón ó!*
> Casadh Peadar de shiúl dhá lae dom,
> *Ochón agus ochón ó!*
> 'A Pheadair, a Pheadair, an bhfaca tú m'aonmhac?'
> *Ochón agus ochón ó!*
> 'Chonaic mé inniu é agus é gaibhte lena namhaid,
> *Ochón agus ochón ó!*
> Agus chonaic mé inné é faoí rópaí cnáibe.'
> *Ochón agus ochón ó!*

[It is time for me to go to the mountain, / It is time for me to mourn [?] my only son. / I met Peter after two days' walk. / 'Peter, oh Peter, have you seen my only son?' / 'I saw him yesterday taken by his enemies, / I saw him today in hempen ropes.']

She is seen by Christ on the Cross and converses with him:

> 'Cén bhean bhreá í seo i leith an fhásaigh?'
> *Ochón agus ochón ó!*
> ''Má tá bean ar bith ann sin í mo mháthair.'
> *Ochón agus ochón ó*
> 'Cén fear breá é seo i gCrann na Páise?'

Ochón agus ochón ó!
'Ní nach n-aithnionn tú d'aonmhac a bhí tú a iompar trí ráithe?'
Ochón agus ochón ó!

['What fine woman is that out in the wilderness?' / 'If it is any woman it is my mother.' / 'What fine man is that on the tree of the Passion?' / 'Do you not know your only son whom you carried for three seasons?']

In a version recorded from Máire Uí Cheannabháin, the famous Máire an Ghabha of An Aird Thoir, Mary tries to break through the guards and is manhandled by them:

Nár ghread sí a bosa agus d'éirigh sí 'n airde,
He mó chona 'gus móchon ó!!
An darna léim chuaigh sí trasna thríd an nGarda,
He mó chona 'gus móchon ó!
Nár crochadh suas í ar ghuaillí arda,
He mó chona 'gus móchon ó!
Nár buaileadh anuas í faoí leacrachaí na sráide.
He mó chona 'gus móchon ó!
'Muise, buailigí mé féin, ach ná bainí le mo mháthair!'
He mó chona 'gus móchon ó!
'Muise, maró' muid thú féin agus buailfidh muid do mháthair!'
He mó chona 'gus móchon ó!
'Muise, 'Mhicín mhúirneach, tá do bhéal 's do shróinín gearrtha.'
He mó chona 'gus móchon ó!

[Didn't she beat her hands together and rise up, / With the second leap she went through the guards, / Didn't they lift her up on high shoulders, / Didn't they throw her down under stones of the street. / 'Musha, let you beat me, but don't meddle with my mother!' / 'Musha, we'll kill you and we will beat your mother!' / 'Musha, my darling little son, your mouth and your little nose are cut.']

Finally, after contemplating each instrument of the Passion, she calls on help in keening her son:

'Níl éinne a chaoinfeas mé leat, a Mháthair.'
Ochón agus ochón ó
Nach geal í a leaba i bhFlaitheas na ngrásta.
Ochón agus ochón ó
Tháinig na trí Mhuire lena trí scread chráite.
Ochón agus ochón ó
'Caoinfear mé leat ar Oileán Phádraig.'
Ochón agus ochón ó

['There is no one with you to keen me, oh mother.'/ Is not her bed bright in the Heaven of grace. / The three Marys came with their three doleful wails. / 'I will keen you on St Patrick's Island.']

In 1975 a young PhD student in Irish, Angela Partridge (later Angela Bourke) heard this song from the seventy-year-old Máire an Ghabha, who knew it under the title 'Caoineadh na Páise', 'The Keening of the Passion'. Máire began to weep as she sang, and broke down on the line 'Muise, 'Mhicín mhúirneach, tá do bhéal 's do shróinín gearrtha.' 'I've gone as far as I can go,' she said; 'Wouldn't any mother be like that with her own son? "Caoineadh na Páise" wounds me deeply.' The experience moved Angela to undertake a profound study of the song, or rather of a group of closely related songs dealing with the Passion, in its local and regional variants, and to trace its roots in two traditions, that of the medieval cult of the Mother of Sorrows and that of the Celtic motif of the triple.

In hope of a glimpse into this rich and complex heritage one could begin by asking 'Who were the Three Marys?' Joe Heaney, who often sang this song, once identified them, with a great deal of hesitation, as 'Mary the Mother of God, Mary Magdalene, and Mary the mother of John and James'. But these three do not figure together in the Gospels; the women who St Mark tells us attended on the crucifixion, and on Sunday morning found Jesus's tomb empty, were Mary Magdalene, Mary the mother of James and Joses, and Salome (not the Salome of the notorious dance). And in European myth it is Mary Magdalene, Mary Jacobi and Mary Salome who sailed from Alexandria and landed on the shore of the Camargue at what is now

Les-Saintes-Maries-de-la-Mer. The relationship of the two last-named women to the three of St Mark's Gospel is or was a matter of tortuous speculations. There is a concocted history of three daughters of St Anna, all by different fathers and all called Mary – a learned genealogical fantasy that does not seem to have entered the Irish oral tradition. But triples of all sorts are omnipresent in Gaelic culture; Angela Bourke quotes a Danish folklorist to the effect that 'nothing distinguishes the great bulk of folk narrative from modern literature and from reality as much as does the number three'. Fodhla, Éire and Banba, the three tutelary goddesses of Ireland, are the supreme Irish example, and for a comparatively modern instance from Iorras Aintheach we have 'Amhrán Mhaínse', in which a dying woman lays it down that she is to be keened by 'three young women from the mountain'. Furthermore the theme of three persons with the same name is widespread in Celtic lands; the tripling of a personage lends him or her a superhuman force, it has been suggested. So, once the classical, dignified and restrained figure of the Mater Dolorosa, statuesque at the foot of the Cross, had been developed by the Middle Ages into a woman of flesh and blood in the extremity of grief, Gaelic culture was not only ready to incorporate but to triplicate her.

Máire an Ghabha learned 'Caoineadh na dTrí Muire' as a child from her grandmother, with whom she shared a bed, as part of a great store of religious songs and prayers; her grandmother made her rehearse them and would waken her with a kick if she fell asleep. Sorcha Ní Ghuairim had the song from her own family, but the version she is known for is based on a text published by Patrick Pearse in 1904. Pearse wrote of it:

This exquisite poem was written down at Feis Chonnacht [a cultural festival] from the recitation of Máire Ní Fhlannchadha (Mary Keady by marriage), from Drom a' Mhacháin, Moycullen. Máire's recitation of it was the finest thing seen or heard at the Feis.

This seems to imply that it was recited like a prayer; but a later (Irish-language) account by Pearse of this (or another) performance suggests it was sung:

It was a joy to listen to her singing the lament so wistfully and musically. Her pity for Mary and her Son was so great she shed tears while saying the verses that her hair and breast were wet. Do not be amazed by this, for the Passion of Christ is often keened tearfully by the Gaels.

And do not be amazed by the fact that Pearse thinks this song to be about the Passion of Christ rather than the Compassion of Mary; deep inside his train of thought the Gaels are being called upon to weep for Pearse himself.

As Angela Bourke remarks, Pearse's is the text one finds reproduced in collections of poetry and especially in schoolbooks, because of the prestige of his name in nationalist circles, because it is short, and because it is unobjectionable linguistically and doctrinally. Its publication and wide distribution was a step in the imposition of conformity on an art form that in its essence is based on a subtle commerce between the performer's faithfulness to tradition and his or her powers of spontaneous invention. Nowadays the tradition is not kept awake by kicks in bed; the concert platform and the singing competition exert a standardizing pressure on transmission of the heritage; the tape recorder and other devices of exact repetition mediate between the learner and a single and therefore authoritative utterance, rather than a lifetime of singing in varied moods and circumstances.

Sorcha Ní Ghuairim's life conceals its own passion, as a recent documentary film researched and presented by Ríonach Uí Ógáin has revealed. She was born in 1911, the youngest of eleven children of a Roisín na Mainiach farmer; she attended the convent school in Carna, and then, most unusually for her time, went on to University College Galway, where she studied under Professor Tomás Ó Máille, but left without taking her degree. She moved to Dublin, perhaps under the influence of Seán Beaumont, a Republican activist, worked as a teacher in a vocational school and then for Beaumont's Irish-language socialist periodical *An t-Éireannach*, translating into Irish news articles illicitly copied from the *Irish Press*. The premises of this courageous and short-lived publication were more like a Gaeltacht visiting house than a newspaper's offices, and the beautiful and passionately committed young Connemara girl with the dark hair and lovely singing voice

was a vivid presence there. She soon became the paid editor of the
newspaper, and later the Irish editor of the *Irish Press*. She 'lived on
her Gaelic nerves', it has been said; she spoke of English as a changeling
left in place of the living Irish language, and blessed her good fortune
in having heard some of the old folk before they left this life and in
having seen the heritage they bequeathed – 'although perhaps it was
ill-fortune to get a sight of a heritage that did not fully come into our
possession and that we would be missing for ever and for ever'. The
pathos of this glimpse of a lost treasure is expressed in her characteri-
zation of the old songs, in a talk she gave at the Oireachtas in Dublin
in 1943:

There is more than Irish words and twiddly little notes to Gaelic music . . .
There is loneliness in this music, loneliness of hill and glen and sea; there is
terror in it – the terror of death – there is weariness in it, the weariness of
the grave. It has every power that is associated with the music described in
the old stories – it would load you with sorrow, it would fill your heart with
pride, it would put your mind into a swoon, if it is but understood.

In 1941 Sorcha was appointed to a lectureship in spoken Irish in
Trinity College Dublin, where she left a profound impression on her
students, as the critic and translator Douglas Sealy later remembered,
on hearing of her death:

Sorcha was a person for whom Gaelic was a fairy lover, a lover nested in the
marrow of her bones and the blood of her heart. For her the sad state of
Irish was a nail in the quick. The long black hair, the lingering green eyes
behind dark lashes, the blood red of her lips and nails, the soft voice that had
sharpness and gentleness in it, even the endless smoking of cigarettes – it
seemed to us these were the very emblems of the Gaelic manner.

Sorcha was close to a number of men, including at one time the
poet Máirtín Ó Direáin. When a young colleague on *An t-Éireannach*,
Eamonn McGrotty, died fighting for the Republicans in Spain, she
wrote a controversial editorial in which she expressed her grief over
the loss of such men to the cause of Gaelic, the subtext of which was

probably her own personal loss. Then a sequence of disasters struck. Her relationship with Beaumont broke up, a young doctor she was in love with married someone else, she fled to An Cheathrú Rua for a while (where Charles Lamb painted her portrait) and then returned to Dublin. One evening she turned up at the home of her brother-in-law, the TD Seán Brady, in great physical and mental distress; the Gardaí were informed of an assault, and her flat was found to have been trashed. Soon afterwards she disappeared to London. Seán Brady's son Ciarán, interviewed in Ríonach Uí Ógáin's film, describes meeting her there and being shocked to see that the vivid young woman had become 'grey', that 'pain was etched on her features'. He speculates that she may have fled to London because she was pregnant through rape, and that if so she went through 'the most awful ordeal, on her own'. But Ríonach tells me that nothing is known for certain about the nature of the catastrophe in Sorcha's life; there may have been a number of reasons for her move to London, including despair over Ireland's neglect of its own language. Whatever the truth is, the subsequent quarter-century that Sorcha spent in Pimlico is lost in degradation and anonymity. She never returned to Ireland, or wrote home; she worked casually in bars, shunned company, and drank, sometimes to the point of incapability. It seems she was engaged in compiling a dictionary of Irish idiomatic phrases, but she lost a suitcase containing her archive in a railway station. She died of pneumonia, alone, in December 1976. It was three days before her body was discovered, and the police had difficulty in finding anyone who knew who she was.

Ochón agus ochón ó!

18 Profit and Loss

If the south side of the road through Roisín na Mainiach is under
the sign of woman, the north side must be under the sign of man
– and as such it is a disaster. An exception might be the playing field
opposite the convent, which was handed over to the state by the
Sisters of Mercy as part of their grudging contribution to the cost
of the redress scheme, under the notorious secret indemnity agreement so manfully negotiated by Sister Helena O'Donoghue on behalf
of the religious orders in 2002. Otherwise the roadside is a depress-
ing factoryscape. Even in its more hopeful days the Údarás na
Gaeltachta industrial estate hardly troubled itself over appearances
or the glorious vistas of bog and mountain it was obscuring from
the road, and now that hard times have returned it is badly neglected.
Some businesses in it are still alive if run-down, some are dead, others
half-and-half.

> Nuair a shiúlaimse síos ag an eastát sin thíos,
> Nuair a fheicim an áit is é folamh,
> Tagann meall ar mo chroí ag an ngeata i mo shuí,
> Is mé ag faire ar an ngrian ag dul i dtalamh.
> Ní dhéanaim aon ól mar níl a'am ach an dól,
> Is iomaí fear atá chomh maith liom a mhair air.
> Ach bíonn sé sách gann ag mo bhean is mo chlann,
> Is a líachtaí ní eile atá ag faire air.

[When I walk down to the estate down there, / And I see the place lying
empty, / I get a lump in my heart as I sit at the gate, / Watching the sun sink
into the earth. / I don't take drink since I only have the dole, / And many a
man as good as myself had to live on it. / But it is little enough for my wife
and my kids, / And the many other things that depend on it.]

A fair sample, this, of the songs of unemployment and emigration being composed these days in Connemara, written and sung in a style that owes more to country and western than to the traditional style, the *sean-nós*. There are songs of celebration too, of places, girls, local sporting and political heroes, in this new genre. For as Micheál Ó Conghaile, founder of the Connemara-based publishing house Cló Iar-Chonnachta, which preserves and disseminates these contemporary songs, has said, we have a totally different Connemara now:

Conamara an discó, an *rock an' roll*, an *chountry and western*, an *walkman* agus an chairíócaí. Conamara na *night clubs*, na *bpotholes*, agus na *mobile homes*. Conamara an bhingó, na *lotteries*, Conamara an chóca cola, na *hotels*, na *chippers*. . .

. . . a new world of cultural means and modes assimilated to various degrees (as the language of this quotation suggests) and subject to abrupt revisions; the Walkman has gone and the iPod has come since Micheál wrote that in 1993, while unemployment has both gone and come again. But this flux of novelty is surprisingly and indiscriminately miscible with the old ways as they have been revivified in recent decades: the traditional boat races, the local pilgrimages, the *sean-nós* singing and dancing. As he says, '*Uaireanta is ar éigean a aithnionn muid muid féin sa tranglam*' ('Sometimes we hardly recognize ourselves in the tangle').

Talking of tangles, beside the untidy back premises of the first of the factories, ACM (roofing contractors), a rubbish-choked path leads away from the road through gorse-bushes; at first it has a high fence on its right – a succession of concrete gallows and ravaged, drooping sheets of wire mesh – but eventually it frees itself from the miseries of failed industry and emerges onto the lonely but invigorating expanses of old turf-cuttings and ice-moulded granite mounds behind the estate. Turning eastwards, it approaches an area of more varied topography, with small hills of glacial deposits and winding sandy tracks and two many-islanded lakes, before rejoining the coast road a mile or so to the south-east of the convent.

The first of the lakes, Loch Síodúch, has a broad, hillocky and heathy headland on its eastern shore called An Chora Dhóite, the burned point, which used to be a favourite resort of the young; it was the place for hunting hares and for sailing toy boats, a sport I am told was taken extremely seriously. The path from beside the factory is known as Bóthar na Nuns, for the Sisters of Mercy used to take their prayerful strolls here, as in a vast conventual unenclosure. But nowadays if they were to complete the circuit they would have to witness another assault on the peaceful earth, for much of An Chora Dhóite and the lake shores south of it have been bared, bulldozed and blasted by over twenty years of gravel and rock quarrying. This is the muddy footprint the recent building boom has left on the earth, the clawmarks of the Celtic Tiger. I estimate that about a dozen acres of commonage have been expropriated and ruined by this example of private enterprise, which a recent court case found to have been a trespass. The judge ordered that some restoration work be done, and a bit of soil has been tipped here and there, but the place still looks like a prevision of some local Armageddon. Meanwhile the county council has post-facto registered some thirty-seven acres bordering on the two lakes as a quarry, without troubling itself about a gross non-compliance with its own Development Plan or requiring an Environmental Impact Assessment. The lakes themselves constitute Iorras Aintheach's prime archaeological site because of the crannógs that have been discovered in them, and some related shore-line sites may have been carted off for road-fill. Since I walk everywhere in Connemara I am inured to coming across its slovenly secrets in out-of-the-way places, but a vandalized signpost at the beginning of Bóthar na Nuns indicates that this particular tour of shame is part of Bealach na Gaeltachta, the long-distance walking route that is supposed to open up the beauties of the locality to the tourist. This little lakeland, so accessible from both Carna and Cill Chiaráin, might have been an asset to both communities; if development were needed, it could have been developed as an epitome of Connemara's natural history, with paths winding through bogland rich in wildflowers, and lake shores with wooden piers for the anglers or hides for bird- and otter-watchers. As it is, the common good has been looted, to immense private profit.

*

Loch Síodúch is the smaller of the two lakes here, and is separated by a narrow bridge of land from the other. The meaning of *síodúch* is unknown, but it is an ancient name, for in the *Books of Survey and Distribution* it is recorded that 'Carme 1 Cartron and Sydogh 1 Cartron', which belonged to a Jeffry Martin before the rebellion of 1641 and ended up in the hands of the great land-accumulator Richard Martin after the Restoration. ('Carme' is a misprint for Carna, and a cartron a measure of land.) The bigger lake is Loch na Scainimhe, anglicized as Lough Skannive, *scaineamh* being the gravel that attracted the exploiters. The lake stretches out into the boglands to the north-west for over a mile, and it is full of islands, three of which are known to be crannógs. In fact the main one, near the south-western corner of the lake, is one of the best-preserved island cashels in Ireland. These crannógs were first investigated by a British ornithologist, Edgar Layard (brother to Austen Henry Layard, the famous excavator of the ruins of Nineveh), who described them in the *Journal of the Royal Society of Antiquaries of Ireland* in 1897. He noted the fair uniformity of size of the stones with which their walls were faced, and surmised that such stones must have been broken to that size elsewhere for ease of transport or building, for it is not easy to find their like in the immediate locality. He also had an ingenious and picturesque suggestion as to how the walls and foundation platforms were built: during the summer months the stones were assembled on the shore, and then in winter when the lakes were frozen they were slid out across the ice; those for the foundations were gathered on the chosen spot and settled to the bottom when the ice melted.

The local name of the principal crannóg is Oileán an Bhalla, the island of the wall. (I learned this during my first explorations here in 1980, from Cailín an Phoist, the post-girl, a cheery little lady whom I used to meet here and there as I trudged the boreens. She was invariably helpful to me and I came to feel an affinity with her; we both carried bags through the rain.) Oileán an Bhalla is a roundish island about fifty feet across, edged by a tumbledown drystone wall a couple of yards thick and up to three yards high in places. Of particular interest is a small stone quay or dock on its northern side, for evidence of the relationship of the island as a dwelling place to the lake-shore territory that must have supported it would throw light on the modes of crannóg life. Traces of a stone jetty several metres long probably represent the corresponding landing place on the lake shore. Near it is a roughly circular layer of stones some ten metres across forming a little grassy island, which the Ordnance Survey map of 1839 shows as the tip of a peninsula; it is either a crannóg or perhaps a fishing platform. There is a similar platform near the western shore of Loch Síodúch too.

Also, close to the south-western point of Loch na Scainimhe there used to be what Layard was told were the graves of 'the people who built the Castle' (i.e. the main crannóg); these small hummocks were pointed out to me in similar terms in the 1980s, but it seems they have since been bulldozed aside. The other archaeological remains in this delicate lake-shore zone are either within the area registered as a quarry or so close to it that they would most likely be destroyed if further exploitation were to be allowed. This would be no small loss, as many questions about the date and purpose of the crannógs remain unanswered, pending detailed archaeological excavation.

Most crannógs were constructed of wood, but stone-built island cashels occur not only in Connemara but also in west Donegal and the outer Hebrides – all glacially scoured landscapes in which lakes would not have had silt beds deep enough to support the piles on which wooden crannógs were built in other regions. Some of them may date from late Bronze-Age times, when perhaps the growth of the bogs was persuading the natives into a lake-based lifestyle, but many may be a good deal more recent, like the island cashel of Ballynahinch, which was a regional power centre in the Middle Ages under the Uí Chadhla or Keeleys and then the O'Flahertys. Most crannógs were probably not defensive, except against wolves and cattle-rustlers, and their supporting economy would have been one of lake-shore cattle-rearing and crop farming; they were single-family domestic sites and, as Layard proposed, would have been roofed with timbers and thatch.

I remember a joyful August day in 1984 spent with the young fieldworkers of the Galway Archaeological Survey investigating crannógs in the two lakes. The local angling club had boats moored on Loch na

Scainimhe; we borrowed the padlock key to one of these, and a pair of oars, from an old man living nearby who had charge of them, and rowed out to the main crannóg, near the south end of the lake. We marooned two of our number there, Olive and Sheila, to measure it up in detail, and the expedition's leader Mike Gibbons and I rowed up the lake to look at another of Layard's crannógs. The lake was very calm, faintly furrowed by an otter swimming away ahead of us. The crannóg turned out to be a tiny island that looked weighted down by an enormous split granite boulder incorporated in its otherwise slight and ruinous wall. The island was very overgrown and to survey it we had to leap to and fro across the cleft in the boulder. This was a highly technical task involving a lot of larking about and admiring the view, in which all colours were rendered psychedelically intense by the late summer sunshine. To the west the far-off crenate silhouette of Erris-beg Hill showed thundercloud-blue over the lake's low, gold-green banks; the burnished bronze cone of Cashel Hill seemed to rise directly out of the levels of bog to the north, with the huge, vague embrace of Gleann Chóchan in the Twelve Pins immediately behind it. Towards the end of the lake we could make out Crompán na bPeelers, haunted by two policemen, McBride and Gloucester, who I am told were drowned while fishing in the lake when their boat sank under them; they once appeared to a man on the run, warning him not to turn up at a certain house that night as it was to be raided, which it was, and they have also been seen by poitín makers.

All this took longer than we had expected, and by the time we came back to rescue them the others were getting fractious (and then we found we had left the Survey's valuable thirty-metre tape measure behind us). Next Olive and I were detailed off to explore a clutter of islands to the west, and the third of these turned out to have a substantial wall round it – a new discovery, we thought, but it transpires Layard was there before us. I stood on the highest point of it and bellowed across the intervening islands to Mike, 'A crannóg!' 'Do it!' came the faint reply. The island was sixty or seventy yards long and half that across, and its wall was very ruinous but in parts stood to four or five feet. We measured it wearily but meticulously, ignoring cries of 'Hurry up!' and great splashings that told us the others were bathing. Then we collected them from the main crannóg and returned the boat to its moorings.

I wanted to question an old neighbour of the boat-keeper about the various islands, so I shouldered the oars and marched off ahead with them; I was bursting with energy in those days. The neighbour was very friendly and full of information. The main crannóg, he confirmed, is called Oileán an Bhalla, the island of the wall; the one in the north of the lake is An Chraoibhín, which I later realized meant the crubeen or trotter, which is what it looks like with its cleft boulder; and the long island is Oileán an Chaca, the island of the shit – why so, he could not or would not say. Then the rest of the party caught up. The old man asked us to get him a *buidéilín trí ghloine fuisce*, a three-glass bottle of whiskey, from a pub in Cill Chiaráin, so I sent them off on this errand while I patted his mental pockets for further information. To prompt him to deliver any *seanchas* he might have about Oileán an Bhalla I asked him if he knew how old it was, and he replied immediately that it was 2,012 years old. This exactitude puzzled me at the time and I could not get out of him how he came to know this with such certainty. Much later it occurred to me that some knowledgeable visitor, perhaps an archaeologist, must have passed by twelve years previously and casually remarked something like, 'You know, that place down there is two thousand years old!'– and my old friend, as custodian of local lore, had been totting up the passing years ever since.

19 Saving Father Miley

Having picked up the name Oileán an Bhalla from Cailín an Phoist I was interested to come across a mention of it, in crudely anglicized form, in connection with the rebel priest Father Myles Prendergast, of whom 'it is said that he spent a short time on his keeping in Illaunavolla'. This occurs in Richard Hayes' book *The Last Invasion of Ireland*, on the 1798 rising and its aftermath. Father Miley, as he was called, was an Augustinian friar who joined the French forces soon after their landing in Mayo, was imprisoned after their defeat by the British army, and escaped to Connemara along with many others implicated in the rising. In *The Last Pool of Darkness* I describe his desperate life as a hunted outlaw throughout north Connemara and his pitiful end near Clifden, but one of his misadventures is so woven into the folklore and topography of Carna and Cill Chiaráin that it fits in naturally here. Hayes had his version of the tale from Seán Mac Giollarnáth, who heard it from two or more of his local sources, but for some reason the detail about the crannóg was omitted from Mac Giollarnáth's own book *Annála Beaga*.

At the time of these events Humanity Dick Martin, as landlord, Member of Parliament and chief of the armed forces stationed at Ballynahinch, was the representative of the Protestant hegemony, but his heart was with the Catholic cause, and when his efforts to arrange a pardon for the priest came to nothing he advised him to take refuge in the obscurities of Iorras Aintheach. At first Fr Miley stayed with a tenant of Martin's, a John Lockhard (of whom I have been able to learn nothing more), in Glinsce, and then moved to Carna, further away from Ballynahinch. Lockhard had advised the priest to look after the small people and avoid the great, but it was the middle sort who betrayed him in Carna. A Liam Barra had the first shop in Carna, and a stillhouse. At first he was friendly towards Fr Miley, but then he decided to make money out of him, for there was a price on his head.

One day when Fr Miley was drinking in Barra's, and perhaps had had too much drink, Barra locked him in a room and sent for the yeomen from Ballynahinch. A servant girl saw what was happening, and she alerted a man called Séamas Nápla Mac Donnchadha, who broke in a window and liberated the priest. By then the yeomen had reached a place called Idir Dhá Loch, between two lakes, less than a mile north of the village.

Fr Miley ran off down to the shore. The tide was out and there were two big hookers dried out on the foreshore at the foot of the river east of Carna, and one of their anchors gave him a bad gash on the shin. He struggled on until he came upon a man called Ó Fatharta tending a kelp kiln on the shore of Roisín na Mainiach. By then the yeomen were within sight. Ó Fatharta persuaded the priest to take off his coat and coroline hat and hide under the seaweed while he drew off the chase. (According to the story as I heard it from Bairbre Bean Mhic Dhonncha of Loch Conaortha in about 1982, Ó Fatharta said that he was nearing death in any case and therefore it wouldn't matter so much if he were caught instead of the priest – a consideration that raises difficult moral questions neither of them would have had time to ponder just then.) Ó Fatharta put on the priest's coat and hat and ran off, through Cill Chiaráin and as far as Ros Dúgáin, a small headland in the next townland, Coill Sáile, a distance of over six miles. There he went into a house where the family were sitting around a basket on the floor eating their meal. When he heard what was afoot, the man of the house told Ó Fatharta to sit down with them while he hid the coat and hat. Soon the soldiers arrived, demanding to know if a man in dark clothing had been seen. The man of the house said that he had seen such a man hailing a boat to take him across the bay to Béal an Daingin, which is five miles away in Na hOileáin. The soldiers carried on up the coast as far as Inbhear, on the boundary of Ros Muc, but couldn't get a boat to take them across the bay; nor did they hear any news of Fr Miley. In the meantime the priest had escaped by boat to Na hOileáin, where he stayed for a short while and then returned to Carna until his leg mended (and it is at this stage of his travails that he may have hidden out on Oileán an Bhalla) before moving to the Clifden area, where he became recognized as the parish priest. From this adventure the descendants of the Mac Donnchadha who liberated Fr Miley were long known by such names as Colm an tSagairt, Colm of the priest. The Ó Fatharta man who bravely donned the priest's coat had to move with his family to Cois Fharraige, but his daughter married into An Aird Thoir, and her son was the famous strongman Seán an Chóta, Seán of the coat.

Trying to imagine Ó Fatharta's heroic scamper, I turn to the Ordnance Survey map of 1839; this is perhaps twenty or thirty years later than the event, but earlier maps show little or no detail of settlement or terrain. The tide was out, so if he ran along the foreshore he had a fine sandy tract to cross in Caladh Fhínse to begin with, but east of that, around An Aird Mhóir, the big point, he would have had to negotiate ankle-breaking rock banks and awkward cliffy edges like Aill na bhFreangach, the cliff of the spotted dogfish. Further on, a serious retardant would have been the slimy mounds of rotting seaweed in inlets such as An Crompán Bréan, the stinking creek, below the village of Aill na Brón. I know these obstacles in my bones, having once forced my way along this stretch of coast in a wintry gale that several times brought me to an exhausted stop, during my obsessive attempt to understand Connemara through the soles of my boots; so I can empathize with Ó Fatharta. If on the other hand he cut overland I see from the old map that there was no road and the few boreens there were answered only to the local needs of the sparse scatterings of hovels he might have passed through, and between which he would have been crossing half-cutaway bog interrupted here and there by knots of field walls. It is possible to sympathize with the yeomanry too, hopelessly chasing resistants through the social and physical labyrinths of a hostile countryside. I shall follow the general trend of Ó Fatharta's course with an eye to what is new and what is unchanged around this corner of Iorras Aintheach.

First of all there is one great enterprise that has come and gone since the time of Ó Fatharta's marathon: the Irish Waste Land Improvement Society. In about 1845 – a year of 'distress', soon to be recognized as the onset of famine – this company acquired various townlands belonging to the Lynches of Barna: An Aird Mhóir, Cill Chiaráin, Coill Sáile and Loch Conaortha along the coast, and inland of them the virtually uninhabited 'mountain' areas, Loch an Bhuí, Seanadh Mhac Dónaill, Beitheach Chatha and Gabhlán Thoir. Their plan was to let smallholdings on terms that would lead to the reclamation of the land:

A settler taking land under the Society, on this estate, has little or no rent to pay for the first three years, for although the nominal rent may be 3s. or 4s. an acre, rising progressively to 10s. or 15s., the allowances at starting are so considerable, that they amount to far more than the rent. In the first place he is allowed £2 per acre for reclamation; next comes £1 for draining; £2 worth of timber and lime for a house; 2s. per perch, for stone fences; 1s. per perch for farm roads: so that the balance of cash is for some time in his favour, while seed is issued to him on loan, to be repaid on sale of his crop. The quantity of corn has increased fourfold, since the property came into the possession of the Society, a period of only four years, during which time, the returns of corn alone have risen from 20 to 80 tons.

This hopeful and benign scenario is from a pamphlet entitled *Remedy for the Impending Scarcity, suggested by a visit to the Kilkieran Estate of the Irish Waste Land Improvement Society*. George Preston White, who quotes this pamphlet in his *A Tour of Connemara*, published in 1849, goes on to say that the society had reclaimed 18,000 acres of waste land for an outlay of £25,000 – but if that is the case it was not on this estate, which amounts to about 9,500 acres only and shows little or no sign of widespread reclamation. The Famine, returning year after year and so acquiring its capital letter, must have swept away this initiative, for Griffith's *Valuation of Properties* shows that by 1855 the lands were back in the hands of the Lynches.

The 'mountain' part of the townland of Cill Chiaráin rises to 552 feet at An Bhinn Bhuí, the yellow peak, which with the hill of Leitir Calaidh two miles off to the east forms a gateway to Cuan Chill Chiaráin; nothing has changed in that grand topography since Ó Fatharta's day. The village below the peak is Aill na Brón, and if that name means, as Seosamh Ó Cuaig suggested to me, the cliff of the great wave, then it is still the same wave that beats on its steep granitic seafront. The Ó Cuaig or Cooke family themselves have been here for some generations and, perhaps through a marriage relationship with the Lydons of Carna, were a family of some standing locally; it was an Ó Cuaig who installed Beartla Ó Clochartaigh as his steward on the island of Bior. Passing along the road one notices a cluster of houses half hidden in trees down by a point of the seashore, fronted by a rather imposing but derelict two-storey building where the 1839 map marks a police station; this is Cora na gCúg, Cookes' point.

These days the brothers Ó Cuaig have houses up by the road. I have mentioned Seosamh's youthful part in the Gaelic civil rights movement and his current status as an independent county councillor. Micheál is a teacher and a poet. He was one of the founders of the Joe Heaney festival, and took up the post of resident *sean-nós* singer in NUIG in 2007. The title poem of his early collection, *Uchtóga*, is a tender reminiscence of gathering *fiontarnach*, the masses of dying *Molinia* grass that turn the hillsides purple in autumn, with his parents, on the eve, one senses, of some life-changing decision. This poetry – allusive and subjective, in the modernist vein stemming from Máirtín Ó Direáin and Seán Ó Riordáin – is far from that of the *sean-nós*; but an *uchtóg*, a measure of straw or the like, is as much as one can gather between arms and breast (*ucht*), and Micheál has gathered the tradition to his heart with the same gesture.

This area, An Aird Mhóir and Aill na Brón, was as notable as An Aird Thoir for its singers and storytellers. The greatest of the latter was Éamonn a Búrc, born in 1866. His family emigrated to the States when he was a child, but after he lost a foot in an accident while working on the railroads he had to return. His disability did not impair his enthusiasm for life and his art; he learned to tie his crutch under his armpit, and could cut turf or even leap a wall with ease, and when out lobster-potting in his little boat he loved to break off from the work in hand to race with the boats going out to Aran with turf. But no doubt his lameness played a part in his taking up the trade of tailor and drawing the village to his house by his apparently limitless store of stories. He saw himself as a link to the lost old days. To Liam Mac Coisdeala, who recorded material from him on Ediphone cylinders for the Folklore Commission which when transcribed amounted to over 2,000 pages of manuscript, he said, 'That's all very well, but if you'd been around here fifty years ago a horse and cart wouldn't be enough to carry all the lore away with you.' One of his traditional stories, 'Eochair, A King's Son in Ireland', took three evenings to tell and is said to be the longest oral narrative ever taken down; I've never been able to get through it, but as the great folklorist Séamus Ó Duilearga has said, 'The art of the folktale is in its telling; it was never meant to be written nor to be read. It draws the breath of life from the lips of men and from the applause of the appreciative fireside audience.' So, what we can experience of the art of an Éamonn a Búrc is to the full expression of it as a pressed herbarium specimen is to the wild-flower blooming in the hedgerow.

Cill Chiaráin today is a rather compact and shapely village, but when the breathless Ó Fatharta passed through it was just a peppering of a score of cottages mainly on the headland between the present harbour and the shallow bay just north of it called Boat Harbour or An Crompán Mór; there were no services or public buildings, and nothing existed on the sites of the present-day centre of gravity of the village or the busy harbour and substantial quay below it. A Fisheries Report of 1836 observes that 'the boats and nets in Kilkerrin district are generally out of repair, owing to the poverty of the people'. At that period rowboats and five- to twelve-ton hookers were used, with nets of locally grown flax; there were abundant fish, but since the nearest road was five miles away there was no market. Development of the fishery had to wait upon the coming of the CDB in the 1890s.

The burial ground and two antiquities, the holy well and ruined church of St Ciarán, are the only features common to the map of 1839 and those of today. The burial ground has expanded from an irregular little plot on the hillside above the village to a large, orderly rectangle sloping up from the modern roadside. The well is reached by grassy paths through heather and brambles above this cemetery; its ancient, oval, stone-lined bowl has been uglified by concrete paving of the D-shaped enclosure around it and the shoddy, old-fashioned fencing of moulded concrete units fronting it. A tall cross of plain white-painted timbers on the hillside above invites one to climb a steep path between hazel thickets, illuminated by wildflowers – purple loosestrife, devil's-bit scabious, bird's-foot trefoil, St Dabeoc's heath, all the everyday wayside charmers. There by the cross is the church, long reduced to a low, featureless mass of stone shrouded in arching bracken fronds; it measures about four yards by three, and at its base perhaps a course or two of masonry can be made out. It is known locally simply as Leaba Chiaráin, Ciarán's bed; the saint is said to have come by here, having got lost on his way to his novitiate in St Enda's famous monastery in Árainn (from which he went on to his great foundation of Clonmacnoise).

This little resting place on the flank of the hill (An Bhinn Bhuí, the yellow peak, which rises to just over 500 feet and begins the chain of heights that runs northwards from here and forms the spine of Iorras Aintheach) is the ideal viewing and listening post for the village. The bright white and cream-washed houses crowd along the road running north, past the modern community hall, the plain little chapel and the premises of the fish-farming cooperative. Nearer at hand a crossroads, from which a side road climbs and winds inland and the harbour approach road falls to the shore, is dominated by a bar and restaurant, Tigh Chadhain. Seawards are a dozen or so black-hulled *púcáin* lying at anchor, all facing into the flowing or ebbing tide; further out, a few little islands, some miles away the low hills of Leitir Móir and the rest of Na hOileáin, and a limitless hinterland of clouds and mountains. From the harbour, where lots of half-deckers and wooden currachs are clustered along the broad concrete pier, one hears the beeping of a truck reversing, probably into the huge, hangar-like store of the seaweed factory, Arramara, that, together with the fish farming, is the source of Cill Chiaráin's prosperous look.

The concocted name 'Arramara' is supposed to suggest the Irish *earraí mara*, goods of the sea, I was told by one of the enterprise's original directors, the late Donald Robb of Cashel. When Ó Fatharta was making kelp in the early 1800s I doubt if he sold it in Cill Chiaráin; it probably went into Galway by boat. But in the CDB era, when the harbour had begun to be developed, there was a kelp agent here, running a business that can be seen as a forerunner of Arramara. From Cill Chiaráin, as from Cashel and similar focal points of many other shorelines, the kelp would be shipped by schooner to iodine factories in Argyle. Kelp-makers and kelp agents were engaged in an ongoing struggle for advantage; the kelp was sold by weight, and if it could be adulterated with stones or sand in such a way as to evade detection, so much the better; also the agent would test it chemically, and as some types of seaweed, the sea-thong for example, contributed great weight to kelp but did not contain as much iodine as others, 'you would try to have it in a part of the kelp that wouldn't be tested', as an old Aran man once explained to me. On the other hand the agent could act very arbitrarily in refusing a load of kelp, and there was no possibility of the sellers checking his weights or his chemical abracadabra. J. M. Synge, in the compassionate reports from the 'distressed areas' he wrote for the *Manchester Guardian* in 1905, criticized the CDB for not assuring the kelp-makers a fair market:

In some places the whole buying trade falls into the hands of one man, who can then control the prices at his pleasure, while one hears on all sides of arbitrary decisions by which good kelp is rejected, and what the people consider an inferior article is paid for at a high figure. When the buying is thus carried on no appeal can be made from the decision of one individual, and I have sometimes seen a party of old men sitting nearly in tears on a ton of rejected kelp that had cost them weeks of hard work, while, for all one knew, it had very possibly been refused on account of some grudge or caprice of the buyer.

More recently the principal value of seaweed has been as a source of alginates, for use as thickening agents in cosmetics, foodstuffs, paints and other products. Alginate Industries (Ireland) Ltd was set up in 1947 and renamed as Arramara in 1955; it was a limited company in which the state held a large majority of the shares, and bought out the other investors, ISP Alginates of Scotland and California, in 2006. At first the old pattern of shipment to Scotland still obtained; a little freighter would come from Girvan for it once or twice a month (and I am told that a taxi-load of Galway prostitutes would be driven out to meet it). Nowadays the seaweed meal product is transported by container lorry to Larne and thence by sea to Scotland.

When I first visited Arramara in 1979 a billowing cloud of steam was drifting out across the bay from its chimney, where the *St Ronan* was being loaded with bags of the end product. There was seaweed heaped everywhere on the road to the quay, and a dumper was loading it into a hopper from which it was fed onto a steep conveyor belt and hosed down before travelling on to the factory shed. Inside – one could wander in at will in those days – the air was full of a salty reek. Two long kilns the size of railway engines, rotating slowly on oily cogs, occupied almost all the space. Every now and then someone appeared and sauntered around looking at dials. I peeped through small windows in the front of one of the kilns and glimpsed its axis of flame and the streams of sparks like glowing chaff streaming down its length. I·sought out the technical chief, Mr MacIntyre, and, in a rush between consulting clocks and taking steaming beakers out of a heater, he told me that they handled a thousand tons a year of sea-rods, the stems of *Laminaria*, a deep-water seaweed. I was very familiar with the sight of sea-rods hung over walls to dry in the Aran Islands, or in stacks awaiting the arrival of Fear na Slata Mara, the sea-rod man, from Cill Chiaráin to collect and pay for them every spring. But since the supply of sea-rods was dependent on the autumn and winter storms to cast them ashore, it was highly unpredictable, and so that business has fallen away. Nowadays the seaweed used is *Ascophyllum*, the knotted wrack known locally as *feamainn bhuí* or yellow-weed. The slipshod old factory has been demolished and replaced by a more modern one, access to which is no longer such a casual matter, and the heaps of seaweed in the road are gone. About twenty are employed in the factory, and the part-time seaweed gatherers supplying it number 250. A declining proportion of the milled and dried end-product, Titan seaweed meal, goes to the Scottish alginates firm nowadays; instead, it is used as animal and poultry feed, as soil conditioner, and as shrimp feed in aquaculture. As I learn from Arramara's glossy brochure, it is organic, rich in minerals, trace elements and vitamins, its source is self-renewing and purified by tides twice a day, and it is in every way a good thing. The only phase of this globalized and automated industry Ó Fatharta, the kelper of two centuries ago, would have recognized is the sheer muscle-work of wrenching wet weed off the rocks, and this too, as I saw in the marine research laboratory in Carna, may be superseded by seaweed farming and mechanical harvesting.

A mile north of the village of Cill Chiaráin my fugitive Ó Fatharta would have crossed a stream now called Abhainn an Mhuilinn, the river of the mill; but the corn mill (long derelict and roofless, up a boreen to the west of the road) was built around the middle of the nineteenth century, and so he would have known it by its alternative name, Sruthán na Teorann, the boundary stream. Beyond it we are in the townland of Coill Sáile, saltwater wood, and the landscape is dramatically different as the great ridge of Cnoc Mordáin rears up ever more steeply on the inland side of the road. Ó Fatharta turned aside here onto a little headland, Ros Dúgáin, Duggan's point, entered one of the very few cottages on it and, so far as the pursuing yeomanry could see, vanished. They pressed on northwards to the sea-inlet or *sáile* from which the townland is named – a severe obstacle in those days, a narrow but deep channel opening out into a muddy lagoon half a mile inland under a slope strewn with enormous boulders fallen from a precipice. These heaped boulders are known as An Ábhach, the lair, and highwaymen once lurked among them to prey on way-farers, according to some lore retailed in *Annála Beaga*; also, an inlet just south of the head of the lagoon is called Crompán Thaidhg na Buile, and the bogeyman-tyrant of Ard Castle is said to have played the robber here.

The first bridge over the inlet, named in honour of the parish priest Fr Flannery, was built in 1887; its stone piers and girders lasted well, but its six-foot-six width was a bottleneck to modern traffic. A proposed new bridge of several spans had to be abandoned when strong tidal currents repeatedly swept away the temporary works for the foundations and two lots of subcontractors pulled out of the job, but in 1954 the construction of an elegant and slender single-span bridge was achieved. At fifty-two metres, it was in its day the longest span of pre-stressed concrete in either Britain or Ireland, I was told by the late Professor Seán de Courcy, whose company, BCR Engineering, together with Messrs Nicholas O'Dwyer and Partners, drew up the final design. A man of infinite anecdote, Seán also liked to recall an incident at the opening of the new bridge: just as the great moment arrived an old man in a donkey cart came rattling down the way and headed across the bridge, and the hoofbeats evidently tickled its resonant frequencies so that it began to sway in time to them, to an extent that alarmed the assembled worthies. Perhaps this was an omen: the second Flannery Bridge did not last the hundred years that had been expected of it. When cracking and spalling was detected in 1995 a temporary bypass had to be provided, and in 1999 a third Flannery Bridge was built, a no-nonsense, arrow-straight affair of concrete beams and reinforced concrete deck, on two moulded concrete piers, bifurcated like elephantine boxer shorts.

Lacking this amenity, the yeomen of Ó Fatharta's day must have floundered around the head of the lake; there was a possible crossing place where the narrow inlet opens out into the lagoon, but by this time I think the tide would have been too high for it to be fordable. Just over a mile further on in the townland of Loch Conaortha they would have faced another obstacle, a short stream that flows out of a sizeable lake into Crompán an Locha, the inlet of the lake. I part from them here and turn inland, while they go blundering on through extremely wet bogs between the steeps of Cnoc Mordáin and the stony coastline, to Inbhear, where they finally give up the chase.

20 The Wizard

Who was Mordán? I have seen on a hill-climbers' website a suggestion that he might be the Welsh wizard Myrddin, out of whom the twelfth-century historian Geoffrey of Monmouth concocted the Merlin of Arthurian legend; but Merlin hardly figures in Irish mythography. The anonymous geologist I quoted when writing about the bogs north of Inbhear records a legend he must have picked up locally about the huge boulder Cloch Choirill:

It was the plaything of a Celtic hero, Corril, who crushed his finger and left the mark in the hollow stone, when he threw it from Mam Turk at Mordan, the father of Goll MacMorna, who stood on his own hill about ten miles off.

This Goll was the great rival of Fionn Mac Cumhaill, and the father of 1,500 sons, but of his own father all I can find is the name Morna. Mordán also figures in a tale that is meant to explicate the name of Loch Conaortha, which I heard from Bairbre, the wife of Pádraic Mac Donncha, a retired schoolmaster, both of them knowledgeable sources of lore. According to this story, Mordán had a herdsman with a fierce dog. When St Ciarán came by, mistaking the way to the Aran Islands, the dog leaped at him, the saint ducked, and the dog flew over his head and plunged into the lake, where it drowned. Hence: Loch Con Aoire, the lake of the hound of the herdsman. None of this satisfies my curiosity about the elusive and intriguing figure of Mordán; nevertheless as I approach the northern limits of Iorras Aintheach I will call on him to magic me out of this Land of Voices.

The long scarp of Cnoc Mordáin rears up immediately inland of the lake, gradually at first and then increasingly steeply, like a vast wave of rock; one could imagine it cresting and crashing down onto the houses scattered along the coast road. Its granite face is deeply weathered into scores of vertical ribs that look rather like the basaltic pillars of the Antrim coast; the local name for these is Na Snáthaidí, the needles. There are some broader gullies called Na hEascachaí, the ravines or gullies, among them, which carry a bit of grass on slopes too severe for anything other than goats or birds; a prominent one above the lake is called An Easca Chaol, the narrow gully; another, further north, I recorded rather ungrammatically as Easc an Ghlasóg, the gully of the pied wagtail.

Pádraic Mac Donncha gave me the names of the various heights overlooking the lake. To its west is An Ghualainn Bhuí, the yellow shoulder. The cliffy slope north-west of the lake is An Anacair; the word has connotations of roughness and difficulty, and in Connemara means a rugged, stony, dangerous place. North of the lake is Binn an Ghabhair, the peak or gable of the goat, with a prominent ravine running down it, Easca Bhinn an Ghabhair. Further along the ridge to the north-east is Binn an Duine, the gable of the person; *duine* is sometimes a euphemism for *duine marbh*, dead person, and here it refers to an eighteen-year-old lad who fell from it, having leaned out too far in throwing a stone at a goat on the cliff-face.

The ascent that avoids all these terrors, though it is steep enough, is an old way, or the after-image of one, alongside a stream that falls to the lake from a dip in the skyline between An Ghualainn Bhuí and An Anacair; the dip is Béal an Mháma, the mouth of the mountain pass, and the old way is called Cosán an Railway, because the Loch Conaortha men used to go this way to work on the building of the Galway–Clifden railway in the 1890s. The easier descent on the other side of the pass, and four or five miles of hill- and bog-walking, would have brought them out of Iorras Aintheach to Cashel, and a few miles more to, say, Ballinafad, if they happened to be employed on sledge-hammering and blasting cuttings through the rocky hillocks of that neighbourhood. For myself, I will follow the ridgeline north-eastwards from the saddle point of the pass, and then in reminiscent/expository mode make an immense circuit through half a dozen uninhabited townlands on the western slopes of the hill.

As one climbs from the top of the pass to the rounded summit above An Anacair, which at 1,164 feet is the highest point on the ridge, with the sea and the tangled fringes and tassels of south Connemara at one's back, the depths of central Connemara come into view ahead. This is a sight one has to watch like a film rather than look at like a painting, it is so responsive to the fickle moods of the Atlantic cloudscapes flowing above it. There is a little lake below in a lap of the hill: Loch na Brocaí, the lake of the badger's den. It empties through a stream falling northwards to the wide lakeland plain that almost insulates Iorras Aintheach from the outer world; when I first saw it, says my diary, it was pouring itself out like tea for the Twelve Pins, which sat around companionably in armchairs beyond the plain. On that day I almost tumbled down the northern end of the ridge, leaning against its steep slant and taking giant, soggy strides, into the knot of fields around the village of Doire Iorrais. This is one of the prettiest villages of Connemara, its houses tucked away among enough trees to justify the *doire*, wood, in its name, thanks to the sheltering mountainside. (Since there is no peninsula in the immediate locality I think the *iorras* refers to Iorras Aintheach as a whole, to which the village is a north-eastern gateway.) But for this present writing I turn the other way, down past Loch na Brocaí into Gabhla, which occupies the north-western corner of the peninsula.

Two rivers form the boundaries of this townland: the Gabhla Mór, flowing out of what the anglers call the Gowla Lake, out on the lakelands to the north, and the Gabhla Beag, which originates as a streamlet high in the pass of Cnoc Mordáin; coming from far apart, they almost meet before falling into neighbouring inlets of Cuan na Beirtrí Buí, and perhaps it is the *gabhal* or fork of which these inlets are the prongs that gives the townland and the little settlement of Gabhla around the mouths of the streams their names. All the mountain-land extent of Gabhla and the townlands south of it used to be open countryside, but now it is patched with forestry and there are some annoying fences across it, too high to step over. How do I treat these? If no stile is provided, the barbed wire implicitly says, 'No trespassers'. But if there were no such prohibitions there would be no such thing as trespassing. So I can do the landowner a favour by ignoring his fences. And thus, by logical wizardry, I find myself on the other side of the fence.

In Gabhla lives Máirtín Ó Catháin, a journalist in print and on radio who, as he puts it himself, does 'bits of community work'. He and I have known each other for years; he occasionally phones me in search of news and the rumours of news, but I think he disapproves of my stance on two or three issues that have seemed to pose a conflict between the preservation of Connemara's naturalness and the development needed to mitigate its endemic unemployment. However, Máirtín summarizes our relationship with the old saying *'Tuigeann Tadhg Taidhgín'*, 'Tadhg understands Taidhgín'; and we get along on friendly terms without worrying who is which.

I met him by appointment recently for a summer day's ramble over the hills he has known all his life, hoping, for my part, to see them anew. Máirtín's house is an expansion of the original small family farmhouse, and is protected from the winds off the bay by dense plantings of the yellow-flowered *Senecio* bush, daisy trees and roses, all growing interlocked and trimmed into tall ramparts above low, mossy stone walls and tunnel-like paths. He has a smallholding that has been in his family for a couple of centuries at least and farms it 'as a mark of respect to past generations'. He keeps some cattle and would like to run some sheep as did his forebears, but does not have a quota for them. We headed up the fields behind his house and crossed a wall out onto the boggy commonage. He named various low hills for me: Cnoc Breac, a shoulder of Cnoc Mordáin that is *breac*, speckled, with pale outcrops of granite; Coill an Gháigín, the wood of the small cleft, whose wood cannot have been much more than a patch of scrub in the centuries since the Bronze Age; Beitheach Chatha to the south, *beitheach* meaning birchwood and the other word more probably from *caoth*, boghole, than *cath*, battle. We came to the smaller river, Gabhla Beag, which was full of yellow waterlilies, and forded it, and approached a stony track, new to me, for when I mapped this area it was the trackless heart of Iorras Aintheach. A dozen or so people on horseback were coming up the track. We swaggered out in front of them and Máirtín announced that we were bandits, come to take their horses – and he certainly looked the part, with his turf-cutter's shorts and solidly muscled limbs. But the leader of the party produced a card on which we read that they were the Galloping Grannies of Indiana, so we quickly stepped aside.

As the brightly dressed riders on their glossy Connemara ponies proceeded up the hill, Willie Leahy, the organizer of such 'Connemara Trail' rides, bringing up the rear in his four-wheel-drive vehicle, stopped to talk to us. Willie, a Loughrea-based breeder of Connemara ponies and Field Master of the famous Galway Blazers hunt, had bought a huge tract of 'mountain' above us to the south-east some years previously, and built the track up to it. He is a small, talkative, humorous man; he needs his sense of humour sometimes to keep his charges happy on days of rain, he told us. He grumbled that he had been refused planning permission for six houses on his mountain, and a proposal for a wind farm had been turned down too – why, he could not understand; these developments would have interfered with no one, as no one ever came up here. So in the end he had forested the land. We went on to talk about the defeat of the first Lisbon Treaty referendum, which had been confirmed the previous day. Máirtín had been reporting on it, and could tell us that the 'no' vote in Connemara had been up to 85 per cent in places, reflecting discontent over local issues that had nothing to do with Lisbon: the prohibition of turf-cutting and of wintering sheep on mountain lands designated as Special Areas of Conservation (such as the one we were then standing in), and the restrictions on salmon drift-netting and other fisheries. Then Willie invited us to join him and his riders for a picnic by one of his lakes above, and drove off to catch up with the Galloping Grannies. Máirtín and I followed on foot.

Willie's land, entered through a gate on the track, lies in the town-lands of Seanadh Mhac Dónaill, the hillside of the MacDonalds, and further up, Loch an Bhuí, the lake of the yellow, so called from a beach of golden sand at the eastern end of a large lake in it, very striking when seen from the hillside above. A stream falls almost from the Cnoc Mordáin saddlepoint into this lake, and other streams link it and five other lakes, all ultimately feeding the Gabhla Beag river. There are two roofless houses close together in Seanadh Mhac Dónaill, stone-built, with high gables and very straight edges to their corners, surrounded by mossy drystone walls and sheltered by ash trees and a young wych-elm that is growing up through the silvery wreckage of its predecessor. It is a superb site, looking down on a small lake with a couple of miles of bog beyond it sloping away to the coast at Gabhla, but until Willie built his track it was extremely isolated. In living memory there were two Ridge families living and farming here, where their nineteenth-century forebears had acted as herds for the owner, a Colonel Newton. Michael and his wife Nan, who was from Fínis, had the house to the east, and Festy and his sons and daughters the house to the west.

The Festys, as they were known, used to cross the bog carrying hundredweight sacks of flour from the shop in the townland of Caladh an Chnoic, the harbour of the hill, two miles away down by the coast. Coming home from the bar in Cashel at night they would have a candle in a jam jar with a handle of string; people living down on the coast road told me of watching these little points of light against the immense blackness of the mountain, flickering, disappearing as the men went down into a dip, reappearing as they crested a knoll. The Festys moved down to the coast, I think in the 1960s. I once called on the last of them in his cottage, which had no path to it, on the shore near Gabhla; he had just returned from the Zetland bar in Cashel and was very boisterous. He searched for a whiskey glass for me and, having found one, filled it with water, which he swirled around with sweeping gestures that sent drops across the room, crying, 'We must be clean, my friend, we must be clean!', and then found some dregs of long-brewed tea in a teapot on the kitchen stove, which he splashed into a mug for me together with a mass of tea leaves. I had hoped to get the definitive versions of the names of the lakes by the old house, most of which are incorrect on the OS maps, but I hurried away as soon as I could escape, none the wiser.

In those days the land around the lakes was a sweeping unity of bog, quite blank on the six-inch OS map, and matching the lakes with the names I had been given by old Mickey Coyne of Gabhla was a puzzle that only repeated visits solved. Once I stood still for so long, study-ing the map and trying to work out where I was, that when I suddenly moved again a startled fox leaped out of the grass a few yards from me, flung itself into a stream and scrambled up the furthermost bank soaking wet. Nowadays Willie's track winds among the lakes, and the conifers, coming down in broken ranks to the lake margins, compose some picturesque landscapes with a Canadian accent that almost persuade me to forgive him the rectilinear, barbed-wired, outer edges of his forestry. At one place the track crosses a stream at its outflow from Loch na nGleannta Móra, the lake of the big glens, and on that day of our meeting with him there were white waterlilies floating in the lake on our right and yellow waterlilies in the stream on our left, and a sandpiper flitting from islet to islet in the lake uttering a brief single note that made the place as lovely and lonely as a primeval forest. A little further on we found the pony trekkers picnicking by Loch an Bhuí, their ponies standing silently and almost motionlessly in a group at the water's edge. We sat down and shared the good things Willie provided. Máirtín kept the Grannies in a giggle of repartee, and Willie got me to tell them the folktale about the man from An Aird and his dream of the otherworldly ceremony (for the Mass rock where that is supposed to have taken place is just above Loch an Bhuí, in the mouth of the pass). Then Máirtín and I took our leave and headed for Gabhla, around the top of the forestry, a long, hard, tussocky slog.

If instead we had continued southwards beyond the chain of lakes and crossed the twin-topped hill called Na Béacáin, the peaks, behind the Ridges' ruined houses, we would have entered into another lonely expanse of mountain land called Glionnán, small glen. Like all these inland townlands this would once have been familiar to the coast-dwelling farmers, and especially the youngsters and womenfolk who booleyed here in the milking season. Now it is wilderness, and for me it derives a certain mystique from its remoteness and also from a most curious piece of folklore that Seán Mac Giollarnáth took down from Micheál Mhac Dhonnchadha of Roisín na Mainiach. I translate:

There is a cliff in Glionnán on which the black raven used to nest, in a place to which no one could climb. Once a man let himself down on a rope from above, and took the raven's eggs. He brought them away with him and boiled them. Then he put them back in the nest. When the raven failed to hatch out its chicks it went and fetched the stone of talents from the north side of hell, and put it in the nest together with the eggs. When the time came the eggs hatched, despite having been boiled. The man went down the cliff again. The raven had gone and had left the stone in the nest. The man took the stone and brought it away with him and while he had the stone he had every talent.

The man steals the eggs and turns them to stone; then the stone of gifts or talents (*'cloch na mbua'*), although it has come from hell, gives them the power of life again; the raven leaves the man the stone, which rewards him for his cruel trick with every gift. As so often with folk-tales one feels that the moral equation would be soluble if some parameter had not been forgotten.

Above this cliff the land rises eastwards to the long ridge of Cnoc Mordáin. This is, I suppose, the way the man from An Aird would have come in pursuit of his dream, crossing the bogs and hills by the most direct route. Having attained the ridge he would have walked a couple of miles along it to the north, and, on reaching the height above the pass, stood in astonishment on seeing the otherworldly congregation assembling in the valley below. The Mass rock is there to this day, a lectern-like shoulder of rock with a few stones on it, by a scattered cairn, a few hundred yards upslope from the mouth of the stream that drains the western side of the pass into Loch an Bhuí.

And as I too stand in imagination and stare down at the Mass rock, my complex circuit of Iorras Aintheach completed, a vast chattering crowd is condensing out of a wisp of mist. They are at once familiar and strange, like faded photographs. I begin to identify characters among them: Tadhg na Buile, for example, playing the bogeyman behind a rock, and Joe Heaney roaring a roaratorio. There's Máire an Ghabha bending over an open coffin, and Miss Moore and her 30,000 circulars, and the Bible reader paying through the nose for a passage to Roundstone, and the Jumpers' soup with the dogfish floating in it. St Mac Dara and his bull and his ram, Myles of the bees with a posy on a stick, and Mr Betts of the bees with his stinking pipe, Miss Betts playing the harmonium under a rainy umbrella, the marine biologists with their intelligent wrasse and dull codfish, His Majesty with a cormorant perched on his head, the bailiff hammering a sod onto a rock with his shoe, Lydon the smuggler felling his masts, Mongan the hotelier laying down 'Carna law', the nuns blasted out of it by the gravel-grabbers, the archaeologists larking about in a 2,012-year-old crannóg, Fr Miley hiding under the seaweed, Ó Fatharta legging it with coat-tails flying, the sweaty yeomen bogged, the saint ducking the leaping dog, the Galloping Grannies and the bandits – all these looking at me resentfully. A leader steps forth from among them, not the priest who celebrated the Mass but a much more ancient and authoritative figure, the wizard Mordán. 'Wretch!' he cries. 'Look at us! Husks made up of folktales, yarns, songs, jokes, anecdotes, rumours, innuendos and libels to populate your pocket universe. Before you came we were persons, we had depths and dimensions you know nothing of; we were the people of the stormy peninsula. Be off with you before you do more damage to truthful memory!'

Well, I could stay and argue my case; after all, if I hadn't given them what voice I can spare, who would have ever heard a word of half their stories? But, seeing the wizard give his herdsman the nod to unleash that monstrous hound, I decide to go. I flit eastwards across the bays, to start another journey, in another mode, that finishes in 'the place that the Lord made last'.

PART III

Anfractuous Rocks

Preface

Fractal Connemara

How long is the coast of Connemara? A reasonable question, it seems, deserving of at least an approximate answer. One's first impulse is to say, it depends on where Connemara starts and stops. But on second thoughts it looks as if changing one's mind on the exact territorial definition of Connemara – for instance, on the question of where its boundary meets the fairly straight coastline stretching westwards from Galway – is only going to make a difference of a few miles to the total length of its shore, a negligible amount compared, for example, to the vast length bundled up into the region of ramifying peninsulas and clustered islands west of the road from Camas to An Tulaigh, eleven miles to the south, in which topographical complexity verges on the paroxysmal. But it will soon become apparent that this second thought is as inadequate as the first to the problem of the length of a coastline.

To begin to understand the question better, let me try to measure on a map that distance from Camas to An Tulaigh, via the boundary between land and sea (including the coasts of the offshore islands that are such a prominent feature of south Connemara). My own map of Connemara is at a scale of one inch to the mile; I can open a pair of compasses or dividers to one inch and step-walk them along the line representing the high-water mark, including the circumferences of as many of the offshore islands as possible. My map gives me a shoreline distance of sixty-four miles. But I have had to omit many islands less than an inch long on the map, and to step over a lot of inlets less than an inch wide. For a more accurate result I can now take the old six-inch-to-the-mile Ordnance Survey maps and once again set off with my dividers opened to one inch, equivalent to a sixth of a mile. This time I find that the coastal length comes to 130 miles, and, judging by the number of little creeks and headlands I have skipped across with my dividers and the hosts of islands too small to take a step on, a measurement made on the 25-inch OS maps would be a lot larger than that. And suppose I decided to walk the shoreline with a pedometer, keeping as close to the edge of the water as possible, my result would be vastly larger again. If, having a spare lifetime to devote to this quest for accuracy, I were to go a stage further and take a foot-rule to all the ins and outs of the water's edge, the only conclusion I could come to would be that there is no conclusion to this process. The sequence of measurements of a coastline surveyed in finer and finer detail does not converge to an answer, the genuine correct distance between two end points; instead it just gets bigger and bigger, indefinitely. Therefore, a coastline does not have a length. Or, our everyday concept of measure is inadequate to the reality of a coastline.

Two caveats. First, this property of coastlines has nothing to do with the ambiguities and variations caused by tides and waves; one can picture the above process as applied to the edge of an ocean frozen at a moment of time. Second, a coastline is a geographical concept, and once one gets down to scales of more interest to the atomic scientist than to the geographer, the question of its length fades out into the mysteries of the quantum world. But what one can claim is that over a large range of scales the length of a coastline increases as if it would never stop, the closer it is investigated.

Coastlines have another surprising quality too, known as self-similarity. Imagine a sketch map on an A4 sheet of the region considered above, in which the edge of the mainland is represented by a wriggling line and the major islands off it by loops. Now imagine another map on an A4 sheet of some part of that coast, say the western shoreline of Leitir Mealláin with some of the lesser islands near it: another wriggling line and a few loops. Finally think of a similar-sized map of part of the shore of one of those lesser islands, with a few nearby rocks in the sea. Someone unfamiliar with the places mapped would be unable to say which of these three represented the largest territory or the smallest. This process could be continued downwards or upwards. Suppose a map of the whole west Connemara coast be added to the pile, and one of western Ireland from Connemara to Donegal, and then one of the Atlantic coast from Norway to Biscay.

In general appearance each map consists of a line and some loops. Any one of them could represent the side of a continent or the margin of a rock pool.

This repetition of form within form, tempting one to credit nature with exuberant prodigality, also occurs in the geometry of river systems, cloud profiles and many other linear features of our world, and is common in matters of area too. Consider a rocky Connemara island; its area might be given on a map as so many acres, but that is to ignore its approximately pyramidal form. One can make an adjustment for this; and then one is on the slope, if not to infinity, then to the indefinitely huge. The slanting sides of the pyramid are of course complicated by cliffs and gullies, and these by jutting rocks and sheep-worn paths, all these surfaces being grooved and pitted and rough with crystals, and so on down to the craggy microcosms an ant has to toil over; all these features immeasurably increase one's estimate of the island's area, and there is no obvious stopping place in this hopeless pursuit of accuracy. The natural world is largely composed of such recalcitrant entities, over which the geometry of Euclid, the fairytale of lines, circles, areas and volumes we are told at school, has no authority.

Some of these apparently anomalous phenomena had been puzzled over by mathematicians before him, but the man who brought them together as objects of empirical study and theorization, and finally unified the field by the brilliant conceptual invention of the fractal, was the mathematician Benoît Mandelbrot; the question with which I opened this preface pays homage to his famous paper of 1967, 'How Long Is the Coast of Britain?' Mandelbrot named his invention with an eye to the Latin, *fractus*, broken. He gives a precise mathematical definition of a fractal, but also allows for a looser use of the term to cover the sorts of things considered above, such as coastlines, that exhibit a degree of self-similarity over a range of scales and are therefore too complicated to be described in terms of classical geometry, which would indeed regard them as broken, confused, tangled, unworthy of the dignity of measure. His mathematically perfect fractals inhabit the Platonic world of forms, and relate to naturally occurring fractals as do Euclid's ideal spheres, circles and straight lines to their imperfect counterparts in reality.

One of Mandelbrot's perfect fractals is simple enough to be discussed in prose, I believe, and can be seen as an idealized model of a coastline. It is constructed step by step starting from a straight line, to which what I will call a sidestep is applied; smaller sidesteps are then applied to each straight bit of the first one, then smaller ones still to each straight bit of the result, and so on to the infinitesimally small, so that if one examined any part of it under a magnifying glass or the most powerful of microscopes, it would look the same, sidesteps upon sidesteps for ever:

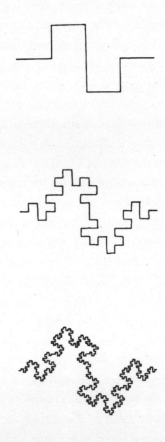

Such an entity is more than a line, which has one dimension, its length, and yet it is not quite an area either, with two dimensions, length and breadth. In fact Mandelbrot showed that it is possible to assign it a dimensionality of one and a half. (I attempt, if not to prove this, then to make it sound plausible, in the footnote or optional sidestep below.★) The difficulty of the concept of fractional dimensions is that our everyday idea of a dimension is a possible direction of movement. Thus within the space of a box we can move an object from side to side, from front to back, and from top to bottom, that is, in three independent dimensions. If the object is to be kept on a tabletop, a plane surface, it can only be moved from left to right, say, and from front to back — two independent dimensions; and if it is strung like a bead on a wire we can only slide it to and fro along that line of one dimension. There is no generalizing that idea to cover fractional dimensions; one cannot have two and a half directions. But there are other ways of conceiving of dimensionality, some of which can be stretched to cover fractals more comfortably; my footnote gives a taste of one of them. It may seem absurd to talk of something having 1.5 or 2.7 or 0.3 dimensions, but it turns out that such concepts are not just the dreams or nightmares of mathematicians; indeed fractional dimensionalities are a feature of many natural entities, from coastlines to curdled milk, systems of arteries, bundles of geological faults, cloud-forms, and even the distribution of the 200 billion galaxies in space.

★ First, in a dull way, straight lines and squares and cubes are self-similar too. For instance a cube can be divided up into smaller cubes, each of which is similar to the whole but reduced by a certain factor, and then the smaller cubes can be dissected in the same way. Think of a cube, with sides of unit length, divided up into little cubes with sides of length ¼. The number of little cubes fitting along one side of the big one is 4, and the total number of little cubes making up the big one is 4^3. Now think of a square, with unit sides, divided up into smaller squares, each of which is the same as the big one but with its sides reduced by the factor ¼. The number of such small squares in the big one is given by 4^2. And for the straight line, the equivalent number is simply 4, or 4^1. In each case the power, 3, 2 or 1, agrees with our idea that the cube has three dimensions, the square two and the line one. If there are N small units in the big unit, $N = 4^D$, where D is 3 for a cube, 2 for a square and 1 for a line. Suppose then we take this equation as *defining* what is meant by dimensionality, and ask what value of D it gives when applied to a fractal form. The simplest case is the sidestepping form described above. Each straight bit of a sidestep is one fourth as long as the line it is applied to, but there are eight such small lengths making up the whole sidestep. By analogy with the other cases, $8 = 4^D$. To find D, note that 8 is 2^3 and 4 is 2^2; so $4^D = 2^{2D}$. Therefore $2^{2D} = 2^3$, whence $2D = 3$ and, finally, $D = 3/2$.

According to Mandelbrot a figure of 1.2 is typical for coastlines. I once did a crude calculation that gave an average-looking stretch of the south Connemara coast a dimensionality of 1.25, and the results of my map-measurements of the Camas to An Tulaigh section suggest a figure of 1.36, an indication of its exceptional intricacy.

The reason for the prevalence of fractals in the natural world, very broadly stated, is this: mathematically self-similar structures are the result of applying a procedure to a simple initial entity, then applying the same procedure to the result, and so on — an iterative process, as in the example of sidesteps applied to the results of previous sidestep-pings, etc.; and nature itself applies its transforming powers again and again to the outcome of previous transformations, thus bringing into being forms that are self-similar over a wide range of scales and of a degree of complexity that pre-Mandelbrot geometry cannot model. Of course nature's operations are usually multiple, various, random and intermittent, and will throw up exceptions to any generalization. Some of Mandelbrot's constructions involve an element of randomness or statistical variation and achieve much closer likenesses to natural phenomena than does the simple repetitive algorithm of sidesteps mentioned above to a real coastline.

Mandelbrot's collation of two ideas, self-similarity and fractional dimensionality, opened up new vistas of thought. What had been an obscure speculation in pure mathematics suddenly became important in physics, the earth sciences, biology and astrophysics, and has proved crucial to one of the great intellectual breakthroughs of the last century, the founding of our ominous new disciplines, Complexity, Catastrophe and Chaos. It also promises to be a rich source of metaphor and imagery in literature and art. Like all discoveries it surprises us yet again with the unfathomable depth and richness of the natural world; specifically it shows that there is more space, there are more places, within a forest, among the galaxies or on a Connemara seashore, than the geometry of common sense allows.

21   Seductive Hills and Devious Shores

Inland of the coastline whose tortuosities I have just described and laboriously measured on maps lies a range of low hills that I associate with happiness, for reasons I do not quite understand. Once, on a bare slope that looks down on Ros a' Mhíl, I saw a pair of golden plovers, a rarity in these depleted days, whose lonely cry took me back to Ilkley Moor in Yorkshire, which I used to quarter in search of golden plover nests when I was young. Another time, on a still summer's afternoon in a nowhere-place, a heathery slope above a patch of hazel wood somewhere east of Camas, I was visited by the *slua sí*, the fairy horde, travelling as is its traditional way in a little whirlwind. This had happened to me once before, in the Burren, where the wind's whispering approach, the sudden cap-snatching play of the air around me, and its retreat into utter silence, seemed sinister; the Burren is often held to be a spiritual landscape, and if it is so, it harbours among others a spirit of malice. But here the invisible vortex spinning across the hillside according to equations of fluid dynamics I've never been able to master, spilling its energy into smaller vortices, and those into still smaller ones, dissipating itself fractally into a pocket of turbulence and the mad gyrations of individual molecules of air, feels in memory like a friendly nod and pat on the back from the incomprehensible system of all things. But perhaps the attraction of these hills is merely that in their soft successions and slow fadings into distance they seem to promise eternity. Three times in my diaries of the time I spent exploring south Connemara some thirty years ago, I find such exclamations as 'I could wander onwards up here for ever.' And so I should and would if I could; but life is finite and art is infinite, and if I am not only to experience Connemara but to share that experience as well as words will let me, I have to impose a boundary. Therefore I will revisit these seductive hills solely to touch upon a geological feature that will both serve as eastern limit to my fractal Connemara and explain something of its intriguing intricacy.

There is a fine wide road running south from Maam Cross via Scríb to Ros a' Mhíl and the shores of Galway Bay, which it then follows eastwards to Galway city; its main purpose is to serve Ros a' Mhíl, which by regional standards is a major port. Travelling along this road southwards from Scríb the hills, rounded and heather-tinted, are a mile or two away to the left, and various enticing minor roads lead towards them – and already, despite my resolve to limit myself, I foresee that I will not be able to refrain from mentioning some of the random beguilements and sidesteps of these ways.

The first of them parts from the main road near Scríb, by a bridge over a river that falls into the head of the last, inmost, twist of Cuan Chamais, the twisty bay. The settlement around the bridge – a national school, the Catholic church that allegedly offended the eyes of the gentry of Screebe Lodge, the premises of an Irish-language summer school and a few houses – is called Foirnís, for there used to be an iron furnace here. The Ordnance Survey map of 1839 shows no buildings in this vicinity, while the road from Scríb stopped just short of the river and did not exist south of it. So this was a remote and secretive place, and it is said that pikes for the 1798 rebels were forged here. The ore used was bog-iron, nodules of oxidized iron minerals that form in bogs where iron-rich groundwater wells to the surface. Perhaps this was gathered locally, but the location of the furnace, at the head of the bay, suggests that it was also brought in from further afield, while the name Molán an Iarainn, the boulder of the iron, a rock off the western point of Camas in the narrowest part of the bay, conserves the tradition of the shipwreck of a boat laden with iron. As if to make this history palpable, the former national school building by the bridge conserves (in a fireplace) a big, black, craggy lump of slag that had for longer than anyone can remember lain in the grass nearby. Little 'bloomeries' like this one, fuelled by timber, were blamed by Alexander Nimmo for the deforestation of Connemara. The side road I am to follow inland now leads to the townland of Leitir Mór na Coille, the big rough slope of the wood, near which a patch of scrub surrounded by naked bog perhaps represents the last of its wood.

This side road soon crosses a stream flowing out of a lake with the relevant name of Lochán an Mhianaigh, the lakelet of the ore, and then another one flowing out of Loch Seanadh Siongán, the lake of the smooth slope of ants. This second crossing is by the irresistibly named Droichidín na Circe Fraoigh, the little bridge of the 'heather hens', i.e. grouse. Before there was a bridge the stream was channelled under the road by Gulletín na Circe Fraoigh, the little gullet of the grouse – but I must not stay for such micro-geography or micro-history. A mile and a half further on lies the hamlet of Leitir Mór na Coille – one couldn't really call it a village, as it has no services and consists solely of a loose clutch of small farmhouses – and, contiguous with it to the south, An Seanbhaile, the old settlement, where there is a small graveyard. Funerals from Camas used to come to the grave-yard across the bog before the road was built, and I have been told of an old faction-fighter of Camas who, when he was dying, instructed his sons to buy a keg of poitín for his funeral, to put down his coffin on Cnocán na Fola, the hillock of the blood, on the way to the grave-yard, and have a great fight there in his honour. On the north side of Leitir Mór na Coille is a low glacial hill with a sparse, mossy old hazel wood on its south flank. They say that the hill has always been green since a Bishop Ó Domhnaill read Mass there; it is called Cnocán an tSoiscéil, the hillock of the Gospel, and I think the 'bishop' is to be identified with the outlawed Abbot O'Donnell who marooned the English soldiery on Cruach na Caoile in Elizabethan times, as told in *Listening to the Wind*. Taller hills, dark and boulder-specked, rise to about a thousand feet to the east and north of the village: Seanadh Mhaoilín, smooth slope of the flat top, and Leaca Donna, brown flags, respectively. And on the south-facing slopes of the latter hill is a small cleft called An Scailpín, out of which a stream descends, and which is the object of my much-distracted expedition.

Just north of this range of hills is the boundary between the granite of south Connemara and the metamorphic rocks of central Connemara, and this little *scailp* marks the track of a major fault that cuts across the granite region to An Cheathrú Rua on the south coast and continues out across the seabed. This is the Shannawona fault, named from Seanadh Bhán, fair slope, another small hill in the vicinity. I came up here once with Paul Mohr, then Professor of Geology at University College Galway, and he pointed out in a rocky recess of the *scailp* a spongy-looking lump of sinter, a concretion of silica that had at some period been deposited by the waters of a hot spring. At what period? The fragile, crumbly sinter could not have survived the Ice Ages when this region was roughed up by glaciers. An Scailpín was formed by erosion after the mile-thick ice-cap had melted away some 13,000 years ago. With the removal of this vast burden of ice the land had risen, fracturing along the line of weakness left by the ancient Shannawona fault. To the east of the reawakened fault the land rose a couple of yards more than it did to the west, a process that must have been accompanied by earthquakes violent enough to shake down the big screes we see on the faces of the Connemara mountains. The spring of An Scailpín was brought to the boil by the heat produced by radioactivity in the underlying granite and accumulated over thousands of years under the insulating ice-cap.

But the Shannawona fault itself long pre-dates these comparatively recent reorderings of the landscape, as is proved by the vast works of erosion since its formation. These works are not particularly obvious to the non-geologist's eye in this mild landscape of level bogs and unemphatic hills. The evidence for them, though, lay to hand at the wayside when we followed up another track about two miles further south, leading into the townland of Muiceanach Choille. (The first word means a hog-back hill, referring to a low glacier-moulded deposit of gravelly material, and the other indicates that this place too had once its woods.) This is a lovely faraway spot, with just two or three houses on a narrow neck of land between two lakes. The track into it is hardly more than a bog road and has branches serving various areas in which turf was being cut; when I spoke to the turf-cutters, I remember, none of them knew the names of the several lakes of the vicinity, for they had been brought in by bus from Leitir Móir and other parts of Na hOileáin that had been stripped of their bogs long ago.

The evidence I mentioned above had been unearthed and thrown aside in the bulldozing of one of these tracks across the rough terrain: a lump of granite, which I lugged back to Paul's car for examination at home. Its striking feature was the huge crystals of feldspar in it,

blocky pinkish-grey chunks an inch or inch-and-a-half long, which
made it quite distinct from the fine-grained granite I was used to
seeing in every roadside wall and rock outcrop in Ros Muc, Carna
and Roundstone. Granite is an igneous rock; it is formed from molten
rock or magma that forced its way up from deep inside the earth's
crust, cooling as it ascended and solidifying before it reached the
surface. The overlying rocks, having been baked, split and thrust apart
by the ascent of the granite, have subsequently been removed by
erosion together with the volcanoes that capped the granite. Here in
Connemara the granite is about 400 million years old, a period more
than long enough for weathering to abolish whole mountains. A
geological map of south Connemara makes it clear that the region's
granite has been emplaced in a number of the great roundish gouts
known as plutons. The Galway granite, also called the Galway batholith (from *bathos*, depth, and *lithos*, stone), incorporates several plutons
of various sizes and stretches across about thirty-two miles from
Galway city to the eastern slopes of Cnoc Mordáin; west of that is
another pluton, the Carna granite, while the Roundstone granite is
exposed in a neatly circular area five miles across and centred on
Cashel Bay.

The Shannawona fault slices through the Galway granite, and fifteen
miles or so to the east, near Galway itself, is a matching break, the
Barna fault; thus the batholith is divided into three sections, and here
at Muiceanach Choille, east of the Shannawona fault, we were in its
central division. The huge crystals in the granite of this division (and
they can be up to five inches long, I read in a geological paper on the
area) must have grown over a much longer period than did the small
crystals of the granite east of the fault, which means that they formed
while deep in the very slowly cooling interior of the batholith. Now,
studies of the strength of gravity in this area show that the earth's crust
is two or three miles thinner in the central division than in the eastern
or western divisions. It follows that the part of the granite between
the two great faults has at some date been forced upwards by that
distance, and has then been planed off to the same level as the rest, as
we see it today, by erosion. That erosion, which removed not only
some great thickness of the 'country' rocks into which the granite was

intruded but two or three miles' depth of the granite itself, has exposed the megacrystals of the batholith's deep-lying and slowly congealed heart.

That does not exhaust the explanatory powers of the Shannawona fault. The difference between the granite east of the fault, toughened by long, slow solidification at depth, and that west of the fault, relatively quickly cooled near the surface and so riven by cracks, may be reflected in the abrupt transition from the sober linear coastline between Galway city and An Tulaigh, to the mad fantastications of the fractal coastline west of that. About two miles south of the Muiceanach Choille turn-off the coast road crosses the fault, which, now on the right-hand side of the road, leaves a more noticeable mark on the landscape than elsewhere along its course in the shape of the narrow lake of Cara Fionnla, Fionnla's crossing place. Very few passers-by on this road would notice that this lovely lake, with its green banks and sedate flotillas of swans, is tidal, but in fact it is linked by a channel hardly wider than a river to Camas Bay, four miles to the north. The southern tip of the lake is only half a mile from the south coast at Casla, so that all the complex ramifications of An Cheathrú Rua and Na hOileáin are very nearly pinched off from the mainland by this stealthy roundabout insinuation of the sea. South of the lake the fault runs on down the eastern side of the peninsula of An Cheathrú Rua (where it takes on a mythological significance, as I will show in its place). Thus it provides a rather convincing boundary between the plain terrains to its east and the topographical excesses to its west. The boundary would be even more satisfactory if the fault ran down Cuan Chasla, Casla Bay, on the east of An Cheathrú Rua – but then it is an oversimplification to think of the fault as a single linear feature; it is a fractal sheaf of faults, the lesser ones splaying off from and remerging with the main ones to form a network, a fault zone, which, I'm sure, can take care of the bay. Granite is a very tough rock, and the small-scale angularity of the Galway Bay shoreline shows that it is well able to resist weathering even by the explosive attacks of the Atlantic, so the proliferation of bays and inlets from Casla to Roundstone is a puzzle, to which perhaps the Shannawona fault tells us the answer: the frequency of joints or fractures that the pounding sea can open up in those parts of the granite that cooled near the surface of the pluton. It is an attractively simple solution, and it gives me a natural boundary from which to start the exploration of the fragmented terrain west of the fault.

The point of land that most exactly separates the simple coastline from the complex coastline is on the east side of the mouth of Cuan Chasla – and quite literally as I finish this account of the fault itself and its determining effect on the form of my book, I notice that I have recorded the name of that little headland as Aill an Bhréagaire, the cliff of the liar. I take this as a reminder that all seductively simple theories will inevitably be undone by the devious nature of Nature.

22 Anathema

'A curse lasts seven years hidden in the lintel of a house,' I have been told. Looking inland from the shore south of the village of An Tulaigh, the broken-down walls and staring window-openings of Cashel House, once the home of the Blakes of Tully, appear above fields abandoned to a sea of gorse. Nowadays one also sees, a little to the east of the ruined Big House, the modest terminal building and hangar of Connemara Airport, my magic bridge to the Aran Islands, just a few minutes' flight away in Aer Árann's little Islander planes. The association with limestone-bright Aran somewhat relieves the grim impression the desolate, wind-racked, rain-soaked, granitic coastal rim of the former Blake estate has left on my mind, which is perhaps only due to the wintery weather I met whenever I came snooping around this way.

Before the time of the Blakes this was Burke territory. In the sixteenth century the Burkes (the Norman de Burgos, gone native and intermarried with the O'Flahertys) had a castle on the shore below Cashel House; it was here that Finola O'Flaherty murdered her stepson Walter Burke, as I tell in *The Last Pool of Darkness* in connection with the O'Flahertys of Bunowen. The castle stood on the east bank of a small river where it reaches the sea; hence the name of the townland here and the next village to the east, Inverin, from *inbhearán*, a small estuary (the local Irish version, Indreabhán, has arisen by metathesis, transposition of sounds, since the Ordnance Survey of 1839, according to the expert I consulted about it). Nothing of the castle stands more than two or three feet high, and it is said that its stones were taken to build the Blakes' residence. The latter family, one of the old Galway mercantile 'Tribes', came to An Tulaigh as a result of the Cromwellian disaster; having been implicated in the rebellion of 1641 and forfeited better estates in east Galway, they were granted bits and pieces of poor land in Connemara. In 1677 under the post-Restoration settlements,

Walter Blake of Drum, near Moycullen, was confirmed in possession of most of the land from the Crumlin river just east of Indreabhán to the Casla river, as well as Inis Ní and Inis Leacan near Roundstone. His great-grandson Valentine seems to have been the first to describe himself as of Tully; he died in 1819, and since, between Larkin's map of that year and the OS map of 1839, the old castle disappears and Cashel House appears, it is likely that the house was built by Valentine's younger brother James Blake and that the stones of the castle went into its making, as local lore maintains. James, it seems, acted as agent in Tully for Valentine's son Patrick, who lived in Drum, and his 'improvements' were very noticeable on the face of the land. The antiquarian artist William Wakeman, coming along the coast road from Galway in about 1850, noted, 'the seat of Mr Blake, whose improvements and clearances give an agreeable repose to the eye, wearied with the interminable succession of rocks, boulder-stones, cabins and loose stone enclosures'.

Those who had been 'cleared' were less impressed. According to the local memory bank, the Blakes emptied the townland of Tóin an Chnoic, on the peninsula south of Ros a' Mhíl, where a cluster of roofless cabins still bears witness to a vanished community that had to cross the bay and re-establish themselves on the hopeless bogs of Baile an tSléibhe, the settlement of the 'mountain'. Similarly the deserted village known as Ballaí Indreabháin, the walls of Inverin, south of the chapel in An Tulaigh, is said to have been the home of people displaced into what is now yet another deserted village on the east of Loch na Tulaí, and thence to Na Creagáin, the crags, a village a mile or so further east. An inquiry was held in Costelloe Lodge, Casla, into evictions carried out by James's sons and locally recruited muscle on New Year's Night, 1847/8, in snow, hail and gales, and Patrick was accused of cruelty and inhumanity. Adding insult to injury, the Blakes supported the Irish Church Mission Society in its efforts to convert their tenants to Protestantism; a chapel was built next to their house, and what a later parish priest referred to as 'a colony of perverts' was settled nearby. The first Monday of each month was 'Silver Monday', when (it was alleged by a Galway periodical) the converts were given cash for attending services. Local oral history concurs, adding that the

'Jumpers', having got their sixpence from the Protestants, would go straight to the Catholic chapel for Mass and contribute a penny, thus making a profit of fivepence (and, one hopes, saving their eternal souls).

It is James Blake who particularly figures, as Séamus a' Bhláca, in local demonology, locked in antagonism with the people's champion, Scorach Ghlionnáin. A *scorach* is a youth, and Glionnán, small glen, is an uninhabited mountain townland four or five miles to the north-east of Indreabhán. There the Scorach lived with his mother in a *scailp*; 'it was eight feet high and seven feet wide, with a boulder on either side and a huge rock above, with a mop of heather growing on it, and not a drop of water got into it from above or below, but all as dry as a mill,' according to what an old workman and storyteller, Peadar Mac Thuathaláin of Cois Fharraige, told Seán Mac Giollarnáth in the 1920s. I translate:

The Scorach was six feet five inches tall. He weighed eighteen stone. He was made like a rock, of bone and skin, broad and strong. His two shoulders were like nothing so much as an oak board, long and wide. He never in his life sowed or dug any potatoes, but grew up on beef and mutton, and not his own either. In the famine times he would walk around the villages enquiring if anyone was in want or distress. When he found there was, he would go and kill a beast. He would give it to the people who were in want.

One day the Scorach and five companions killed Séamus a' Bhláca's bull, a mighty beast so broad a man could sleep on its back. They made four quarters of it, gave two to a household in want, and hid the other two in a bog-hole. Then, knowing that Blake would be going to fetch the 'Revenue', the Scorach crossed the hills to Galway at a mighty pace, drank a mug of buttermilk in the market place and set off for home again. Above Salthill he met Séamus a' Bhláca and his wife in their coach. 'My God!' said Séamus; 'There's many a man hanged in error. I was sure that was the man who stole my bull.' So he got off on that occasion, but in the end he was caught and gaoled. The prison governor was troubled that so fine a man should be in prison, so he wrote to the Queen and got him a pardon. On his release he was asked if he would like to join the army, and he said he would prefer that to the hare's life he had been leading. He was given four days to visit his relatives before he left, and that was the time he composed a song about his exploits. I translate a few verses:

> I got up in the morning and I didn't break my fast,
> I made that expedition to Boar's Wood Glen,
> I looked around me and I saw a lovely beast,
> I hit it on the forehead with my hammer without a handle.
> . . .

> I bore it on my back through the hills and the valleys,
> Over hillocks that were steep and mountain that was soft,
> I skinned it in the morning on a Wednesday
> Far from the villages in the Badgers' Stony Place.

> This is the Scorach who never saw a person hungry
> If there was a goose in the yard or a beast on the hill,
> For my knives were always sharp and brightly shining,
> They would shave a hundred men without drawing blood.

> That day will come when all the folk will see
> Smoke on the mountains and hares running free;
> And for my friends I leave my blessings,
> On Neachtan, Caena, Cearra, and on Ned.

And that, according to Peadar Chois Fharraige, was the last that was heard of the Scorach in Ireland. Peadar takes the story no further, but my friend Mícheál Bairéad, who was also from Cois Fharraige, had two episodes from the Scorach's army career. Once his companions wanted to try his famous strength, so they rested the barrel of a cannon on his back and fired it. He was well shaken, but did not fall. And finally, in the Crimean War, his head was taken off by a chain-shot. He was smoking his pipe at the time, and his head was seen to take three more puffs of the pipe before it fell from his mouth.

Mícheál also had the story of the last days of the Blakes of Tully:

One day a woman and her family were roasting potatoes in a fire by the roadside. Blake's daughter came by on her saddle-horse, and when she saw what was going on she walked her horse over the fire and put it out, and made mud of the potatoes. The woman said, 'May you not live to play that trick again!' And according to the *seanchas* the Blakes came to no good end. Some priest pronounced the Anathema, 'Salm na Mallacht', against them. He wrote it on a piece of paper, put it in an envelope, put that envelope in another, and so on, seven envelopes in all. He gave it to a lad to deliver, telling him to take a good horse and get as far away as he could while Blake was opening all those envelopes.

The carnage wreaked by this moral letterbomb is clear. Patrick died in 1857, his uncle James soon followed him; James's son Arthur (a boxer and bully – when the priest in An Spidéal spoke out against boxing he threatened to make smithereens of his head) left the house in the 1870s. Rents were then paid to Patrick's son Pat Minor, who was in the lunatic asylum at Ballinasloe. The Blakes' bailiffs, the Wallaces, lived in Cashel House for a while, and then one of the last of the Protestant missioners, until the 1920s. Now the church that stood just in front of the house is hardly traceable; the 'colony of perverts', and the little society of the Blakes' hangers-on, their coachmen, butlers, cooks, gardeners and so on who lived nearby in the area still called An Caisleán, has long been reabsorbed into the community. The Catholic faith reigns: the old chapel in Indreabhán, which the Blakes are said to have burned, was replaced in 1874 with a better one in An Tulaigh, and that in its turn gave way in 1962 to a people-friendly post-Vatican-II church – the first in Ireland to have the altar facing the congregation – with abstract stained glasswork and charming pseudo-naïve Stations of the Cross. Cashel House is gapped to such an extent that one can drift through it like a wraith. The orchard beside it still has its twelve-foot walls but it is a mere field, a few days' grazing for two or three cows, with just one apple tree, which once sheltered me from a shower, and a bank of such old-fashioned herbs as comfrey and elecampane.

Mícheál Bairéad, who gave me the saying with which I began, on the lasting power of a curse lodged in the lintel of a house, also told me that 'A curse falls on the one cursed, on the one who curses, or on the place in which it was made.' Has the priest's curse spilled over the townlands west of Teach a' Bhláca? Hassled by October winds and discouraged by squalls as I tried to map the boreens threading through the tattered fabric of stone walls enclosing countless stony plots between the main road and the shore, I could almost have been persuaded to believe it; but then, again and again, I met farmers of this ungenerous terrain who were happy to stand in the rain, jackets hitched up to hang from their weather ears, and tell me tales of the Blakes, Colm Cille and Conán of the Fianna, and who loved the place, which made me more tolerant of its bleakness. The subjects of these stories, although immersed in a time-worn past largely composed of gaps and of distinctly less than one dimension, have left definitive marks on the landscape. The Blakes I have dealt with; Colm Cille made landfall from the Aran Islands in An Chloch Mhór, three miles to the west of Cashel House; and Conán, the glutton and buffoon of the Fionn cycle of legends, paused in Caorán na gCearc, another mile along the coast.

Coming down the side road to An Chloch Mhór by a mile-long lake that had broken into fields on either side of it, I found three men peering disconsolately over a bridge at the swollen stream that was supposed to empty the lake to the sea. 'That's the stream that's causing the trouble!' said one of the men; the council was to dredge the stream-bed but hadn't done so, and now his crop of oats was drowned. (The note on the stream's name in the 'field name books' of the 1839 Ordnance Survey reads 'Sruthán Weirs, a hybrid name'; but there are no weirs on it, and these men could tell me that the name is rightly Sruthán Mhaorais, the stream of Maoras, i.e. plain-promontory, a district comprising three neighbouring townlands of this low and level coastal strip. As to An Chloch Mhór, the huge boulder from which it has its name (*cloch mhór*, big stone) had been blasted when the road was being built, and the remaining fragment of it was to be seen in a field further down the road near the old cemetery, Reilig Mhaorais. I don't know what their feelings about this were, but the vague memory of a biblical proverb came back to me: 'Remove not the ancient landmark, which thy fathers have set.' Here Nature had set a mark notable enough to become an iconic presence in the neighbourhood, and it should not have been removed.

The old burial ground at the foot of the road is dedicated to St Colm Cille and is said to have had a church on it, but nowadays the oldest-looking structure there is the family vault of the Wallaces, bailiffs and rent collectors to the Blakes. There are also two holy wells on the foreshore below it, I had heard, and it was in search of these that I had come. Obviously these were not spring wells dispensing fresh water but wave-worn potholes. After some splashing about in the receding tide I found a likely-looking rock pool a yard or so across, a smoothed-off triangular basin with its outer side bowed outwards, like a font, about 300 yards south of the burial ground, and when I plunged my arm into it up to the shoulder I could feel coins jammed into a crevice in its depths. This identification by the sense of touch pleased me, for it is only through the immemorial work of hands upon these shores that such potholes, which are usually obscured by seaweed, have been found, as I have explained in connection with the cylindrical holy wells of Inis Ní. But I failed to find the other well, which the OS map marked rather nearer the graveyard. Instead I set off, a little wearily as it was the end of a long day's work, to walk the length of an unpromising shingle bank stretching endlessly south-eastwards. And after half a mile of tramping, to my delight: a score or so of sea-kale plants, with their big cabbage leaves and bizarre proliferations of globular seed-pods on branching stalks, like models of complex mol-ecules – a species then unrecorded in the wild from Connemara and which I knew of from a single shingle bank in Árainn. (I later found another colony, in An Caorán Beag on the western shore of Cuan Chasla.) So I was justified in my insistence on walking every stretch of these dreary shorelines; my sore ankles and aching thighs forgave my will.

On returning to the graveyard I saw a farmer knocking down the boulder-filled 'gap' in a wall to let his cattle into a field nearby, and ran across to talk to him. He gave me directions to the well I had missed – it is another large basin, difficult to find as it is down near the low-water mark and often full of sand – and he also pointed out the great canted slab of rock called Bád Choilm Cille, Colm Cille's boat, on which the saint sailed across from the Aran Islands. It does in fact look like the foredeck of a foundering boat. The farmer pointed out the grooves worn in its edges by the working of the oars, and the track of the anchor chain, as well as the saint's gigantic handprints. As we discussed these things the setting sun suddenly burst through the western clouds and put their ragged fragments into gilt rococo frames. 'This is the time of day when it's worth being down here,' he said.

On my next visit I took a boreen that comes down to the shore a little further west, in Caorán na gCearc. A *caorán*, at least in Connemara Irish, is a small hill of rough land, and the *cearca* or hens in question would be grouse, which no doubt were once plentiful in this townland on the moors north of the road. The placename reminds us of what was, and points out what the botanists would describe as the depauperate nature of the overgrazed plant community. In fact a history of poverty, famine and clearances haunts the human community of Caorán na gCearc too. Today's houses are higgledy-piggledy by the roadside, and just over half a mile to the south, down the boreen, are the pathetic ruins of An Seanbhaile, the old village, deserted since, I am told, the 1860s. The OS map of 1839 shows about twenty-one buildings in use here – half of them look smaller than the rest and were perhaps outhouses – in unpatterned neighbourliness by a small lake. One can stroll in and out of the tiny garden plots, the grass-carpeted floor-spaces, the narrow 'streets' around each cabin. Apart from a few gables all is reduced to a tight little maze of low walls that merges into the slightly looser maze of fields and boreens covering this coastal plain for mile after mile.

Here, in the rain, I met an elderly man peacefully walking behind his six cows and smoking his pipe. He told me there was a green hummock on the shore below that would be worth my while going to see. Unenthusiastically I continued down the boreen, and there, close to its foot, was indeed a smooth, barrow-like, grassed-over mound eight or so feet high and perhaps forty long, very conspicuous against the dark, seaweedy shore. Rabbits had burrowed into it, spilling thousands of periwinkle shells. It was a midden, no doubt prehistoric and perhaps the result of generations of periodic communal feasting or even of some regular exploitation of shellfish for dyestuff, as I have described apropos of Dog's Bay near Roundstone. It was by far the most striking midden I had come across, though I have heard that there was one big enough to have a name on the shore of An Caorán Beag south of An Cheathrú Rua, which unfortunately has been taken for burning to lime; it was called An Caisleán Cruinn, the round castle. This one in Caorán na gCearc turned out to have a name too. That evening on my way back to my lodgings I fell into conversation with a man who came out of a run-down mobile home as I passed, with a bottle in his pocket. Amidst a welter of incomprehensible stuff from an ancient prophetic text, *Cogadh an Dá Ghall*, 'The War of the Two Foreigners', the prophecies of Colm Cille and those of an old woman about a chapel in An Tulaigh that will never be finished, he told me that the mound marked the spot where Conán once stopped to empty his pocket, and that it is called Toit Chonáin. (*Toit* is a dialect word for a feed of shellfish, and Conán Maol is a comic and rather pathetic figure, fat, greedy and boastful, in the tales of Fionn Mac Cumhaill and his magical band of warriors.) I had not expected to meet the Falstaff of the Fianna on these disheartening shores, but looking back it is as if, over several visits to them, I had opened an envelope of gloom and found another within, and so on, and in the last, to reward my persistence, the curious details here noted.

23 The Whale

Imagine a world in which time and space are hardly separated, when there are pools of time landlocked in space and islands of space cut off in time, and everywhere and everywhen is blanketed in a boggy mixture of the two. A hunter-gatherer comes splashing and slipping, sweating and swearing, through this world which is her world, and stops on a little promontory between a sea full of islands and a land full of lakes, to draw breath. And the breath she draws is loathsome, fetid, corrupted. Wedged between sea-licked boulders nearby is a huge carcass. The pioneer picks her way around it delicately, respectfully, never having seen such a monster before, dead or alive; half her tribe could huddle under the vaulted roof of its skeleton. Perhaps her conception of the edge of the future is different from ours: rather than a wave for ever breaking over us from ahead, as it seems to be for us, it may form a mist-circle around her that accompanies her in any direction she chooses. But she might already have an inkling of a beginning here, a tendency for time to trickle in one direction only. She will report to the others what she sees and smells on the promontory of the beast, or of the whale, and the phrase will be repeated, and become a placename, a marker of a place fixed in its place and resistant to the flux of time so that it will be translated from language to passing language, to reach our age as Ros a' Mhíl, the promontory of the whale.

When the Stone Age forests of Connemara were invaded and over-whelmed by the slowly deepening bogs of the Bronze Age, the fallen tree trunks mostly rotted away under the weather, while the roots were preserved in anaerobic bogwater and buried in depths of peat. Then the sea level rose, and high tides carved channels into the bog. These narrow, soft-bottomed creeks were perfect little harbours for cowhide currachs, and many have twisted bog-oak roots protruding from their black cliffy banks that make handy bollards. Descendants of the first lady of Ros a' Mhíl, prowling along the coast by sea, happened to note a particularly serviceable such harbour, tucked into the inmost corner of a small bight and sheltered by an islet, near where she had seen the whale, on the eastern shore of the easternmost of south Connemara's four great bays. They settled there, and life took its irresistible course, as the old song, 'Ros a' Mhíl', tells us:

I Ros a' Mhíl cois cuain tá rúinsearc mo chléibh;
Néal ní chodlaím suaimhneach le mórchumha 'na déidh,
A' déanamh lionndubh in uaigneas nach trua libh fear mo scéil,
Ach 'sí mo leaba an uaigh mara bhfuasclaí sí mé.

[In Ros a' Mhíl by the bay is the love-secret of my breast; / I don't sleep an easy wink for great sorrowing after her, / Making melancholy in loneliness don't you pity a man in my state, / But the grave is my bed if she does not release me.]

Over the generations one of the region's most populous villages grew up, first south of the landing place, and later inland to the east of it, living off fishing and the export of turf to the city and to the Aran Islands. Officialdom had to take some notice of it when the French were on the seas after the Revolution and again in Napoleon's time, as it was realized that an invading force landing in Galway Bay could be threatening Dublin within six days. Three Martello towers, one of them at Ros a' Mhíl, the others at Aughinish and Finnevara on the south coast of Galway Bay, were built in about 1815, to supplement the chain of signal towers around the coast that I have already mentioned. The Ros a' Mhíl tower, a stout stone drum some forty feet high and thirty in diameter, stands by the shore just over half a mile south of the landing place. It would not be easy to take by force: its walls are thick and its cut stone-work unshakeable, and the slot-like door-opening is twelve or fifteen feet above ground level. It had an ample water tank in the basement, a magazine and stores above that, accommodation for an officer and thirty soldiers on the first floor, and on the flat, parapeted roof, a large cannon commanding a field of fire of 360 degrees. Grim and determined, aloof from the chaotic boulders and rock outcrops around it, it waits to this day like a giant's chess piece ready to make its move.

Then in the early 1820s Nimmo swept through Ros a' Mhíl, leaving plans for a pier of local granite, to be coped with blocks of limestone shipped in from the Aran Islands. The new quay (nowadays known as An tSeanchéibh, the old quay, having been rendered old by younger developments) would have obliterated my hypothetical aboriginal creek. By 1824 the harbour of Ros a' Mhíl was being used by nearly a hundred fishing boats. Then time turned cruel. *Pailitéirí*, landless people, moved into Tóin an Chnoic, the rear of the hill, at the end of the peninsula, building *bráicíní*, little huts, for themselves and cultivating the bog. It is said they used to strip off the upper layer of sods, dry them and burn them to ash, which they spread on the ground to feed it, a practice that eventually wore out the land. In the famine time the landlords, the hated Blakes, drove the people of Tóin an Chnoic across the little bay on its east to the even more barren bog of Baile an tSléibhe, the settlement of the 'mountain'. The husks of a deserted village in Tóin an Chnoic, and their children's burial ground, a knoll by the eastern shore, have been pointed out to me.

The picturesque old Seanchéibh, with its stacks of turf awaiting shipment, its pipe-puffing boatmen scrutinizing the sky and its clutch of hookers and *púcáin* bobbing alongside, having delighted the eye of painters and photographers since what felt like time immemorial, gradually fell behind the times and was superseded. As part of an EEC-funded development project a concrete pier was built to the west of it in the 1970s, with a cold store and a hall for fish auctions. It seems that the more space is taken up with concrete the more narrowly is time channelled into inexorable progress. But then, in a curious little vortex in time's flow, a fish-processing factory that was built in hardly more than three months in 1985, on a little point of land behind the western quay, totally vanished again after a short spell of intermittent operations. During its brief existence I wrote about it with an enthusiasm that surprised those who saw me as an inveterate objector to any modern developments:

The new factory, Prótéin Éisc, concentrates fish offal into a foodstuff for salmon and mink farms, a process that does not sound as if it would give rise to good architecture. But here the ideas of the sort of Romantic-High-Tech engineering (as seen, for instance, in the Beaubourg art centre in Paris) in which the functional parts are exposed and emphasized with colours instead of being hidden away behind walls, have been applied with great boldness, and the result is a building that does not try to 'harmonize with the landscape' as if it were guilty about being there at all, but inhabits it proudly. Lars Aglen, the Norwegian inventor of this way of using fish offal, also designed the layout of the factory. He has arranged its fourteen tall silos in two rows of seven, and linked them with narrow glazed panels to form its side-walls, so that the roof appears to be borne on monumental columns. And as the end-on profile of the very low-pitched roof is like that of a classical pediment, the whole is reminiscent (almost parodically) of a Greek temple. The exuberance of the conception is enhanced by the choice of a bright blue for the great blank end walls, a choice made by Winnie Joyce, the wife of the Irish partner in the enterprise, I am told. This, to my eyes at least, is the most exciting building in Connemara since Mitchell Henry's Kylemore Castle of the 1860s, which also has a touch of absurdity about it, and it deserves its magnificent site out on a headland in the airy expanses of Cuan Chasla, where it rears up like a temple before the fishing boats bringing in their tribute.

Unfortunately function lagged behind form; the factory stank like the hypothetical whale on which I have founded this brief history of Ros a' Mhíl, and its effluent polluted the waters of the bay. Very soon it was abandoned. Men had to go in and chisel out the fishy mess solidified in the silos, then the whole structure was dismantled, and the great marine temple ceased to be.

Very soon the old pier became overcrowded and quarrelsome as the Galway and Aran fishing fleet acquired bigger trawlers and rival ferry services to the Aran Islands fought it out during the tourist boom years. In 1989 another development project, to cost £6 million, was begun; the Seanchéibh was lengthened, and the auction hall, cold store and ice plant were relocated on a desert of concrete extending from the back of it (in the depths of which, perhaps, is the original bog-oak root to which I moored this history of the harbour). The Galway and Aran Fishermen's Co-op, founded in 1974, has its offices here now, and there is a proper waiting room for passengers to the islands, and a nearby car park for over 300 vehicles. Dredging of the harbour has brought an end to the ancient moon-linked regime of departures on high water; nowadays sailings to Aran, up to eight of them a day, in fast, two-tiered ferries, are precisely scheduled. There are also plans for a small-craft harbour to be built on reclaimed land in the middle of the bay, while a deep-water harbour for ever-bigger fishing vessels is under discussion.

Over the past few years €15 million has been spent on a brand-new harbour to the east of the Seanchéibh to facilitate Island Ferries' five big vessels in the handling of some 300,000 passenger journeys a year. I went down to see it on the day it was completed, in April 2010, and was astounded by the acreage of paved esplanade and the three great pontoons that rise and fall with the tides and are accessed by long covered ways, all as fresh as paint and as alien in this amphitheatre of ancient mountains and ageless waters as a newly landed space station. The contrast between the machinery of mass tourism deployed at Ros a' Mhíl and those tender flakes of limestone out in the ocean is painful. This is a tremendous public investment in the profitable private business of piping as many day-trippers into the Aran Islands as they can hold, regardless of its effect on those national treasuries of precious, ancient, delicate things: their boreens carpeted with wildflowers, their sainted ruins, their language and its memories.

Meanwhile, what used to be a ghastly blackish old fish factory by the approach road to the harbour has been refurbished and now looks relatively acceptable in a bland, anonymous way. But even as I write, I read of a threat to the jobs of forty fishermen and thirty factory workers; six trawlers are tied up and the factory is idle. As fish stocks have declined, so quotas are reduced, and while this local row will no doubt be resolved, it is symptomatic of a worldwide collapse of fish stocks. Is there an alternative future for Ros a' Mhíl in connection with the oil importation and storage facilities presently located in Galway, or in servicing the new energy industries to be founded on the Atlantic's winds and waves? Or could the whole harbour someday find that its time is up, that the Aran Islands are no longer open to exploitation and the fish have gone, and then lie here like a beached whale for a while before following the temple into oblivion?

In that encyclopaedia of absurdities, Georges Perec's 1978 novel *La Vie mode d'emploi* (the English version is *Life, A User's Manual*), we read of an English millionaire, Bartlebooth, who devises a discreet, logical and totally gratuitous programme for passing the remainder of his days. First, starting in 1925, he will spend ten years learning to paint (for which he has no talent) at the rate of a lesson a day; then he will travel the world for twenty years and paint 500 watercolour seascapes at the rate of one a fortnight, each to be posted to a craftsman who will glue it to a thin board and cut it into a jigsaw puzzle of 750 pieces. Finally the returned wanderer will, over another twenty years, reassemble the jigsaws at a rate of one a fortnight, and have each seascape treated so that it can be removed as a whole from its backing and returned to its place of origin, where it is to be dipped into a detergent solution and so reduced to a blank sheet of paper. Needless to say this plan of perfect futility is disrupted by the contingencies of life and death, but not before our hero has painted his first port of call, Gijon in the Bay of Biscay, and his last, Brouwershaven in Zeeland, and at some period in between, 'the little harbour of Muckanaghederdauhaulia, not far from Costelloe, in Ireland's Camus Bay'.

Since Perec was under the spell of spelling (he also wrote a novel without using the letter 'e', and another using no vowels but 'e'; and if all the 'e's evaporated out of his own name no vowels would be left other than 'o', a void, which is perhaps fortuitously the title, *A Void*, of the English version of his 'e'-less novel) it is certain that he was drawn to mention this obscurest corner of Connemara by its name, as reduced to comic inanity by anglicization, rather than by any quality of the place itself. I will now unpack the name, which gives us the basics of what is properly called Muiceanach Idir Dhá Sháile. The first word means a hog-backed hill, as mentioned earlier; it comes from the obsolete adjective *muicineach*, pig-like. The last means salt water, or an arm of the sea. The whole therefore means the hog-back between two arms of the sea.

Muiceanach Idir Dhá Sháile is in fact a small townland occupying a narrow promontory jutting northwards from the rim of the immense uninhabited bogland north of An Cheathrú Rua. To its west is Cuan Chamais, and to its east the string of lagoons and channels by which tides percolate southwards almost to Casla. A smooth glacial hill or drumlin occupies the centre of the peninsula. Thus the placename is a thumbnail sketch of the topography. Old maps show a tightly clustered settlement here, with the trackless bog to the south and the sea on all other sides. Until a footbridge was built in about 1900 linking it to the townland of Cinn Mhara, head of the sea, on the east, and then at some more recent date a road reached across the bogs from the south to run up the peninsula, all traffic must have been by boat or by one or two tidal fords. Nowadays a shrunken and still rather isolated population lives by farming or fishing or both in a small way.

I am sure that in spring, when it lies in the arms of Connemara's sparkling waters and catches the sun in its cupped hayfields, the place is delightful, but my several map-making visits in the 1980s were made in harsh weather and left me with an overriding impression of dismal, wet little fields and desolate stony shores; my diary even likens the peninsula to 'some poor famine victim lying down on the shore and going to sleep with a thick blanket of seaweed drawn up to his chin'. But the people I met were friendly; turf-cutters were ready to chat as we crouched over a few smouldering sods out on the bog, and even a dog that ran down a boreen to bark at me was content to join me under a bush and look out at the rain for quarter of an hour. The Ó Máille family, I remember, gave me cups of tea and a small store of placenames, and directed me to where Diarmaid of the Fianna made a bed for his Gráinne and left his gigantic footprint on a rock on the Cinn Mhara shore. (Many of the so-called beds attributed to the eloping couple are in fact megalithic tombs, but this one, disappointingly, was just a small rectangular hollow and purely natural so far as I could see.) Since then I have learned that the excellence of Muiceanach Idir Dhá Sháile lies in its traditional singers, that something as warming and pungent as brandy has been brewing for generations in these little farmhouses, potato plots and nooks of the shoreline. To hear Sarah Ghriallais sing, even in the sterile setting of a TV studio, is to realize that the *sean-nós* is still an open road from the past. She is one of twelve siblings, among whom she, Nan and Nóra have each won the prestigious Corn Uí Riada, the *sean-nós* singing competition at the annual Oireachtas – in fact Nóra has won it three times. When asked to sing Sarah will say, in Irish, 'Well, I'm not as good as I used to be, but I'll have a go,' and without getting up from her chair will perform as unselfconsciously as if she were in her own kitchen, in the style of inward woe, of the unshed tear in the heart, that I gather is characteristic of Muiceanach Idir Dhá Sháile.

But it is the bridge that is for me the main character of the village. As mentioned above, a footbridge was built in 1900 or so, a strange lanky contraption of timber and concrete on several tall spindly supports, just wide enough to drive a fat pig across. For farmers heading to the fair at Maam Cross it saved having to ferry stock across an 'arm of the sea', but I have heard that the local poitín-makers were not happy with it as it enabled the police from Oughterard to descend on them with little or no warning. In 1955 the question of its repairs was raised in the Dáil, and I am told that TDs took great pleasure in bringing it up repeatedly, with histrionic hesitations over 'Muck . . . Mucky . . . Muckannegg . . .' until the Honourable Members were falling about with laughter. In 1980 the bridge finally fell down, nearly carrying to their deaths a couple of girl students from one of the Irish summer schools. For a long time it lay there like a gigantic broken stick-insect, while plans were drawn up for a proper road bridge that would cross the tidal channel in a single 42-foot span. This project was anxiously debated locally. During this period I met a *stumpa fir*, a little stump of a man, on the road in Camas, who told me that the old bridge had had twelve or sixteen openings (he must have been counting the little apertures in its parapets), whereas the new one was to have but one – '*súil amháin*', 'a single eye', as he put it, gazing up at me solemnly and with an immensely impressive length in the word '*soooool*'; and '*Tá mise á rá leat!*', 'I'm telling you', he kept repeating with tremendous emphasis, '*Tá mise á rá leat . . .*' that the first time a spring tide came together with a wind from the north-east the bridge would surely be swept away.

Soon after that my partner M and I had to make a life-changing decision that is indelibly associated in our minds with the famous bridge. Our eleven-year spell in the Aran Islands was coming to an end, and our plan was to resettle ourselves in London, whence I would return now and again while finishing off my research towards a map of south Connemara. But before we did so I wanted to show M my new-found land, and so we came across by the little open ferryboat of those days to Ros a' Mhíl and set off to cycle around Connemara. Under September sunshine and showers the countryside was at its most seductive; M was amazed and appalled by the beauty and amplitude of the terrain I had rashly undertaken to map. In Roundstone we happened upon the Industrial Development Authority's craft estate, where there were a studio and a little house available to rent. In no time at all M worked it out that we should make this the base, not for the mapping of south Connemara but of the whole of Connemara; while this was in progress – which would surely only take a year or so, said I, underestimating by a factor of seven, as it turned out – she could go and earn some money as a temporary office worker in London. I felt faint at the sudden prospect, and had to sit down on the bare stairs of the house we had gained entrance to. That evening we climbed Cashel Hill, and in sight of a multitude of mountains confirmed our decision.

The next morning we set off for Ros a' Mhíl, as we wanted to get back to the Aran Islands to vote in one of the great human-rights referenda of that obnoxious period in Irish history during which not a craw remained unthumped. A rising north-west wind seemed to hurry us on our way. In Camas, tousled from the gale, I ducked into the former national school that serves as the offices of An Comhlachas Náisiúnta Drámaíochta, an association for the promotion of Irish-language drama, and asked in Irish if I might use their phone. I remember the eyes of the girl in the office growing rounder and rounder as she overheard this weather-beaten bicyclist arranging an appointment to discuss leasing premises with the IDA. 'What should we bring with us?' I asked, thinking of references and samples of publications. 'Just bring yourselves!' was the amiable reply. By the time we were whizzing southwards again it was obvious that the Aran ferry would not be sailing that day, so we decided to divert via Muiceanach Idir Dhá Sháile to a friend's house in An Cheathrú Rua, and go into Galway the next day to see the IDA.

We took a side road that leads over the little hill of Cinn Mhara, where the wind met us head-on and forced us to dismount, and came down to the bridge. It was far from finished, funds having run out as we later learned, but the body of it was there, without parapets or approach ramps. A large notice forbade crossing. Nobody was about, so I scrambled up onto it, M heaved the bicycles up to me and then I pulled her aboard. The wind was shrieking down the channel; later M told me she had clearly seen the headlines, 'English couple blown off the bridge of Muckanaghederdauhaulia'. We dropped the bikes off the other end of the bridge and set off across the utterly shelterless bog to the south; the gusts were so strong that we had to push the bikes all the six miles to An Cheathrú Rua. The next day the residue of the gale blew us into Galway, where the IDA gulped us down like a sea anemone ingesting a shrimp, for reasons I have explained apropos of our settling in Roundstone, in *Listening to the Wind*. Thus it was that the bridge came to stand for a diversion of our lives, a way taken that has led us to – well, 'M's is her own story,' as I wrote at the beginning of my book on Aran, but for myself, what it has led to is a quarter of a century of work on a project that for the most part has been supremely soul-fulfilling, and at times has felt as eccentric as Bartlebooth's scheme for the employment of life.

25 The River

Apart from the little-used bridge of the last chapter, all vehicular access to South Connemara's densest complexes of habitation, An Cheathrú Rua and Na hOileáin, is through the village of Casla, on the isthmus between the head of Cuan Chasla, to the south, and Loch Cara Fionnla, to the north. Since 1972, views of that locality have been dominated by the mast of Raidió na Gaeltachta, the mere sight of which fills the air with the invisible heartbeat of the Irish language. The service's HQ is here in Casla and there are also studios serving the Gaeilgeoirí of Donegal, Mayo, Meath, Waterford, Cork and Kerry, as well as Dublin. It is operated by RTÉ but has its own advisory council and controller. It attracts some 150,000 listeners a week, and one of its crucial functions is to bring the far-scattered Gaeltachtaí within earshot of each other and break down provincial rivalries and prejudicial attitudes to regional dialects. The invaluable 'RnaG' is a neighbourly presence; one hears the rattle of jigs and reels and the familiar voices of its presenters from houses as one passes. Make a humorous remark to one of its team met on the road and it will be aired to the Irish-speaking world that same day.

The village gets its name from a *casla* or small creek: the mouth of the river, Abhainn Chasla, that flows into the bay east of the village. The name is frequently anglicized as Costelloe, not from the family of that name but from a mispronunciation of *casla*, which it seems Alexander Nimmo was the first to commit to paper, in his piloting instructions for this coast. Doire Né, more correctly Doire an Fhéich, the wood of the raven, is the name of the townland in which Casla lies. In the *Books of Survey and Distribution*, which record changes in land ownership over the Cromwellian period, I read that 'Derrynea' belonged to the Frenches before the rebellion of 1641 and to the Blakes after the Restoration.

Who were the early inhabitants? Perhaps an old woman called

Sadhbh Ní Shúilleabháin was one of them. Her name has been preserved in a folktale about Aill na Graí, the cliff of the stud (i.e. a place where horses were bred), which rises from the roadside opposite an old quay a mile or so west of the river. Like the very similar roadside cliff in Cashel that I described in *Listening to the Wind*, this was reputedly a fairy dwelling, and a threat to passers-by. One evening Sadhbh was walking past by herself and the fairies snatched her into it. The first thing she saw inside it was a corpse on a bed. A fairy woman said, 'Who will wash this corpse and lay it out?', and another answered, 'Who will wash it and lay it out but Sadhbh Ní Shúilleabháin?' Sadhbh got into a rage and shouted, 'To the demon or the devil with it ['*Don deamhan nó don diabhal é*'], Sadhbh Ní Shúilleabháin won't wash it or touch it!' And because of her cursing they threw her out onto the road again. (Fairies are extraordinarily touchy about bad language.)

Until well after the Famine the only road in the district was the coast road from Galway, and it terminated at the bridge over the river. But it was the river that was the goal of most of the place's few visitors, for it teemed with salmon and sea trout in season. In pre-Famine days the fishery was leased from a Mr Cottingham, who lived near Oughterard, by a consortium of wealthy anglers. A Mr Belton, in his book *The Angler in Ireland* (1834), expressed his astonishment at the river's productivity:

The late Sir R. Staples, a most superior sportsman, took lease of this river for thirty years. He built a small but very comfortable house on its banks, where he usually spent three or four of the summer months, employing ten watchers to guard the sacred waters from every kind of poaching . . . The number and weight of fish that Sir R. Staples often killed would seem incredible to anyone only acquainted with the streams of South Britain. We succeeded in basketing forty-three white trout, of from three quarters of a pound up to five pounds, and weighing altogether seventy-three pounds, besides losing a vast number more, and rises beyond all count.

From another angler, writing in 1840, we have a lip-licking description of the hospitality of the Staples' lodge:

We soon entered the lodge, and in a short time sat down to a dinner, to which we were well inclined to do ample justice. 'Jack Mulloy', with his greyhounds, had crossed the mountains, the day before, to give notice of our approach, and had brought in a brace of hares, which had been reduced to most palatable soup. One of the keepers had been up the river about five o'clock, and in proof of his success, at the head of the table smoked a splendid fresh run salmon, of twelve pounds weight, which, three hours before, had been swimming in Corrigmore Pool. Some of the fishermen from the bay had called and left a fine turbot, with a couple of lobsters to keep him in countenance; there was a saddle of five-year-old mountain mutton, with chickens and bacon to retire upon. Nor were we without a glass of genuine sherry, just, as old G . . . . said, 'to dry our feet' after the mountain walk. The ubiquitous Guinness had contrived to transmit a barrel of XX to this almost inaccessible region. And who that has ever sat over the turf fire at Costello, after a hard day's exercise, and long-continued wetting, will fail to appreciate, and gratefully remember, the mountain-dew which the faithful John Connor produced from some mysterious depository, about which no one made any particular inquiry.

In the 1850s the lodge and the fishery were in the hands of the Hon. Richard Hely Hutchinson, a prominent Conservative politician who succeeded to the title of Lord Donoughmore in 1851 and went on to become a president of the Board of Trade and a member of the Privy Council. Mr Balfour, Chief Secretary for Ireland, and his party were the guests of the 'Costello Fishing Club' in 1890, when touring the famished coastal districts of Galway and Mayo, in which the lodge must have been an oasis of comfort and prosperity. Soon after that date improvements to the fishery – reparation of a sort for the decades of unthinking slaughter – were undertaken by a V. P. Laing, who cleared the tributary streams and established a hatchery, which remained in operation until about 1920. Laing was exceedingly rich, or seemed so to the impoverished locals, among whom 'as rich as Laing' became a formula of comparison that has outlasted the man himself.

The next owner of the lodge was a man who had come to Connemara to hide from infamy. Bruce Ismay, President and Chairman of the White Star Line, had been on board the company's liner, the *Titanic*, on its inaugural voyage in 1912. The huge ship was an epitome of the class society of that age: a layer cake of privilege with poor emigrants from Ireland packed into steerage down below, the second-class and the first-class accommodation above that, and twenty-eight staterooms of fabulous opulence as icing on the cake. When the magnificent unsinkable brushed up against an iceberg at full speed and began to fill, the proletariat found itself trapped in the belly of the leviathan; the number of lifeboats had been reduced to the legal minimum to make room for luxury, they were all on the first-class deck, and many of the staircases were locked. According to the findings of a subsequent inquiry, Ismay assisted many women and children into a lifeboat, and then, as it was being launched, there being no more passengers in the vicinity, got into it himself. He must have spent the rest of his life, like Conrad's Lord Jim, in reliving that moment, whether it was one of decision or of automatism. His was the last lifeboat to get away; over 1,500 were left to drown. In the lifeboat he was, it appears, in deep shock; he did not turn to watch as his proud creation upended and plunged. Many felt that he should have gone down with his ship, as the captain did, especially when it became known that he had a radio message warning of ice in his pocket at the time, and that the ship was a kettle of design faults. Hounded by the Hearst press in America and ostracized by London society, slandered by the accusation that he had disguised himself in woman's clothes in order to get away, Bruce Ismay retired to Connemara.

To the local people Mr Ismay and his wife Julia were of course distant figures in the social landscape, but they were well regarded as sources of employment and charity. The womenfolk worked for them as maids and cooks, and the schoolchildren were occasionally given sweets and clothes by Mrs Ismay – 'like Our Lady in Heaven with stuff you wouldn't get in any shop out here'. The boatmen took them out fishing, and it is remembered that on Sundays Ismay would enquire before setting out as to whether they had been to Mass. (The Ismays themselves, I am told, attended services at 'Teachín na bPrayers' near Scríb.) The lodge, a two-storey thatched building, was burned down by the IRA in the Troubles, and was rebuilt in 1925 on a much grander,

10,000-square-foot scale, with eight bedrooms, four reception rooms, conservatory, a games room and so on; a spiral staircase designed by Ismay, which unfolded at the press of a button, was an object of wonder to the servants. The *Titanic* was a forbidden topic in the lodge, and perhaps the family was unaware of the cruel pun on Bruce Ismay's name circulated among their Irish-speaking neighbours: *Brú síos mé*, lower me down (i.e. into a lifeboat).

After twenty-five years Ismay moved back to England, suffering from diabetes. He underwent a leg amputation, and died in Mayfair in 1937. His widow stayed on in Connemara for many years, and erected a monument to her husband in the garden, a romantically rugged chunk of limestone, with a rather enigmatic inscription:

He loved all wild and solitary places where we taste the pleasure of believing what we see is boundless as we wish our souls to be.

Those solitary places were surely witnesses of much agony of mind; the wilderness must often have been full of the screams of those abandoned to their doom on his foundering dream-palace.

One can be sure that throughout the history of the Casla fishery there has been nocturnal war between the owners and their bailiffs on the one hand and local men and boys (including some of those same bailiffs) who naturally considered they had as good a right to nature's bounty as the gentry. A mile or so west of the lodge is (and has been for perhaps a century or more) Derrynea courthouse, where many a case of poaching was tried. The song 'Cúirt Mhallaithe Dhoire an Fhéich', 'The Accursed Court of Doire an Fhéich', is a raw account from the 1930s of the sufferings of a man sent from the court to Galway prison for a 'big long month'. On arrival its gates open before him like those of Hell, and he is stripped as naked as he was at birth. The food is yellow meal stirabout and lumps of bread as hard as a millstone (but in the third week he gets a little cocoa with a drop of milk through it). His worst care is that back at home his ass is not under the straddle and his little horse is in the hay and his seaweed scattered on the shore. When the turnkey asks him what brought him there he answers, 'Musha, trouble that came upon me and I say no lie, but whatever I did, I'll not tell before I die.' Perhaps I go too far beyond evidence in imagining that his trouble involved the river and its fish.

The next owner of Costelloe Lodge, as it is now called, was Colm Ó Lochlainn – a man so committed to the Irish cultural and political project, and especially to the language, that it was a surprise to me to learn that he is ill-remembered in Casla for having evicted a family from a cottage they had occupied for generations. Ó Lochlainn was born into a prosperous Dublin family in the printing business; his father was a Kilkenny man and spoke Irish. He taught briefly at Pearse's Scoil Éanna, and studied Old Irish under Eoin Mac Néill. He took lessons in piping from Séamas Ennis's father in return for tuition in Irish, and when still a student became Secretary of Cumann na bPíobairí, the pipers' association. A member of the IRB and the Volunteers, he was ordered to Kerry in April 1916, when Roger Casement and a cargo of arms were due to be brought in by yacht from a German submarine – a plan that miscarried when the yacht was captured and Casement arrested. Three young Volunteers driving behind Ó Lochlainn went off the road and were drowned in a lake – a chaotic end to an escapade that Colm later looked back on as 'a boyish adventure'. Shortly before this he had been asked by certain of the revolutionaries to print a document they said had originated in Dublin Castle, listing people the government intended to arrest. Suspecting that it was a forgery intended to win Mac Néill's support for the forthcoming Rising, Colm showed it to him, and it was one of the reasons Mac Néill tried to stop the Rising at the last moment. Disillusioned by such duplicity among the Pearse faction, Colm lost enthusiasm for the revolutionary cause, and his subsequent career was devoted to the service of Irish culture.

His publishing imprint, At the Sign of the Three Candles, was founded in about 1926; its best-known productions are two collections of Irish street ballads (which set Ronnie Drew singing). With the help of an artist, Karl Uhlemann, he designed the elegant typeface Cló Cholm Cille, which brought the Gaelic script used in medieval manuscripts into the era of Eric Gill. A lecturer in UCD's Irish department, a singer often heard with his sister on Radio Éireann and a committee member of the Gaelic League, Ó Lochlainn was, most probably, the

first master of Costelloe Lodge to appreciate the culture of his neighbours. No doubt it was some impediment to his enjoyment of his other
passion, fishing, that led to the eviction of the occupants of Teach an
Droichid, Bridge House, in 1954. As he was a member of the Connemara Board of Fishery Conservators, it was amusing to discover that
he himself had been up before the court in the previous year for un-
licensed use of a fixed net. He and his employees had been netting the
river, and, according to his account of it, after he had gone home to
bed they had fixed the net in position, which was illegal in the absence
of a licence, and had been caught in the act by the water keepers. He
got off on appeal with the time-honoured defence that he had intended
to get a licence the next day.

The first time I called into the lodge, it was in the possession of the
late Jack Toohey and his wife Agnes. Toohey, born into a Limerick
Jewish community in 1909, had been highly successful in the ladies'
wear business and at one time was Ireland's largest exporter of clothing, employing some 200 workers in his Dublin concern, Ascot Models.
He was also a sportsman, winning motor races for Ford in the 1930s,
and in more recent times a benefactor of the Connemara Isles golf
course in Eanach Mheáin. He was also an art collector. (A statue he
bought from Edward Delaney and presented to the nation was recently
installed in the Formal Garden of the Irish Museum of Modern Art.)
He retired in 1979, when he bought and restored the lodge, and he
died there in 2002.

All this I learned later; on the day I walked up the drive, clanged
the big bell that hung from a tree, as if in a castle forecourt, and looked
around me astonished by the symmetries of the lawn and shrubberies
and the complex roof slopes, tastefully profiled gables and round-
arched doorways of this grand Arts-and-Crafts-style mansion, so
sedulously hidden from the road by dark conifers, the servant girl who
eventually appeared told me that the family was away, and she knew
nothing of the place's history. More recently, therefore, I asked my
friend and mentor in Irish-language matters, Liam Mac Con Iomaire,
to show me round the locality as I knew he had been born nearby, and
then learned to my surprise that Liam's name in the old Irish system
of patronymics is Billy Mháirtín Mhaidhc Thomáis Pháidín an

Droichid (of the bridge), and that it was his parents who with their young ones had been evicted from Teach an Droichid. So far as the family understood they had been the owners of the cottage ever since the ancestral Páidín an Droichid; but the law deemed otherwise, and although they won some compensation in a court case they had to set about building a new house on land they owned half a mile to the north-west by Céibh Aill na Graí, and were forced to move into it before it was properly habitable. The cottage by the bridge then became the fishery manager's office. Nowadays the premises of the modern hatchery and the new manager's office are located behind it.

Not surprisingly, given this history, my tour with Liam had something of the covert nature of a poaching expedition. First he led me down a muddy and grassy track to a small stone pier, Céibh an Tí Mhóir, the quay of the big house, by the dark still waters of the estuary, the *casla*, itself. From there a slight path sneaked round behind the grounds of the lodge to the bridge. We peered over the demesne wall into a dense little wood, through which we could glimpse a complicated corner of the lodge with a balcony over a sun lounge or conservatory. The trees – cypresses and pines – are wind-blasted and grey to seaward but flourishing landward, with branches flying as if in remembered onshore gales. An ancient, squat, barrel-trunked Monterey pine overhangs the wall, its upper branches matted into layers tenanted by herons; six or eight of the great birds floated out above us, their broad wings black against the sky, a perfect Japanese moment. Below the bridge and the cottage is a broad tidal pool; Liam remembered how his father, a keen angler, would sometimes come home at midnight, change into his oilers and wellingtons and go down to this pool, and Liam would accompany him carrying two big ewers, which with their rounded bellies and narrower necks were ideal for keeping the catch in. Sometimes sea trout were so plentiful his father would catch them three at a time with the three flies on his line; then Liam would go to bed delighted at the prospect of fresh trout for breakfast the following day.

The bridge nowadays links the huge developments of Ros a' Mhíl in one direction with the industrial estates of Casla and An Cheathrú Rua in the other; so the once idyllically perched cottage is within a few feet of heavy traffic. We crossed the road from it and climbed through a stile to follow the river bank upstream into the lonely bogs it drains, the roars of the road soon falling into deep silence behind us. The river is lively, wrigglesome, playful, rich in incidental places. Liam showed me a pool where some big seabird he and his young friends took to be a gannet used to catch fish, and the lads would hide behind a gorse-bush and leap out to scare it away and seize its prey; they soon learned not to strike too soon lest the fish escape, but to wait until the 'gannet' had given it a few good pecks in the neck. We passed Carra na nEascannaí, the crossing place of the eels; he remembered how eels used to come squirming on their bellies out of the water to eat the offal when fish were being gutted on the bank. Further upstream we looked into a little brick-built shed that used to house 'The Ram', a pump that thumped away all day long supplying the lodge with water drawn from the stream just above the tidal limit. After about three-quarters of a mile we came to a deserted lunch house for anglers, in a snug hollow among moss-covered boulders and old ash trees, over-looking Cottage Pool. This perfect gravel-bottomed spawning place was carefully guarded by the water keepers, and was the site of the early hatchery. The present hut, on the site of a thatched homestead that had been there for generations and, like Bridge House, was rather suddenly abandoned, dates from some thirty years ago. It has a pantiled roof knobbed with golden-green moss, and the sides of its roof kick outwards slightly just above the eaves as if in respectful allusion to the lodge itself, which has the same nicety of design. Through a broken window we could see graffiti of very competently drawn Galway hookers on an interior wall.

Finally we climbed out of the hollow onto a plain that seemed to stretch for miles northwards towards the Mám Tuirc mountains, or a hazy reduced image of them. It was the first day of a belated spring; masses of dried-up purple moor-grass gave the vast extent of the bog a blonde pallor, and half a midday moon hung high before us, pale almost to invisibility. There were discreet signs of life, though nothing moved but a skylark singing high above: otter spraints by the river, the empty cocoon of an emperor moth lying on a tussock of heather. A faint path, making use of the tawny outcrops of granite where they ran in the right direction and augmented by sequences of stepping stones in muddy places, led us on towards the little stone-built hutches or *brácaí* the bailiffs used to lurk in by night. This must have been one of those 'wild and solitary places' Bruce Ismay loved, where, according to his epitaph, 'we taste the pleasure of believing what we see is boundless as we wish our souls to be'. That wish is not an option for me; souls are not boundless, they have their particular ends and in the end all drown in the boundlessness of what happens; but I can taste the pleasure of the make-belief that such a place and time might go on for ever.

26 Views of An Cheathrú Rua

The name An Cheathrú Rua, anglicized as Carraroe, is loosely applied to the whole of a low-lying peninsula about four miles long and a variable mile or so across. It means 'the reddish quarter', and reflects the generally starved and unprofitable nature of the land. The shore-side fields are half stony hummocks and half wet dells, and when a heather fire licks swiftly across the low hills of the interior it reveals acres of granite from which the peat has been stripped over the centuries and shipped as turf to the Aran Islands and Galway city, while the scraw, the topmost layer full of living roots, was burned at home, such was the pressure of want.

More particularly An Cheathrú Rua is the name of a large village – by Connemara standards a town – the public face of which mainly shows along a road obliquely crossing the neck of the peninsula, while much of its private life is hidden away down two side roads and a net of boreens extending southwards towards the headland. There is an old harbour on either side of the peninsula: Sruthán, stream, at the east; and Caladh Thaidhg, Tadhg's harbour, to the west. Both were once busy ports, the delight of photographers and painters, with men in traditional garb flinging turf into the bulging bellies of hookers moored by picturesque old stone quays. By the end of the 1960s just two veterans of the Aran turf trade were still making the crossing: *An Tónaí* from Sruthán and *An Mhaighdean Mhara*, 'The Mermaid', from Caladh Thaidhg. Since then, though, the revival of the workboats for purposes of fun and sport has meant that nowadays one can see a gaggle of them in either little harbour; the old quays, on the other hand, have been denatured with concrete, a stuff with which Connemara, in revolt against its stony past, has an addictive relationship.

The event that gives the village its little place in history, Cath na Ceathrún Ruaidhe or the Battle of Carraroe, took place in 1880. At that period, while the eastern half of the peninsula was part of the vast

Berridge estate, the western half was the property of the Kirwans of Blindwell, Tuam. Like most of their neighbours in Connemara the people of An Cheathrú Rua were in a state of 'distress' after several bad harvests; Michael Davitt, the Fenian and IRB member who, with Parnell, founded the Land League in 1879, had visited the locality in that year and reported that the people were reduced to eating their seed potatoes, which were in any case of poorest quality and vulnerable to blight. A few days after the following New Year there were disturbances on the Kirwan estate when notices of ejectment were being served by Mr Kirwan's henchmen, supported by a flying column of sixty constables. Missiles were thrown, the police made a charge, cabins were closed and the ejectment notices nailed to their doors. As the situation worsened a force of 200 constables was sent down to Galway by rail and every public vehicle was requisitioned to take them out to An Cheathrú Rua. These events were widely reported. The *New York Herald*'s Irish correspondent describes how on the following day Fenton, the process server, in the midst of a little army, tried to execute his mission:

The first house visited was that of William Faherty. Women surrounded the door, and, as Fenton advanced to effect service, they clutched the process and tore it to shreds. The police then charged all round with their sword bayonets, wounding several severely. The women were bayoneted right and left; and one of them, Mrs Conneally, sustained such injuries that the last rites of the Church had to be administered to her by the Rev. P. J. Newell, the Catholic priest of the place, who was an eye-witness of the scene.

At another house, that of James Mackle, the police used their bayonets again and were showered with sticks and stones.

The police became much excited, and at last fired some shots over the heads of their assailants. Then the process server attempted to deliver the document. The women, as before, snatched it out of his hand and destroyed it. Sub-inspector Gibbons rushed into the house, and, as he advanced to the hearth, Mrs Mackle lifted a blazing turf, and smashed it on his neck . . . The commanding officer considered that the situation was now too critical to act without the presence of a magistrate, whose orders would relieve the constables of the legal responsibility of a conflict with the peasantry. Accordingly the whole force was withdrawn, and concentrated at the police barracks in the village, where the process server remained for protection.

Another newspaper, the *Galway Vindicator*, reported that 2,000 or so people, some of them coming from a distance, assembled on all the eminences within a mile or two of the barracks; this intimidatory presence evidently persuaded the unfortunate Fenton to write to the agent, Robinson of Roundstone, declining to serve any more notices. No reply was received, and the people then dispersed quietly. Finally a steamer, the *Citie of the Tribes*, came out from Galway to collect the entire force of police.

This popular revolt did not stop evictions, but it did make An Cheathrú Rua an unmissable stop on the distress-tourism trail, as a new parish priest, Fr Conroy (of the Conroys of Garafin), who arrived a few years later, wrote in his memoirs:

. . . great estrangement continued between Mrs. Kirwan and her Carraroe tenants and rents were not paid for some years. During this unhappy period I came to Carraroe and Lettermullen. Other evictions of Mrs. Kirwan's tenants took place. Visitors from England came to see Irish evictions and were directed by the Land League to Carraroe . . . The evictions of Carraroe and the great struggle of the people to hold their homesteads against the landlord and forces of the Crown were again and again referred to by Mr. Parnell and Mr. Davitt in their efforts in America to collect money to help the Land League as well as to relieve the partial famine.

In the end the priest succeeded in bringing about a settlement between Mrs Kirwan and her tenants, in recognition of which she donated the site for a presbytery. Local memory preserves a strange detail of those tumultuous days. It is said that many unfamiliar faces were seen among the throngs that gathered: the dead of the Famine times, come up from the old graveyard of Barr an Doire south of Sruthán. Traditionally Irish rebels have summoned the past generations to their side only metaphorically; thus the Fenians derived their name from the Fianna of old, and thus we have Cú Chulainn in the Dublin GPO. The Land Leaguers of An Cheathrú Rua, it seems, brought this recurrent trope a shade nearer reality by convoking the actual ghosts of their ancestors.

To give a brief overview of the village as it strikes the visitor today, I will start from the east, following the road from Casla past Sruthán harbour. On the left here is a side road leading into a charming valley, An Gleann Mór, the big glen, which immediately contradicts what I have written above on the barrenness of the area, as if the shelter of the hill (a sacred height, as I shall explain later on) to the west had cast a beneficent spell on it. There are trees and cornfields; I remember meeting the cooperative thresher going from farmyard to farmyard here, leaving pools of golden, fragrant chaff. Here we are in the townland of Barr an Doire, the head of the oak wood, and it is not unimaginable that there was an oak wood in this valley once upon a time.

The main road leading on to the village from Sruthán has Lochán an Mhuilinn, the lakelet of the mill, on its north or right-hand side. The mill, hardly traceable nowadays, stood on the *sruthán* itself, the stream that empties into Sruthán harbour and whose full name is Sruthán an Bheannaithe, the stream of the blessing – a hint of a legend I will attend to later on. Between the road and the lake is a building that originated as a CDB lace school, perhaps around 1900, and in the 1970s and '80s housed Bob Quinn's film studio and cinema, Cinegael; here originated a range of films as various as *Poitín*, a grim Connemara tragedy, the first feature film in the Irish language, and *The Atlantean Quartet*, a study of Gaelic Ireland's hypothetical affiliations with the exotic Mediterranean.

As one travels on westwards, houses become more closely spaced south of the road, their gardens opulent with hydrangeas in summer. Then comes the surprisingly big chapel, much extended in 1947 but still incorporating one built largely by local labour in 1892–3, under the guidance of the parish priest, Fr Walter Conway, who at the same time oversaw the building of a school close by. This priest was long remembered for his crossness – he used his blackthorn stick on anyone he saw loitering idly – and for treating his workers and visitors to glasses of poitín of twice the usual strength. He had distillers make this potent brew for him in a shed by the priest's house, and once sent a keg of it by horse and car to his Archbishop, in a box addressed to the Archbishop's servant girl, Bridgie Mogan, c/o Lord MacEvilly, Tuam, and labelled 'Jam with care'. The church is known as Séipéal an Chillín, 'An Cillín' being the old name of the eastern half of the peninsula, derived from a medieval chapel and graveyard down by the shore in Barr an Doire. Similarly the next side road to the south, just beyond the church, is Bóthar an Chillín. A few hundred yards down this road is the large comprehensive school dating from 1968; one of the earliest such schools in the country, it incorporates the former Presentation Convent, opposite it.

The nub of the village lies around this turning to the south and another to the north a little further on. Clustered here are a bar called Tigh an Táilliúra (the tailor's house); the Irish-language school Coláiste Cholumba; and an eye-catching modern building with an ambitious curving roof, opened in 2001 and rather oddly named An Scailp Chultúrtha, which houses a public library and serves as a venue for community occasions. Just up the turning to the north are: Tigh Nan Dooley, a day-centre for children with learning difficulties, the only such to be run through the medium of Irish; next to it, the former technical school, now Áras Uí Chadhain, an outpost of NUI Galway providing courses in Irish and named after the language's great modernist Máirtín Ó Cadhain; opposite, the Garda station, and the hotel Óstán Cheathrú Rua with its attendant clutch of holiday cottages. Further west on the main road are Áras Mac Dara, an old people's home; another bar, An Réalt (the star); another hotel, Óstán an Dóilín; and, on the turning to the left leading down to the sports field, an industrial estate of several factories.

A little further on there are turnings to the right, of which the second runs down past a pretty lake to the harbour, Caladh Thaidhg, built in 1842 by a Tadhg Ó Catháin, who owned boats trading to and from Galway; there is a derelict seaweed factory, a gloomy concrete hulk, beside it, which was operative only for a decade or so from about 1947. At the beginning of the side road down to the harbour was the old barracks, once the only slated building in the locality, and which too was built by the enterprising Tadhg. It was the focus of the Battle of Carraroe of 1880, was burned out in the Troubles of 1922–3, but survived sufficiently to provide the setting for Bob Quinn's *Poitín*. The main road continues westwards in a minor vein as An Bóthar Buí, the yellow road, so called because it used to be surfaced with reddish-yellow sand from a nearby quarry. It winds up a hill and down again past lots of houses and lots of hydrangeas (the saving grace of An Cheathrú Rua), and sheds the last of the village to run through rough little fields to a beach, Trá an Dóilín, the strand of the creek, better known these days by the touristic name of An Trá Choiréalach (the 'coral' being the washed-ashore twiggy scraps of a seaweed with lime-stiff fronds, as found on the Coral Strand in Mannin Bay).

That, then, is An Cheathrú Rua in summary – higgledy-piggledy, assembled as if by successive throws of dice rather than according to a plan. The artists who discovered the village as a reservoir of the traditional and authentic a century ago would be astounded and dismayed by it, but it is animated by a self-confident community that still treasures the Irish language and includes a remarkable number of well-known *sean-nós* singers. It has its Saturday-night scene and attendant troubles as do all villages; there are discos in the hotels and sessions in the bars and chippers open late. It is only as contradictory and untidy as life.

Now for a more personal and inward view of An Cheathrú Rua I start with a particular house and then follow a train of thought out into the hinterland and around the hintershore to the south of the village. The house in question is on the north side of An Bóthar Buí; it has a distinctly English, or more exactly a Home Counties and Edwardian air to it, which the tourist might not notice in passing as it is tucked away behind old trees. This is Tigh Lamb, Lamb's house, where the artist Charles Lamb had his studio and painting school. In it I have found welcome ever since I first called and was entertained on the doorstep by Lamb's five-year-old granddaughter Doireann.

Charles Lamb, son of an Ulster Catholic house-painter and decorator, born in 1893, first studied art in evening classes in Belfast, and won a scholarship that took him to the Dublin School of Art in 1917. A close associate there was Seán Keating, the heroicizer of Aran Man, the IRA of the Civil War, and the construction of the Ardnacrusha hydroelectric power station. If Keating – a noisy painter, thrusting everything into aggressive proximity with the viewer – was an ideologue of the headline themes of Irish nationalism, Lamb soon adopted a more reflective and quieter mode for himself, in a sustained and loving observation of the craggy charms of a fading way of life in the Connemara Gaeltacht. Perhaps, though, he shared Keating's fixed belief that modernism was humbug, for his work never steps out of the province of rural naturalism. It was Pádraic Ó Conaire who steered him towards Connemara; the pair of them came out to An Spidéal in the 1920s, and Lamb went on to tour Connemara on horseback and find in An Cheathrú Rua a landscape that fired his imagination and became for him a world of lime-white, golden-thatched cottages that nestled into their settings and were inhabited by people formed by the simple dignity of their tasks: *The Turfcutter*, *Connemara Harvesters*, *The Lobster Fisherman* (to quote some of his titles); also *The Young Connemara Girl*, in a round-eyed fireside trance over some traditional song or tale, and *The Quaint Couple*, who have survived much and sit together like two boulders in one of their stony fields.

Charles Lamb and his wife Katherine, daughter of the novelist Ford Madox Ford (and so great-granddaughter of the pre-Raphaelite painter Ford Madox Brown), built the house on the Bóthar Buí in 1935 – a good-hearted, right-thinking house, harking back to the Arts and Crafts movement in its clarity of form (for instance the fall-pipes are all hidden in the thickness of the walls), fidelity to materials (the walls being built of variously shaped polygonal blocks of local granite ingeniously fitted together, unplastered, golden in the evening sunshine) and the touch of the human hand (although the craftsmen had to be brought in from Armagh and East Galway as their skills were not to be found locally). It is a one-and-a-half-storey house with little dormer-windowed bedrooms under the steep slate roof, no porch but a few steps up to the plain front doorway, and three chunky chimney stacks. There are some stylish adjustments of one form to another: the slight flaring of the roof as it descends to the eaves, and the blunting of the upper edges of the chimneys, making them slot easily into the sky – a motif Lamb brought back from a painting tour in Brittany.

Behind the house was the studio, the hub of the painting school Lamb conducted for many years. He himself was a small fiery man. The locals remember Leaimbín na Féasóige, little Lamb of the beard, as being *crosta* when hung-over, but he hated being dragged out to the pubs by the heavy-drinking artists grouped around Gerard Dillon on Inis Leacan. '*Fear lách grádiaúil*', 'a kind, charitable man', is another judgement I hear of him, and his employing local children in his vegetable garden and paying boatmen to take his students out to the Aran Islands were appreciated by the penurious community. Despite his high regard for traditional ways he never mastered the Irish language; his wife acquired much more of it but never lost her English accent.

Charles Lamb died in 1964, and the house is now the summer home of his daughter Laillí, her husband the wildlife film-maker Éamon de Buitléar, and her brother Peadar Lamb, the well-known Abbey actor. I came to know it as a relief from the rigours of the road when mapping the neighbourhood in the 1980s. Here many strands of a regional culture seemed to knit themselves together into a mutually sustaining web. The Connemara landscape had its presence through the many paintings on the walls by Laillí's father and his pupils. Éamon brought in not only the voices of birds and mammals (quite literally, being a brilliant mimic) but that of traditional music too, having played the button accordion in Seán Ó Riada's group Ceoltóirí Chualann and gone on to found his own 'company of musicians', Ceoltóirí Laighean. The thought of the sea was never far away: Peadar had a *gleoiteog* moored in Caladh Thaidhg, and Cian, Éamon and Laillí's son, was later to work with his father on films celebrating the old Galway workboats and recording the building of his own hooker, *Star of the West*. Tigh Lamb was talkative in Irish and English, and as busy as a hive with comings and goings – Peadar off down to secure his boat when the wind threatened to rise; Doireann, the little de Buitléar daughter, a non-stop comic turn; the elder children preoccupied with their cryptic teenage concerns; Éamon awaiting a telephone call to say that a family of otters had been spotted in Killary Harbour; his film crew and their bulky equipment filling the hall; and my M, on one of her rare visits, trying to protect the late Mrs Lamb's precious old china teacups from their manly grasps.

I have a snapshot I took (curious art, that conserves me a memory of an occasion in which I seemingly do not figure – thus showing how things will be when I am gone) of Laillí, Éamon and M with Walter Verling, who had been the last of Charles Lamb's pupils, and his elegant wife, sitting around a little folding table crowded with teacups and cake on the gravel sweep before the house: Laillí in full anecdotal flow, Éamon bare-chested and bronzed, Walter in smart tweed jacket sitting slightly apart, pipe in mouth and hands on knees, apparently studying the group as if for a painting. Walter was still committed to marching out *en plein air* and snatching the *motif* live from the jaws of time in a brisk and bold shorthand of brushstrokes. Aidan Dunne in an appreciative review of his exhibition in the Limerick City Art Gallery in 2008 writes of him as 'a representative of an Ireland that predates not only the Celtic Tiger but also the era of Seán Lemass and T. K. Whitaker', and whose work 'reflects some of the more positive aspects of pre-modernised Ireland'. He was such a familiar of the boreens and shorelines of An Cheathrú Rua, Éamon tells me, that another visiting artist was told by a local man that he had come too late: '*Tá chuile* view *tógtha ag an Máistir Werling*!' ('Every view has been taken by Master Verling!') Not only a painter of the Old School (to quote Dunne again), he is also a dedicated teacher, and, I would imagine, an exacting one. Later during that visit, when Éamon was driving M and me to catch our ferry home to Aran, we saw Walter with his easel by the roadside in Ros a' Mhíl village; he had some message for Éamon, and signalled to us to stop with curious precise right-angle turns of a pointed finger, as if he were marshalling a fly to a landing place. But, looking around the village, bristling with telegraph poles and banjaxed by bungalows, I wondered what of Old School beauty he might hope to find by peering under the wires at a ruined landscape from which indeed every view had been taken. West of Ireland naturalism is reaching the end of a narrowing outlook. It will be driven into ever-greater selectivity, and so fall into untruth by omission, unless it takes on modernity in all its ungainly contradictions.

No, I exaggerate. There are still plenty of lovely views in An Cheathrú Rua, and one that remains with me is the panoramic outlook from the peninsula's highest hill, which rises eastwards from the comprehensive school to a modest 228 feet. To the north, beyond the immediate busyness of the little town below the hill, the bogs stretch away and rise into hills inland of Ros Muc, with the Mám Tuirc range and the Twelve Pins overtopping them in the distance. To the east, trawlers and the Aran ferries negotiating the bends of Cuan Chasla to and from Ros a' Mhíl. To the west, Cuan an Fhir Mhóir or Greatman's Bay (more on this giant later on), separating An Cheathrú Rua from the next peninsula, which is broken up by narrow windings of the sea into the archipelago of Na hOileáin; there is perhaps a tiny currach with an outboard engine unzipping the stillness of the waters. All the coastal reaches of this complexity of place are densely settled; there are so many houses – mere dots of white from here – that I can scarcely credit that I have at least looked at each one to mark it on my map, and have drunk tea and talked about this strange, self-obsessed coun-tryside in a fair proportion of them. Within these rims of settlement are heather-tinted inlands of bog or silvery barren hills. And to the south, away across the sun-spattered ocean, the long blue-grey-cloaked forms of the Aran Islands lie prostrate, like postulant monks, on the horizon. A tiny little tab fitting into the sky on the profile of the biggest of the islands, Árainn itself, is – I work it out – the house M and I lived in for so many spellbound years. My heart flows out to it.

Perhaps there is a connection between this hill and Aran. Its name is Cnoc an Phobail, the hill of the congregation, and the midsummer or St John's Eve bonfire is lit on it; there must be a whole congregation of flickering points of light visible from this height as each village lights its own fire. There is a dark little tarn full of waterlilies in a fold of the hill near the summit, Loch na Naomh, the lake of the saints, who, I was told by a local man, stopped here on their way to Aran; one of them stooped to drink a little rainwater lodged in a cow's hoof-print, and it grew into this beautiful and slightly mysterious lakelet. They had come from the north, leaving holy wells at each of their stops, including those I have mentioned in Casla and Cladhnach. In the harbour of Sruthán is a knob of rock called An tOileáinín Bean-naithe, the blessed islet, which was another of the saints' resting places. All such sites are protected by supernatural sanctions, as local folklore well knows. When the quay at Sruthán was being enlarged the foreman ordered one of the workers to blast the islet out of the way. The man refused to obey, until the parish priest, happening by, assured him that it was all right to carry on – but of course when he went to pick up the charge it exploded, and he lost several of his fingers. Similarly for the well in Casla: it was destroyed in the course of quarrying there, and the man who did the deed fell and broke his ankle, and a year to the day later he fell and broke it again.

From Loch na Naomh the saints moved on to An Rinn near the south-westernmost point or *rinn* of the peninsula, where there is another holy well, and whether they went on to Aran by boat or by miracle I do not know. But as he reached the shore at An Rinn their leader realized he had left his prayer book at the lake. Word was passed back along the line of saints, who were so numerous that the last of them was able to pick up the book as he left the lake. Once when I was geologizing on Cnoc an Phobail a tall silent figure with a staff came stalking up the hill, who could have been one of the saints come back to collect some forgotten relic, but turned out to be a grazier looking for straying cattle; he did not know the place's legend as he was from Leitir Mór na Coille, but he had a similar tale concerning Cnocán an tSoiscéil there and the old graveyard in An Seanbhaile. So perhaps one can reconstruct a single legend of larger scope, with the saints marching in from beyond the pass in Leitir Mór na Coille – in which case they were following the line of the Shannawona fault fairly closely, that great earth-crack so significant for the topography of south Connemara. Here on the south flank of Cnoc an Phobail the fault manifests itself as intrusions of white quartz that appear in the granite as dazzling sheets, fiercely worked, and contorted veins of it like thick ropes knotted into a rough carpet. The miraculous-looking skein leads southwards, towards Aran. I know of two dykes of quartz in Leitir Mealláin that are regarded as saints' roads leading out to Aran, and so perhaps I can add to the reconstructed legend that this quartz carpet on the saints' hill is also the road they took, imbued with the spiritual radiance of their footfall.

The last well of the saints' march is one of the few holy wells marked on the old six-inch Ordnance Survey sheet, but in the wrong place; the map has it twenty yards or so above the high-water mark, whereas in fact it is down on the foreshore and only accessible when the tide is out. It is of course a round, sea-worn pothole rather than a spring well. A woman I once met on the road in An Cheathrú Rua first told me about it. If someone of your family was away in America, she said, and you had had no news of them, you could go down to the well and scatter some crumbs on the water, and a *breaicín*, a little fish, would appear; if it swam the right way up, your loved one was well, and if it swam upside down he or she was dead. Her simple account, a harsh light on the heartbreak of emigration in preliterate days, remained with me; I was anxious to see this well, and had already failed to find it once, even with the help of quite a few men from the nearby hamlet of An Rinn. However, a friend of Lailí's, Peadar Tommy Mac Donncha, had an elder brother in An Rinn who was said to know exactly where it was, so we arranged to meet up with him. Together with an elderly bachelor, Máirtín, who had already shown me some other wells, Peadar and I walked down to An Rinn (a scattered few houses and bungalows; the most striking feature of the place on that first acquaintance was a magpie's nest, a huge ball of twigs full of squeaky chicks, precariously lodged between three wires at the top of the last telegraph pole, there being not a tree in the vicinity). There we collected Joe Tommy, and after some groping about in the seaweed he found the well, a neat oval bowl about two feet across. It was full of mud and pebbles, which we began to scoop out. Then the fabulous fish came to light; Joe Tommy held it out to me on the palm of his hand and I stroked its head. I felt I had never come so close to magic. It was what they called a *donnánach*, a little rockfish. Joe put it aside casually, and no doubt it found its way back into its pool with the next tide, for small shore fish are very territorial.

This handling of the spirit of the rock pool made me conscious of the immensity of the hidden interface between land and sea. A fish the size of the *donnánach* has access to holes and crevices the surface area of which is many times greater than that of the foreshore as we would measure it, in acres, say. Within those retreats are smaller ones, home to little creeping things that enjoy still larger areas, not just in inverse proportion to their own size, but absolutely. Extending this thought to the single-celled population of the seashore, it seems that our acre contains within it thousands of acres. Since thought has access everywhere, rightly considered the nondescript rocky shore is cavernous, labyrinthine, unfathomable. Add to these fractal dimensions the echoing linguistic space opened up by placenames and oral lore, and the mythic realms inhabited by prophetic fish and wonder-working saints, and it is clear that my account of it, even if I wrote volumes on this one dog-eared corner of land, would be a mere footnote to reality.

When we had finished at the well the lanky Joe Tommy led us at a vigorous pace down the coast, he and Máirtín closely inspecting every bullock in the little fields and at the same time calling out placenames which I tried to scribble down as I tussled with maps in the breeze. The area around the well is An Mullán, the boulder, or Mullán na Naomh, the boulder of the saints; but there was no prominent boulder nearby to anchor the name; if it was one of the stone boats the saints used in the days of faith, it had long set sail for Aran. Just south of the well the fractal structure of Irish toponymania seemed to reach crisis: a cleft in the shore hardly big enough to berth a currach in was called An Ing Chaol, the narrow notch or groove; forty yards away was An Ing Mhór, the big notch; and in between them were a few pinches of sand – An Tráighín Idir Dhá Ing, the little beach between two notches. We scrambled along past An Crompán Sliogánach, the shelly creek, and An Meall Glas, the green knob, and Barr na Cora, the tip of the rocky point (the southernmost extreme of the whole peninsula), and Na Muiltíní, the small boulders, and Caladh an Uisce, the harbour of the water, and lots of other plainly and practically named shore-forms; then we turned inland, crossed a few stone walls to reach a track to the village, and so home. But for this writing I will continue along the south and east coasts of the peninsula, putting together some of the findings of my several expeditions.

After about 1,200 yards of the variously shelly, knobbly, bouldery and watery foreshore of the south coast one comes to the mouth of Sruthán na Teorann, the stream of the boundary, which has its western bank in the pre-Reformation parish of Kilcummin and its eastern bank in that of Killannin. At one time this was also the division between the Kirwans' land to the west and the Martin, later the Berridge, estate

to the east; also that between the Diocese of Galway to the west and
the Diocese of Tuam to the east. Here at least the last-named boundary was clearly defined, but the rest of its ramble through south
Connemara was as intricate and disputatious as any theological crux.
Like Gladstone, who used to boast that he was the only person who
understood the Schleswig-Holstein Question, so, after many an hour
poring over a very obscure map kindly supplied by the Archbishop's
secretary in Tuam, I could at one time claim to have understood these
ecclesiastical divisions – but certainty has evaporated and I am not
minded to take up the puzzle again. Even the present parish boundaries here and in Na hOileáin made more sense in the days when it was
easier to cross the arms of the sea by boat than to drive around them
in a pony trap. Enough to say that in the Church's good time the two
halves of the Ceathrú Rua peninsula were welded together as the parish
of Killeen or An Cillín, and since 1890, with the islands of Garomna
and Leitir Mealláin, form Paróiste an Chillín agus Gharomna, in the
Diocese of Tuam, while the island of Leitir Móir and its satellites made
up the small Paróiste Leitir Móir, formerly part of Paróiste Chill Bhriocáin (i.e. Ros Muc), in the Diocese of Galway. And throughout all
this, Sruthán na Teorann just kept rolling along.

A little further to the east the road from the village of An Tismeáin
comes down to a beach, Trá an Tismeáin (or, more correctly, Trá na
Tismeána). *Tismeáin* isn't in the dictionaries, nor is it understood
locally, but Professor de Bhaldraithe told me it means 'exact middle';
and here we are about halfway along the south coast. There is a little
memorial by the rocks at the western end of this beach, which I pass
by for the moment with a muttered blessing, although I have no faith
in prayer, and to which I will return.

To the east again is An Dólainn, the creek; compared to the other
creeks of this unemphatic coast it is large, with room for hookers to
come up to a little quay at its head. Two broken-down dams there
were obviously intended to keep the tide out of some useful grazing
inland of it; they are marked as 'floodgate' on the OS map of 1839.
The remains of a huge shell midden can be seen on a tiny cape of land
between the two dams. What age it was one can only guess for the
heaps of limpet and periwinkle shells have long been carted off for

burning to lime to sweeten the land, but it was notable enough to have been given a name, An Caisleán Cruinn, the round castle. Three or four hundred yards inland of the dam are some broken remains of the walls of what the OS maps of 1839 and 1899 name as Keeraun House, once a place of some standing; the clutch of houses a little further north are still known as An Diméin, the demesne. In the 1790s this was the seat of Máirtín Mór Ó Máille or Máilleach an Chaoráin. (A *caorán* is a round heathy hill, and here we are in the townland of An Caorán Beag.) He was the acknowledged head of the smuggling business in Connemara, as a Galway magistrate, Mansergh St George, reported to government; he lived here 'in a state of permanent defence' and ingratiated himself with the local people by dispensing lavish hospitality. His landlord was the profligate Humanity Dick Martin of Ballynahinch, who, according to St George, had borrowed large amounts of money from Ó Máille. The fame of his hospitality lasted long; Seán Mac Giollarnáth was able to collect this lore about An Máilleach from a Garomna boatman in the 1930s:

There were few houses in Ireland finer than his house. He was a tenant of Colonel Martin, and an honour to him. It was the highest honour Martin enjoyed, having him as a tenant. This Ó Máille was shipping from Guernsey, and he always had a barrel of wine in the house, its lid off and permission for anyone to drink the full of his cup from it. When he killed an ox or a sheep none of it was salted for he shared out the meat and it would be eaten before it needed salting.

Ó Máille died in a duel over a nothing. He was entertaining the Bishop of Galway and others once, and as it was a Friday the Bishop was eating fish. When a servant thoughtlessly poured meat gravy on it the Bishop simply waved the dish aside, but the Bishop's cousin Sir Thomas French made an affair of honour out of it. Where I learned these details I cannot now recall. Mac Giollarnáth's old storyteller had a slightly different version, and provided a memorable end to the story:

Máirtín Mór Ó Máille said something impolite in the presence of the Bishop of Galway, and the Bishop hit him on the mouth with the back of his hand.

A cousin of the Bishop's, Sir Thomas French, challenged An Máilleach to a duel. An Máilleach was killed with the first shot. When Col. Martin heard the story he said that Ó Máille had preferred a hole in his guts to a hole in his honour, 'But,' he said, 'there would have been a hole in neither if he had let me know of it.'

And that was the end of the great Ó Máille. The next generation of the family moved out to the Aran Islands (where I track them down in *Stones of Aran: Labyrinth*), and by degrees the old house in An Diméin fell apart.

From An Dólainn the coast trends southwards to the south-eastern extremity of the peninsula, on the other side of which is another former landing place for smugglers, An Cuan Caol, the narrow bay; the iron spikes they used to moor their boats to can still be seen, set in the rocky shore. There is a substantial quay here, and a clutch of small fishing boats, and the village of An Pointe looks down on it from a little height. Immediately to the east is Aill an Chlogáis, the cliff of the tower, bearing a small automated lighthouse to guide shipping into the mouth of Cuan Chasla. The eastern shoreline of the peninsula is a succession of low stony capes and little sandy beaches; just beyond the lighthouse is An Trá Bhig, the little beach, then Trá na Boilgeoige, named from some sort of small swelling or *bolg* – a blister, a submerged reef, a bubble; the dictionary gives plenty of alternatives and local opinion is undecided. Next, Trá an Chaoráin Bhig, the beach of the small moorland hill, where I found the sea kale growing, a great rarity in which I am told Laillí's mother took an interest. Round the next little headland is Trá na Reilige, the beach of the graveyard, and just inland of it, the ancient *cillín* or burial ground from which the parish has its name, An Cillín, full of sea breezes and the wildflowers that thrive in them, and gravestones that lean towards each other, gossiping about the dead.

Nearby is a medieval chapel, roofless, robbed of some cut blocks from one of its doorways, its gables shrouded in ivy, its interior full of brambles and fallen stone. A lancet window in the east gable has an ogee limestone head to it with sunburst patterns carved on its spandrels, oddly refined in contrast to the rough granite wall it is set into. The church has a strange and suggestive name: Teampall Inis Mac Adhaimh, the temple of the island of the sons of Adam, for which Roderick O'Flaherty is the prime source:

Between Casla Haven and Fearmore, or the Great Man's Haven lyes the land of Killin, about four miles, where stands a church by the sea-side, which antiquity named Inismacaw church, the feast day whereof is on the 15th of March.

Hardiman, his nineteenth-century editor, comments on this, 'When or by whom it was built, or why "antiquity named" it so, we are ignorant.' I am told by a researcher that *inis* can mean, not an island, but a holm or water meadow, and that there are no early ecclesiastical mentions of Mac Adhaimh. The opinion of An Cheathrú Rua is that the church was built by a Naomh Smocán or Mocán, who came across from the Aran Islands; people living nearby heard the sound of building, and in the morning the church was there. It is at least obvious that the cut limestone blocks of its window and door surrounds came from Aran, but scholarship holds that St Smocán or Mocán is a will-o'-the-wisp, a mere echo of the phrase 'Inis Mac Adhaimh', and the question of the origin of that name rests with 'antiquity'.

The next landmark (omitting a thousand wrinkles of the coast, important to boatmen and seaweed harvesters) is a house, placed to admire a vast expanse of the bay and the shores and hills beyond, that reminds one of Charles Lamb's. In fact it was designed by Lamb for his friend of Dublin days, Arland Ussher, the philosopher-essayist. Ussher was the TCD- and Cambridge-educated scion of an old Ascendancy family and a student of the Irish language (but no revivalist). A sometimes savage ironist, when his income from the family farm was curtailed by De Valera's Economic War with Britain, he wrote an application for the post of public hangman, 'as there appear to be no other openings for young men of good family and liberal views in the Twenty-Six Counties':

I may mention that as a translator of Gaelic poetry I should hope to pass the bilingual test, necessary for all appointments in the Free State, and doubtless essential for taking down the last remarks of prisoners, which are made, presumably, in Irish only.

Tigh Ussher shares a look with Tigh Lamb, but by the time it was built, in 1946, cut granite could no longer be afforded, and the house is built of concrete blocks and dashed with pebbles from the nearby shingle bank. Perhaps such a house, of English affinities constrained by Irish-British animosity, was appropriate for the rueful portraitist of *The Face and Mind of Ireland*.

One final curious feature to finish this view of the shores of An Cheathrú Rua, before I return to that little monument by Trá na Tismeána. Just inland of Tigh Ussher a forest of strange forms that remind me of the instruments by Mace Head meteorological station rears up in a field behind a small studio-house. This is the Sculpture Park created by Edward Delaney, who died here in 2010 at the age of seventy-nine. Delaney is best known for two public monuments to national heroes in Dublin, the Wolfe Tone memorial in St Stephen's Green, and the Thomas Davis fountain opposite Trinity College. He won many prizes and prestigious commissions, but his work was often vigorously criticized (in fact Wolfe Tone was blown up in 1971, perhaps by Loyalists intent on revenge for the IRA's demolition of Nelson's Pillar), and Delaney responded with equally vigorous criticisms of the Irish public's critical faculties. He was, by all accounts, a roistering, vociferous, contrarian figure around town in his younger days, but in the mid 1980s he retired to Connemara, where he abandoned his representational, expressionistic bronzes for the abstract works in steel that now puzzle visitors on their way to the beach. Local opinion of them is summed up by the man who, as Éamon de Buitléar likes to recall, said, 'They're no good at all! I've been watching them for a year, and the crows don't take a blind bit of notice of them.'

27 The Waste Shore

'Paint me a cavernous waste shore,' demands T. S. Eliot in the sonorous introductory verse of his 'Sweeney Erect', a poem in which I now read hatred of women, hatred of the Irish, hatred of the working class, hatred of the body, but which has echoed in my head ever since I read it as a youngster, drunk on modernism, to whom it was not yet hateful but cryptic and therefore probably profound. And it still resonates, especially in the phrase 'the bold anfractuous rocks'. I have come across this valuable word, 'anfractuous', nowhere else; it means, according to the *OED*, sinuous or circuitous, but with the sound of fracturing in its heart it seems to answer not just to the winding course of the south Connemara coast but to its intimate texture, with its heaps of boulders worn into smoothly curving rims and basins by the almost ceaseless pounding of the waves.

In his second verse Eliot makes brief mention of Ariadne, her hair tangled by the gales that speed her false lover's ship away from her. Ovid tells us that Ariadne, having eloped with Theseus from her parents' palace in Crete, was callously abandoned by him on Naxos in the Cyclades, where Bacchus found her and made her his bride. Catullus adds a soft-porn account of her state of near-naked vulnerability as she watches Theseus's ship flying off to Athens. Her 'rescue' was a rape, as Titian's gorgeous painting in the National Gallery, London – still gorgeous despite the rape the restorers perpetrated on it – makes plain: Bacchus is accompanied by his drunken, libidinous rout of fauns and satyrs, and is shown leaping from his chariot, his whole body a stiff, urgent little phallus; Ariadne's magnificent gesture spiralling from heel to raised hand is a vain attempt to ward him off.

On a Saturday night in December 1998 three girls, Siobhán, her sister and a friend, were given a lift into An Cheathrú Rua from their home in Leitir Móir. The other two were let into a disco in the hotel Óstán an Dóilín, but the men on the door knew that Siobhán was only seventeen and turned her away. She went off down the village street, which was probably quite animated at that time of a Saturday night; perhaps she was heading for a chipper. A 23-year-old man, John, from one of the little clusters of houses on the boreens south of the main road, was also around town in his car. He had just seen his ex-girlfriend queuing up for the disco, and had struck her on the head and punched her new boyfriend. A Garda had told him to go home, and he had answered, 'It's a free fucking country.' Towards one o'clock in the morning John picked up Siobhán near one of the pubs – perhaps he offered her a lift – and turned down one of the roads to the south. Meanwhile the Garda, concerned about John's aggressive manner earlier in the night, had driven down to his family home and knocked at the door, but got no answer; on his way back he probably just missed meeting John's car coming down the road. At a place where high field walls hid the deed, John raped Siobhán horribly. Then he carried or dragged her a few hundred yards down to the shore and dumped her in a channel between great boulders. He went home, and at around two o'clock was seen in town again, without the white jumper he had been wearing earlier. Two or three hours later the rising tide reached Siobhán; whether she was still conscious by then is uncertain. The following afternoon a man hunting for rats and crows on the shore was led to the body by his spaniel.

The tone of early newspaper reports of her death suggests that the community soon deduced who was responsible; only a local would have been able to negotiate the web of boreens between the town and the isolated strand where Siobhán was found. The heart-shaped silver pendant she had been wearing was discovered too, in the roadside field where the rape took place. John was questioned twice, and a few days later his house was raided and the jumper he had been wearing on the night of the murder taken for examination. Fibres found on it matched those from the girl's clothing. When the Gardaí came to rearrest him in mid January his mother was heard to say, '*Ná habair tada leo agus seasfaidh mise leat*' ('Don't tell them anything and I'll stand by you'). She was arrested on suspicion of withholding information, but apart from admitting that she had washed her son's jumper since the murder, she said nothing and spent most of her time in detention singing *sean-*

nós songs. A neighbour of the family later told reporters that he had been asked to tell the Gardaí that he had seen John in An Cheathrú Rua at the time the murder was thought to have been committed, but refused to do so as he had not been in the village that night.

John was finally tried in June the following year. His parents and siblings supported him throughout the trial, at which he admitted nothing. When he was found guilty he exclaimed, 'Oh, for fuck's sake, *ní dhearna mé é*' ('I didn't do it'). He was sentenced to life imprisonment. In 2007 he appealed unsuccessfully against the conviction. The people of An Cheathrú Rua, who stood by Siobhán's family throughout, built the little memorial by Trá na Tismeána that I passed by in my previous chapter.

I have no words adequate to these facts. The waves breaking on the waste shore will have to speak for me.

28 Going Native in Bungalowland

When the journalist Frank McDonald began his 'Bungalow Blitz' campaign against bad planning in rural areas, in 1987, the photograph used to accompany his full-page spread in the *Irish Times* was an aerial shot of the coastal region north of An Cheathrú Rua. It shows a road following its old twisty way, with houses – mainly bungalows, but also some cottages of traditional layout with multiple extensions – adhering to it in random clumps like barnacles on a piece of driftwood. Immediately behind the houses and largely invisible from the road is the well-known landscape of stone-walled fields fading away into a vista of bays and islands and distant hills. 'Driving through the area,' McDonald wrote, 'is a shocking experience':

The blight of bungalows is spreading right around the coast, consuming almost everything in sight and leaving only the boggy hinterland in a passably unspoiled state . . . Connemara is littered with the ruins of sturdy old cottages, often side by side with the brash new bungalows . . . stark reminders that the present inhabitants of Connemara have emphatically rejected their past, and the poverty associated with it, in favour of pervasive vulgarity.

Since then the situation has worsened. Misuse of the notorious 'Section 4' procedure under which, in cases of 'essential housing needs', councillors could override their own planning officers' objections to building in areas of 'outstanding scenic amenity' amounted to a secular selling of indulgences. The very name of An Taisce, the voluntary National Trust organization, which resolutely opposed such practices, became a hate-word in the mouths of clientelist politicians. The social costs of dispersed housing have become clear – the contamination of drinking water by leaking septic tanks in this terrain of shallow soils and impenetrable rock, the increase in road traffic, the expense of supplying electricity, telephone service, water, rubbish collection, school buses and so on. Nevertheless, today's bungalows, crowned with dormer windows and multiple gables, are twice as big and twice as numerous as those McDonald deplored, and a large proportion of them are holiday homes empty for most of the year.

I happened to bump into Frank McDonald at some official function soon after his article appeared, and when I suggested to him that there might be something positive to be said about this new form of settlement, he smilingly told me I had 'gone native'. But 'driving through the area' is the key phrase in McDonald's article, and the quality I was beginning to become aware of is not one visible from the window of a car. At that time I had just finished mapping the Ceathrú Rua sprawl, pushing my bike along each road and boreen as I marked every house on my wind-torn photocopies of the old Ordnance Survey six-inch maps, often being appalled by their ugliness and the clumsiness of their siting, but at the same time finding a certain fascination in the vagaries of their coexistence with the traditional, and above all talking to everyone I met. I knew I had taken on local colour – a rain-stained, wind-chapped lichen grey – when a couple of boatmen, eyeing the big black shoulder bag in which I carried maps, camera, binoculars and specimen jar, asked if I was selling anything, and on three occasions a Traveller, trawling the laneways in a battered van stuffed with wife and children and towing a little horsebox from which a pair of grey furry ears stuck out behind, asked me if I had any old donkey for sale. (But how I resent the appropriation of that fine word 'traveller' by one small sect of us gentlefolk of the road!)

Actually, gossip was my stock in trade. In visiting every townland, often carrying greetings from one family to another, I accumulated a stockpile of information that was of passionate interest to people who often lacked an excuse for roving about and would have been accused of snooping had they done so. My knowledge of the Aran Islanders, among whom the boatmen in particular had many friends and business contacts from the days of the turf trade, was a particularly choice line of ware. Gossip matures into *seanchas*, old lore, with time: to elicit tales of the saints of Connemara all I had to do was to tell some tale of the saints of Aran, and local pride did the rest. Sometimes an old story was enough to repay an otherwise unrewarding day of exploration. A man with a funny little dog I met on the road told me of a holy well, Tobar Anna, which had a cure in its water if you saw a fly floating on it; the people of the house beside it had improved it ('*chuir siad caoi air*'), he said – a bad portent, usually meaning concrete and an ugly cross. I found the well, hidden away in a mesh of boreens; it was a little spring in a diamond-shaped hollow at the foot of a small scarp of rock, and indeed it had suffered from updating with concrete. But its legend was pure illumination. A woman who had committed a great sin was told by her priest to visit wild and lonely places and to light a candle at each one, and that she would find forgiveness at the place where her candle stayed alight. So she visited various holy wells all over Ireland and her candle kept blowing out, until she came here, where it burned on even though there was 'a terrible storm of wind'. So too I occasionally found, if not forgiveness, a validation of my researches in this anomalous territory disputed between today's economic headlines and yesterday's old tales.

Sometimes in this bicycle-powered world of roadside and hearthside conversations I felt I was inhabiting my own nostalgic fantasy of bygone Ireland. At other times it came to me that I was entering dangerously far into the countryside's own fantasies. One elderly bachelor (long gone now to his lonely grave), down at the holy well to which he had guided me, asked if I'd had any 'biteen' since I came to Connemara. It soon became apparent that he was in want of a wife, who would be someone to talk to, and wondered if I, as a sort of *spailpín fánach* or roving labourer, in and out of every kitchen, might find him one – 'any woman, up to fifty-five, Protestant or Catholic'. I took this seriously; the quest wasn't impossible, for his was just the sort of hard case that the marriage bureau associated with the shrine of Knock in County Mayo undertook with occasional success. On our parting he gave me a hug and a peck on the cheek. I didn't mind that – I have deep sympathy for the many such isolates stranded between modernity and a traditional way of life – but I found myself avoiding him on subsequent forays in his neighbourhood. The problem was that his little cottage was right next to the only road to various places and people I wanted to visit, but fortunately there was a long decline before it on which my bike and I could pick up speed so as to pass his door like a meteorite. Even then, about a year later, he suddenly materialized at my side, pedalling furiously and crying, 'Listen! Did you find me a woman yet?' 'Still looking!' I replied as the momentum of my heavy conscience carried me off towards the horizon.

The old world, so far sunk into desuetude that it is hardly distinguishable from the other world of ghosts and fairies, still subsists in nettly banks and briary ditches in the interstices of the modern. I used to enquire – very tentatively, knowing what painful memories I might evoke – after children's burial grounds, having found that almost every townland or village had one tucked away in some unfrequented or marginal spot, unrecorded and in danger of being itself buried, not in ground consecrated by grief but in the concrete of foundations. One wild day a very elderly couple invited me into their caravan for shelter, tea and bread and marmalade, and when I asked for directions to one such little plot I had heard of in the vicinity, the husband pointed up the sloping fields behind the caravan saying, 'Some of my own are buried there.' It was not the one I was looking for but another, even more obscure and seemingly associated with the one household alone. I climbed over walls and stamped around in undergrowth looking for a telltale cluster of small boulders set in the ground, while the old man shouted directions that were torn away by the wind, but I failed to locate it precisely.

As well as marking all the new houses on my old OS maps I also had to cross off those that no longer existed, except perhaps as ruins. This I found a trying task, but to indicate all these absences on the map I went on to publish would have blackened it with the shadow of the past. Famine graves too were depressingly numerous familiars of this terrain disputed between today and yesterday, and I regret to say that I eventually stopped recording them. I remember looking for one I had been told of, behind an isolated cottage down a boreen. There I found a tall, long-skirted elderly lady digging potatoes, and put my question to her. '*Níl sé i bhfad uaim*' ('It's not far from me'), she replied unsmilingly, parting the bushes along the field edge to show me a couple of small stones. She remembered the name of the man buried there: Peadar Keehan. In 1995 I wove this episode into a talk called

'Weeping for Connemara', which I gave to a conference in New York commemorating the Great Famine. Much of the material that had been presented on that occasion was at once dry and harrowing (I remember in particular an analysis of mortality statistics by a European expert who referred to his subject throughout as the 'decomposition' of mortality statistics, which added an extra note of morbidity). So, when I had mentioned Peadar Keehan I departed from my script to ask the audience if he was the first famine victim to be given a name in these proceedings. It seems it was so, and years later someone who had been present told me that the interjection had been a shock. So Peadar had his posthumous moment of recognition, even if I could only apologize for knowing nothing of him beyond his name and the place of his resurrection among the bushes and the bungalows.

29 The Inordinate Isles

If Plato is right and the things of this world are imperfect copies of ideal forms, then the archipelago of Na hOileáin, the islands, must have its celestial counterpart in a realm of absolute goodness, beauty and truth. In a wild flight of fancy, born of hard days of bog-hopping and shore-stumbling, I came to associate it with the mathematical object known as the Mandelbrot set. This astounding form was first evoked in 1980 by the genius who gave us the concept of the fractal. As it was built up for the first time, pixel by pixel on a primitive computer screen through the endless reiteration of a very simple calculation, it loomed into view, slowly revealing more and more of its details. Its initial bug-like appearance as a kidney-shaped region with a circular bud just touching it at its round end, and vague spindly antennae, was not engaging. But then its finer features gradually became visible, or perhaps, one should say, came into existence. Its boundary proved to be studded with circular buds like the first but ranging downwards in size to invisibility. With today's computers one can see that each of these buds is rimmed by endless numbers of lesser ones, and so on ad infinitum, all of them issuing in filaments that ramify, coil into exquisite curlicues and clasp together like barbaric ornaments. Choose any tiny fragment of this tissue of forms and magnify it a thousand-fold, or a million-fold, and you find inexhaustible treasures: hyperdaisies, superCeltic spirals, spilt galaxies, celestial seaweed beds. Caught in this paradisal tangle like jewelled clasps in the hair of archangels are countless reduced versions of the original set, each of which has its own ever-more-minute simulacra, down to the infinitesimally small, giving the whole a degree of self-similarity that makes it the mother of all fractals. A flight into the endless complexities of this psychedelic fantasia through the medium of the computer screen is one of the signature experiences of this age, an enchantment, revelatory of the richness of pure form, and mortally frightening.

And on the other hand, one has the messy confusion of Na hOile-áin, the result of repeated geological faulting and the ever-renewed attack of the ocean. One can pick form out of it, including a notable degree of self-similarity in the hierarchical concatenation of its islands. Garomna, a battered disc some four miles across, is its heart. At the north, north-west and south-west, Garomna is linked by causeways to rather smaller islands, each of them linked to two or three still-smaller ones. Every one of these islands has an irregular halo of islets and offshore rocks, many of which can be reached when the tide is out. The fringes of these exhibit the usual interdigitation and mutual inclusion of sea and shore: headlands riven by creeks, bays forking around promontories, rock pools with rocky hummocks standing in them, rocky hummocks with rock pools hollowed out of them. Nevertheless, to compare the general form of the archipelago with that of the Mandelbrot set exposes it as stunted, lopsided, ridiculous, falling far short of the Platonic ideal. But this is to read it as a mere outline on a map, and if the cartographical image is abandoned in favour of direct physical contact with the place, supplemented by attention to its unwearying account of itself in placelore and song, the actual asserts its superior powers of fascination. So I will indulge my extravagant comparison, and erect the Mandelbrot set as a little folly from which to survey this ultimate extravagance of Conne-mara's topography.

The true fractal, washed in the streams of pure thought, is a hier-archical structure, each level of which contains a lower level – with the paradoxical feature that all the levels are identical; enter, and there is no way of telling what level you are at. In the next chapter I visit, among many other places, a *glasoileán*, a tidal almost-island that is acces-sible at low water from a certain islet that itself is subsidiary to an island that is, because it is almost deserted, a social appendage of a well-inhabited island that is functionally part of the mainland by virtue of a causeway. Common sense, science and art tell me to discriminate between these levels, to allot each only its due share in my book. If I sometimes neglect this sensible advice it is because of echoes from those other levels, up to the planetary (explicit, as will become clear in my explorations of Na hOileáin) and down to the subatomic (implicit here but salient elsewhere in the book), echoes that inform and perhaps confuse my consciousness of the scales of everyday.

Since the softening cover of peat has long ago been stripped off these islands and burned in the hearths of Aran, Galway and County Clare, one level of reality is immediate and demanding. Treeless, rugged, low-horizoned, the terrain directs attention to what is underfoot. Oddities and anomalies of bedrock and boulders have been exhaustively commented on, named, explained by myths. The bleak outer reaches of the archipelago – the southern third of Garomna, the southern half of Leitir Móir, the ultimate westernmost island, Gólam – are of a geology so visibly different from the pale glistening granite of the rest, so dark, crabbed, written-through with ancient catastrophes, that it demands elucidation (and is in fact evidence of the collision of two continents). All this, with a patchy cloak of humanity thrown over it: roads, villages (dozens of them), old churches, trades (kelp, boats, poitín), ill-remembered history, well-remembered songs . . .

To make sense of it all – but no, to make sense of it would be to belittle it; let me say, to avoid total bewilderment and paralysis at its innumerable crossroads – I must follow a simple topographical trend, and thread any temporal diversions, whether into personal reminiscence or geological millennia, onto that one spatial continuity. Like any bicycle-borne visitor I'll enter the maze from the north-east, where it is linked by a causeway to the mainland, and work my way down and around to its south-western extremity.

The road from Casla to Na hOileáin, roughly speaking, separates the dispersed suburbia of An Cheathrú Rua, on the left, from almost un-inhabited bogland, on the right. It is called Bóthar na Scrathóg, the road of the scraws, the sods cut from the topmost layer of the bog. J. M. Synge travelled this road in 1905 together with Jack Yeats, the former having been commissioned by the *Manchester Guardian* to write a series of articles on the distressed districts, and the latter to illustrate them. As Synge noted, the road had been 'built up in different years of famine by the people of the neighbourhood working on Govern-ment relief works'. His compassionate description of the relief workers incidentally explains the road's curious name:

We drove many miles, with Costello and Carraroe behind us, along a bog-road of curious formation built up on a turf embankment, with broad grassy sods at either side – perhaps to make a possible way for the barefooted people – then two spaces of rough broken stones where the wheel-ruts are usually worn, and in the centre a track of gritty earth for the horses . . . Some of the people were cutting out sods from grassy patches near the road, others were carrying down bags of earth in a slow, inert procession, a few were breaking stones, and three or four women were scraping out a sort of sandpit at a little distance. As we drove quickly by we could see that every man and woman was working with a sort of hang-dog dejection that would be enough to make a casual passer mistake them for a band of convicts.

Bóthar na Scrathóg eventually reaches the coast at Béal an Daingin, where there is a scattered settlement with a quay and a big bar, its surrounding tarmac made all the more desolate-looking by a tall bottle-shaped monument stuck all over with big pebbles. From here a causeway and bridge crosses a strait some 500 yards wide to the first island of Na hOileáin. The mouth of the stronghold or secure place is the meaning of the name; there never was a fort here to justify it, so the *daingean* in question must be the almost landlocked anchorage to the north of the crossing place. Before the causeway was built people would have to wait for low water to cross into or out of the island, while boats would have to wait for high water to sail through the narrows. Lewis's *Topographical Dictionary* of 1837 states that there were sometimes 200 boats waiting for a passage here, and that the government was proposing to clear the channel. For boats coming down the bays from Ros Muc or Camas, it used to be said, '*Tá an dá bhealach ann, an Daingean is an Ceann – bealach díreach is bealach cam*' ('There are two ways, by the Daingean or the Head – the straight way and the crooked way'), for the alternative to the pass here is a wide detour out into Cuan Chill Chiaráin and around the ocean-face of the archipelago, Ceann Gólaim or Golam Head. The causeway was built in 1892 as part of the scheme to link all the larger islands of the archipelago to each other and to the mainland. (Traces of an earlier and much slighter causeway, marked on the Ordnance Survey map of 1839 as 'Dangan Pass', can be made out on aerial photographs of the tidal shallows south of the present one.) There used to be a small opening span or swing bridge in the causeway, through which the turf boats heading for Aran or Galway could pour themselves out on a flowing ebb; Dick Scott praises the skill of those old boatmen 'who disdained any idea of warping if they had a breeze' to take them at speed through this narrow gap. But as the turf trade fell away in the 1950s the swing bridge was replaced by a fixed span, and it is no longer possible to take *an bealach díreach*, the straight way – a little history that reads like a homily on the decline of morals.

Eanach Mheáin: an *eanach* is a relatively dry bit of bog, the sort of place one might spread turf on to dry; *meáin* is the genitive of *meán*, 'middle'. The island is flat and fairly boggy, with a handful of houses and B&Bs, and a cluster of holiday cottages built by the local development organization with funding from Údaras na Gaeltachta and later controversially sold off to a private buyer. There is also a nine-hole golf course, which boasts Ireland's only thatched clubhouse, the ancestral home of John, Tony and Cathal Lynch, who founded the Connemara Isles Golf Club in 1993. I don't play golf, but I would enjoy a walk around this course with its northwards outlook onto a panorama of distant mountains and, closer by, a bewilderment of forking seaways. (A friend of mine who lives in the south of Ros Muc likes to tell his visitors that there is a golf course within a mile or so; however, the road to it would take them a good twenty miles round the head of Cuan Chamais and along the chain of tidal lakes to Casla.)

I spent a day or two loitering around Eanach Mheáin once, investigating its coastal ins and outs and its satellite islets; the best part of this time was an hour of dozing in the sunshine on a rock while waiting to see if anyone could take me across to Inis Treabhair, nearly a mile off to the north-west. (The name is corrupted: a will dated 1656 by which the O'Flaherty chieftain Murchadh na Maor left the island to his son Murchadh na Mart names it as Inniscrevar, i.e. Inis Creabhair, gadfly island, or perhaps woodcock island.) I would have wanted to visit it in any case, but it looked singularly attractive, with more trees than is usual in these parts, and a few cottages peeping out from among them. Whereas Eanach Mheáin is tethered to the mainland and in tow to progress by virtue of its causeway, Inis Treabhair has been cast adrift. Once it was densely inhabited; the population reached its peak well after the Famine, in 1871, when 158 persons, in twenty-two households, somehow lived off its 191 stony acres. At the time of my visit there were just three households left, and as I write today it has but one inhabitant.

Eventually a wooden currach with an outboard engine emerged from one of its little inlets and came scooting towards me across the milky calm, the boatman singing blithely. Pádraig Ó Loideáin had come across to collect his dole and a newspaper, and as soon as he had done that, he rowed me out to the island. He was, as his voice had announced over the waters, a big-bodied, big-hearted man, full of life and talk. He told me he had spent some years in Chicago, but loved the peacefulness of the island. It was a memorable little voyage. We diverted to look at Oileán na nGeabhróg, tern island, a low grassy hummock where we saw a dozen or more nests – slight hollows with a few wisps of straw with one, two or three brown-blotched eggs in each – and a cloud of terns and a few black-headed gulls clamorous above. Then, on docking in the island's little harbour, we walked up a green lane to Pádraig's house. He and his mother were one of the three remaining households. (A recent documentary film on TG4 has shown us his present solitary but still cheerful life, now that he is alone on the island.) He pointed out cattle on the skyline further inland to indicate where there was a children's burial ground I wanted to visit, and we agreed to meet up in two hours' time.

I found the little school, opened in 1900 according to a plaque on it, closed in 1980, and now reduced to an abstraction, an empty volume, an unattended geometry lesson. I walked all round the island, failed to pinpoint the children's burial ground among innumerable stony hummocks, and met one of the other families, busy at pitchforking seaweed out of a boat onto the quay. Father and son just about filled in my map with island placenames, and mother invited me in for tea. Then I saw Pádraig walking down to his boat, and hurried to rejoin him. I mentioned a holy well the other family had told me of, on an uninhabited islet half a mile away to the north, and he immediately turned the boat in that direction.

There are in fact a pair of islets here, known as Na Beitheacha, the birch woods (perhaps there was some scrub on them formerly, although they are quite bare now). The larger is An Bheitheach Gharbh (rough); with a good ebb tide one could walk to it over 300 yards of rock and mud from the north-east point of Inis Treabhair, and it has a few fields on it. The other, An Bheitheach Mhín (smooth), is smaller and could be reached via another few hundred yards of intertidal rock; it is undivided commonage which the Inis Treabhair families each had rights to, for instance the 'grass of two cows', and would ferry their quota of cattle out to it for a few weeks' grazing at some agreed time of year. And on the south shore of this lesser islet is a sliver of rock, a *glasoileán* in that it is part of the islet when the tide is out, on the bare slanting southern flank of which Pádraig pointed out two round potholes side by side like a pair of eyes, each about a foot across, and having a little cleft above it stuffed with coins and rosaries. I forgot to measure their depths, but I am told (though do not believe) that one cannot reach the bottom in them; also that they were made by some saint as baptismal fonts. They had a presence. On this tidal supplement to an islet off an islet off an island off an island off an obscure headland of the main, they asserted that this was a place, therefore central. (More of this mystery when I come to write of the holy wells of Garomna, which has an extravagance of them scattered along its shores and in its barren granite heartland.)

On the way south again I rowed too (and felt an unfamiliar weightiness in my shoulders that evening). A seal periscoped at us from close by, and Pádraig told me seals were *an-bheannaithe*, very blessed. Then we bumped into a submerged rock he said was called An Córa Mór, the big coffer; this accident caused a lot of laughter and enabled me to mark the rock accurately on my map. I was happy, my boatman was happy; it had been a good day, one that made up for many an hour of crouching behind field walls in the rain trying to hold my map upside down above me to write on it, with time to observe how the grey scarves of hail hang vertically from the tail ends of black squall-clouds and are then swept obliquely ahead of them by the gale.

Later on I learned more about the island by correspondence with some of its former inhabitants, so that I have lists of placenames covering every little inlet and headland of this jagged patch of land – many more than I can write about here – with details of the significance of each to the farm and fisher folk. As an example, Carraig na nÉan or Bird Rock, off the south coast. I translate from the Irish:

They say there are birds perched on this island every day of the year. I often heard people say that birds going to An Doirín [in Leitir Móir] from Inis Treabhair rest on this rock because it is about halfway between the two places. People used to read the state of the tides by it. For example, by looking at it you would know if there was enough water to float the boats in An Caladh ó Dheas [the south harbour].

This little insight into the inhabitants' hour-by-hour awareness of the waters and the other lives around them I owe to Inis Treabhair's notable son, Micheál Ó Conghaile. Micheál was born in 1962 and attended the island national school before going on to Coláiste Éinde and NUI Galway, and a career in teaching Irish. In 1985 he founded Cló Iar-Chonnachta, which has its offices in Indreabhán and is now the most productive publisher of Irish-language books and traditional music CDs. Micheál himself is a writer of short stories and novels that have gathered many awards; as a gay Irish-language writer he is in a minority of a minority; as an islander he has made himself 'a part of the main'.

It was from an article by Micheál that I learned that one of Connemara's oddest songs was composed in Inis Treabhair:

> D'fhág mé lá an baile amach
> is chuaigh mé ar oileán farraige;
> Tháinig mé i dteach geanúil –
> ba bhréag dom athrú a rá.
> Ba socair céille aigeanta
> an beag 's an mór d'ár casadh liom;
> Bhí múnadh ar fhear is bean acú
> nach bhfaca mé ar a lán.
> Gach uile ní dár thaithnigh liom
> gan gársamhlacht, gan grabaireacht,
> Gan focal ar bith arranta,
> ach a ndéanaimis de ghreann.
> Dá gcaithfinn ráithe an earraigh ann,
> chomhairfinn nach mbeinn seachtain ann,
> Ach is ann a cóireadh leaba dom
> is mé ag comhrá leis an mBás!

[I left my home one day / for an island in the sea; / I came into a decent house – / I would lie to say the opposite. / Steady, sensible and lively / were young and old I met there; / Manners on each man and woman / I have not seen on many. / Everything that pleased me / with no coarseness and no prattling, / Not an angry word, / but what we said in fun. / If I spent the whole of spring there, / I'd count it but a week, / But it's there they made me up a bed / in which to talk with Death!]

The author was Na hOileáin's famously long-lived rhymester Colm de Bhailís (1796–1906!). Colm was something of a builder and carpenter and used to go from house to house doing odd jobs and extemporizing songs. A peculiarity of many of these old songs is that, to make any sense of them, one has to know circumstances of their composition not explicit in the song itself; the song is the kernel of a nut, the shell of which is a dense fabric of personal histories and placenames – not always the most digestible of stuff, but without it the kernel loses its savour. One day he came to a house in Inis Treabhair (one of the many of which only the walls stand today), expecting to have a bed for the night. There was an itinerant tailor in the house too, a miserable little fellow whose nickname was An Bás, death. Then some other guests arrived, and Colm to his disappointment found he had to share a bed with the tailor. The lady of the house noted this, and promised him a quart, no less, of poitín if he could make up a song about it overnight. The next morning Colm sat down opposite the tailor and sang this song. In the second verse he asks his bedmate who he is: Jupiter, Hercules, Neptune the god of the sea, or perhaps Goll Mac Morna? The tailor says he is none of these:

> Ach is mé an Bás atá faoi ghiúin,
> A bhí ní bhfearr ná iad uile.
> Tá mé ag comhrá leatsa anocht,
> Agus beidh tú agam dom féin.

[But I am Death who is being mocked, / Who got the better of them all. / I am talking to you tonight, / And you will be mine alone.]

After this menacing exchange they fight, and cause so much disturbance that men are sent out to catch them both, tie them to two stones and fling them into the tide to be carried off without return. This is not the only one of Colm's cheery nonsenses to have a sinister undertone, as will appear when we come across his traces in Leitir Móir and Garomna. He was well used to talking with death, as he outlived his wife and son, saw his neighbours go down into the pit of the Famine and lived on into deep and solitary poverty, before his own death in the Oughterard workhouse.

Perhaps the island folk really were, in Colm de Bhailís's phrase, 'steady, sensible and lively', and are so still. I asked Micheál if he had written anything autobiographical about growing up in this tiny community, and in particular growing up gay. He said that he had not, but that some of his fiction reflected the experience; in particular he mentioned the short story 'Athair', 'Father'. This is largely a halting and pain-filled dialogue. A young man has just come out to his elderly father, who is at first shocked into a brief fit of snivelling, which he soon swallows like a big bitter pill. While he questions his son anxiously – do his sisters, now living in London, know? Did his mother know, before she died? Do the neighbours know? – the father moves around the kitchen, distractedly preparing to go out to milk the cows. To his son's surprise he goes on to ask about his health, showing that he has acquired, perhaps from the continuous background chatter of the television, an unexpected degree of information about the matter. Then: 'And do you think you are going to stay around here?' This could be a plea, or a sentence of banishment. Normally it would be the young man's part to stay and look after his ageing father, being the youngest of the family and the only son. He is at least willing to stay, knowing that if he is driven to leave he will probably never see his father alive again, and that the old man will have a solitary death. The father puts the kettle on to boil, scalds the milk bucket, warms milk for the calf, while the son thinks of his mates in Dublin and their variously unhappy lives after being disowned by their families. Finally the father goes to the door, crosses himself with holy water from the stoup hanging beside it, opens the door and, turning slowly to his son, says, 'Will you come and stand in front of that jumpy cow for me while I milk her? She still has a sore teat . . .'

31 Two Songs from Leitir Móir

From the south-western corner of Eanach Mheáin another 600 yards of causeway carries the road across tidal flats to Leitir Móir. A *leitir* – from *leath*, half, and *tir*, land – is a rough, wet slope, and the other word is probably *mór*, big, in some fossilized form, perhaps the obsolete 'locative' case, which several linguists have failed to explain to me. Another theory is that the name refers to the mythological female figure Mór of Munster, who originated as a goddess of the land and dwindled down into the subject of the odd saying used of an ostentatious person, '*Cailín ag Mór, agus Mór ag iarraidh deirce*' – 'Mór has a maid, and Mór begs for alms.' Leitir Móir is both the name of the island and that of the easternmost of the two townlands on it; the western townland is Leitir Calaidh, or, more faithful to the pronunciation, Leitir Caltha, the harbour *leitir*. Each townland consists mainly of a hill and its skirts; since the two hills are of a height (Cnoc Leitír Móir, 388 feet; Cnoc Leitir Calaidh, 364 feet), and both rather smooth and rounded, the island makes a pleasant focus to views of Na hOileáin from the surrounding lands of Iorras Aintheach, Ros Muc and An Cheathrú Rua, especially as their coverings of bog have long been harvested for fuel, leaving granite to catch the sun's rays. The main settlement is in Leitir Móir townland; this is a proper village with a chapel, shop, bar, Garda barracks and so on. The causeway to Garomna, Droichead Charraig an Lugáin, named from some rock with a hollow or *lugán* in it, takes off from just south of the village, while minor roads leading from it make a circuit around the island, linking a large number of hamlets which nowadays tend to merge into a loose knot of ribbon development. From east to west the island is just over three miles long; from north to south it is a variable mile to a mile and a half.

Two songs define Leitir Móir for me. The best-known is a charming lullaby, or more accurately a baby-bouncing song (it rattles along to a bouncy tune), 'Peigín Leitir Móir', and I begin with that as it incidentally gives me a back door into local history. Peigín, I am told, was a baby born into the village of Croiminne, near the end of the causeway from Eanach Mheáin. The song gives its name to an annual beauty competition, originating in the 1970s, in which the winners of local heats held throughout Connemara, the Aran Islands and further afield compete for the title of Peigín Leitir Móir. (A photograph that looks as if it dated from some much further-off age of innocence shows Na Peigíní, as they are called – seven laughing, curly-headed girls in white blouses and knee-covering skirts – arriving by *púcán* for the adjudication. And now in August 2010 I see in the *Connacht Tribune* the current Peigíní sitting on the sea wall, as demure as ever in long traditional skirts of black with two yellow bands round the hems to match their yellow sashes.) Here is the chorus and a few verses of 'Peigín Leitir Móir', with a literal translation:

> Is ó gairim gairim í, is gairim í, mo stór,
> Míle grá le m' anam í, 'sí Peigín Leitir Móir.

> Tá Bríd agam, tá Cáit agam, 'sí Peig an bhean is fearr,
> Cibé fear a gheobhas í nach air a bheas an t-ádh.

> Tá iascairí na Gaillimhe ag teacht aniar le cóir,
> Le solas gealaí gile nó go bhfeicfidís an tseoid.

> Chuir mé scéala siar aici go gceannóinn dí bád mór,
> 'Sé 'n scéal a chuir sí aniar agam go ndéanfadh leathbhád seoil.

[And oh I praise her, and I praise her, my treasure, / She is the thousandfold love of my soul, is Peigín Leitir Móir. / I have Bridget and I have Kate, it's Peig is the finest woman, / Whichever man gets her won't he be the lucky one. / The fishermen of Galway are coming from the east with a favouring wind, / By the light of a bright moon to see the jewel. / I sent messages back to her that I'll buy her a *bád mór*, / The message she returns is that a *leathbhád* would do.]

There are lots of other rather witty verses on the modesty of Peigín's demands: her suitor offers her a big house, and she says a sod hut would do; he offers a feather bed, she says a straw in a corner would do; he would make her a big fire, she would be happy with a couple of turfs; he would buy her 'button boots' (in English in the original), 'slipper shoes' would be enough; and so on. And then:

Nach cumasach 's nach ceannasach an rud aduirt Frank Óg,
Dá dtéigheadh sí amach a' Daingean uaidh go leagfadh sé 'n Teach Mór.

[Wasn't that a strong and masterful thing Young Frank said, / That if she went away from him by An Daingean, he would knock the Big House down.]

Who was this intemperate admirer? The Teach Mór, the Big House, stood a few hundred yards north of the crossroads in the village of Leitir Móir, near the present Garda barracks. In the mid nineteenth century it was occupied by Sinéad ní Sheachnasaigh (Jane O'Shaunessy), a Dublin lady who married Éamonn Ó Flaithearta from Garomna, and to whom the small tenants of Leitir Móir, Eanach Mheáin and most of Garomna paid rent (or failed to pay rent, as appears). Jane O'Flaherty, as she became, and her husband were the royalty of the islands. After the spring sowing the tenants had to burn kelp for this couple, who owned hookers to ship it to Galway; after Sinéad's big two-masted boat sank with forty tons of kelp on its first voyage, it used to be said of any loss, '*Bá mhó an chaill bád Shinéad ní Sheachnasaigh ná í*' ('Sinéad ní Sheachnasaigh's boat was a bigger loss than that'). The kelp workers used to camp on Inis Léith, grey island (?), an islet half a mile east of the village, where they were fed by Sinéad; when potatoes were short she imported some from Skye:

Fataí Inis Sgéith
Ag teacht go hInis Léith,
Agus an fear atá ina gclé
Is air atá an léan.

[Spuds from Skye / Coming to Inis Léith, / And the man who depends on them, / He's the one in want.]

Sinéad and Éamonn had two sons, Máirtín Óg and Frank Óg, both of whom died young; Frank Óg was the handsome one, and after his death his mother could not bear to hear 'Peigín Leitir Móir'. Éamonn died too, and after that Sinéad returned to Dublin.

But Sinéad was not the owner of the Garomna estate; she and a female relative (who appears in the records as E. O'Shaunessy) in turn paid rent (or, again, failed to pay it) to Christopher St George, son of Arthur French St George, of Tyrone House near Kilcolgan. This imposing three-storey Palladian mansion still stands, aloof and haughty even though roofless and windowless, on a bare rise of land at the head of Galway Bay. The Frenches of Tyrone were famous as the best huntsmen and worst landlords of the region; Christopher St George kept his own pack of foxhounds, and hunts at Tyrone gave rise to many tales of daredevil jumps over six-foot-six walls and spiked iron gates taken by such bucks as George Moore of Moore Hall and Lord Clanricarde.

Christopher St George stood as Tory candidate for Galway in the general election of 1847; his election address in that year of famine deplored the government's failure to heed 'not only the voice of the landed proprietor, but even the poorest inhabitant of this country, as to the mode of expenditure of the large sums of money that have been lavished on works chiefly of a useless description'. Soon after his election those 'poorest inhabitants' made an unwelcome appearance in person. The Poor Law Inspector at Galway reported that 'no less than eleven boats, loaded with destitute persons' had come in from Connemara, most of them from the estates of St George, 'who, I am told, is ejecting them without even a rag to cover them'. It was also reported that his bailiff had employed men for a day at 2s 6d each to level the houses of the evicted. In April 1848 St George defended himself in Parliament against such charges. He explained that Jane O'Flaherty and her relative had obtained their lease in 1836, the rent being set at £837, and by 1847 they owed £1,256. He was therefore obliged to serve them and at least 600 householders on the lands with ejectment notices, and also to pay Mrs O'Flaherty £150 for immediate possession. On visiting the territories himself, he had found that outcasts from other estates had moved onto his land, due to Mrs O'Flaherty's neglect, and he was informed by 'the more respectable portion of the tenantry' that these squatters had killed and carried off many cows and over 600 sheep. It transpired that the tenants owed the two ladies as much money as the latter owed to him.

I stated that I had the full ability of dispossessing them all. They entreated me not to do so. I considered their sad position, and at length informed them, that if I was paid £400, within three months, I would remit £1,100. The tenants and the priest considered my offer most liberal. The tenants informed me they would pay me £400, provided I got rid of the squatters and all bad characters. I engaged them to do so. I have now to say I have not as yet received £400, as promised me.

He had accompanied the Sheriff to the lands, where possession was taken of some dwellings, whose inhabitants were allowed to return as caretakers. A few who were pointed out as objectionable characters were given money to enable them to remove elsewhere.

I am quite averse to acts of cruelty. I regret the state in which my property is in Connemara. Such is chiefly ascribable to middlemen. I have borrowed £6,000 under the Land Improvement Enactment, and appropriated £1,500 to Lettermore and £1,000 to all parts of Connemara. I am not receiving my rents, and have paid an immense poor-rate . . . I feel indignant at being accounted a bad landlord.

St George never raised his rents again after the general reduction he made at this time, but he didn't go short. As a breeder and racer of champion horses he was very successful; his jockeys in their sea-green jackets and white caps were stars of the scene at Epsom, Ascot and Goodwood until 1866, when he fell sick and all his horses were sold off. Christopher St George died after years of ill health in 1877. His widow lived on in an increasingly decrepit Tyrone House until 1905, by which time most of the estate had been dissipated and the tenants of Na hOileáin were, as elsewhere, on the way to becoming owners of their little patches through the CDB and the Land Commission. The house then lay abandoned. In 1912 the forlorn sight of it and local gossip about the once haughty family's decline into local liaisons and irregular parenthood inspired Violet Martin to write to her cousin Edith Somerville – 'If we dared to write up that subject . . .' – which they did, in their novel *The Big House of Inver*. As a final ignominy Tyrone House was burned by the local tenantry during the War of Independence when there were fears that it might be used by the Black and Tans as a base. Various proposals for its rescue and renovation have since come to nothing.

The second song originated halfway along the northern coast of Leitir Móir by An Sruthán Buí, the yellow stream, a thread of water running out of the bog between the island's two hills. Colm de Bhailís was caught in the rain here once, and made himself a little shelter of sticks and clods of grass. Then, to pass the time, he composed a song praising this 'court' in wonderfully high-flown terms:

> Is deas an féirín gabhtha gléasta
> Cúirt an tSrutháin Bhuí,
> Ar talamh déanta ar dheis na gréine
> I bhfoscadh ó 'chuile ghaoith,
> 'Bhfuil a ghairdín pléisiúir le n-a taobh
> A dhéanfadh óg de'n aois,
> 'S go bhfuair na táinte bhí gan sláinte
> Fóirithint ann le mí.

[How fine an ornamental treasure / Is the Court of the Yellow Stream, / Built on land blessed by sun / And sheltered from the wind, / So that the pleasure garden by its side / Would make the old feel young, / While hosts of invalids / Found succour there for the last month.]

And so on it goes, heaping up extravagances for verse after verse: Queen Victoria is mad with rage since hearing praise of its roof, sailing ships with favouring winds bring the Queen of Sardinia, all is prepared with golden gates and company fit for a king, and finally

Martin Luther himself comes begging for pardon at the Court of the Yellow Stream. The strange thing is that this fantasy is sung to an air of passionate, almost tragic intensity – but one could understand the implicit tragedy to be the disproportion between these people's material circumstances and their life-capabilities. While Tyrone House is a hollow wreck and Leitír Móir's own Big House is marked on the Ordnance Survey map of 1899 only by the open rectangles that indicate roofless walls, the poet of Na hOileáin built a house, a court in fact, that no agent could raise rent on and that shows symptoms of literary immortality. The artistry that goes into singing its merits, even today, is as glorious as the furze that blossoms on his granite island.

In the centre of Garumna nothing can be seen but bog interspersed
with rocky tracts of bare granite, rounded and marked by glacial
action, and studded here and there with large boulders of granite,
many of which are from ten to fifteen feet, or even more, in diameter. Turn which way one will, great stretches of bare stony ground,
thinly covered with peat in the hollows, meet the eye . . . A more
utterly barren, dreary looking region could hardly be imagined.

That was written in 1898 by Dr Charles Browne of the Anthropo-
logical Laboratory of Trinity College Dublin, who came here with
his callipers and tape measure to study what he termed 'probably the
poorest and most primitive population in Ireland'. There were then
1,706 people living on this island's nine square miles, of which area
nearly four square miles were reckoned to be 'utterly unproductive
moor and rock'. The chain of causeways and swing bridges linking the
principal islands of the archipelago to each other and to the mainland
had been completed in the previous year with the opening of Droichead Charraig an Lugáin between the north-eastern corner of Garomna
and Leitir Móir. Before the building of the causeway the 500 yards
between the two islands could be crossed, with some danger, by means
of a *pas*, a raised footpath, at the very low ebb tides that occur near the
time of a full or a new moon. On the shore below the causeway some
scattered stones have been pointed out to me as marking the graves of
famine victims who died while waiting to walk out of the island,
waiting for the moon.

This miserabilism of landscape and history is vigorously contradicted
by contemporary social developments. A short way south of the causeway is a fine new sports centre and the football pitch, Páirc an Mháimín
(what little pass or *mám* is in question here I have not learned, but in
fact Máimín is the name of a townland stretching diagonally across

Garomna to the bridge leading into Leitir Mealláin). Then comes the village of Tír an Fhia (its evidently very ancient name means 'the land of the deer'), where the principal institutions of the islands cluster. Here are the headquarters of Coláiste na nOileán, the Irish-language summer school, and the community hall; also a new services centre for various development agencies, notably Muintearas, which was founded in 1980 with funds from Údarás na Gaeltachta and an international charity, the Van Leer Foundation, and whose mission is to advance the Gaeltacht community through education at all levels, training in computer skills, etc., while protecting its language and culture; under its wings are a crèche and a Youthreach centre. Close by are An Chlúid, 'the nook', a communal restaurant; the premises of Morenet Teo, which provides services to the fish-farming industry such as the defouling and repair of fish cage nets; Irish Sea Spray, a fish-smoking enterprise; and the offices of Comhairle Ceantair na nOileán, the elective council of Na hOileáin. This last was founded in 2000, superseding another development agency, deep in the past of which was Comharchumann na nOileán, dating back to 1976 and in its day one of the most successful and enterprising of the Gaeltacht co-ops.

Here it was that I met Pól Ó Foighil for the first time. A small whirlwind of a man, vital, restless, Balzacian, full of schemes, trailing controversies behind him as he moved rapidly from post to post, he had already run a co-op in Cois Fharraige before he came to manage the one in Tír an Fhia, and was to go on to manage another in Inis Meáin in the Aran Islands. He was also a politician: at one time or another he was an elected member of Údarás na Gaeltachta, a Fine Gael member of Galway County Council (where he had a provision to protect the Irish language incorporated into the county development plan, under which applicants for planning permission for houses in the Connemara Gaeltacht had to prove their fluency in Irish) and a member of the Seanad (where he refused to speak English and insisted on wearing a traditional white woollen jacket or *báinín* despite all objections). Seeing him at work in Tír an Fhia in the 1980s – when it seemed there was only one telephone in the building and it was on his desk, so that at one moment he was dealing with some Norwegian firm for the supply of many thousands of pounds' worth of fishing equipment and the next answering a query from a little girl about the Irish summer school, while leafing through a pile of letters and trying to persuade me to apply, or better still let him apply on my behalf, for a huge loan from Údarás na Gaeltachta – I got the impression that he operated under centrifugal strain. He was clearly enjoying himself enormously but often rubbed his hands over his face, and he tended to get ahead of himself; he congratulated me on the improvement in my Irish, and I could not persuade him that we had never met before. I learned later that he held things together by his furious energy, so that as soon as he moved on and was no longer whipping it into a spin whatever structure he had set up would totter to a fall like a slowing top.

I had called in at the co-op because, having seen my map of the Aran Islands, he had written to me to suggest I make a map of Na hOileáin, an idea that had taken root and, by the time of that meeting, grown to be a projected map of the whole of south Connemara. It is ironic that it was he who started me on that road, in view of my later rows with him over two projects he supported with irrepressible populist rhetoric and stand-up verbosity: the airport to be built on Roundstone Bog (which never materialized) and the three wind turbines powering a desalination plant on Inis Meáin (which, sadly, did). When Pól Ó Foighil died in 2005 aged seventy-eight, the then Minister for the Gaeltacht, Éamon Ó Cuív, said that Pól had fought for the things he believed in, and was 'a man who spoke out strongly on many subjects, but was fair-minded, courteous and gentle'. Well, *de mortuis*, etc.; but I knew him as a ranting demagogue, and I do not forgive him for spreading the perception that I wanted Connemara emptied of its human inhabitants in favour of the landscape.

Just south of Tír an Fhia's cluster of utilitarian if not harmonious buildings (for there is indeed a problem to be faced about the human contribution to the landscape, especially in this denuded terrain that offers no soft vales, sheltering trees or other absolution for architectural sins) there is a crossroads. Three ways lead onwards; I shall take the main road first, which runs diagonally across the island, and then explore the turnings to left and right.

Immediately past the crossroads is the former Presentation

Convent, founded in 1935 by four nuns sent in by the Archbishop of Tuam in response to the parish priest's expressed concerns about the declining educational and moral state of the community. The sisters ran a renewed national school, and a vocational school for girls, which later became an adult learning centre before its closure in 1956. When the last sister had returned and none were ready to come to this isolated area to replace her, the convent itself closed in 2006; the building is now used for spiritual retreats. The Catholic chapel, dating from 1932, is about a mile further on; it is officially called 'Bricawna Church of the Immaculate Conception', although the name Bricawna (from *briceanach*, speckled place?) is not known from this locality. It seems that the diocese was left a sum for a church to be built at Bricawna, and being unable to identify the place applied the money here. (In fact I know a place of that name in Ros a' Mhíl, if it is of any help . . .)

After that the road runs out across a blasted heath – many a time have I and my bicycle groaned our way against the wind here – where the only shelter is a huge broken boulder known as Cloch an Tortáin, the stone of the hillock, the king of the stones of Garomna, which is said to have been split by lightning. A lake appears to the left, and then one to the right; this last is 'Loughawallia' on Ordnance Survey maps, which would suggest that the Irish original is Loch an Bhaile, the lake of the village. However, on passing it one day when the water level was low I noticed that a small round island near its southern shore has traces of tumbled stonework around its rim. I mentioned this to a local man who had become a good friend, Pádraic Ó Cualáin, whose family had a shop a little further west in the nearby village of Baile na Cille. Pádraic immediately said, 'Shall we go and look?' and led me down to the lakeside, where we borrowed a little boat that was lying on the shore. I jumped onto the island, which was densely overgrown with low, scratchy scrub, and struggled around it in clouds of midges. It clearly had been improved if not built up as a whole by walling, so it is definitely a crannóg. Later I heard from another most generous source of local lore, Pádraic Ó Maoilchiaráin, the story of an old lady who had been sentenced to burning for witchcraft but was banished to the island instead. One day a Cromwellian soldier (or a Dane, say some) came out to the island (on stepping stones, which it is said were set so far apart one had to jump from one to the next), with the intention of robbing her, and the old lady killed him by hitting him on the head with her skillet. I also learned that the lake is called Loch an Bhalla, the lake of the wall, referring to the island. (Thus the lake's name should have been anglicized as 'Loughawalla'. John O'Donovan, who decided on these anglicized forms on the basis of the Irish names as recorded from the indigenes by the sappers of the 1839 Ordnance Survey, was slack about visiting sites in Connemara, being impatient to get away to the more spectacular archaeology of the Aran Islands, and this is a clear instance of information being endangered by the brutal process of anglicization.)

The best thing Pól Ó Foighil did for me was to introduce me to Pádraic Ó Cualáin, who at that time was overseeing a Van Leer project, the recording of memories from the elders of the island, for he gave me unstinted help while I was working in Garomna. I remember that evening of the crannóg with gratitude to life. It was the finest evening of the year; the lake was breathtakingly beautiful and breathlessly still. After our bit of archaeology we took to the boat again and rambled around islets in the northern reaches of the lake, Pádraic rowing backwards gingerly and as if dreamily, bumping gently into submerged rocks now and again. Then we returned the boat to its place and went back to Pádraic's house, where we had a sup of poitín punch and a long evening of storytelling with an old neighbour of his called Beairtle and Pádraic's young sons, who listened in silence before taking themselves off to bed one by one. Sometime after midnight, having swapped Aran legends for Garomna legends, I walked down the dark road with Beairtle to my lodgings, through a companionable, villagey silence broken only by the tapping of his stick.

Dr Browne of Trinity College Dublin, the anthropologist whose dismal general impression of Garomna I quoted at the beginning of this chapter, has a paragraph on cases of longevity in the islands in which he says:

One old man was met with who had walked several miles to get some goods at the shop, as he frequently does, though, to use his own expression, 'weak in the legs now'. He said he was born on the 2nd of May, 1796, so that he is now over 102 years old.

This can only be Colm de Bhailís, Baile na Cille's most famous son, to whom Pádraic has had a little monument erected at the village crossroads. Remnants of his house can be seen, in a little glen (Gleann Bhailís) on a hillside a few hundred yards north of the crossroads, made noticeable by the very high walls Colm built around his three potato plots. (An elderly man living near the crossroads told me exactly how many baskets of potatoes used to come out of those plots, but I have mislaid this historical detail.) Dr Browne may have measured Colm's head in all dimensions, calculated his cephalic index and categorized him as dolichocephalic, mesaticephalic or brachycephalic, but derived no sense of what was in that head.

In 1902 Patrick Pearse discovered that the poet he had assumed was dead for decades was alive, if not well, and in the Oughterard poorhouse, and through *An Claidheamh Soluis* he raised money to establish him in a cottage and publish his works. Pearse described him as 'a naive, sprightly, good-humouredly satirical personality, a peasant living among peasants, who sings like the lark from very joyousness and tunefulness of soul'. This was near the truth, but fails to register how under that good humour the realities of deprivation show, like bones sticking out. 'Amhrán an Tae', 'The Song of the Tea', is a comic dialogue between wife and husband, she addicted to tea and he to tobacco. He says, 'Musha, you're always talking about tea, and when you have it no one else sees any of it; be off and get me some tobacco or I'll give you a touch of the spade-handle!' She replies, 'How can I do that but by selling two chickens that laid yesterday? The stuff you got on tick at Christmas isn't paid for yet, and that's running short for the children.'

An Fear   Maise, bíonn tusa i gconaí 'cur síos ar an tae,
             'S an lá bhíos sé agat, ní fheictear a'at é;
             Imigh leat 's faigh tobac dam ar mhaithe leat féin,
             Nó roinnfidh mé leat feac na láí!

An Bhean   Cia an tslí atá a'am-sa? Cá bhfaighinn-se duit é,
              Acht ag ceangal dá chirc a raibh ubh aca aréir?
              Rud a thóg tú faoi Nollaig, níor íoc tú fós é,
              'S tá an méid so sách gann ag na páistí.

After a dozen verses of argument they go to law and end up as laughing stocks, and Colm's final comment is '*Ach ceapaim gur cailleadh na páistí*' ('But I think the children died').

A story about Colm is told in the Aran Islands, where he used to do odd jobs (he had a great reputation for building chimneys that drew well). On this occasion he was in Inis Meáin, where he had work to do on several houses. It was the custom in those days to do a few hours' work before breakfast. Colm finished the job on the first house before breakfast time came, and the woman of that house assumed, or pretended to assume, that he would get his breakfast in the next house. But the people there took it that Colm had had his breakfast already. So Colm worked away quietly for a bit, and then he turned to the man he was working for and said, 'What is the name of this island?' 'Why, this is Inis Meáin!' he replied. 'Ah,' said Colm,

> 'Inis Meáin, inis gan 'rán
> Inis gann, gortach;
> Tabhair leat do chuid 'ráin
> An lá 'mbeidh tú a' dul ann,
> Nó beidh tú an lá sin i do throscadh!'

['Inis Meáin, island of hunger and wanting; / Have bread in your pocket / The day you make your visit, / Or you'll spend that whole day fasting.']

The poet's satire was a fearsome weapon in the Gaelic word-world, and Inis Meáin has never forgotten Colm's little verse. Perhaps that is why its penury has not stopped it being the most hospitable of places, as Synge found when he stayed there.

The Baile na Cille of today is strung out along the main road, which here follows the northern shore of a third lake, Loch Bhaile na Cille. Formerly the village was further south, on the east side of the lake, where its empty rooms are now just so many more cells in a network of tiny fields. The *cill* in question in these names is an ancient ruined church in a little burial ground south of the lake; I shall visit that place of years gone by in another chapter. Returning to my explorations in the 1980s, here and there among the houses of today's Baile na Cille I noticed some that were better situated with regard to shelter and less besmattered with stuck-on multi-toned stone facing than the rest. These, I learned, showed the hand of Derek Hawker, an English art teacher (he had been principal of Middlesbrough Art School, and later went on to head the Dublin College of Art and Design and then Lincoln School of Art and Design). Derek and Liz had a house up a twisty boreen in the little rocky hills south of Baile na Cille. I called in there on impulse once, having been tramping bogs in the rain; Liz opened the door and to my surprise greeted me by name; she had heard of my being in the vicinity. In no time at all I was sitting by a glowing turf fire, in dry clothes and slippers. After this home-from-homecoming I stayed with them for some days, and was gloriously fed by Liz and entertained by an endless flux of their visitors.

Derek put the sad standard of local domestic building practice down to the lack of art classes in the schools, and tried to remedy it by advice and example. In particular he inveighed against applied stone facing ('dog-biscuits!') and the perching of houses on hillocks to catch the view, where they suffered from wind-howl and window-rattle. Indeed we are far from Paul Henry's Connemara, in which, I note, the little whitewashed and golden-thatched cottages seem to be sinking shyly away from the viewer as if nuzzling into the ground for protection. Nevertheless, when one looks into the depths of the landscape on a clear evening from a lowland such as Garomna, the scene is composed of three strata: the sunlit golden levels of the bog, the distance-blue silhouette of mountains and a limitless upward extent of sky. These three elements Henry hardly had to simplify at all in composing his works, which at first glance are almost abstract but in fact answer faithfully to reality, at least in these distant perspectives. His near-at-hand Connemara, which always had a degree of wishful thinking in it, is gone, but even the modern bungalow, usually painted white, at a sufficient distance becomes a lime-bright Paul Henry cottage and takes its place as a dot of human persistence at the foot of the eternity of mountains. It is as if Henry's Connemara has receded not only in time but also in space, and preserved a truth in so doing. Only his rather stodgy and immobile piles of cumulus are false to the wind-spun dramas, the fractal multiplicity, the Atlantic wilfulness of Connemara's skies.

The last building in Baile na Cille is the bar, Óstán na nOileán, which a century and more ago was the Hotel of the Isles, patronized by, among others, Roger Casement, the great humanitarian who was as concerned with the oppressed of Connemara as he was with those of the Belgian Congo and Peru. Casement had been informed in 1913 by his sister Nina Hamilton of the plight of Garomna and Leitir Mealláin, where, it was claimed, fifty people had died of typhus. He opened a relief fund and persuaded the *Irish Independent* to open another, inaugurated by his famous letter likening the sufferings of the islanders to those of the Peruvian Indians on the rubber plantations of the Putumayo:

I have learned of the appalling state of things in Connemara owing to the absence of anything like civilized government in that part of the world. Were this in truth a United Kingdom the press of its capital would contain some reference to a state of things so near its doors; but I have not seen a single word in any London daily of this dire need of our plague-pestered fellow-subjects in Connemara. I hope very soon to be able to leave London for Ireland, and, if possible, to visit Lettermullen and see whether something lasting can be done to remove the stain of this enduring Irish Putumayo from our native land. One thing is clear to me – only Irishmen and Irishwomen can clear it up.

A sum of £2,440 was soon gathered, the Quaker chocolatier William Cadbury, anonymously, being among the chief contributors, and it was arranged for the children in infant schools of one of the islands to have a free meal every day for a year. Augustine Birrell, the Chief Secretary for Ireland, visited the islands at this time, and called on a smoke-filled hovel in which a boy had recently died of the fever; it was, Birrell said, the worst dwelling he had ever entered, and the man of the house was given £2 out of the relief fund. But the *Irish Times* feared that Casement's 'lurid' letter would ruin the tourist season in

Connemara, as readers would not know that Leitir Mealláin lay far off the tourist itineraries. There was fever, it agreed – forty cases, including five deaths, in a dispensary district of 10,000 persons – but such recurrent outbreaks were the fault of the Congested Districts Board, which was failing to remedy the 'frightfully low' standard of life:

The people are housed like pigs; they draw their water from stagnant pools. It would be a miracle if typhus fever did not flourish in such conditions. It will be eliminated, not by gifts to unhappy sufferers, but by the provision of decent houses and a pure supply of water.

While the *Irish Times* persisted in believing that despite their failings the agencies of the powers-that-be could reform the state of Connemara, Sir Roger went on to act on his faith that only Irishmen and Irishwomen could clear up such filthy corners of the so-called United Kingdom. Soon after his visit to the islands he helped to found the Irish Volunteers. His role in the subsequent Easter Rising, his condemnation to death for treason, and the debate over the so-called 'Black Diaries' are one of Ireland's most often rehearsed and least understood stories.

Beyond the Óstán the road network throws itself out into the sea to haul in one more draught of islands – but there is more to be seen in Garomna yet, and so I return to the crossroads in Tír an Fhia, and this time take the road running around the north and west coasts of the island. This leads past Loch an Ghainimh, sand lake, and down to the shore through Gleann Trasna, the crosswise glen, which is a greener and more habitable-looking locality than the rest, thanks to some slight glacial deposits such as the sand that gives the lake its name. The road now follows the coast closely through Na hUaimíní, an area thought to be named from its numerous little sea-caves (*uaimh*, a cave).

For me the most significant feature here is Bóthar na nOileán, the road of the islands, a sequence nearly a mile long of broken-down causeways, seaweedy stepping stones and thicketed islets by which it is possible to reach Inis Bearcháin if the tide is low enough. Waiting for this possibility to be granted, as attentively as if it were a supernatural permission, while watching the water that had gorged the ramified bays and channels between Garomna and Leitir Móir pour out like an unhurried river, until by degrees the first of the stepping stones loomed up to the slowly sinking surface, was one of the experiences that gave me the dream-writing of 'Walking Out to Islands', my first essay on Connemara, and I will not attempt to recapture its mood here.

Inis Bearcháin is a substantial island, nearly half a square mile in area, rather hilly and resistant to exploration, with inland clifflets, marshy bottoms and – from a glance at the old OS map – well over a hundred minute stone-walled fields, mostly abandoned to briars and bracken. The deserted one-roomed national school bears a plaque reading, 'Scoil Inis Barr an Chuain 1934'. (This version of the island's name, meaning island of the head of the bay, is a clumsy misinterpretation; tradition holds that it is named from a St Bearchán who came here from the Aran Islands.) There were twenty-three families on the island in the 1920s, I am told, some of which were among the twenty-seven from Na hOileáin and An Cheathrú Rua that set out for the bland pastures of County Meath in the Ráth Cairn resettlement scheme of 1935. When I visited Inis Bearcháin in 1980 there was one elderly couple there, and one single man, Máirtín Chóilín Choilmín Seoighe of the indefeasible currach-racing team of the 1970s, the Joyces of Inis Bearcháin. Their link to the outer world was by boat to Céibh an Rosa in the south of Leitir Calaidh, and Bóthar na nOileán was long disused. The island community's history, then, has been a slow, inexorable bleeding to death. Amazingly, a third of a century later Máirtín is still there. He is a craftsman, and as the quintessential many-skilled island man he has been the subject of several TV documentaries; when I called on him he was making a spinning wheel to decorate the bar in Leitir Móir and three canvas racing currachs for the Aran Islands. But from that visit principally I remember the sequence of *céimíní*, vertical slits in the field walls just wide enough to step through one leg at a time, that defined a crooked way from the old couple's house to Máirtín's. Formerly all the houses would have been linked by a network of such rugged but delicate trails, which now are walked by none but ghosts.

Back on Garomna and going on from Na hUaimíní one comes to a little hill that emphasizes the outermost, north-western corner of the island. It is called Cnoc Chathail Óig, and Seán Mac Giollarnáth recorded the following oral history of it: a Spanish boat spent some time in Cuan Chaisín off this headland, and its captain, Cathal Ó Flaithearta, met and married a local woman. Later he and his wife sailed off, never to return, leaving money for their son Cathal Óg, young Cathal, to be brought up by the woman's father. Cathal Óg's son Brian Dubh went to live in Leitir Móir, and Brian's grandson Éamonn married Sinéad ní Sheachnasaigh; these Flahertys and O'Shaunessys were the middlemen of most of Na hOileáin until the Famine, when the tenants could pay them nothing, as I have told apropos of the Big House in Leitir Móir. But in real-time history the name of the hill is much older than this oral lore would suggest, for one can read in the *Composition of Connaught*, the great treaty which formally wrote the Irish chieftains into the feudal hierarchy, that 'Clocke McCahill Oge' was one of the 138 quarters of a subdivision of Moycullen Barony called Gnomore belonging to a Gilleduffe O'Flaherty, as far back as 1585. Oral genealogy enjoys a high degree of credibility, especially among its bearers, and is often simply wrong, or (as here) elides the generations.

At An Cnoc, as it is called nowadays, the road turns south, and then runs around the head of Cuan an Mhuilinn, mill bay. The mill itself was on Abhainn an Damba, the stream of the dam, which flows out of the nearby Loch an Mhuilinn; later on I shall have tales to tell of another mill on a stream flowing into the same lake. Further south, the waterway between Garomna and the bewilderment of islands to the west narrows and shallows to a hundred yards or so of tidal rock and mud: An Cuigéal, the bottleneck, which is crossed by the bridge into Leitir Mealláin.

I revert again to the crossroads in Tír an Fhia, and this time take the left-hand turn. The road soon finds the coast at Céibh Ghlais na nUan, the quay of the stream of the lambs. This is a late nineteenth-century quay, smaller than that of Máimín, a mile to the north, which is one of Nimmo's works of the 1820s. Máimín was Garomna's great turf quay, with much coming and going to and from the Aran Islands, but the other eclipses it now, being the site of one of south Connemara's yearly regattas for traditional sailing boats and currachs.

Following the road southwards through the village of An Pháirc, the park, one sees a gaunt, derelict barn of a church on a bare rise by the shore: An Seanséipéal, the old chapel, or Séipéal na Leacrachaí Móra, the chapel of the big flags, so named from the great sheets of bare rock on the shore below it. One of the big churches that replaced the little old chapels and Mass houses in the confident days after the Catholic Emancipation Bill was passed in Westminster, it was built by Fr Peter Conboy (who also built the church in Carna in 1845) to serve the teeming villages of Tír an Fhia, which however are some way inland, leaving it a dispiriting presence on this already desolate coast. Before the complicated boundary changes of 1890 Garomna came under the Diocese of Tuam, while An Cheathrú Rua and Leitir Mealláin were in that of Galway. Fr M. D. Conroy of An Cheathrú Rua used to manage to serve Mass in both parts of his cure by dint of '2 miles walking, 2 miles on horseback and 2 miles sea crossing', in which latter the church on the Garomna shore was his landfall. (Looking at a map, I think he underestimates these distances considerably, unless he was using the big old Irish miles.) He describes one particularly difficult journey, starting on Christmas Eve:

Having arrived back at Carraroe after a Station in Rosmuck I set out for Lettermullen to say First Mass on Christmas Day. After a rough passage by sea and the long walk to Lettermullen I found to my surprise I had forgotten my watch and tried in vain to get a watch in Lettermullen. I had to depend on my landlord Thomas Lee to call me in good time for early Mass 8 o'c. Early next morning he called and reported to me that the people had assembled in large numbers at the new church nearby and that probably I was late for the morning was very bright. Without much ado I proceeded to the Church and said Mass. I then started on my walk to Rakins Pass [this must be an old name for An Cuigéal] expecting to find there my horse and saddle, but finding them not I resigned myself to the 2 miles walk through Gorumna. The morning was wild and showery. When I had almost completed my 2 miles journey and a fierce shower had passed, the appearance of the sky led me to think that it was just break of day, a surmise I soon realised was correct. On coming to Tiernea Church I had ample time under the shelter of a rick of turf to think out the problem. What was to be done should my curragh not come to me from Carraroe on such a wild day, and the easiest solution I thought would be that if the Tuam priest [of An Cillín, the eastern half of the Ceathrú Rua peninsula] were unable to cross for Mass at Tiernea, he could say Mass for me at Carraroe and depend on me to say the Tiernea Mass. Eventually he came and I crossed. Landing at Carraroe I said my second and third Masses . . .

After all that, just as he is setting off to Cill Bhriocáin in Ros Muc for his Christmas dinner he is called to Daingean to visit two typhus patients, whom he finds comatose; then he goes on 'a long tramp through the bogs' to the priest's house in Cill Bhriocáin, but finds him not at home, so he walks on to his family home at Garafin and partakes of the remains of their Christmas dinner, 'thinking not at all of the danger of carrying the infection to the family'. (I have often shared the shelter of a turf rick with this heroic priest's shade, but at least I did not have to visit comatose typhus cases.)

English was less familiar in Garomna than in Leitir Mealláin, because, say local people, the landlords or middlemen lived in Leitir Mealláin, or more likely because of Archbishop MacHale's long-sustained refusal to permit the establishment of national schools in his diocese. Hence a funny tale about the Tír an Fhia priest's pig that I heard from a merry old lady of Eanach Mheáin. One day the pig escaped from its sty and the priest's housekeeper could not get it to go in again. But when the priest came out with his horsewhip and shouted in English, 'Get in with you,' it obeyed, and the housekeeper said to herself, 'I'd forgotten that pig came from Leitir Mealláin!'

After another couple of miles on the roads leading southwards one comes to the village of An Trá Bháin, the white beach, which sprawls down a gentle slope to the shore near the south-eastern point of the island. Here is a neat little harbour, and, only just above high-water level, the walls of a late medieval church that Roderick O'Flaherty calls 'Olither church, or the Pilgrime's church' (*oilithreach*, a pilgrim), and which was probably a gathering place for pilgrims to the Aran Islands'

monasteries. An Trá Bháin is and was one of the densest settlements in
Na hOileáin; the 1839 map shows forty or so cabins within a few
hundred yards of the harbour, and as each dwelling has grown by extension or replacement on the same small patch the village is tightly
clustered. Nevertheless, with its bright-windowed school, well-kept
gardens and sea-breezy setting An Trá Bháin looks spruce, cheerful and
up to date. In the nineteenth century such hives of humanity as this
fishing village at the latter end of nowhere were hardly known to the
outside world, though the landlord's agent and the priest would have
kept a close eye on them. Dr Browne in the 1890s describes the poorest
of the dwellings as having one little room, a door of straw matting or
a bundle of furze in a wooden frame, two little window-holes stuffed
with rags or sods of turf, no chimney apart from a hole in the roof,
furniture consisting of one or two small benches and a rough table,
and perhaps some banks of stones built up to form seats, no bed apart
from a litter of dried bracken and some tattered blankets on the floor
or on a pile of stones, and no utensils other than a pot, a tub, some
baskets, a tin lamp and a few mugs. That is, all the appurtenances of
domesticity scratched together out of the detritus of heath and bare
rock, to make the little white homes that in a distant view so enchanted
Paul Henry and a subsequent generation of landscapists.

This is the end of the road; there is not even a path along the barren
southern shore of Garomna, although boreens reach down from the
main road to little quays in its numerous creeks. But that southern face
of Na hOileáin, born out of almost unimaginable geological cata-
clysms, is so different from the rest that it calls for separate treatment.
I end this tour of the roads of Garomna with words from the lament
– one of the great south Connemara songs, part of the magnificent
furnishings of the hovels Dr Browne describes – 'Amhrán na Trá Báine',
or 'Amhrán an Bhá', 'The Song of the Drowning'.

The incident happened off the point here: three young brothers of
the Ó Máille family were returning in their currach with goods from
Galway when it was rammed or run over by a sailboat (I have been told,
almost as if it were a secret, that the boat was from Aran); they were
drowned, and the bodies of at least two of them never found. It is said
that the crew of the big boat had a grudge against the Ó Ceallaigh

family of An Trá Bháin, that they asked the lads in the currach if they were Ó Ceallaighs, and as there was intermarriage between the Ó Ceallaighs and the Ó Máilles, they answered, 'That's us all right.' Passengers in the big boat who saw what had happened were put under an oath not to reveal it as long as they were 'alive in Ireland' (a set phrase meaning simply 'alive'), and so it was generally accepted that the drowning had been accidental; however, one of them emigrated to the United States and felt that as he was no longer 'alive in Ireland' he could tell the truth. All this has been hotly disputed over the years.

A sister of the drowned men, Bríd Ní Mháille, had emigrated to Boston before the event, and it is said that when she heard the news she shed no tear until she had composed the song. She begins by regretting that she did not die the day she was baptized, for she has been left a lone bird with not a creature to talk with; she has neither brother nor sister, her dear mother is dead, her old dad weak with age, and, she says, 'Oh Christ, it's no wonder.'

> Céad faraoir ghéar nár cailleadh mé an lá is ar baisteadh mé go hóg,
> Mar fágadh i mo chadhan aonraic mé gan feithide an bhéil bheo,
> Níl deirfiúr agam is níl deartháir agam is níl mo mháithrín beo,
> Is tá mo dheaide bocht lag aosta is a Chríost cén t-íonadh dhó.

She curses the boat, she upbraids the currach and the seas off An Trá Bháin; she pictures her brothers tossed from breaker to breaker and from rock to rock; she regrets leaving her home, for it is lost to her, and for nothing, since the man who was to have kept it for her is dead and an in-law has possession of it. The song has a simple rocking rhythm – one can picture a drifting corpse in gentle waves – and it ends:

> Tháinig na maidí isteach ar an duirling, agus an churrach ar an trá.

> [The oars came in on the shingle bank, and the currach on the strand.]

– a line that seems to breathe resignation, as if to a law of nature.

33 Holes in Reality

There is much that cannot be seen from the roads in this at first sight bare and boring island of Garomna. I begin with some minor works of faith or of muscle on its eastern foreshore.

I first heard of Tobairín 'P' from a boatman I was chatting to about rock-pool holy wells and other marvels, on the quay near the old church in An Trá Bháin. It is so called, he said, because it is the shape of the letter 'P' for Patrick, and I would find it 1,000 or 1,200 yards along the shore to the north. From experience I knew that I was highly unlikely to find it in the seaweed-covered wastes without further directions. 'Well,' he said, pointing, 'do you see that dot? That's a sheep. It's a hundred yards beyond that sheep.' But by the time I had got round the head of the harbour inlet and onto the open shore again the dot had vanished. I pressed ahead, and on rounding a bend of the shore I saw the sheep running away ahead of me. How far back had it been when it started running? I went on until I began to feel I must have gone too far. Then the sheep turned and ran back past me. A black squall was coming up the bay as I worked my way south again along the rocks, looking at hundreds of rock pools of all shapes and none. Suddenly at my feet was a pool the outline of which was unmistakably a capital 'P' about a yard high. As if to swear to its identity there was a metal crucifix jammed under a stone beside it and a plastic holy-water bottle in the shape of the Madonna bobbing about in it like a bath toy. I looked up, and there was the sheep sitting in the lee of a field wall just a hundred yards back along the shore, grinning at me. What counts as a significant feature of a geography? Here the seaweed gatherers and winkle pickers of centuries past had recognized a letter of the infinite alphabet of rock-pool shapes and read it as an initial attempt to spell out the nature of place: here, one could imagine, some follower of St Patrick had paused on his way to the pilgrims' church and embarkation for holy Aran, had bent his head and looked at this pool, and by the intensity of his interpretive attention made a nowhere into a place for ever more, or at least for as long as its story is handed down.

It was probably on that same day that I found another interpreted rock pool, this one not the work of a saint. Cuinneog an Fhir Mhóir, the big man's churn, is a fine, smooth, tub-like pothole in the south flank of a deep cleft in the upper shore, about 200 yards north of Tobairín 'P'. Greatman's Bay, Cuan an Fhir Mhóir, is named after the same big fellow. O'Donovan in his letters concerning the Ordnance Survey of 1839 takes note of it:

It is called Cuan an Fhir Mhóir in the annals of the Four Masters at the year 1600, which is the name still in use among the *Cois fhairge* [seaside] people, but those who speak English always call it '*The Great Man's Bay*'. Of this great man tradition remembers nothing more than that he was one of the giants who lived here so long ago that no one knows how long, and who plundered all the boats and ships that passed the way. The natives still point out a large hollow rock called his churn – Cuinneóg an Fhir Mhóir – and three large rocks called Branraidh an Fhir Mhóir, which supported the three legs of his pot in which he was used to boil the whales caught by a fishing rod! He was equal to Rabelais' giant. I firmly believe in his existence, though I have no historic evidence to prove the period at which he lived, or whether he was one of the Fomorians or of Bolgic or Danaan colony.

I have not identified Branra an Fhir Mhóir, the giant's tripod, but a little over a mile further north, by a side road leading down to the roofless carcase of the nineteenth-century church, is a huge granite boulder, An Chloch Mhór, or more accurately, it is said, half a boulder, the other half being Cloch Chormaic, which lies on the opposite shore of An Cheathrú Rua; it seems that Cormac and the (nameless) Garomna giant threw the boulder back and forth at each other until it split in two and was no longer worth the trouble of throwing.

As well as its foreshore holy wells – there are another five that I know of, all beautifully smooth cylindrical potholes – Garomna has some inland ones, and of these three turned out to have a curious characteristic in common: they are triangular. The first such well I visited was Tobairín Naoimh Anna. (St Ann or Anna is the mother of the Mother of God, and indeed of the Three Marys according to some legends; she is the patroness of women in labour.) Some men I met on the shore of Tír an Fhia, where they were cutting long strips of sea-washed turf to cover potato pits with, told me of it; they said that it was by a lake they called Loch Tan, just under a mile inland. Whether the name of the lake, pronounced as I have spelled it, has something to do with St Ann, or merely comes from *tanaí*, shallow, I was not able to ascertain. The old Ordnance Survey field-name books record it as Loch na bhFeadán, the lake of the watercourses, and the men knew this name too but seemed to think it referred to the water horses that are said to haunt the lake.

Having heard this much I made my way to the lake, and walked up a grassy boreen to an isolated cottage near its north shore to ask for further directions. Two old ladies came out to greet me, one of them on metal crutches. As soon as I mentioned what I was looking for the more mobile lady seized me by the elbow and ran me around the east side of the lake until she could point the way to the well. I could not understand much that she said as she had no teeth, but there was no mistaking the warmth of her welcome: '*Fáilte romhat, a dhuine uasail, fáilte romhat!*' I picked my way onwards through little fields invaded by seepages from the lake until I found the well. It was most striking: a neat and regular triangular hole in a wide, flat outcrop of granite, its sides measuring about ten inches. There was a low U-shaped shrine of drystone walling around it, with some little crosses and holy statu-ettes of the Virgin Mary, and two oval enclosures about three feet high, planted with nasturtiums, asters and other cottage-garden flow-ers. I was very pleased with the place: the bare stony brink of the rippling, shallow lake, the empty plateau of central Garomna stretch-ing away to the west, even the little pump house muttering to itself nearby, its broken window hung with a slightly sinister black rag of clothing. I circled the lake back to the cottage to thank the ladies, and was invited in for a cup of tea. The lame lady was the more dominant and conversational, but both of them glistened with animation; I got the impression that they had few visitors. The cottage was very bare, but they would not accept the little sum I offered them for their trouble. They told me that a lame Mayo man had dreamed of the well and spent a month in walking to find it. He was cured, but then he didn't like to leave his crutches, so he took them away with him, and his leg was as bad as ever. The little flower gardens were made by a local woman in memory of a child she had lost. I later heard that a *fear siúil*, a 'walking man' or tramp, had dreamed that there was a well even holier than this one on a tiny island in the lake, but this has never been found.

How I learned about the second of Garomna's triangular wells I cannot now remember. It is called Tobairín Ghleann an Uisce, the little well of the glen of water, and it is in an exceedingly watery location in the interior of the island. About a mile south of the village of Tír an Fhia a track leads out onto the patchwork of bare rock sheets, little lakes and soggy hollows west of the main road. A bit more than half a mile out, where this track dips into the wide and shallow glen, there is a large boulder on the left; the well is about sixty yards to the south-west of the boulder. This triangle is about a foot and a half across, and it is surrounded by a little ring of stones and small stakes. I noted several small holy leavings: coins, beads, wooden crosses, nails, a pen, a sardine-tin opener, medallions, a bottle of Lourdes water in the shape of the Madonna. That first visit was made in early summer sunshine, when a tender wilderness of water-loving flowers such as lady's smock, marsh orchids and yellow flags stretched all around. But, as I found out on another visit, in mist and rain this central plain of Garomna appears a dreary, wet desert, its loneliness even enhanced by a solitary turf-cutter picking away at the last scraps of its worn-out peat banks.

That the simple triangle (or, better, the triangular emptiness) has such weight in this elemental landscape serves to remind me that one can tire of Mandelbrot's fractal epiphanies with their eternal spirals winding into eternity. Perhaps one could claim that fractal geometry is to Celtic art as Euclid is to classical art. While the mainstream of European culture has pursued its magnificent course, another perception has been kept in mind by the Celtic periphery, all the way from La Tène Iron Age ornament to Jim Fitzpatrick's kitsch-Celt goddesses – in a word, that a fascinating sort of beauty arises out of the repetitive interweaving of simple elements. The beauty of nature is often of this sort. In Connemara, which is pre-eminently the land of 'dappled things' – drizzly skies, bubbly streams, tussocky hillsides – one recognizes the texture. But after a thorough soaking in this dappled Celtic bewilderment, one is tempted to run for shelter in classical temples. Perhaps this is why I have taken so inordinate an interest in the round and triangular holy wells, treating them as major reference points in a landscape that otherwise teems with ungraspable reiterations of details. Perhaps too something of this same feeling arose in the *seandream*, the old folk of vaguely ancient days, who found and named and speculated about these exceptions to the phenomenological flux, thus adding to the realms of the real and the ideal the imaginary in all its incalculable dimensionality.

The third of the triangular wells is Tobairín an Átha Leacaigh, the little well of the flaggy ford, a mile or so north of Baile na Cille. A flag in this context is a flagstone, a flat rock outcrop, and such an outcrop provides a natural crossing place on a stream flowing out of Loch an Bhalla westwards to Loch an Mhuilinn, the mill lake; the well is a small, neat, triangular hollow in this flag. There was, as I have mentioned, a mill on the outflow of this last lake, as well as which the 1839 OS map shows the 'Slateford Corn Mill' on its inflow, a hundred yards downstream from the ford itself. (A slate, in Connemara, is another term for a flat outcrop.) The old mill wheel, I am told, used to lie near the site of the mill, but was taken to decorate a garden in Tír an Fhia. The mill belonged to a Féilim Mac Dhubhghaill, or Mac Dhúill, or Mac Chuthail, according to various sources – but however he is to be spelled, he was a fine rollicking song-maker and impromptu versifier. Féilim's father Labhcás, who lived in Inis Ní, was a poet too. Once when he came to stay with Féilim at the flaggy ford he was woken in the morning by shafts of sunlight piercing through holes in the walls, and sat up in bed to complain in verse. Féilim replied sharply:

> Is iomaidh óigfhear múinte tréitheach
> A ghabh an gleanntán sléibhe seo an Átha Leacach,
> Ach níor fríoth aon locht i gcaitheamh an tsaoil air
> Go dtí an mhaidin chéanna a dtáinig m'athair.

[It's many a well-mannered, accomplished young man / Came to this mountain glen of the flaggy ford, / But no fault was ever found with it / Until the very morning my father came.]

If Féilim's house was of the flimsiest sort, it was well furnished with merriment. 'An tIolrach Mór', 'The Big Eagle', is one of Féilim's well-remembered songs. The occasion of its making was this: While Féilim was away from home one day his wife had a visit from a woman relative of hers, and having nothing else to offer her guest to eat she killed and cooked the cock that used to wake Féilim every morning. The next morning, not hearing the usual cockcrow, Féilim overslept, and when he asked his wife what had happened to the cock she said that the big eagle had taken it to feed its chicks. But Féilim heard the truth from the neighbours, and made up a fine fantasy about his revenge on the eagle:

> D'eirigh mé go feargach ar maidin mhoch Dé Domhnaigh,
> Chuir mé orm mo bhróga is mé ag goil go Tír an Fhia,
> Ag goil thrí Ghleann an Duine Mhairbh dhom casadh
>   an tIolrach Mór dhom,
> Is ba gheall le dúchán móna é go prámhaí ina shuí.
> Thug mé straoill is strachaille air, amadán is óinseach,
> Cinéal Bhriain 'ac Lóbais de phór Chathail Bhuí,
> Sin agus mo sheacht mallacht go bhfeara sé go deo air
> A thug mo choileach óg uaim a ligfeadh dhom a ghlao.

[I got up angry on the Sunday, / I put on my boots to go to Tír an Fhia. / Going through the Dead Man's Glen I met the Big Eagle, / And it was like a turf-stack boldly standing up. / I called it streel and grabber, fool and silly woman, / Of the tribe of Brian 'ac Lóbais and the seed of Cathal Buí, / And may my seven curses fall on it for ever / For taking my young cock that used to crow for me.]

The eagle denies the charge and tells him to go home and ask his wife Nóra the name of the young woman who plucked the cock; Féilim refuses to believe it and says that he has a store of history books to show that the eagle's father was the greatest rascal in the land. The eagle puts on its suit of mail and takes up the sharpest sword it can find, while Féilim has his scythe and wears nothing but his shirt. They fight like two bulls in a mountain glen from early in the morning until half an hour before sunset, and neither could say who was the better man. The next day the eagle sends him a written challenge and they fight again; but in the end the eagle has to plead for its life and promises to praise him for ever for defending the fame of Ireland.

Féilim's 'Marcaíocht an Phúca', 'The Ride of the Púca', starts off rather mysteriously at the ford itself:

> Chuaigh mé ar mo ghlúna, 's gan caint ar mo dhearnacháin,
> Ag lámhacán siúil ag an Áth Leacach;
> An ránaí púca (an deamhan d'á chumhdach)
> Rinne m'uachta, a's bhain díom m'amharc.

[I went down on my knees, not to say my palms, / Crawling about at the flaggy ford; / The skinny púca (may the Devil keep him) / Made my will, and robbed me of my sight.]

Whether the poet was paying his respects to the holy well, or was in the befuddled and belated state that often seems to provoke the púca's attacks is not clear. But as is its wont the púca slung him onto its back and took him off on a terrifying ride through streams and pools, over the peaks of Na hUaiminí and down Gleann Trasna; they would have got as far as England had not the púca cast a shoe in Úraid. Dumped far off in a place called Baile an Tuaiscirt, the town of the north (which I cannot identify), Féilim got supper and a bottle of something from a friend, and set off to walk home. He fell in with the Cruitirín Ceoil, the little harpist, one of the fairies of Cnoc an Dúin in western Connemara, who angrily urged him to get back to Connacht. But then he met the harpist's enemy Finnbheara, king of the fairies of Cnoc Meá near Tuam, who was drilling his army with a gun in his hand; what happened then is left unsaid, but for Féilim that day was 'longer than the season of spring'. There the mad caper ends, as suddenly as it began, as happens to drunks and poets.

*

Now that I have done with the humble but engaging literary tradition of the flaggy ford – a place that is nowadays marginal to the marginal, being far from roads or houses and reached by a path that is in part untraceably lost to bog through disuse – two questions arise for me regarding the triangular wells of Garomna. Why are there such phenomena, uniting the utmost simplicity of geometry with a naïve tradition of sanctity? And then, why am I '*ag lámhacán siúil ag an Áth Leacach*', 'crawling about at the flaggy ford' – that is, what has led me to devote so much time, thought and energy to searching them out?

The objective question first. The *leaca*, the flat sheets of bedrock bared by turf-cutting and ages of overgrazing in such places as Garomna, are criss-crossed in all directions by long straight cracks (and – to pursue the causal chain a little further into the concatenation of all things – the reason for the fissuring is that the granite exposed to the west of the Shannawona fault is from the upper or outer layers of the pluton, and as it cooled and hardened into a crust it contracted, and then as vast tonnages of rock were removed from above it by erosion, it flexed itself and expanded, and in one way or another was repeatedly faulted and riven). Here and there three of these cracks, happening to cross one another at about sixty degrees, will outline a triangle sufficiently regular to catch the eye. But these cracks are merely the surface manifestation of what the geologists would call joints: planar breaks extending deep into the body of the rock, vertically or aslant. Three planes, if no two of them are parallel, meet in a point, says one of the basic rules of incidence in solid geometry. If that point happens to lie a little way below the present-day ground level, the three planes will isolate a tetrahedron, an inverted triangular pyramid, of rock. A loose piece like this would easily have been plucked out by the glacier that gave these outcrops their final polish. What is left is a neat triangular hole, usually containing rainwater, sky-reflecting. Among the vague, unintelligible chaos of forms underfoot it is a beacon of order, a promise of rationality, an effect so simple that it calls for a simple explanation, which the sense of wonder supplies and tradition hallows: it is a font, the work of a saint.

The second question, the subjective one, I cannot fully answer. If I could crack open the crust of my own rationalism and release the magma of spontaneous association within, then I would write better about these, for me, paradigmatic places or nodes of being. When I first became aware of the triangular wells and of the cylindrical holy wells of the foreshore they suggested stars widely scattered in a dark sky, motes of almost tangible meaning in the endlessness of the incomprehensible. I should have symbolized them on my maps by asterisks, little stars referring one to a footnote, for each has its story, ceremonial rite and delusive promise. If these regular figures are the points at which the character of the landscape can be grasped, it is through paradox. Galileo says that the language of nature is triangles and circles, but as I have shown it is more often the fractal. But here the fractal, through its fractures, throws up the Euclidean. A collusion across aeons between fire and ice — a granitic pluton of 400 million years ago and a glacier of 12,000 years ago — brings forth the schoolroom geometry of points A, B and C. Even the designation of these features as wells is paradoxical. Holy wells, one feels, should be springs that originate deep down and channel chthonic energies, as they did long before the Christian era, tapping into the water table that lies under the surface of the land like an inexhaustible reservoir of the possibilities of life. (This is the feature that gives a spring well the allure and mystery of another person's being, that welling up of a common humanity.) From this point of view the Garomnian holy well is a mere puddle.

Let me not, by omission, suggest that these considerations came to me on first seeing these wells. All I gathered then was the collocation of an object — a negative one, a hole — and a legend, explicit if such a tradition still persisted, or implicit in the title of holy well. The realization that these geological curiosities could become icons of a way of looking at the world came later, in the course of puzzling over what it is that I see in them, or perhaps of constructing something to see in them. (This second formulation is the better one: it frees the wells to revert to being simply hollows in stone, on which no saint or scholar has laid a hand.)

If I now take these obscure triangles as the basis of a subjective triangulation, in place of the lofty mountain peaks of the Ordnance Survey's Primary Triangulation of Ireland in the 1830s, what are the dimensions, the chains of associations, along which other locations could be situated in relation to them? Some of these are the simply mensurational, which I prefer to express in feet and yards and miles, measures that still retain the imprint of the human body, handling, spanning, striding, marching; the geophysical, as in the jointing that relates these wells to the Shannawona fault; the mythic, their humble entry into the vast domain of tradition regarding the acts of the saints, the prehistory of Christianity, and behind that the archaic sacredness of the land; their anchoring of a chain of placenames linked by a narrative, as in the Ride of the Púca taking flight from the Flaggy Ford. So, from these wells, as from the hundreds of other places that I mention in this book, a web, an interweaving of many modes of cognition, stretches out across Connemara. And if I privilege the holy wells – the genuine springs and the foreshore potholes together with the triangles of Garomna's interior – in my literary reconstruction of Connemara, it is for reasons I can hardly explain to myself (though it pleases me that, in fluid dynamics ,'del', the mathematical expression used in calculating the divergence and vorticity of a flow, is symbolized as ∇). The output of Garomna's little dels is purely notional, a flux of the imagination, an ideal irrigation of the real. What exactly wells up for me at this moment of writing, in these triangular sources? I used to think it was 'meaning' – but that is a mere gesture, a waving to the reader to come to my help, for meaning is always specific; one can always ask, 'What meaning?' Now I take it to be the primitive precursor of meaning, difference. Without differences, distinctions, discriminations, no world, no language, no meaning. Surely these wells dispense difference in sparkling profusion, being so odd, so remote from all modern practicalities, and so little known to the world outside of strictly local tradition? (And, as the first to recommend them to the attention of a readership, I claim priority for whatever interpretations or projections I invest in them!) They are therefore the purest springs of what makes Connemara itself, in the three dimensions I have highlighted, the intimacy of settlement with wilderness, the persistence of the deep past, and the echoing treasure house of its language.

Theories of flow must consider sinks as well as sources. There are locations – by definition they are not places, though we know too well where they are – that swallow up difference, leaving a desert of toxic sameness, an atmosphere of depleted possibilities of meaning, a dull residue of differences that make no difference. Our civilization produces them; it even needs them. We need them in Connemara – I am no purist in this – but must not allow them to drain away its essences. That should be the principle at the core of arguments around particular cases. And if the web of associations I have spun around these quaint landmarks in Garomna should lap out beyond the vague confines of Connemara to envelop more and more of the world, it might bring with it the suggestion of a way of looking at places as sources of difference; and surely taking note of the particularities of a place is the first step in taking care of it.

This conceptual Ride of the Púca is as much as I can offer to justify my work, as a citizen of troubled times.

34 Subduction

The ground in the southern third of Garomna and the southern half of Leitir Mealláin is utterly different from that of the rest of Na hOileáin. The eastern end of the geological boundary is close to the little harbour of An Trá Bháin; there one walks off the bright smooth sheets of granite, which look as if they have been settled in place since the beginning of time, and steps into a zone in which the rocks underfoot seem to be resting for a moment between bouts of hand-to-hand fighting. The outcrops are glacially polished as elsewhere, but in their smooth surfaces one can trace a static turmoil of forms – gnarled lumps, twisted and clenched veins, heaped gobbets – that are evidences of some profound convulsion long anterior to the Ice Ages. In fact to begin to comprehend what has happened here one has to adopt a perspective of hundreds of millions of years. And what does 'here' mean? None of today's landmarks existed, not even the mountain ranges and the oceans whose shapes we know from maps; the crucial events took place dozens of miles down in the dark beneath this sunlit skin-deep surface made up of what we recognize as places. For example, in the e-mails I exchanged with the geologist Paul Ryan, who undertook to explain these titanic processes to me, he states that at a certain period Connemara 'was buried to depths of 20–25 km' where its sedimentary rocks 'were deformed and folded and then rapidly heated to temperatures of ~600 C within 5 Ma [million years]', which, he adds, is 'an impossibly short time geologically speaking'. We live on a floating world subject to sinkings, a shifting jigsaw of transient geographies, but our senses, unless aided by science, are too quick to see it.

The scientific context of these considerations is the theory of plate tectonics, which I summarize as best I can for my purposes in this chapter. Parts of the earth's crust consist of ocean-floor basalts some three to six miles thick, and other parts are of the less dense rocks that form continents, twenty or thirty miles thick. Under the crust is the mantle, consisting of rock rendered plastic by heat – not properly molten, but as fluid under pressure as white-hot steel under the hammer. The interior of the earth is heated by radioactivity, and the resultant convection currents in the mantle have broken the crust into eight major plates and a lot of lesser ones, which are constantly shifted about, welded together and torn apart by the sea of hot rock they float on. Most plates consist of both oceanic and continental crust. Where two plates are moving away from each other, molten basalt wells up between them and hardens into new ocean crust, spreading out on either side of the divide. Where plates collide, if the leading edge of one of them is ocean floor it will be forced beneath the other and plunge into the mantle to be melted at great depth. (When I say 'plunge' I think of a phrase from one of the great exponents of this theory, Preston Cloud: 'The plates glide . . . at rates comparable to that at which an anvil might settle through solid asphalt.') If the leading edges are continental, they will be crunched together and their rocks folded and heaped into mountain ranges. Thus the earth's heat is dissipated by extrusion of hot ocean floor and absorption of long-cooled ocean floor; this is the engine that drives geography through time; it used to do so more vigorously than it does now and someday it will stop as the last few radioactive atoms disintegrate, having lost their game with chance.

As I explained in *Listening to the Wind*, Ireland was born in the fusion of two tectonic plates. Four hundred and forty million years ago the northern half of Ireland-to-be, including the makings of Connemara, lay on the edge of a continent called Laurentia (which, roughly speaking, comprised what is now North America and Greenland), and the rest of it lay on the shores of Avalonia, a minor fragment of continent close to Baltica (which is now Scandinavia). The ocean separating these continents has been named Iapetus after one of the Titans, the son of Uranus and Gaia. (The Atlantic did not exist at this period; it only began to open up some 220 million years ago.) As a result of a change in the pattern of convection currents in the underlying mantle, Iapetus began to narrow as ocean floor on the Laurentian plate dived southwards under that of the plate carrying Avalonia and Baltica. Some of that ocean-bed rock, rich in hydrated minerals and entrained ocean water, melted in the hot depths, forming a light and fluid magma which rose in plumes, punching through the Baltican ocean floor and forming an arc of volcanic islands like those of today's south Pacific. As Iapetus continued to shrink, the continent of Laurentia eventually came up against this rampart of volcanoes, and the 'subduction', as the geologists call it, of the Laurentian plate came to a stop. So far as concerns the little local detail of Ireland-to-be, the line of this suture runs from Croagh Patrick to Fair Head in north-east Ulster. The rocks that would form Connemara were part of the great collision zone of Laurentia and the volcanic arc – a pile-up that built the mountains of the Grampian orogeny, a Himalaya-high range across what are now Norway, Scotland, Ireland and Appalachia.

In the later convulsions of the subduction, proto-Connemara was tossed around like a pancake: first it was driven down under the volcanic arc to a depth of fifteen miles or so and stewed by magma that heated it up to 600 degrees centigrade over a period of 5 million years, and then spewed out again to be thrust a dozen miles southwards over part of the arc (as I have described apropos of the Mannin Thrust west of Roundstone). What happened then defies imagination. The whole stupendous tectonic process flipped: the ocean floor on the Baltica plate began to plunge northwards under the collision zone piled high along the leading edge of the Laurentian plate. Connemara was in the thick of this; the trench into which the Baltica plate descended ran along what is now Galway Bay and across Ireland to Clogher Head north of Dublin, and thence across the Southern Highlands of Scotland. As the Baltican ocean floor scraped under the edge of the collision zone, various volcanic structures and sediments were chiselled off its back and accumulated into a wedge of rocks that slowly grew out southwards, until, 416 million years ago, Iapetus finally closed, with Avalonia rammed up against these new extensions of Laurentia. The Shannon estuary marks this last suturing, which left Ireland in the middle of a vast new continent. The South Connemara Group, as the geologists term the rocks of the southern coast of Na hOileáin, are some of those scrapings off the bed of Iapetus; they include lavas spouted out into ocean depths by submarine volcanoes, concretions of volcanic ash, and conglomerations of boulders or sand-grains of varied origins – if one can talk of origins in a world that has been remoulding itself for billions of years.

That was not the end of the processes that gave rise to this dark conflicted stuff of south Garomna. Molten granite came up in slow surges beneath it, and what we walk on here once formed a pendant, a downward-pointing excrescence, of the rock that lay above the granite pluton like a roof. The pendant would have been particularly intensely baked and kneaded by the granite welling up around it, and its component minerals have been thoroughly deformed and recrystal-lized. This happened some 400 million years ago, and in the unimaginable lapse of time since then the rest of the roof has been removed by weathering, leaving a cross-section of the pendant exposed for us to stroll across.

Such a stroll might start at the quay of An Trá Bháin, from which an old track leads across a little headland to the craggy south-facing shore of Garomna. I took that way recently, to see what had changed on the human scale since my explorations in the 1980s. It was mid March. The track is edged with blocks of stone, but between these rims its surface is a smooth grassy sward, sparkling that day with daisies and primroses. It winds between little stone-walled plots of shaggy pastur-age and knolls of stripy rock – lavas veined with metamorphosed calcite – that looked as if they had been woven out of thick rope. The boulders just above high water mark were badged with brilliant orange lichen. The surface of all things seemed to rejoice in the light of the sun. The first change a cartographer would have to note was at An tAircín, where a narrow road comes down from An Trá Bháin to what I dimly remembered as a small stone-built jetty in a steep-sided inlet (an *aircín* being a place where the sea seems to break into the land). Now there is a working harbour with a long concrete pier borne across a branch of the creek on a broad semicircular arch of moulded concrete, a clutch of currachs, a little trawler, heaps of lobster pots and, on props by the roadside, an immense Galway hooker – the largest ever built, in fact – the *St Barbara*.

This is the dream-boat of a Garomna man, Steve Mulkerrins, who emigrated to Boston and then Chicago as a lad, worked as a builder, carpenter and boatwright, and spent three years building this 47-foot-long, 26-ton vessel of imported Irish oak and larch, and christened it after his mother's name-saint. In 2006, with an Aran Islands skipper and Connemara crew, he sailed her through Lake Michigan, Lake Huron, Lake Erie and the Erie Canal, then down the Hudson river to New York and across the Atlantic via the Azores to Céibh an Mháimín. What her future is I have yet to learn; she must be the only hooker with a website address on her bows, but the site just bounces back e-mails as the huge emptiness of her hull re-echoes a knock on her timbers. For now she looms on stilts, a glossy black beetle, astonishing the occasional passer-by, who could shelter from a shower under the rigid bulge of her bows. Her sheer size seems partially to exempt her from reality, like an emigrant's memories of childhood that fail to take into account the subsequent growth of the child and so enlarge every-thing in retrospect. For me at least she is the emblem of the impossibility of return.

Half a mile or so beyond An tAircín one comes across a rare memento of the kelp industry that for two and a half centuries used to wreathe this coast in smoke. The widely enquiring geologist G. H. Kinahan, writing in 1869, sets the scene:

This smoke is very peculiar; it does not ascend like other smoke, but hangs near the surface, creeping along the ground, and lying in heavy clouds in the cooms and hollows among the hills. The natives consider it very whole-some; but strangers generally find it heavy and oppressive, and usually contract a headache from its smell . . . The kelp fires can be seen on all sides – out on the islands, in on the bays, north, south, east and west; and unless there is a good breeze, the horizon will be formed of a heavy cloud of brownish-grey smoke.

There are two structures left over from the industry on this Garomna shore, just above high-water mark: a half-ruined drystone wall three or four feet high enclosing a circular patch of grass and brambles, about twenty feet across, and a rectangular bank of heaped-up blocks of stone. This latter was, when I first came across it, clearly a kelp kiln of the type introduced by the Free State authorities in the 1930s, when specimen kilns were built on various seaweed shores, together with circular enclosures for seaweed stacks. Today it is hardly identifiable, having fallen in on itself and probably having had more stone piled onto it to clear a little grazing in its vicinity. These innovatory kilns were carefully built, with a hearth-like opening at either end and smaller holes at ground level on either side through which the burning seaweed could be stirred with rakes. This one in Garomna measured about sixteen feet by four and stood three or four feet high. Whereas in the earlier and more rudimentary kilns the fire was kept going for up to two nights and a day, and the ash allowed to fuse into a slab that then had to be broken up for transport, in the new ones the firing only lasted for eight hours or so, and the ash was bagged up as a powder. The old kelp-makers, once their rooted conservatism was overcome, appreciated the less toilsome regime of the new kilns, but I have been told they complained that it was difficult to dry weed in the walled stacks. In fact the stack platforms were intended only for newly gathered weed, to let the seawater drain out of it, while it could be shielded from rain by a covering of thatch or a layer of old weed if necessary, and the final drying had still to be done by pitchforking the weed out like hay.

However, the trade, always vulnerable to developments far beyond the horizons of Garomna, was in its last days by the time of these innovations, and finally died out in about 1948 as iodine was outdone by modern antibiotics. Now very few of the 1930s kilns survive, the seashore being a fiercely self-destructive environment; I know of one in Árainn and another in Inis Oírr, and in my fairly exhaustive walking of the southern Connemara shores the Garomna specimen was the only one I came across. (I have subsequently seen one on Inis Duga, near Slyne Head.) The earlier kilns, being hardly more than a shallow trench with a rim of stones a foot or so high, have long been brushed aside by winter storms and have left scarcely a trace on the shores of today. So the storm-battered stony mound on this lonely shore is probably the best memorial of Connemara's contribution to Europe's smoky centuries.

Further west, the shoreline lies more remote from the settlements inland, from which narrow roads come down here and there to a few inlets and small unfrequented quays. After three miles or so of scrambling – shingle, boulders, little cliffs, sand, mud – it may be a relief to turn inland by a soft old grassy track to the ruined church from which Garomna's westernmost village, Baile na Cille, derives its name. It lies rather isolated in a little glen south of Loch Bhaile na Cille, surrounded by graves, some a century or two old, some recent. The old Ordnance Survey maps mark it as 'abbey', but nothing is known of its origins or affiliations. An old man crippled with arthritis whom I met nearby told me that it is said to have been built in a night (like the chapel south of An Cheathrú Rua), which he found difficult to believe as 'it would have been a big job even by daylight'; also, he said, its stones were brought from Aran – and in fact the jambs of the lintelled doorway and the surrounds of the remarkably tall and narrow window in the east gable are of cut limestone and more than likely did come from Aran. Many of the older gravestones are nobly proportioned slabs of Aran limestone too, while others are home-made slabs of concrete. Some give the names of the grieving relatives who erected them as well as of those lying below; I was touched by one that read 'inserted by' instead of 'erected by', the wording of a published death-notice having evidently been taken as guide. Both church and graveyard used to be choked with millennial overgrowth (I had to force my way up through a hanging thicket of ivy to check by touch that the head of the slit window was indeed rounded, as reported), but a community employment scheme in the 1980s has left them clear, cared for and somehow bereft of centuries of experience.

The surroundings, though, reserve a certain melancholy magic. We are still in the zone of the South Connemara Group here, and the contorted shadows of ancient catastrophes show in many humps and shoulders of rock. Odd things have happened in this locality, it seems. Dr Browne was told that a woman living by the lake surprised a water horse, and it shook drops of water onto her, which left her paralysed. And Pádraic Ó Cualáin told me that some smooth green fields sloping to the lake shore just north of the old church have the (irresistibly suggestive, if grammatically unconvincing) name of Gort an Mhoill, because a man was abducted by the fairies there and held for three days, which caused the *moill* or delay.

I spent some time there myself once, rather exhausted from a long day's walking, and let my mind lose itself in the faintly mysterious terrain, grey-green under a low grey sky, in which nothing moved apart from a few cows munching, and in the distance the black and white blades of breakers rising out of a flat grey sea, with a lone currach faintly rising and falling. I tried not to think of the list in which we will all be inserted one day or the next, and turned my meditations to the less personal and almost consolatory theme of the vast, ongoing, minute-by-minute subduction of the past, which swallows church-yards, industries, languages, geographies and all.

35 Loose Ends of the Earth

When I look at the fat wad of file cards on which I have recorded placenames from Leitir Mealláin and its five satellite islands, and the long handwritten lists of placenames I received from people I met there and later corresponded with, I feel my veins loaded with ore – precious stuff, but it impedes the flow of writing. Since much of it has found its place on my map of Connemara and the rest will ultimately be available to anyone who is interested through the Hardiman Library at NUI Galway, I merely allude to it here in order to validate my finding that the smaller the place the more there is to be said about it. (This means that, like Achilles pursuing the tortoise, I can never quite cover the gap between me and my goal, the end of this book, which I will have to bring to an arbitrary close very soon.) The overload of detail is also due to the generosity of the people of these ultimate islands of the archipelago, where, my diary notes, after a few days of exploration I felt not only overwhelmed with topographical detail but 'plodaithe [stuffed] with tea and bread and butter'. Typical was my reception in a very traditional house at the end of the long stout arm Leitir Mealláin reaches out to the west, where I called in to enquire about the offshore islet of Gólam, the outer point of Ceann Gólaim or Golam Head.

Gólam (a curious name, not understood locally, which perhaps derives from gualann, a shoulder) is one of the principal seamarks of Galway Bay because of the ruined signal tower on it, one of the chain of such towers built around the west coast of Ireland in 1804–5 when Napoleon was a menace. From any sufficient height in south Connemara one can see the tower as a little stump, golden or black according to sun and cloud shadow, around which huge expanses of land and sea seem to pivot. Each tower could signal to the next in the chain and to shipping by means of flags and 'black balls' (canvas-covered hoops) hoisted on an eighty-foot mast. The Gólam tower was in sight of four similar towers: two of them still extant, on Árainn and Inis Oírr, to the south; and two that have vanished, on Cnoc an Choillín and Doon Hill to the north-west. This last-named tower could communicate with one, now a ruin, on Cleggan Head ten miles further north. Thus the chain strode around Connemara like a giant, or like the first and crudest attempt to measure the length of its coast.

As soon as I mentioned Gólam, the elderly man of the house detailed a young lad to row me out to it. It only took a few minutes to cross from a little quay below the house to a small beach on the lee side of the islet, which is a spray-blasted rocky knoll. The tower, built of granite blocks, is remarkably fresh-looking but lacks its roof, which I am told was robbed for its lead by the Mac Donnchadha family of the nearby island of An Chnapach. Like the other towers I have seen, it is a square, two-storey building on the scale of one of the O'Flahertys' medieval tower houses. There is a doorway facing south-west in the upper storey, which was obviously reached by a ladder that could be pulled up in times of danger. Above the doorway and accessible from the parapeted roof is a bartizan, a projection like a balcony without a floor through which shots could be fired downwards. Other bartizans above each of the rear corners of the tower covered the other walls, and it was clear that such a fortification could withstand a sea raid for long enough to summon help. There is a hearth and chimney in the north-east wall. I saw a big stick nest high up in a cleft of the masonry, and a raven circling above us watchfully.

However, it is not the tower that I remember most vividly from that expedition. The islet itself, like the whole of the southern half of Leitir Mealláin, is of the dark and contorted South Connemara Group rocks. The youngster led me scrambling up a steep fault scarp near the south-eastern corner of the islet to show me a row of smooth depressions, the footprints of a saint. In a crevice running diagonally up the scarp was a round pothole, the saint's holy well. And nearby was the road the saint trod, a five-foot-wide exposure of pale porphyry running like a fantastically pyramid-paved path or a miraculously frozen wake across a choppy sea of blackish rock, heading south-south-westwards towards the horizon-hugging profile of the Aran Islands. If the saint had proceeded in that direction, whether over or under

the waves – we did not know which – his exact landfall would have
been on Cill Mhuirbhigh beach in Árainn, down the hill from 'The
Residence' in the village of Fearann an Choirce, which was at that
time my home. (When I returned to Aran after this expedition I found
that the saint's road could just be made out from our house as a faint
pale streak on the opposite coast, which is about eight miles away.) All
the peninsulas and archipelagos of south Connemara seem to yearn
towards Aran, which has an almost transcendental status in their
consciousness. Looking out along the saint's road my young Virgil
said with the utmost simplicity, '*Áit dheas í, Árainn. Áit bheannaithe*'
('A nice place, Aran. A blessed place'). Thinking now of the luminous
cleanliness and bell-like resonance of Aran's limestone rock sheets,
their parallel fissures pointing one to the edge of clear-cut cliffs, and
the solace on a summer's day of its spring wells that image the perfec-
tion of the wildflowers attendant on them, I realize what a difficult
terrain is south Connemara: multidirectional from every point, so
complex in form it verges on the formless, disputing every step with
stony irregularities, leachlike softness of bog or bootlace-catching
twiggy heath. Often when visitors ask me what they should see in this
region I am at a loss. A curious hole in the ground? The memory of
an old song about a drowning? Ultimately I have to tell them that this
is a land without shortcuts.

Then we regained the mainland, or the island that counts as mainland for Gólam, and walked up to the house. There the lad's father,
Tomás, and I sat on tiny stools on either side of the turf fire in a wide
fireplace recess that, being half insulated from the room by a canopy
of oilcloth hanging to below head-height from the mantelpiece above
us, seemed designed for the almost secretive passing-on of lore, while
his mother made me a mug of tea and a welcome pile of bread and
butter. Refreshed, I went off to search for yet more holy wells and
another saint's road Tomás had told me of, down on the wave-battered
rocks of An Tóin Dhubh, the black bottom, to the south of the house.
Unfortunately I forgot to ask Tomás if he knew anything of an Ó
Mealláin or Mallon from whom Leitir Mealláin might have got its
name, a matter that I have not seen discussed anywhere.

The question of the island's history is raised by the remains of a small castle, a thick, jagged shard of masonry five or six yards long and up to three yards high, on a little rise commanding the narrows between Leitir Mealláin and Garomna. The earliest power in the island that we know of was that of a branch of the O'Flahertys, the MacHughs. *The Annals of the Four Masters* mentions Murrough, grandson of Edmund MacHugh of Leitir Mealláin, as among the supporters of the western O'Flahertys who were pursued to Aran and killed there by the eastern O'Flahertys in 1584, in the course of the feud over the island castle of Ballynahinch that I wrote of in *Listening to the Wind*. In the *Books of Survey and Distributions*, which track the changes in land ownership over the Cromwellian period, 'Leater and Mallan' is described unenthusiastically as follows:

2 Qu^{rs} of Rocky heathy Mountain with divers parcels of Arrable diged with Spades with a little Castle in reasonable repair and a new House with stone walls the afores^d 2 Qu^{rs} is very rocky and not above ¼ pt profitable.

For what it was worth, the island was confiscated from an Ervan Flaherty and disposed to a Steephen Lynch, and the Lynches of Bearna were its absentee landlords for generations. In the 1850s Leitir Mealláin and a scattering of other properties from bankrupt estates in County Galway and Clare were bought up through the Encumbered Estates Court by a Galway carpenter, Henry Comerford, who had set himself up as a merchant and raised a huge loan to make these purchases. It was said of him that:

If he had ascertainable sympathies, they lay probably in the matter of remunerative investments. He had an intelligent appreciation of the rent producing capabilities of the western peasantry. He recognized and respected the power vested by law in the landlord to utilize those capabilities.

No wonder, then, that his memory as a bad landlord lives on in Leitir Mealláin.

So far as I can unpick local lore, it seems that a Comerford married a woman of the O'Flahertys of Na hOileáin, and lived in An Teach Mór, the big house, now the post office, near the north-west corner of the island. Seán Mac Giollarnáth recorded some information about a Captain Comerford, who was engaged in smuggling American tobacco; the tobacco was hidden in baulks of timber that were thrown overboard and picked up by boats from Kinvara and Bell Harbour on the south side of Galway Bay. The Comerfords also owned a little island well-named An Chnapach, the lumpy place, just offshore from An Teach Mór. Here lived the Mac Donnchadha or McDonagh family, who leased the island from the Comerfords. (The *seanchas* is that they were from Claddaghduff near Clifden. One of them, a coastguard, bought a wreck for £5, found gold in it, came to Leitir Meálláin with his horse and cart, and bought An Chnapach for a few pounds. He set up a store there, built some little houses and a shop, and acquired eighteen tenants.) Antoine Mac Donnchadha of this family captained a smuggling vessel for the Comerfords, and laid the foundations of the family fortune by his seamanship: he evaded the King's cutter by sailing through the narrow channel between the island and Inis Oirc, the next island to the north, and landing his cargo of Spanish wine, brandy and tobacco below his father's house. I think he is the Antoine Mór I hear of who was lost in Leitir Meálláin's great marine disaster of 1849, when the brig *St John*, owned by a Toona Ó Conaola of Leitir Móir, crowded with emigrants from Galway, was wrecked on the Grampus Ledge off Cohassett near Boston; ninety-nine were drowned, including Antoine, while two Comerfords, one of whom was first mate of the ship, were saved.

The McDonaghs' ascent continued. A generation later Dr Browne noted that there were only two carts in Garomna and Leitir Meálláin, both belonging to a P. M'Donough, JP. One of the family moved to Galway and opened a shop there, selling eggs and fish brought in by Connemara hookers, an enterprise that grew into a commercial power in the town, Thomas McDonagh and Sons' huge hardware store and timber yard on Merchant's Road. An Chnapach, though, is long deserted; the McDonaghs sold it to a local man who has built a large concrete causeway out to it, erected an ugly cattle shed and put up notices: 'Keep out' and 'Beware of the bull'. When I visited it in the 1980s I walked out to it on a little tidal footpath. I found the ruins of the old shop, with a little quay below it. The island is largely rocky hummocks and marshy hollows, and when I was down in one of the latter I heard two men talking; I was surprised, as I had thought I had the place to myself. One of the men, hidden from me by a knoll, said very clearly, '*Maidin bhreá*' ('fine morning') – which it was, still and bright. I wanted directions to Leaba Dhiarmaidín, a ledge in the low cliff of the northern shore I had heard attributed, like many bed-like prehistoric tombs and natural nooks, to the legendary wandering lovers Diarmaid and Gráinne. But when I ran up the knoll and looked around, nobody was there. I recounted this event as a ghost story in the house I was staying in at the time; it caused quite a sensation, and I hope it has become part of the lore of the lumpy island.

North of An Teach Mór there is a bridge into Foirnis, outer island, the last of those accessible by road. A salmon-farming concern, MuirAchainní Teo, has its offices on the right just before the bridge, where its predecessor Bradán Mara, one of the first salmon farms to be set up in Connemara, used to be. On the day of my little adventure on An Chnapach I sat for some time on the small quay east of the bridge watching the men rowing to and fro among the rather decorative hexagonal fish cages in the bay there, throwing a few handfuls of fishfood into each. When they came ashore we talked, and soon they took me into the office where, they said, was someone who could answer my enquiries. He turned out to be Pádraic de Bhaldraithe, a robust, bearded marine biologist and owner of the *Banks*, a traditional *gleoiteog*. Having a trained ear for Irish phonetics he was able to settle several placename puzzles for me, and later he and his wife Máire and their baby made me welcome in their house in Foirnis.

Also working in Bradán Mara was a young man in an immaculate white sweater, Tom Folan, whose family used to live on Inis Oirc, and who agreed to row me out there the following day. It was a memorable trip. We poled under the bridge on a high tide and out into the bay to the west in an absolute calm under soft, gentle rain; it felt as if we were between two sheets of glass, slow-moving dot-like creatures on a microscope slide. Ins Oirc (pig island, sea-monster island, whale island – there is no agreement on the meaning of the name) is roundish, half a mile across, with several houses clustered on the southern shore, where pale smooth granite shelving into the water gives it a faint glow of welcome. There was just one family living on the island at that period, headed by the matriarchal old lady known as Peigín de Valera or the Queen of Connemara; they were to leave in about 1992. Some little lads goggled at us from behind the corner of their house. We rambled all over the island and Tom named its coves and hummocks for me; but there was an uneasy feeling about the place, the reasons for which became clear later on, and we did not stay long, or call on the de Valeras.

After we had threaded our way back through the bridge I asked Tom to show me Oileán Chaisín, an uninhabited islet that cleaves to the eastern shore of Foirnis like a calf to its mother. (Caisín, little bend, is the name of the curved bay between Foirnis and the north-western point of Garomna.) Again there was a slight atmosphere of constraint about our visit. These outer islands are or were centres of the poitín trade, and close enquiry is not encouraged. In unfrequented corners of Na hOileáin and elsewhere in south Connemara I had already come across certain stone-built bowl-shaped structures, three feet or so in depth and four or five across, that at first glance looked like the sort of limekiln single families used to build for their own use. But lime-kilns were usually by the shore since the limestone burned in them came from the Aran Islands as ballast in turf boats returning empty, whereas these were tucked away in the secretive web of field walls or in glens out on the commonage. Also, where the limekiln has a simple opening at its base to admit air and allow the lime to be raked out, these had a little extension like a stove to which the rest of the struc-ture formed a big chimney. I had soon gathered that these were *áitheanna* or corn kilns, used in the hardening of malted barley for poitín. (Some of these obscure items of field furniture are marked on the 1899 OS maps and in two or three cases misidentified as limekilns, whether in error or as a matter of discretion, I do not know.) I had also come across a few stillhouses in the course of my pokings-about in unfrequented marginal spots, and it had seemed wise to assume they were all of purely archaeological interest. They usually amounted to nothing more than a bit of sheltering wall, a hearth and a few stones to support a barrel, by a spring in a secluded hollow or a cleft among the rocks of the shore. Now in Oileán Chaisín Tom showed me one such shelter, clearly long disused, and then another more recent one. As we stood looking into the latter in the thin rain, I asked Tom to explain exactly what went on there. The following is based on his account, supplemented by a couple of published articles on the topic.

The secretive trade of the poitín-maker was literally the water of life to many Connemara communities, and is celebrated in songs and stories.

> Nach deas an rud poitín sa tír seo,
> D'íocfadh sé cíos agus *poor law*.
> Leigheasódh sé casacht na hoíche,
> Agus dhíreodh sé seanduine cam.

[What a fine thing is poitín in this land, / It would pay the rent and the poor-law tax. / It would cure the night-time cough, / And straighten the bent old man.]

Poitín cemented engagements and marriages, baptized the babe, eased the grief of wakes, cured the wobbliness of newborn lambs. It also caused fights and murders, shortened the way to the graveyard and pauperized families. Men from Na hOileáin would walk miles by night with a keg of it to sell to shebeens all over Connemara, or smuggle it to Aran and Galway buried in boatloads of turf or kelp. It was sent to County Meath to the Connemara folk who had been resettled there in 1935, and was posted to homesick relatives in the States, labelled 'Holy Water from Knock'. A good poitín, as clear as *deoir aille*, 'the drop from a cliff', in which the bubbles that appeared when you shook it took their time to come to the surface, was the product of a proudly conserved craft. As it was said, 'You would drink it out of a goat's arse.' And here is the recipe for making it.

First soak some hundredweight bags of barley in a well or a pond for two nights and a day, and leave the grain in a heap on a floor until it begins to sprout. When the green shoots are about half an inch long spread it on the floor and turn it over until the shoots shrink back into the grain again. The next stage is to harden this malted grain in a kiln of the sort I have described. The open top of the kiln is covered with branches and a layer of clean straw on which the malt is spread, with a roof of grassy sods, or an old boat sail, to shelter it from the rain, and a turf fire is lit in the hearth to send its hot smoke up through the malt. Then the hardened grain is hand-ground with a quern consisting of a thick disc of granite eighteen inches or so across, resting on another and turned by a wooden handle – a laborious, muscular task. Next, take the ground malt to the stillhouse, discreetly.

Now for the crucial stage, the distillation. Bring a fifty-gallon iron pot of water to the boil, empty it into a tub of twice that size and top up with cold water. Stir in half a hundredweight of malt for an hour to extract the juice, which is then to be drained off through a tap near the bottom of the tub into a keeler, a shallower tub, taking care not to let any of the boiled grain through. Next, add yeast, and when the mix (the 'ale') has stopped foaming throw in some of the boiled malt or some wholemeal flour to form a crust to keep the wind off it while the yeast continues to work. After a day the ale will be ready for its first distillation. The still is a pot with a lid from the top of which a pipe leads to the worm, a long coil of copper tubing running down inside a barrel to a tap on the side of the barrel. Fill the barrel with cold water, put the ale in the pot and light a fire under it. Steam will condense in the cooled worm and the 'singlings', as the condensed liquid is called, will drip out of the tap. Clean out the still and pour the singlings into it for a second distillation, the *dúbláil*. The poitín is now ready for consumption, though putting it in hiding for a time improves it. *Tús an phota*, 'the first of the brew', is the strongest, clearest and tastiest, and traditionally the distiller keeps it for himself. All this has to be done in secret, of course. It is advisable to have trustworthy neighbours on the lookout for peelers; if working on an island keep an eye open for signal fires warning of their approach by boat.

That is how it was done in the golden age, but from about 1935, what with the maledictions of the priesthood and especially of such Savonarola-fierce missioners as Fr Ó Conghaile from Aran raining down on the heads of the poitín-makers, and the likelihood of finding themselves picking *ócum an phríosúin* if caught by the Gardaí and brought up before Justice Seán Forde, there came a decline in the trade. When in the 1960s and 1980s poitín experienced a revival it was associated with a degree of thuggery and counterfeit. Soon the lorry-driving lads were using citizens' band radio to evade police checks. One heard stories of poitín 'baptized' with water to bulk it up, of the use of soap to put bubbles in it, and whatever else it took to make something that looked like poitín out of the cheapest ingredients. Tom said that in the old days the poitín would come out of the worm drop by drop, but now it flows as from a tap. However, he dismissed talk of the use of domestic bleach and methylated spirits as a slight on the trade, decadent though it may be.

After these considerations we looked at a *clochar*, a natural heap of glacial boulders, in which foxes bred, Tom told me, or did so until they were all shot. I have been told that there used to be no foxes in Na hOileáin because the old swing bridge in the causeway at Béal an Daingin had a slatted base and they didn't like to cross it; but when the bridge was replaced by a fixed span they began to spread and are now common throughout. Then we rowed back down the bay in time for the salmon's 3.30 p.m. feed.

Foirnis itself is a remarkably hilly little island, a bit more than a mile long and a third of a mile across. I bucketed up and down its narrow roads and boreens on my bicycle, following directions to its three half-forgotten holy wells. When I asked Pádraic the name of the hillock his house is perched on he said that when he came to live there a neighbour told him it was called Cnocán Rúscaire, but he was never sure whether this was a genuine name or a satirical dig at himself, a *rúscaire* being a slapdash, hasty worker. (Whatever the truth about that, I published the name on my map without fear or favour, reasoning that many a placename has originated as a bit of fun.) In one household I called on unannounced, the family conferred in whispered Irish; was I a spy on the track of illegal stills? I managed to reassure them, and then, as so often happened in my travels, my powers of literacy were called upon. They showed me a letter about a car they thought they had won in a draw organized by something called Leisure Arts Ltd, but which they had not received. At first on leafing through the pages of ambiguous blether the book club had sent them, I thought indeed that they had won a car, so I wrote a stiff letter on their behalf demanding to know when they could expect delivery. But on reappraisal I was fairly sure that all they had won was a little Dickens anthology. They were impressed by the speed of my writing, however, and I had to explain that that was my trade.

The last fraction of land to be visited by this volume is Daighinis (or perhaps Daimhinis, stag or ox island, according to several authorities). It is separated from the north-west shore of Foirnis by a narrow but deep channel. J. M. Synge and Jack Yeats were ferried out to the island in the course of their tour of the distressed districts. Although Synge complained that the nature of their commission from the *Manchester Guardian* precluded him from writing as he would have wished, his prose portrait of 'The Ferryman of Dinish Island' is a fine piece, in which the smooth musculature of his descriptive prose controls the expression of his deep sympathy for the people of these neglected marginal places, and unclenches to allow the ferryman himself to rail against his lonely fate in the songlike language Synge had constructed out of the Hiberno-English of the countryside. The ferryman had spent years as a sailorman in America and a labourer in Britain, and deeply regretted that he had had to come back to the island:

'And isn't it a queer thing to be sitting here now thinking on those times, and I after being near twenty years back on this bit of rock that a dog wouldn't look at, where the pigs die and the spuds die, and even the judges and quality do come out and do lower our rents when they see the wild Atlantic driving in across the cursed stones.'

'And what is it brought you back,' I said, 'if you were doing well out beyond in the world?'

'My two brothers went to America,' he said, 'and I had to come back because I was the eldest son . . . I have a young family now growing up, for I was snug for a while; and then bad times came, and I lost my wife, and the potatoes went bad, and three cows I had were taken in the night with some disease of the brain, and they swam out and were drowned in the sea . . . And I don't know what way I'm going to go on living in this place that the Lord created last, I'm thinking, in the end of time; and it's often when I sit down and look around on it I do begin cursing and damning, and asking myself how poor people can go on executing their religion at all.'

For a while he said nothing, and we could see tears in his eyes . . .

One of the ferryman's discontents was that he used to bring the schoolmistress in and out of the island, and ten or so little children

Bibliography

Andrews, Allen, *The Splendid Pauper: The Story of an Eccentric Victorian Empire Builder, Moreton Frewen* (New York, 1968).

Anon., *Frost and Fire: Natural Engines, Tool-marks and Chips, with Sketches Taken at Home and Abroad by a Traveller*, vol. II (Edinburgh, 1865).

Anon., review of Revd J. P. Garrett, *A Brief Memoir of Miss Moore, Late of Warren Cottage, Lisburn*, in the *Gospel Magazine*, 1 July 1884.

Berry, James, *Tales of the West of Ireland*, with introduction and ed. Gertrude M. Horgan (Dublin, 1966).

Bigger, Francis Joseph, 'Cruach Mac Dara, off the Coast of Connemara; with a Notice of Its Church, Crosses, and Antiquities', *Journal of the Royal Society of Antiquaries of Ireland*, Part II, Second Quarter (1896).

Blake, Martin J., *Blake Family Records* (London, 1905).

Blake Family, *Letters from the Irish Highlands* (published anonymously, London, 1825; republished Clifden, 1995).

Bolger, Patrick, *The Irish Co-operative Movement* (Dublin, 1977).

Bowen, Desmond, *Souperism, Myth or Reality* (Cork, 1970).

Breathnach, D., and Ní Mhurchú, M., *Beathaisnéis*, vols. 1–9 (Dublin, 1983–2002).

Browne, Charles R., 'The Ethnography of Carna and Mweenish', *Proceedings of the Royal Irish Academy*, 3rd series, vol. 6 (1900–1902).

Callaghan, Brian, 'Locating the Shannawona Fault: Field and Geobarometric Studies from the Galway Batholith, Western Ireland', *Irish Journal of Life Sciences*, 23 (2005).

Cashel, Alice M., *The Lights of Leaca Bán: A Story of Recent Times in Ireland* (Dublin, n.d.).

Cashman, D. B., *The Life of Michael Davitt, Founder of the Land League, To Which is Added, The Secret History of the Land League* (n.d.; facsimile reprint. Cork, 1979).

Cloud, Preston, *Oasis in Space: Earth History from the Beginning* (New York, 1988).

Conroy, Fr M. D., *Lifetime Memories*, typescript (1943).

Coulter, Henry, *The West of Ireland: Its Existing Conditions, and Prospects* (Dublin, 1862).

D'Alton, Right Revd Monsignor, *History of the Archdiocese of Tuam* (Dublin, 1928).

de Bhailís, Colm, *Amhráin Chuilm de Bhailís*, ed. J. H. Lloyd (Dublin, 1904); ed. Gearóid Denvir (Indreabhán, 1976).

de Bhaldraithe, Tomás (ed.), *Pádraic Ó Conaire: clocha ar a charn* (Dublin, 1982).

De Paor, Máire and Liam, *Early Christian Ireland* (London, 1958).

Delaney, V. T. H. and Delaney, D. R., *The Canals of the South of Ireland* (Newton Abbot, 1969).

Dunleavy, John, 'John Yates, a Traveller in Connemara, 1875', *Journal of the Galway Historical and Archaeological Society*, 43 (1991).

Dunlop, Andrew, *Fifty Years of Irish Journalism* (Dublin, 1911).

Edgeworth, Maria, *Tour in Connemara* (1833), ed. H. E. Butler (London, 1950).

Edwards, Ruth Dudley, *Patrick Pearse: The Triumph of Failure* (London, 1977).

Eliot, T. S., *The Complete Poems and Plays of T. S. Eliot* (London, 2004).

Fallon, Niall, *The Armada in Ireland* (Middletown, Conn., 1978).

Fennell, Desmond, *Beyond Nationalism* (Dublin, 1985).

Finlay, Revd T. A., 'The Economics of Carna', *New Ireland Review* (April 1898).

Gibbons, Michael, and Higgins, Jim, 'The Island Habitation Sites of Connemara, Co. Galway', unpublished MS.

Griffith, Richard, *Valuation of the Several Tenements in the County of Galway* (Dublin, 1855).

Gwynn, Stephen, *A Holiday in Connemara* (London, 1909).

Hall, S. C., and Mrs Hall, *The West and Connemara* (London, 1853).

Harbison, Peter, *Pilgrimage in Ireland, the Monuments and the People* (London, 1991).

Hartmann, Hans, Tomás de Bhaldraithe und Ruairí Ó hUiginn (eds.), *Airneán, Eine Sammlung von Texten aus Carna, Co. na Gaillimhe*, Text 3 (Tübingen, 1996).

Hayes, Richard, *The Last Invasion of Ireland* (Dublin, 1939).

Herity, Michael (ed.), *Ordnance Survey Letters, Galway* (Dublin, 2009).

Higgins, F. R., 'An Appreciation', in Pádraic Ó Conaire, *Field and Fair* (1929).

Inglis, Brian, *Roger Casement* (London, 1973).

Irish Church Mission Society, *The Banner of the Truth in Ireland*, vol. I (1851); vol. VI (1856).

Joyce, P. W., *Irish Names of Places*, vol. III (Dublin, 1913).

Kerrigan, Paul, 'The Defences of Ireland 1793–1815', Part 12, *An Cosantóir* (February 1982).

Kilfeather, T. P., *Ireland: Graveyard of the Spanish Armada* (Dublin, 1967).

Killanin, Lord, 'Notes on some of the Antiquities of the Barony of Ballynahinch, Co. Galway', *Journal of the Galway Historical and Archaeological Society*, XXV, Nos. 3 & 4 (1953–4).

Kinahan, G. H., 'The Sea-weeds of Yar-Connaught, and Their Uses', *Quarterly Journal of Science* (July 1869).

——, 'Notes on Antiquities in Yar-Chonnacht', *Journal of the Royal Historical and Archaeological Association of Ireland*, II, Series 4 (1872–3).

Lane, Pádraig G., 'Some Galway and Mayo Landlords of the Mid-Nineteenth Century', *Journal of the Galway Archaeological and Historical Society*, 45 (1993).

Layard, Edgar L., 'Fortified stone lake-dwellings on islands in Lough Skannive, Connemara', *Journal of the Galway Historical and Archaeological Society*, 2 (1897).

Longford, Elizabeth, *Jameson's Raid* (new edn, London, 1984).

Lucas, A. T., 'The Horizontal Mill in Ireland', *Journal of the Galway Historical and Archaeological Society*, 83 (1953).

Lynam, Shevaun, *Humanity Dick Martin, King of Connemara* (Dublin 1989).

Mac Aonghusa, Criostóir, *Ó Ros Muc go Rostov* (Indreabhán, 1972).

Mac Aonghusa, Proinsias, *Gaillimh agus aistí eile* (Dublin, 1983).

——, *Ros Muc agus Cogadh na Saoirse* (Dublin, 1992).

MacCoisdealbha, Liam, 'Seanchas agus Scéalta ó Chárna', *Béaloideas*, 9 (1939).

Mac Con Iomaire, Liam, *Breandán Ó hEithir, Iomramh Aonair* (Indreabhán, 2000).

——, *Seosamh Ó hÉanaí: Nár fhagha mé bás choíche*, Indreabhán (2007).

——, photos by Bob Quinn, *Conamara, An Tír Aineoil / The Unknown Country* (Indreabhán, 1997).

—— and Robinson, Tim, *Camchuairt Chonamara Theas / A Twisty Journey* (Dublin, 2002).

Mac Con Iomaire, Séamas, *Cladaí Chonamara* (Dublin, 1938), trans. Pádraic de Bhaldraithe as *The Shores of Connemara* (Kinvara, 2000). (The author's name is incorrectly given as Mac an Iomaire in later editions of the original Irish text.)

Mac Dónaill, Peadar, *West Connemara I.R.A., Organisation and Operation*, typescript (n.d.)

McDonald, Frank, 'Bungalow Blitz', *Irish Times*, 12 September 1987.

Mac Donncha, Cóil Neaine Pháidín, 'Pluid Dhorcha Leára', in Micheál Ua Ciarmhaic, *Guth an Ealaíontóra* (Indreabhán, 1993).

Mac Donnchadha, Máirtín, 'Amhráin na Trá Báine', *Bliainiris* (2001).

Mac Giollarnáth, Seán, 'Tiachóg ó Iorrus Aintheach', *Béaloideas*, 3:4 (December 1932).

—— (ed.), *Peadar Chois Fharraige: Scéalta Nua agus Seanscéalta d'Innis Peadar Mac Thuathaláin* (Dublin, 1934).

——, *Annála Beaga ó Iorras Aithneach* (Dublin, 1941).

——, *Mo Dhúthaigh Fhiáin* (Dublin, 1949).

——, *Conamara* (Cork, 1954).

Mac Liammóir, Micheál, *All for Hecuba* (1946; republished Dublin, 2008).

MacLysaght, Edward, *Irish Life in the Seventeenth Century* (Cork, 1950).

MacNeill, Máire, 'Poll na Seantuinne and Poll Tigh Liabáin', *Béaloideas* 39–41 (1971–3).

MacPiarais, Pádraig, *Gearrscéalta an Phiarsaigh*, ed. Cathal Ó hÁinle (Dublin, 1979).

——, *Filíocht Ghaeilge Phádraig Mhic Phiarais*, ed. Ciarán Ó Coigligh (Dublin, 1981). See also under Pearse, Patrick.

Mandelbrot, Benoît, 'How Long Is the Coast of Britain? Statistical Self-Similarity and Fractional Dimension', *Science,* New Series, 156:3775, 5 May 1967.

——, *The Fractal Geometry of Nature* (New York, 1982; revised edn of *Fractals*, c.1977).

——, 'Fractals and the Rebirth of Iteration Theory', in H.-O. Peitgen and P. H. Richter, *The Beauty of Fractals* (Berlin, 1986).

Mark, Gordon St George, 'Tyrone House', *Quarterly Bulletin of the Irish Georgian Society*, XIX, Nos. 3 & 4 (July–December 1976).

Martin Estate Sale, *The Third Section of the Galway Estates of the late Thomas Martin, Esq.*, particulars of sale (August 1849). Also: 'Auction of the Connemara Estates', *Farmer's Journal* (November 1849). Also: *In the Court of the Commissioners for the Sale of Incumbered Estates in Ireland. Connamara. Martin Estates*, particulars of sale (July 1852). (Public Records Office)

Maude, Caitlín, *Dánta*, ed. Ciarán Ó Coigligh (Dublin, 1984).

——, *Drámaíocht agus Prós*, ed. Ciarán Ó Coigligh (Dublin, 1988).

Micks, W. L., *History of the Congested Districts Board* (Dublin, 1925).

Moffitt, Miriam, *Soupers & Jumpers: The Protestant Missions in Connemara, 1848–1937* (Dublin, 2008).

Mulloy, Sheila, *O'Malley People and Places* (Whitegate, Co. Clare, 1988).

Ní Chlochartaigh, Máire, 'Fínis agus Bior', *Tiachóg* (June 1993).

Ní Dhomhnaill, Cáit, *An Cheathrú Rua* (Léacht an Oireachtais, 1983).

Ní Fhlathartaigh, Ríonach, *Clár Amhrán Bhaile na hInse* (Dublin, 1976).

Ní Mhainnín, Cáit, *Cuimhní Cinn Cháit Ní Mhainnín* (Indreabhán, 2000).

Nimmo, A., 'Report on the Bogs . . . to the West of Lough Corrib', *Report of the Commissioners of Bogs in Ireland*, Appendix 12, House of Commons, London (1814).

——, Coast Survey, in *First Report of the Commissioners of Enquiry into the State of the Irish Fisheries* (Dublin, 1836).

Ó Ceallaigh, An tAthair Tomás (ed.), *Ceol na nOileán* (1931; new edn, Indreabhán, 1990).

Ó Ceannabháin, Peadar (ed.), *Éamon a Búrc. Scéalta* (Dublin, 1983).

Ó Ceoinín, Seán, *Seoltóireacht Ghéar, Amhráin Sheáin Cheoinín* (Béal an Daingin, 1988).

Ó Ciosáin, Éamonn, *An t-Éireannach 1934–1937, Páipéar Sóisialach Gaeltachta* (Dublin, 1993).

Ó Conaire, Pádraic, *M'Asal Beag Dubh* (Dublin, 1944).

——, *Seacht mBua an Éirí Amach* (Dublin, 1918; new edn, 1970).

——, *Aistí Phádraic Uí Chonaire*, ed. Gearóid Denvir (Indreabhán, 1978).

Ó Conaire, Pádraic Óg, *Ceol na nGiolcach* (Dublin, 1939; new edn, 1976).

——, *Déirc an Díomhaointis* (Dublin, 1972).

Ó Conghaile, Micheál, 'Poitín agus Stiléaracht in Inis Treabhair', *Macalla* (1981).

——, 'An Poitín a Fuair Colm', *Glór na nOileán* (1985).

—— (ed.), *Croch Suas É!* (Béal an Daingin, 1986).

—— (ed.), *Gaeltacht Ráth Cairn, Léachtaí Comórtha* (Béal an Daingin, 1986).

—— (ed.), *Up Seanamhach, Amhráin* (Indreabhán, 1990).

——, *Gnéithe d'Amhráin Chonamara Ár Linne* (Indreabhán, 1993).

——, 'Athair', in *An Fear a Phléasc* (Indreabhán, 1997).

Ó Conghaile, Seán, *Cois Fharraige le mo Linnse* (Dublin, 1974).

Ó Cuaig, Micheál, *Uchtóga* (Indreabhán, 1985).

Ó Curnáin, Brian, *The Irish of Iorras Aithneach, County Galway* (Dublin, 2007).

Ó Direáin, Peadar, *Sgéalta na nOileán* (Dublin, 1929).

Ó Dochartaigh, Liam, 'An tAmhrán Bréagach', *Foinn Agus Fonnadóirí; Léachtaí Cholm Cille*, XXIX (1999).

Ó Faoláin, Seán, *An Irish Journey* (Dublin, 1940).

O'Flaherty, Roderick, *West or H-Iar Connaught* (1684), ed. James Hardiman (Dublin, 1846; facsimile reprint, Galway, 1978).

O'Fotharta, Domhnall, *Siamsa an Gheimhridh; nó cois an teallaigh in Iargconnachta* (Dublin, 1892).

Ó Gaora, Colm, *Mise* (Dublin, 1943; new edn, 1969).

——, *Obair is Luadhainn nó Saoghal sa nGaedhealtacht* (Dublin, 1937).

Ó Glaisne, Risteárd, *Scríbhneoirí na Nua-Ré*, vol. I, *Ceannródaithe* (Dublin, 1974).

——, *Raidió na Gaeltachta* (Indreabhán, 1982).

Ó hÓgáin, Dáithí, *Myth, Legend and Romance: An Encyclopaedia of the Irish Folk Tradition* (London, 1990).

O'Leary, D., and Murphy, C., 'Design and Construction of a Pre-stressed Bridge', paper read to the Institution of Civil Engineers of Ireland (1955).

Ó Lochlainn, Colm, *The Fishery at Casla, Conamara: Its History and Records 1684–1956* (Dublin, 1957).

—— (ed.), *An Claisceadal*, No. III (Dublin, 1933).

Ó Máille, Mícheál, *Diarmuid Donn*, ed. Tomás Ó Máille (Dublin, 1936).

Ó Máille, Tomás, *An Béal Beo* (Dublin, 1936).

——, *An tIomaire Rua; Cogadh na Saoirse i dTuaisceart Chonamara* (Dublin, 1939; new edn, ed. Máirtín Ó Cadhain, 2007).

Ó Máille, Tomás agus Mícheál, *Amhráin Chlainne Gaedheal* (1905; new edn, Indreabhán 1991).

Ó Máille, T. S., 'Four County Galway Placenames', *Journal of the Galway Historical and Archaeological Society*, 25 (1952–53).

——, 'Muicineach mar áit-ainm', *Journal of the Royal Society of Antiquarians of Ireland*, 85 (1955).

——, *Liosta Focal as Ros Muc* (Dublin, 1974).

Ó Maoilchiaráin, Pádraig, 'An Brig St. John', *Glor na nOileán* (n.d., *c.*1983).

Ó Móráin, An tAthair Tadhg (ed.), *Séipéal Cholm Cille, An Tulach*, pamphlet (n.d.).

Ó Nualláin, C. (ed.), *Éamon a Búrc. Eochair, Mac Rí in Éirinn* (Dublin, 1982).

Ordnance Survey Field Books (MS notebooks of placenames recorded in the 1830s for the first Ordnance Survey, with, for Co. Galway and elsewhere, anglicized forms due to John O'Donovan; microfilm copies in the National Library of Ireland.

Osborne, Hon. and Revd Godolphin, *Gleanings in the West of Ireland* (London, 1850).

O'Sullivan, Sean, ed. and trans., *Folktales of Ireland* (London, 1966).

Otway, Caesar, *A Tour in Connaught* (Dublin, 1839).

Partridge, Angela, *Caoineadh na dTrí Muire, Téama na Páise i bhFilíocht Bhéil na Gaeilge* (Dublin, 1983).

Pearse, Patrick, 'About Literature', *An Claidheamh Soluis*, 26 May 1906.

——, 'The Irish-Speaking Child', *An Claidheamh Soluis*, 5 January 1907.

——, *The Literary Writings of Patrick Pearse: Writings in English*, ed. Séamas Ó Buachalla (Dublin and Cork, 1979).

Plunket, Revd W. C., *A Short Visit to the Connemara Missions* (Dublin, 1863).

Póirtéir, Cathal, *Glórtha ón Ghorta* (Dublin, 1996).

Previté, Anthony, *A Guide to Connemara's Early Christian Sites* (Oughterard, 2008).

Ridge, Seamus, *Conamara Man*, Englewood Cliffs (N.J., 1969).

Robinson, Sir Henry, *Further Memories of Irish Life* (London, 1924).

Robinson, Tim, *Setting Foot on the Shores of Connemara* (Dublin, 1984).

——, *Setting Foot on the Shores of Connemara and Other Writings* (Dublin, 1996).

——, *Connemara: Listening to the Wind* (Dublin, 2006).

——, *Connemara: The Last Pool of Darkness* (Dublin, 2008).

Ryan, P. D., Max, M. D., and Kelly, T., 'The Petrochemistry of the Basic Volcanic Rocks of the South Connemara Group (Ordovician), Western Ireland', *Geological Magazine*, 120:2 (1983).

Scott, Richard J., *The Galway Hooker, Working Sailboats of Galway Bay* (Dublin, 1983; revised edn, 1996).

Synge, J. M., 'In Connemara', in *Collected Works II: Prose*, ed. Robin Skelton and Alan Price (Oxford, 1966).

Tiachóg (local periodical), June 1993.

Thomas, Br. Conal, *The Land for the People: The United Irish League and Land Reform in North Galway, 1898–1912* (Corrandulla, 1999).

Uí Ógáin, Ríonach, 'Cruach na Cara', *Sinsear* (1979).

———, '"Is í an Fhilíocht Anam an Cheoil", Sorcha Ní Ghuairim, Amhránaí Roisín na Mainiach', *Bliainiris* (2002).

Vendries, J., *Lexique étymologique de l'Irlandais ancien* (Paris, 1987).

Vignoles, Julian, 'Shame of the *Titanic*', radio programme, RTÉ, 23 February 1987.

Villiers-Tuthill, Kathleen, *Beyond the Twelve Bens: A History of Clifden and District 1860–1923* (Clifden, 1986).

———, *Alexander Nimmo and the Western District* (Clifden, 2006).

Wakeman, William, *A Week in the West of Ireland* (Dublin, n.d. [*c.*1850]).

White, George Preston, *A Tour in Connemara, with Remarks on Its Great Physical Capabilities* (London, 1844).

Wigger, Arndt (ed.), *Caint Ros Muc* (Dublin, 2004).

Wilkins, Noel P., *Ponds, Parcs and Passes: Aquaculture in Victorian Ireland* (Dublin, 1989).

Sources

Part I: Roads to Freedom

Preface: This Road Before Me

Pages

3   (Pearse's kingdom) Mac Giollarnáth, 1954.

(Pearse's writings) Ó Gaora, 1943.

1. The Roads

Pages

10   (Pádraic Ó Conaire) Mac Aonghusa, Criostóir, 1972.

11   (Orson Welles) Mac Liammóir, 1946. Colin Murphy, writing in the *Sunday Tribune*, 12 October 2008.

12   (Pádraic Ó Conaire) Higgins, 1929.

(roses) http://archives.tcm.ie/businesspost/2007/03/04/story21465.asp

(influence of Pearse) Gearóid Denvir's introduction to Pádraic Ó Conaire, 1978.

13   (folklore) Pearse, 1906.

(Pan of Gaelic) Tomás Ó Cléirigh, in *The Capuchin Annual*, 1936, reprinted in de Bhaldraithe, 1982.

14   (death) Mac Aonghusa, Proinsias, 1983. Liam O'Flaherty, in *Comhar* (April 1953), reprinted in de Bhaldraithe, 1982.

15   (Pádraic Óg Ó Conaire) Breathnach and Ní Mhurchú, vol. 3, 1992.

17   (Coláiste na bhFiann) Uinsionn Mac Dubhghaill, in *Cuisle* (October 1998).

18   (Ó Lúbhlaí) *Irish Examiner*, 1 October 1998. *Cuisle*, 1:1 (September 1998).

19   'Treall', in Maude, 1984; quoted with the kind permission of
            Cathal Ó Luain.

20   (Tobar Bhriocáin) Tomás Ó Conaire, 'Fios Feasa', *RosC, Iris
            Phobail Ros Muc*, No. 2, 1977.

21   (An tOileán Iarthach) Pádraic Ó Conchúir, 'Cora Leis', *RosC,
            Iris Phobail Ros Muc*, No. 3, 1978.

24   (attack on minister) Deasún Breathnach, writing in *Amárach*, 18
            June 1982.
            (ancestral language) 'An Dá Thrá', in Maude, 1988.

2. The Junction with History

Pages

25   (Mannion) *Glór Chonamara*, 19:2, 27 February 2009.
            (Ó Flatharta) Criostóir Mac Aonghusa, 'An Pobal Inniu', *RosC,
            Iris Phobail Ros Muc*, No. 2, 1977.

26   (Criostóir Mac Aonghusa) Breathnach and Ní Mhurchú, vol. 8,
            2001.

27   (Proinsias Mac Aonghusa) Breathnach and Ní Mhurchú, vol. 9,
            2002.

29   (proportion) Synge, 1966.
            (Pearse's cottage) Mac Aonghusa, Proinsias, 1992.

30   (Pearse's arrival) Ó Gaora, 1943.

31   (Irish-speaking child) Pearse, 1907.

33   (Pearse's sexuality) Edwards, 1977. 'Why Do Ye Torture Me?', in
            Pearse, 1979.

34   ('Renunciation'), in Pearse, 1979.
            (manoeuvres) Proinsias Mac Aonghusa, 1992.

3. The Gentry's Roads

Pages

39   (O'Hara) Ordnance Survey Field Books, 1839; Martin estate sale
            documentation, 1852.
            (Doohulla fishery) Wilkins, 1989.

40   (gentry's roads) Ó Máille, T. S., 1974.

40   (Frewen) Andrews, 1968.

(Jameson Raid) Longford, 1984.

41   (Lord Dudley) Robinson, Sir Henry, 1924.

(United Irish League meeting) Ó Gaora, 1943.

42   (Inver Lodge) Gwynn, 1909.

(visiting gentry) Ní Mhainnín, 2000.

44   (fight in Glinn Chatha) Wigger, 2004.

47   (crows) Information from Paddy Folan, Scríb, 1980s.

(Doire Bhanbh) The three sources, in order, are current Ordnance Survey maps, Ordnance Survey Field Books, 1839, and Ó Máille, 1974.

48   (Lynches) Ordnance Survey Field Books,1839.

(Fuge) Martin estate sale documentation, 1849; Griffith, 1855.

(first motor car) Wigger, 2004.

(Teachín na bPrayers) Information from the late Tomás Ó Conaire, Glinn Chatha, 1980s.

49   (Ramsbottom) Wilkins, 1989.

(drowning) Letter from Helen Spellman, Galway, 2008.

50   (Gertie Miller) Seosamh Ó Cuaig, *Taibhsí na Staire*, documentary, TnaG, 1998.

4. Crossing the Bog

Pages

51   (Ó Gaora's crossing) Ó Gaora, 1943.

(*criathar*) Vendries, 1987.

52   (Cloch Choirill) Anon., 1865. My thanks to Paul Mohr for this *trouvaille*.

(poitín) Wigger, 2004.

57   (thunder) Wigger, 2004.

58   (hoky poky) Ó Gaora, 1943. The first poem is like an English one about ice cream (see Wikipedia under 'Hokey Cokey'), which has been said to derive from an old parody of the Latin Mass ('*hoc est enim corpus meum*'); the second is a garbled version of a poem attributed to the mythical Amairgen (see Alwin and Brinley Rees, *Celtic Heritage* (London, 1961)).

59   (Úraid Joyces) Mac Giollarnáth, 1954.

            (Limerick bridge) *Tom Pheaidí Mac Diarmada ag Scéalaíocht*, cassette
            CIC L17, Cló Iar-Chonnachta, Indreabhán. Another version in
            O'Fotharta, 1892.

60   (Limerick man goes to Boston) Mac Giollarnáth, 1941.

5. *A Hiding Hole and a Public House*

Pages

63   (Henry Blake) See 'Moaning About the Chimneys', in Robinson,
            Tim, 2008.

64   (Dunton's stay) Letters of John Dunton, quoted in MacLysaght,
            1950.

69   (steamer at Mám) Delaney, 1969.

70   ('hare soup') Edgeworth, 1833.

            (the Halls on O'Rourke) Hall and Hall, 1853.

            (Lord Leitrim) Typescript copy of a memoir of Arthur Gough
            by Fred Ashley, in possession of Mary Keane, Mám.

            (Lord Carlisle) Dunlop, 1911.

            (Ann King, the Wallaces) Information from Mary Keane, Mám.

            (lease) Coulter, 1862.

71   (the Keanes at Mám) Information from Mary Keane, Mám.

            (Máire Ní Aodáin diary) Quoted in Edwards, 1977.

6. *The O'Malleys and the Joyces*

72   (Na Braonáin) Information from Michael O'Toole, Leenaun.

            (Míliuc) Information from Dónall Mac Giolla Easpaig, Placenames
            Branch, Dept of Arts, Heritage, Gaeltacht and the Islands,
            Dublin.

            (Kilcreevanty) D'Alton, 1928.

            (Evie Hone window) Plaque in church porch.

73   (O'Malley family) Mulloy, 1988.

74   (Mass) Quoted in Hall and Hall, 1853.

            (Grace O'Malley) Mulloy, 1988.

            (Breathnach) Information from Michael O'Toole, Leenaun.

74   (Pádraic na mBan) Wakeman, n.d. [*c.*1850].

       (twelve cradles) Mac Giollarnáth, 1954.

       (Mícheál Ó Máille) Ó Máille, Mícheál, 1936.

77   (Joyce Grove church site) D'Alton, 1928.

78   (Henry Blake) Blake Family, 1824.

80   (Big Jacky Joyce's lodge) Edgeworth, 1833.

       (Jack in prime) Otway, 1839.

81   (Leenaun Hotel) Osborne, 1850.

7. *The Battle of the Red Ridge*

Pages

83–94   (War of Independence) Ó Máille, Tomás, 1939; Ó Gaora, 1943; Villiers-Tuthill, 1986.

       (Peadar Mac Dónaill) *West Connemara I.R.A., Organisation and Operation; Statement by Captain P.J. McDonnell, Newcastle, Galway.* (I am grateful to Marie Reddon, Hardiman Library, NUI Galway, for a copy of this typescript.)

85   (drunken Tans) Information from the late John Barlow, Roundstone.

86   (Scríb ambush) The curate's account is in a local periodical, *RosC, Iris Phobail Ros Muc*, No. 3, 1978.

93   (Eilís Ní Chaisil) Cashel, n.d.

8. *The Long March*

Pages

97–103   (civil rights) I am indebted to Donncha Ó hÉallaithe, archivist of the movement, for copies of newspaper articles on the activities of Cearta Sibhialta na Gaeltachta.

       (Ó hEithir) Mac Con Iomaire, Liam, 2000.

       (Gearóid Ó Tuathaigh) Quoted in Ó Glaisne, 1982.

99   ('Israel in Iarchonnacht') Fennell, 1985.

       (Bob Quinn) http://conamara.org/index.php?page=essay-on-bob-quinn.

99–100   (pirate radio) *Irish Times*, 5 October 1987; Donncha Ó hÉallaithe, *Ó Theilifís na Gaeilge go TG4*, typescript (October 2006).

100   (opening of RnaG) Ó Glaisne, 1982.

    (fish-ins on Erriff, etc.) *Connacht Tribune,* 21 June 1971.

101   (Jack Lynch) *Irish Post*, 14 June 1969.

102   (Faroes) Included in Fennell, 1985.

103   (fate of Irish language) Ó Curnáin, 2007.

Part II: A World of Words

Preface: A Tale Out of Time

Pages

108   (unrecorded folktales from Carna) O'Sullivan, 1966.

    (cooperative movement) Bolger, 1977.

    (Finlay) Finlay, 1898.

109   (songs from Ballynahinch) Ní Fhlathartaigh, 1976.

    (Éamonn a Búrc) O'Sullivan, 1966.

9. The Castle

Pages

113   (Tadhg building in Maínis) MacCoisdealbha, 1939.

    (turf cutting forbidden) Browne, 1900–1902.

    (roof of castle) Mac Giollarnáth, 1941.

    (death of Tadhg) Mac Giollarnáth, 1941; my translation.

114   (inquisition) Hardiman's appendices to O'Flaherty, 1846.

115   (Lord Deputy) Quoted in Kilfeather, 1967.

116   (Connacht Council) Quoted in Kilfeather, 1967.

118   (fire to lure ships) Local testimony recorded in Irish from a Cosgrave (Ó Coscardha) and published in English in Fallon, 1978.

    (Spaniard's revenge) Mac Giollarnáth, 1941; my translation.

10. *The Song of Granite*

Pages

120   (singers of Na hAirdeanna) Local lore collected by Liam Mac
Con Iomaire. The news of Johnny Sheáin Jeaic's tragic drowning
came shortly after I had written this, in September 2009.

120–27   (Joe Heaney) All biographical information is from Mac Con
Iomaire, Liam, 2007.

122   (interview) www.mustrad.org.uk/articles/heaney.htm. I am
grateful to Virginia Blankenhorn, Áras Shorca Ní Ghuairim,
Carna, for permission to quote from her corrected transcription
of this interview, and other details on Joe Heaney's career.

127   (photograph) Reproduced in Mac Con Iomaire, Liam, 2007.

11. *Religious Storms*

Pages

131   (church dedicated to St Mac Dara) O'Flaherty, 1846.
(altar stone) Killanin, 1953–54.
(origin of saint's name) Uí Ógáin, 1979.

132   (meaning of *ceithearnacha*, and Raghnall and his dog) Mac Giollarnáth, 1941.
(tradition of friars) Mac Giollarnáth, 1941.
(scripture reader) Plunket, 1863.

133   'Soup-House Mhuighruis') MS in Roinn an Bhéaloidis, University College Dublin, vol. 74, pp. 241–2; I thank Dr Lillís Ó Laoire
for locating the words of this song for me, and Dr Ríonach Ó
hÓgáin for permission to quote them. See also Póirtéir, 1996.

134   (foundation of Protestant church) Anon., 1884.

135   (occupation of school) Bowen, 1970.
(Hamilton) Hartmann, 1996.

137   (attacks on church, school, boat) Moffitt, 2008.
(Seán Mhac Con Raoi) Mac Giollarnáth, 1936, 1941.
('Capall Sheáin') University College Dublin Folklore Archive
MS 461 and MS 1281.

138   (donkey and bell-rope) Hartmann, 1996.

138   (Miss Betts) Information from the late Anthony Betts. For the Betts family see Chapter 6, 'Bee Flight'.

140   ('Sionnach') Herity, 2009.

        (Oileán Mhic Dara) O'Flaherty, 1846.

        (punishing the disrespectful) Mac Giollarnáth, 1941.

12. The Sheltering Island

Pages

142   (drownings on saint's day) Mac Giollarnáth, 1941; Scott, 1996.

        (building of saint's church) Mac Giollarnáth, 1941.

145   (An Fhuaigh Leanúnach) Mac Giollarnáth, 1941.

        ('petrified wooden construction') De Paor, 1958.

146   (finial) Bigger, 1896.

        (date of chapel, shingles) Harbison, 1991.

147   (last burial on island) Uí Ógáin, 1979.

        (Páidín Rua) Mac Giollarnáth, 1941; my translation.

148   (rite at holy well, etc.) Uí Ógáin, 1979.

149   (missioners' vist to island) Irish Church Mission Society, 1851.

        (boat damaged) Irish Church Mission Society, 1856.

150   (the Ark) Scott, 1996. Dick Scott told me that the date for the Ark given in his book was reversed in error.

13. The Song of Wonders

Pages

153–4   (An Seangharraí) Family lore from Sgt P. Ó Conghaile, An Coillín.

154   (Garraí Pholl an Chiste) Mac Giollarnáth, 1941.

        (Maolra na mBeach) Mac Giollarnáth, 1941.

155   (Tóin Naigín) Sgt P. Ó Conghaile, An Coillín.

156   (horizontal mill wheel) Lucas, 1953.

        (holy well) Mac Giollarnáth, 1941: family lore from Sgt. P. Ó Conghaile, An Coillín.

        (Deer Island) Mac Giollarnáth, 1941; see 'Ogygia Lost', in Robinson, Tim, 2008, for this story.

157–8   ('The Song of Wonders') O'Fotharta, 1892.
            (An tAmhrán Bréagach) Ó Dochartaigh, 1999.
            (Carna version) Ní Fhlathartaigh, 1976.
            (European background) Ó Dochartaigh, 1999.

14. Bee Flight

Pages

160   (crannóg) Kinahan, 1872–3.
            (a later enquirer) Layard, 1897.
161   (Knockboy forest) Micks, 1925.
            (phosphorus deficiency) letter from Niall O'Carroll, author of
            Forestry in Ireland – A Concise History (COFORD, 2004).
167   (Maoilre Dhonnchadha an Tuistiúin) Mac Giollarnáth, 1941.
            (Martins) Martin estate sale documentation, 1849.
            (Mac Dhonnchadha na Céise) letter from John McDonagh,
            Mountbellew, Galway, 2000.

15. The Town of Tall Tales

Pages

171   (Berry) Berry, 1966. The tales first appeared in the *Mayo News*,
            1910–13.
172   (building of church) Mac Giollarnáth, 1934.
172–4   (Martin Ryan Institute) I am grateful to Richard Fitzgerald and
            Kieran O'Halloran of the MRI for showing me these and other
            projects in hand.
174   (Lydons, Mongans and Mylottes) Mac Con Iomaire, Liam, 2007,
            and interviews with Seosamh Ó Cuaig quoted in it.
            (Mongan's Hotel) Ó Faoláin, 1945.
            (smuggling) Mac Giollarnáth, 1941.
175   (economics of Carna) Finlay, 1898
            (compensation payment) *Galway Vindicator*, 2 June 1880.
176   (policeman's ghost) Browne, 1900–1902.
            (Carna law) Seosamh Ó Cuaig, quoted in Mac Con Iomaire,
            Liam, 2007.

177   (life of Mac Giollarnáth) Ó Glaisne, 1974.

           (obituary) Quoted in Ó Glaisne, 1974; my translation.

178   ('Ócum an Phríosúin') Mac Donncha, 1993.

16. *A Necklace of Islands*

Pages

181   (date of causeway) Browne, 1900–1902.

182   (dispute with Nolan) Thomas, 1999.

183   ('The kelp makers') Mac Con Iomaire, Séamas, 1938, trans. de
           Bhaldraithe, 2000.

186   (*Conamara Man*) Ridge, 1969.

187–90   (hookers) Scott, 1996.

191   ('An Hunter') Ó Ceoinín, 1988.

192   (Fethernagh) Joyce, 1913.

194–5   (products of Fínis) Ní Chlochartaigh, 1993.

196   (*seantuinne*) Angela Bourke pointed this out to me, and directed
           me to MacNeill, 1971–3. For Lí Ban, see Ó hÓgáin, 1990.

199   (kelp smoke) Mac Con Iomaire, Séamas, 1938.

           (Inis Múscraí) Mac Giollarnáth, 1949.

201–2   (history of Bior) Mac Giollarnáth, 1949; information from Pádraic
           de Burca; Griffith, 1855; Martin sale documentation, 1852; Ní
           Chlochartaigh, 1993.

203   ('out beyond the Briolla') Ó Máille, T. S., 1974.

           (Oileán Mana) I am grateful to Dr Dáithí Ó hÓgáin for this
           story (MS 202 in the University College Dublin Folklore
           Archive).

17. *Sorrowful Mysteries*

Pages

204   (meaning of Roisín na Mainiach) Ó Máille, T. S., 1952–3.

           (foundation of convent) www.sistersofmercy.ie/ireland_britain/
           western/i_tuam.cfm.

           (Yates) Dunleavy, 1991.

205   (parish priest's letter) 'A Famishing People', *The Nation*, 10 January 1880.

207   (Áras Shorcha Ní Ghuairim) For information about the Áras I thank Séamas Ó Concheanainn, administrator, Acadamh na hOllscolaíochta Gaeilge.

208   (attack on Col. Forbes) *Nenagh Guardian*, 15 January 1868.
        I am grateful to Seán Ó Guairim of Acadamh na hOllscolaíochta Gaeilge for the Irish text from Mac Giollarnáth, 1932.

211–15 ('Caoineadh na dTrí Muire') *Sorcha*, (CD) CEFCD 182, Comhairle Bhéaloideas Éireann / Gael Linn, Dublin. My treatment of the song tradition depends on Partridge, 1983.

214   (Pearse's publication of poem) Partridge, 1983.

215–17 (life of Sorcha Ní Ghuairim) Uí Ógáin, *Bliainiris* 2002. *Ar Lorg Shorcha*, television documentary, TG4, director Bríona Nic Dhiarmada, presentation Ríonach Uí Ógáin, 2007.

216   ('Gaelic nerves') Risteárd Ó Glaisne, quoted in Ó Ciosáin, 1993.
        (loss of heritage) Sorcha Ní Ghuairim, quoted in Ó Ciosáin, 1993.
        (Gaelic music) Sorcha Ní Ghuairim, quoted in Mac Con Iomaire, Liam, 2007.
        (Douglas Sealy) *Scéala Éireann* (January 1977); also in Ó Ciosáin, 1993.

18. Profit and Loss

Pages

218   (indemnity agreement) Among countless press reports see Vincent Browne's column in the *Irish Times*, 27 May 2009, and 'Properties Fully Handed Over to the State', *Tribune*, 24 May 2009.
        (song on closed factory) From Ciarán, Ó Fátharta, 'Dífhostaíocht', in Ó Conghaile, Micheál, 1990.

219   (modern subject matter) Ó Conghaile, Micheál, 1993.

220   (quarry) Clifden Circuit Court, 13 February 2008.

221–2   (crannógs) Layard, 1897. Gibbons, Michael, and Higgins, Jim, unpublished MS.
        (local lore) I am indebted to Eoghan Ó Néill of Dumhaigh Ithir

and Josie Gorham of Roisín na Mainiach for many stories and placenames from this locality.

19. Saving Father Miley

Pages
225   ('Illaunavolla') Hayes, 1939.
227–8   (Irish Waste Land Improvement Society) White, 1844.
229   ('Uchtóga') Ó Cuaig, 1985.
229–30 (Éamonn a Búrc) Ó Ceannabháin, 1983.
          ('*Eochair*') Ó Nualláin, 1982.
234   (bogeyman-tyrant Tadhg) Information from Pat Sullivan, Coill Sáile.
234–5   (Flannery Bridge) O'Leary, D., and Murphy, C., 1955, in *Flannery Bridge, Kilkieran, County Galway*, Galway County Council documentation, 1995.

20. The Wizard

Pages
236   (Myrddin) *Mountain Views*, http://mountainviews.ie/mv/index.php?mtnindex=897.
          (Cloch Choirill) Anon., 1865. My thanks to Paul Mohr for a copy of this passage. See also Ó Máille, T. S., 1974, under '*cloch*'.
237   (Anacair) Ó Máille, T. S., 1974; Ó Máille, Tomás, 1936.
          (Cosán an Railway) Information from Pat Sullivan, Loch Conaortha, who supplied me with many placenames in this locality.
242   (Glionnán) Mac Giollarnáth, 1941.

Part III: Anfractuous Rocks

Preface: Fractal Connemara

Pages
249–52 (coastlines) Mandelbrot, 1967.
250   (sidestep construction) Mandelbrot, 1982.

21. *Seductive Hills and Devious Shores*

Pages

254   (pikes) Ó Máille, T. S., 1974.
        (cargo of iron) Ó Máille, T. S., 1974.
        (deforestation) Nimmo, 1814.

255   (faction-fighter) Story from Peter Flaherty, Camas.
        (Mass) Ó Máille, T. S., 1974.

257–8   (Shannawona fault) Callaghan, 2005.

258–9   (coastlines in granite) I thank Prof. Paul Mohr and his successor Prof. Paul Ryan of the Geology Department, NUI Galway, for suggestions on this question.

22. *Anathema*

Pages

260   (curse in lintel) Information from Mícheál Bairéad, Roundstone.
        (murder) 'Who Owns the Land?', in Robinson, Tim, 2008.
        (Indreabhán) Dónall Mac Giolla Easpaig, then of the Placenames Office, Ordnance Survey, personal communication, 1989.

261   (Walter Blake) Acts of Settlement and Explanation, quoted in Blake, Martin J., 1905 (Vol. II, App. E.).
        (Blake family history) Blake, Martin J., 1905 (Vol. I). Information from Padhraic Faherty, Barna, and Seán Ó Mainnín, Indreabhán.
        ('improvements') Wakeman, n.d. [*c*.1850].
        (Ballaí Indreabháin) Information from Fr Audley, former curate in An Tulaigh, and the late Johnny Chóil Mhaidhc, Indreabhán.
        (Costelloe Lodge inquiry) Parliamentary (Distress) Papers, 1848.
        (colony of perverts) Conroy, 1943.
        (Silver Monday) *Galway Mercury*, 29 April 1854, quoted in Moffitt, 2008.

262–3   (Scorach Ghlionnáin) Mac Giollarnáth, 1934.

263   (death of the Scorach) Mícheál Bairéad, *Fadó Fadó*, unpublished MS in my possession.

264   (Anathema) From notes taken down by me in Irish and English from Mícheál Bairéad, Roundstone, *c*.1989.

264   (date of An Tulaigh church) Inscription on old font, preserved
           in the sacristy of the present church.
           (1962 church) Ó Móráin, n.d.

23. *The Whale*

Pages

270   (song) Ó Ceallaigh, 1990.
271   (Nimmo's pier) Nimmo, 1836; Villiers-Tuthill, 2006.
           (landless people) 'Agallamh le Beartlaí Ó Maoileoin', *Ros a' Mhíl
           Cois Cuain* (local periodical), Easter 1978.
271–2   (fish-processing factory) 'Mapping South Connemara: Part 50',
           in the *Connacht Tribune*, reprinted with Irish version in Mac Con
           Iomaire and Robinson, 2002.
273   (new ferry harbour) *Galway Independent*, 6 April 2009. I thank the
           Harbour Master, Captain John Donnelly, for plans and informa-
           tion on harbour development.
           (strike and layoffs) *Connacht Tribune*, 28 January 2010.

24. *The Bridge at Muckanaghederdauhaulia*

Pages

274   ('Muicineach') Ó Máille, T. S., 1955.
276   (Griallais family) Mac Con Iomaire and Quinn, 1997.
           (bridge) Photograph in *Connacht Tribune*, 5 June 1991.

25. *The River*

Pages

279   (Raidió na Gaeltachta) Ó Glaisne, 1974.
           (Nimmo) Hardiman's notes to O'Flaherty, 1846.
280   (Aill na Graí) Told to me by the late Mícheál Bairéad, Round-
           stone, and translated literally from his Irish; the tale is also well
           known in the Casla area.
           (Cottingham) Martin estate sale map, 1853; Wakeman (n.d.)
           [*c.*1850]; Griffith, 1855

280   (Belton) quoted in Ó Lochlainn, 1957.

       (another angler) 'Recollections', quoted in Ó Lochlainn, 1957.

281   (Hely Hutchinson) Griffith, 1855.

       (Balfour) Villiers-Tuthill, 1986.

       (Laing's improvements) Wilkins, 1989; (his riches) information
       from Liam Mac Con Iomaire.

281–3 (Ismay) Vignoles, 1987; Pádraic Ó Catháin, interview with Julian
       Vignoles, Raidió na Gaeltachta, 14 February 1994.

284   (Ó Lochlainn) Breathnach and Ní Mhurchú, vol. 4, 1994; *Irish
       Times*, 16 January 1953.

285   (Toohey) Obituary, *Irish Times*, 3 June 2002.

       (Costelloe Lodge) *Sunday Independent*, property section, 16 Janu-
       ary 2005.

26. Views of An Cheathrú Rua

Pages

289   (turf boats) Scott, 1996.

290   (Davitt) Cashman, 1979.

290–91 (Cath na Ceathrún Ruaidhe) *New York Herald*, quoted in Cash-
       man, 1979; *Galway Vindicator*, 3 and 7 January 1880.

291   (Mrs Kirwan's evictions) Conroy, 1943 (copy of typescript kindly
       supplied by Fr M. Lang, An Cheathrú Rua).

       (the dead) Local lore from Mícheál Bairéad, Roundstone.

292–3 (poitín) 'Séipéal an Chillín', agallamh a rinne Gráinne Seoige le
       Johnny Mhicil Charley Ó Loideáin, *Tiachóg* (a local periodical),
       An Cheathrú Rua (June 1993).

293   (Caladh Thaidhg) Information from Martin J. O'Connor.

294   (singers) Mac Con Iomaire and Quinn, 1997.

294–6 (Lamb) Information from Laillí Lamb.

297   (Walter Verling) *Irish Times*, 23 June 2008.

298–9 (Loch na Naomh) Information from Beairtle ó Flaitheartach,
       Barr an Doire. A similar story is told of St Brendan and his
       followers in Kerry.

301–2 (parish boundaries) Conroy, 1943.

303–4 (Mairtín Mór Ó Máille) Lynam, 1989; Mac Giollarnáth, 1941.

305   ('Inismacaw church') O'Flaherty, 1846.

305   (Mac Adhaimh) Information from Dónall Mac Giolla Easpaig,
           Placenames Branch, Dept of Arts, Heritage, Gaeltacht and the
           Islands, Dublin.
           (Smocán) Ní Dhomhnaill, 1984.

27. The Waste Shore

Pages
307–9   (Siobhán) *Irish Independent*, 12 December 1998 and 24 June 2001.

28. Going Native in Bungalowland

Pages
310   (Bungalow Blitz) *Irish Times*, 12 September 1987.

29. The Inordinate Isles

Pages
315   (first sight of Mandelbrot set) Mandelbrot, 1986.
           (flight into the set) A particularly druggy one is *Fractal Zoom
           Mandelbrot Corner* on YouTube: http://www.youtube.com/
           watch?v=G_GBwuYuOOs&feature=related.

30. Islands Tethered and Free

Pages
318   (Synge) Synge, 1966.
319   (boats at Béal an Daingin) Scott, 1996.
           (causeways) Information from Michael Gibbons, Clifden.
           (golf club) www.oneclickireland.com/golf_clubs/connema-
           raisles/index.htm.
320   (*creabhair*) Ó Máille, T. S., 1952–3.
323   (de Bhailís) Ó Conghaile, Micheál, 1985.
325   (coming out) Ó Conghaile, Micheál, 1997.

31. Two Songs from Leitir Móir

Pages

326   (Mór) Ó hÓgáin, 1990.

327   (Na Peigíní) Ó Conghaile, Micheál, 1986.

327–8   ('Peigín Leitir Móir') *An Claisceadal* III, 1902.

328–9   (Sinéad) Mac Giollarnáth, 1941.

329–31   (St George) Mark, 1976.

331   ('Cuirt an tSrutháin Bhuí') de Bhailís, 1976.

32. Garomna by Road

Pages

333   (central Garomna) Browne, 1900–1902.

335   (Ó Cuív) RTÉ News, 21 March 2005.

336   (Presentation sisters) *Tírnea – The Story of Our Community* (http://
           www.presentation-sisters.ie/content/view/106/131).

           ('Bricawna') Information from Fr M. Lang, letter, 1980s.

338   (Pearse on de Bhailís) *An Claidheamh Soluis*, 8 August 1903.

           (Amhrán an Tae) de Bhailís, 1976.

341   (Casement) Inglis, 1973.

           ('Famine Ravages Irish Islands') *New York Times*, 22 May 1913;
           Irish Times, 24 May 1913, reprinted in 'From the Archives', *Irish
           Times*, 24 May 2010.

342   (sea-caves) Ó Máille, T. S., 1974.

343   ('Walking Out to Islands') Robinson, Tim, 1984, included in
           Robinson, Tim, 1996.

           (St Bearchán) Piaras Ó Conaire, *RosC, Iris Phobail Ros Muc*, No.
           1, 1976.

           (Ráth Cairn) Ó Conghaile, Micheál, 1986.

344   (Cnoc Chathail Óig) Mac Giollarnáth, 1941.

           (*Composition of Connaught*) Hardiman's appendices to O'Flaherty,
           1846.

345   (Fr Conboy) Mac Giollarnáth, 1941.

345–6   (Fr Conroy) Conroy, 1943.

           (late medieval church) O'Flaherty, 1846.

347–8   (drowning) Mac Donnchadha, 2001.

348   (shed no tear) Local lore from Dr Angela Bourke.

33. Holes in Reality

Pages

350   (giant) Herity, 2009.

352   (well on the island) Information from the McDonncha, An Doirín Darach, Tír an Fhia.

353   (versions of Féilim's family name) Ó Direáin, 1929; Ó Máille, Tomás agus Mícheál, 1991; Ní Fhlathartaigh, 1976.
           (Féilim and his father) Ó Máille, Tomás agus Mícheál, 1905.

353   ('An tIolrach Mór') Ó Máille, Tomás agus Mícheál, 1905; O'Fotharta, 1892.

355   ('Marcaíocht an Phúca') O'Fotharta, 1892.

34. Subduction

Pages

360–63   (subduction) I am grateful to Prof. Paul D. Ryan of NUI Galway for information on recent research findings, on which my account is based.

361   (tectonic plates) Cloud, 1988.

363   (pendant) Ryan, Max, and Kelly, 1983.
           (hooker) www.sailingsaintbarbara.net

364   (kelp) Kinahan, 1869.

364–5   (kilns) Ó Gaora, 1937.

366   (community employment scheme) Previté, 2008.

35. Loose Ends of the Earth

Pages

368   I especially thank Pádraig Ó Maoilchiaráin, Pádraic de Bhald-raithe, Tom Folan and Tomás Ó Maoláin for information about these islands.
           (signal towers) Kerrigan, 1982.

371   (Comerford) Lane, 1993.

372   (Captain Comerford) Mac Giollarnáth, 1941.

           (origins of Mac Donnchadhas) P. Ó Maoil Chiaráin (letter).

           (Antoine) Mac Giollarnáth, 1941.

           (*St John*) Ó Maoilchiaráin, Pádraig, *c.*1983, and personal letter.

375–6   (poitín) Ó Conghaile, Micheál, 1981; Ó Conghaile, Seán, 1974.

378–9   ('The Ferryman of Dinish Island') Synge, 1966.

380   (ivory) Ó Direáin, 1929.

           (*Bruiser*) Robinson, Sir Henry, 1924.

Index

All plants, apart from seaweeds, are listed under 'plants', hookers and similar boats under 'hookers', and songs under 'songs'.